THE SOCIOLOGY OF KNOWLEDGE

The Sociology of Knowledge

ITS STRUCTURE AND ITS RELATION TO THE PHILOSOPHY OF KNOWLEDGE

A CRITICAL ANALYSIS OF THE SYSTEMS OF KARL MANNHEIM AND PITIRIM A. SOROKIN

BY

Jacques Maquet

University of California at Los Angeles

TRANSLATED BY
JOHN F. LOCKE

WITH A PREFACE BY
F. S. C. NORTHROP

BD
175
.M343
1973

GREENWOOD PRESS, PUBLISHERS
WESTPORT, CONNECTICUT

208371

Library of Congress Cataloging in Publication Data

Maquet, Jacques Jérôme Pierre, 1919–
    The sociology of knowledge, its structure and its
relation to the philosophy of knowledge.

    Reprint of the 1951 ed., which is a translation of
Sociologie de la connaissance.
    Bibliography: p.
    1. Mannheim, Karl, 1893–1947. 2. Sorokin, Pitirim
Aleksandrovich, 1889–1968. 3. Knowledge, Sociology of.
I. Title.
[BD175.M343 1973]   301.2'1   70–168963
ISBN 0–8371–6236–X

Originally published in 1951 by The Beacon Press, Boston

Reprinted with the permission of Jacques Maquet

Reprinted by Greenwood Press,
a division of Williamhouse-Regency Inc.

First Greenwood Reprinting 1973
Second Greenwood Reprinting 1974

Library of Congress Catalog Card Number 70-168963

ISBN 0-8371-6236-X

Printed in the United States of America

Contents

FOREWORD TO THE REPRINT EDITION ix

FOREWORD, *by Jacques J. Maquet* xi

PREFACE, *by F. S. C. Northrop* xiii

1. INTRODUCTION 3

PART ONE

KARL MANNHEIM

2. MANNHEIM'S SOCIOLOGY OF KNOWLEDGE
   Introduction 19
   Origin of the Sociology of Knowledge 21
   Some Positive Research 23
   The Three Essential Elements in Mannheim's System . 28
   The Explanation 33
   The Method of Research 35

3. EVALUATION OF MANNHEIM'S SOCIOLOGY OF KNOWL-
   EDGE
   First Stage: The Research into Facts 37
   Second Stage: The Results of Empirical Observation . 42
   Third Stage: The Scientific Theory 47
   General Significance of Mannheim's System . . . 49

4. MANNHEIM'S PHILOSOPHY OF KNOWLEDGE
   Introduction 57
   The Point of Departure 58
   First Solution 59
   Relativism 61
   Relationism 62
   The Criteria of Truth 64
   General Consequences 74

5. EVALUATION OF MANNHEIM'S PHILOSOPHY OF KNOWL-
   EDGE
   Introduction: Epistemology and Gnosiology . . 75
   Direct Criticism 79
   Implicit Metaphysics 86

6. CONCLUSIONS DRAWN FROM THE STUDY OF MANN-
HEIM

Philosophic Significance of a System of the Sociology of
Knowledge 92
Contribution of Mannheim's System to the Sociology
of Knowledge 98

PART TWO

PITIRIM A. SOROKIN

7. GENERAL FRAMEWORK OF SOROKIN'S SOCIOLOGY OF
KNOWLEDGE

Introduction: The Scientific Career of Professor Sorokin 107
Outline of Sorokin's System of General Sociology . . 111

8. SOROKIN'S SOCIOLOGY OF KNOWLEDGE

The Three Truths 124
The Independent Variable 133
The Dependent Variables 135
The Type of Relationships 153
The Explanation 157

9. EVALUATION OF SOROKIN'S SOCIOLOGY OF KNOWLEDGE

Criticism of the Method of Positive Research . . 163
Criticism of the Conclusions of Sorokin's Positive Re-
search 174
Criticism of the Theory 177

10. SIGNIFICANCE OF SOROKIN'S SOCIOLOGY OF KNOWL-
EDGE

Is It a Real *Wissenssoziologie?* 187
External Limitations for Sorokin's System of *Wissensso-
ziologie* 189
Internal Limitations for Sorokin's System of *Wissensso-
ziologie* 195
Conclusion: What Is the Most Important Factor? . 201

11. SOROKIN'S PHILOSOPHY OF KNOWLEDGE

Introduction: Sorokin's Position in Regard to Philo-
sophic Implications 204
How the Problem of Truth Arises 206
First Reply: Integralism 206
Second Reply: Relativism 208
The Double Principle of Sorokin's Solution . . . 209
Conclusions 214

12. EVALUATION OF SOROKIN'S PHILOSOPHY OF KNOWLEDGE

    Introduction: Reminder of the Hypothesis of Criticism   215
    How Is Integralism Ambivalent?   216
    Separability of the Two Aspects   217
    Remarks and Conclusion   222

13. CONCLUSIONS DRAWN FROM THE STUDY OF SOROKIN

    Sorokin's Contribution to the Sociology of Knowledge .   224
    Relationship between the Sociology of Knowledge and
        the Philosophy of Knowledge   227

PART THREE

GENERAL CONCLUSIONS

14. THE SOCIOLOGY OF KNOWLEDGE AND THE PHILOSOPHY
    OF KNOWLEDGE

    Structure of a System of the Sociology of Knowledge .   231
    The Philosophy of Knowledge   240
    Relationship between the Philosophy of Knowledge and
        the Sociology of Knowledge   243

15. RESULTS AND PROSPECTS FOR THE SOCIOLOGY OF
    KNOWLEDGE

    Clarification of the Notion of the Sociology of Knowl-
        edge   250
    Unity of the Sociology of Knowledge .   .   .   253
    Idealistic and Marxist Approaches   .   .   .   256

NOTES   261

BIBLIOGRAPHY   298

INDEX   312

TWENTY YEARS LATER

Foreword to the Reprint Edition

The First American edition of this book, published in Boston in 1951, has been out of print for about fifteen years. Here is the reprint edition. Like the second French edition, published in 1969 by the Brussels University Press (*Editions de l'Institut de sociologie de l'Université libre de Bruxelles*), it is identical to the first edition.

Of course, I had the temptation to revise it and to bring it up to date. First, because Sorokin had added to his bibliography, already impressive twenty years ago, about ten other works published up to 1968, the year he died. However none of these books brings a significant change to the Sorokinian system of sociology of knowledge as I described and analyzed it in 1951. Yet a few interpretations of secondary matters are likely to be enlightened by Sorokin's recent publications. Mannheim died in 1947. His posthumously published works include six titles: three collections of essays and articles that had previously appeared in print, and three books respectively devoted to democratic planning, general sociology, and the sociology of education. Here again, Mannheim's essential contribution to the sociology of knowledge was completed before I wrote this study. Yet, it would be satisfactory to take into account Mannheim's posthumous publications.

Moreover, research in the field of sociology of knowledge has been progressing during the last two decades. The Laboratory of Sociology of Knowledge, founded by Georges Gurvitch at the *Ecole pratique des Hautes Etudes* of Paris, and to which he has devoted the last years of his life, has grown up and brought forth results. This group, continuing their studies under the direction of Roger Bastide, produce a periodical, *Contributions à la sociologie de la connaissance,* whose first number was issued in 1967. Beside these—and other—developments in the sociology of knowledge, the methods used in the sociology of literature and the new perspectives offered by aesthetic anthropology are stimulating contributions that I would have liked to introduce in the appraisal of the Mannheim and Sorokin systems.

Finally, since 1951 my views have somewhat evolved. Twenty years ago I was so anxious to avoid any undue introduction of metaphysical assumptions in sociology that I refrained from adopting either the Sorokin idealistic theory or the Mannheim materialistic one. I recognized an equal explanatory value and an equivalent capacity for pro-

ducing valid research hypotheses in both. My subsequent anthropological fieldwork in Black Africa has convinced me of the unequal value of
the two theories. In particular and limited field research as well as in
overall syntheses, a materialistic theory has proved to be more useful
than an idealistic one. My anthropological publications may be said to
belong to the trend of cultural materialism, notoriously illustrated by
Leslie White. Obviously I would have liked to reexamine Mannheim's
and Sorokin's theories in the light of my anthropological experience.

Ironically, all these reasons in support of a revised edition made it
impossible. If I were to take into account Sorokin's and Mannheim's
writings published during the fifties and the sixties, the recent developments in the sociology of knowledge and related fields, and the assumptions of cultural materialism, a revised edition would not be enough. A
new book should be written. Now it happens that it is the *Sociology of
Knowledge* as published in 1951 that some colleagues and students
would like to have available again.

They think that this book, in spite of its date, is not obsolete. The
dichotomy between the materialistic and the idealistic approaches remaining crucial in the social sciences, it seems to them that a micro-
analysis of specific systems clearly representing the two perspectives
keeps its relevance in the seventies. It has also been pointed out that the
framework used for comparing the two systems (independent and dependent variables, conditioning relationships) is a conceptual tool
whose application to the Sorokinian and Mannheimian sociologies indicates its potential without exhausting it.

The future will let us know if these kind critics were right or wrong.
In any case, I came to be convinced that a book like this cannot be
dissociated from the year it was born. An attempt at updating it would
disregard one of the conclusions of the sociology of knowledge: a content of knowledge cannot be separated from the perspective of the
observer who expresses it. For similar reasons, a painter does not
"revise" a picture he made when he was young even if, twenty years
later, the landscape and he himself have changed.

Jacques Maquet

University of California
Los Angeles
January 1973

Foreword

MORE THAN ANY OTHER SCIENCE, sociology prompts the author of a book to be aware of the immense debt he owes to his predecessors. I am fully conscious of the extent to which the present study is beholden to the sociologists and philosophers I have had the privilege of meeting in person or through their works. But the mere enumeration of these influences would be an impossible task — they are too many. Moreover, so complete is the assimilation of some of these ideas that it would be very difficult to indicate their origin.

For fundamental intellectual attitudes and the framework of my thinking, I feel particularly indebted to the professors and scholars of Louvain and Harvard. I am especially grateful to two of them: Professor Jacques Leclercq, who guided my sociological and philosophical development; and Professor Pitirim A. Sorokin, who, during the eighteen months I spent at Harvard, kindly lent himself to many discussions of his theories.

I am conscious of the great honor done me by Professor F. S. C. Northrop of Yale University, in prefacing this book with such an important contribution to the sociology of knowledge.

I thank Mr. John F. Locke for his great help in translating the French text and the staff of the Beacon Press for their patience in editing the manuscript.

This book is, rather than an individual enterprise, the result of close collaboration with Emma Maquet, my wife, in intellectual elaboration as well as in the presentation of ideas.

I feel grateful to the Belgian-American Educational Foundation, Inc., for the help I received from that institution during my stay in the United States.

For permission to reproduce many quotations from Karl Mannheim's *Ideology and Utopia,* I wish to extend my thanks to Harcourt, Brace and Company of New York. For similar authorization to quote from the writings of Pitirim A. Sorokin, I am indebted to the following publishers: American Book Company, New York (for *Social and Cultural Dynamics,* vols. I, II, and IV); Duke University Press, Durham, N. C. (for *Sociocultural Causality, Space, Time*); E. P. Dutton and Company, New York (for *The Crisis of Our Age*); and Harper and Brothers, New York (for *Society, Culture and Personality*).

J. J. M.

Preface

IT IS NOT EASY to overestimate the importance of the inquiry of this book. Its implications are far-reaching, touching not merely the social sciences and philosophy, but also the practical problem of war and peace and even the fate of our civilization.

Its problem is that of the relation between the facts of social existence and the ideas making up human knowledge. That social scientists and philosophers have taken positions upon this question is evident. That statesmen making important decisions with respect to international policy affecting the peace of the world have taken similar positions is equally obvious.

Again and again we hear it said by social scientists, historians, philosophers, statesmen, and laymen that the solution of the problems of peace and the causes of war centers in economic factors. Laymen and social scientists often assert that the ideas of men are but afterthoughts, merely rationalizing — in the derogatory sense of the word "rationalize" — the group interests, the class aims, or the forces of power politics which supposedly determine the beliefs and the behavior of men, both as individuals and as groups.

Suppose this popular opinion rests on error or is only partially true. It is easy then to appreciate the implications for social science and the concrete political decisions of statesmen which such a conclusion would entail.

Conversely, suppose that the afore-mentioned scholars and laymen are right. Then, clearly, much that is being done at present in carrying on the traditional practices in education, with their emphasis upon cognitive rather than merely hortatory meanings, should be changed. Also, many present efforts to set up international organizations and to seek for a truly international law which require for their success social principles and beliefs going beyond local, provincial class interests and the present socio-cultural premises and existential facts of our world should be

branded as misguided and a waste of time. Men attempting to
ameliorate or resolve the problems of our world by constructing
new economic, political, and legal norms different from those of
the present or the past should also be discouraged and branded as
misguided, scientifically uninformed folk who are attempting the
impossible. This follows because, according to the foregoing conception of scholars and humanists, the ideas of men but reflect the
facts or forces of the culture in which they are immersed or those
of a unique future which will succeed the present culture in an
inevitable manner.

Clearly, an inquiry which deals with these matters afresh and
which in part at least reaches conclusions which are somewhat
more informed and subtle than the traditional answers is important.
Such is the nature of the inquiry of this book.

Because, in this atomic age, time is short and because of the
attendant urgency of the problems faced by this book, I shall not
merely note the issues which it so sharply focuses, but also bring
additional considerations to bear upon certain questions which its
reading generates.

Dr. Maquet indicates that the problem, as traditionally understood under the continental European name of the *sociology of
knowledge,* involves three factors: (1) the conditioning social
facts; (2) the ideas making up human knowledge which are conditioned; and (3) the relation joining the former factor to the
latter.

The investigation of the problem therefore involves asking of any
given sociological theory three main questions: (1) What, specifically, are the conditioning social factors? More concretely:
Are they purely economic? Are they physical circumstances such
as climate or natural resources? Are they the military establishments of the groups in question, etc.? (2) What are the ideas conditioned? Is every idea in human knowledge conditioned by sociocultural facts or are merely some? And, if merely some, which
ones? To put the matter in more detail: Are all ideas and theories
of the humanities and the social sciences thus conditioned, whereas,
as Mannheim notes, the concepts of mathematics and mathematical
physics are not? Is even one's philosophical theory of knowledge
thus conditioned, in which instance even this thesis itself becomes
not a cognitive proposition but a purely emotive and instrumental
one? (3) What is the precise nature of the relation by means of

which the facts of social existence determine the ideas of human knowledge? Is it a completely deterministic relation, such as that of rigorous cause and effect between the states of physical systems at different times in mathematical physics, or such as the formal relation of logical implication? Or is it the weaker form of the causal relation as designated by Mills' methods which give merely observed, repeated sequences and rather weak empirical correlations? Or is it something even weaker than this, a mere compatibility or harmony, such as Dr. Maquet reveals to be the case in certain instances, as for example, Mannheim's position when it is carefully analyzed?

Furthermore, in answering all these questions, what method is to be used? Is one to use nothing but the purely inductive method of the historian, noting merely temporal sequences? Also, if the historian's method is used, what guarantee is there that, in the inevitable selection from the infinite number of facts in history, all those relevant to the inquiry have been examined? Or is some more powerful method of analysis to be applied to the inductive data? It is at this point that Dr. Maquet's choice of Professor Sorokin as well as Mannheim for consideration is a happy one. For Professor Sorokin brings much more powerful methods of inquiry, more like those of the natural scientists, to the discussion than does Mannheim.

This book forces its readers to ask an even more important question: Is the frequently asserted determination of human knowledge by social existence a determination which operates only in one direction? Put more technically, is this relation of determination insymmetrical? Is it the case that the facts of social existence determine ideas, and that ideas never determine the facts of social existence? Again, Dr. Maquet's study of the sociology of Professor Sorokin as well as that of Mannheim is fortunate.

The full force of Professor Sorokin's findings must not be missed. They reveal that a scientific study of any culture leads one to a connected set of basic predominant premises from which all the different predominant factors of that culture follow, exactly in the manner in which a scientific study of nature by the mathematical physicists leads to a connected set of theoretical principles from which the facts of nature and the instruments of technology derive. It is not an accident that the difference in the conclusions of Mannheim and Professor Sorokin are accompanied thus by a correspond-

ing difference in their methods of inquiry. Nor is it an accident
that the correspondingly more powerful conclusions of Professor
Sorokin are achieved by the correspondingly more powerful methods analogous to those of the mathematical physicists. The
historian's methods, excessively inductive, purely empirical and
descriptive, seem to be as weak and insufficient, even though necessary, in social science as they have proved to be in the natural
sciences.

A further thesis of Professor Sorokin's sociology must also be
noted. Not only does a specific culture obtain its definition and its
unity from an underlying set of premises, but these premises turn
out also to be philosophical in character. One of the most notable
developments of our time in the field of the cultural sciences is the
independent demonstration of this conclusion by a large number
of investigators who have approached the subject from quite different starting points. Professor Sorokin's sociology is one example.
Recent study in the philosophy of the world's cultures such as my
Meeting of East and West[1] is another instance. The investigations
of the cultural anthropologists, such as Professor Clyde Kluckhohn,
have demonstrated that even the behavior and objective institutions
of so-called primitive people such as the Navaho Indians cannot be
understood until their philosophy is determined.[2]

One additional point first emphasized by Professor Sorokin is
becoming increasingly clear. Values turn out not to be objective,
irreducible data appearing as common factors through different
cultures. Instead, one's philosophical theory of the ultimate nature
of reality and of man as a factor in reality defines one's values.
Thus the word "good" is not an idea within the total set of ideas
making up one's ultimate philosophy. It is, instead, but a short-
hand name for one's ultimate philosophy. This is the real point of
Socrates' dictum "Know thyself" and of Plato's thesis that there
will not be good government until philosophers are kings. The
point of the latter thesis is not that Plato wanted philosophers in
political positions. It is, instead, that one's philosophical theory of
what is primary or ultimate in experience is one's criterion of the
good. Hence, only those who have a true philosophical theory of

---

[1] F. S. C. Northrop, *Meeting of East and West,* Macmillan Co., New
York, 1946.
[2] See symposium volume *Ideological Differences and World Order,* Chapter XVII, Yale University Press, New Haven, Conn., 1949.

ultimate reality can be good statesmen. Hence Professor Sorokin's findings which show that cultures resting on different philosophical conceptions of reality have radically different aims and values.

Dr. Maquet's analysis makes it clear also that one must watch the different definitions of the *sociology of knowledge*. One definition conceives it as "the study of the relationship between society and mental productions." Another defines it as the consideration of "mental productions in so far as they are influenced by social factors." It is to be noted that the first of these two definitions leaves the question open as to whether the relation of determination between social facts and human ideas operates only in one direction, whereas the second formulation does not. It appears that Mannheim's definition is the second one, whereas Professor Sorokin's is the former of the two.

One is, of course, free to define the *sociology of knowledge* in any way that one chooses. It is also probably the case that its original definition was the second or more restricted one. Nevertheless it is not to be overlooked that, if one takes the more restricted, traditional definition, then one can draw from it only very restricted and partial conclusions concerning the implications of the *sociology of knowledge* for the philosophical theory of knowledge. Clearly, if one has defined the *sociology of knowledge* as an inquiry into the determination of human ideas by social existence, then all that one can possibly conclude, so far as general philosophical epistemology is concerned, is that sometimes social existence determines ideas. It does not seem to be a misrepresentation to say that those who have defined the *sociology of knowledge* in the restricted sense have not restricted themselves to the limited conclusions so far as philosophical epistemology is concerned which such a restricted definition entails.

A consideration of the definition of culture is most relevant in this connection. Sociologists are well aware, as biological scientists frequently are not, that there is a fundamental difference between the biological organization of society and its cultural or social organization. Biological social organization and behavior are the organization and behavior which result solely from the genetical inheritance of the material bodies of the people in society and the effect upon these bodies of external stimuli. The cultural and social organization of society, on the other hand, is built on top of this. The fundamental differentiating factor is symbols and learned behavior in response to social symbols. This appears in the definition of culture as socially learned behavior. This is the key also to Professor Sorokin's emphasis upon cultural social behavior as meaningful.

This inescapable presence of symbols which are stimuli, often continuous, standing for factors other than themselves and hence having an intentional character or, in other words, a meaning, has implications not always noted. Since culture is learned behavior toward symbols and since learned behavior conditioned to a symbol always involves a stimulus taken as an idea referring to something other than the stimulus itself, it follows that culture is learned ideas embodied in individual behavior. From this it follows that the restricted thesis of the *sociology of knowledge* to the effect that cultural or social existence determines ideas is merely the tautology that a learned idea entails the idea that is learned. Thus when one pays attention to the definition of culture used by those who define the *sociology of knowledge* as the conditioning of ideas by cultural existence, it turns out that the thesis rests upon a definition of culture which makes cultural existence the effect rather than the cause of ideas — the effect because culture, as opposed to merely biological society, is by definition the product of an idea or symbol to which one's behavior has become conditioned.

There is now experimental evidence combined by Drs. Warren McCulloch and Walter Pitts with the appropriate theoretical analysis which demonstrates the manner in which particular existences become turned into universals by the human nervous system, due to reverberating neural nets in the central nervous system, and how such universals can through their particular embodiments fire motor neurons, thereby determining human behavior and, through human behavior, social existence.[3] It appears, therefore, that Dr. Maquet's analysis, making more precise the traditional possibilities and opening up new possibilities of conceiving of the relation between social existence and human knowledge, especially when supplemented with the latter considerations, results in novel and very important conclusions.

One explicit result of Dr. Maquet's inquiry into the relation between social existence and human knowledge merits special atten-

---

[3] *Ideological Differences and World Order, la. cit.,* Chapter **XIX**. See also *Science*, April 23, 1948, pp. 411-417.

tion. His examination of Mannheim's findings leads to the verdict that social conditioning means little more than coherence, correlation, or harmony. This mitigates the limitation of Mannheim's definition of the *sociology of knowledge* which identifies its subject matter with a study of the way in which social existence determines ideas. For to find that this determination is mere correlation or harmony is practically to assert that the relation is symmetrical rather than insymmetrical.

Dr. Maquet's study escapes from the error of begging the latter question in another respect. He suggests that the definition of "the existential determination of knowledge" as mere correspondence or harmony may mean that "ontologically" ideas and social existence come from a common factor.

There is historical evidence in support of this conclusion in the case of the relation between Roman law and existential Roman society. A recent investigation of this topic by the lawyer Mr. Gray L. Dorsey[4] has brought out that any correspondence or correlation between the universal principle in later Roman law and existential Roman society is due to the fact that the ideas of Stoic philosophy not merely went into Roman law as it was finally codified by lawyers (practically all of whom were Stoical philosophers) but also went independently, through the ethical teaching and conditioning of children in the family, directly into Roman society. When to this is added the fact that existential family life and Roman law, by way of the common Stoic philosophy, were regarded as cognitively valid in their common ethical and legal norms because these norms reflected the law of nature as derived by the Stoics from Greek science and natural philosophy, it becomes clear that the basis of the validation of human knowledge and its cultural norms may be in existential nature rather than in social existence. In this connection, Mannheim's observation that human knowledge in mathematics and mathematical physics escapes relativity to cultural facts for its existential source and validation takes on a new importance.

Such a theory of the existential source of human knowledge and its non-culturally relative cultural norms must, however, face the crucial question put by Dr. Maquet in this volume.

---

[4] *Ideological Differences and World Order, la. cit.*, Chapter XXI.

Let us suppose [he writes] that we have shown that the principle of causality, a fundamental category of our logic, does not exist in Chinese thought and that what is closest to it is a sort of principle of harmony. The question of validity with regard to these two categories claims our attention in these terms: Are there in reality relations of causality or rather of harmony? How could the philosopher who would discuss this subsumability of the real in these two categories reject as irrelevant the fact that his own mind has been formed by a tradition in which people are accustomed to see the world in terms either of causality relationships or of harmony relationships?

The answer to this question is that Mr. Gray L. Dorsey, in his afore-mentioned study of the source of universal ethical and legal principles in both Chinese and Roman law, finds that in both instances the ideas involved in these principles were grounded for their verification and cognitive meaning in the existence of nature rather than in cultural social existence. He has pointed out also that in my *Meeting of East and West* it was shown that for the Chinese and the Orient generally, nature was known primarily, if not solely, by the intuitive method of immediate empiric apprehension, whereas in the West, nature has been known not merely in this way but primarily by means of theoretically designated, indirectly verified, deductively formulated theory. Now it can be shown, as Hume made clear, that empirically known reality gives only the notion of temporal succession or correlation, or harmony, just as the Chinese maintain. It has been demonstrated similarly by Kant and more recently by Henry Margenau[5] and the present writer,[6] that causality, as applied to the states of systems in nature by Western mathematical physics, can be known only by the Western methods of knowing nature in terms of indirectly verified, deductively formulated theory. Thus one is not driven, in order to explain the difference between the Chinese intuitive notion of harmony and the Western technical concept of causality, to cultural existence for the cognitive source and validation of these different theories. They have their basis instead in two different scientific ways of knowing nature, each of which is correct for the component of nature which it grasps — both components of nature being real.

---

[5] Henry Margenau, *Journal of Philosophy of Science*, I (1934), 133-48; IV (1937), 337-370.

[6] *The Logic of the Sciences and the Humanities*, Macmillan, New York, 1947, Chapters 11 and 12.

These are some of the crucial contemporary questions upon which this book focuses and which it illuminates. It is clear that they are both important and fundamental. It is becoming clear also that man through knowledge can be something more than a loudspeaker for the particular class or the provincial culture in which circumstances happen to place him. Nature exists one and the same for all men, as well as the many classes and cultures. Hence there is another source for the existential validation of philosophical knowledge and its attendant norms than either class or culture.

F. S. C. NORTHROP
Sterling Professor of Philosophy and Law in Yale University

THE SOCIOLOGY OF KNOWLEDGE

CHAPTER ONE

Introduction

THE SOCIOLOGY OF KNOWLEDGE has not yet reached the stage of development in which the limits, content, structure, and methods of a discipline are fully determined. Therefore any study in this field must necessarily begin by defining what the sociology of knowledge is. An exhaustive critical study of this point would require a long monograph, but we will be satisfied with a rapid description: a few particulars with regard to its nominal definition, its history, and certain psychological attitudes which are systematized by this new division of sociology. In the second part of this introductory chapter, we will show how the problem which forms the subject of this monograph claims our attention and how we propose to solve it.

I

The expression "sociology of knowledge"— which is a translation of the German *Wissenssoziologie* — indicates that our discipline is concerned with knowledge. The English term has a greater denotation than the German one (*wissen*) which it translates. *Wissen*, taken as a whole, means science, whereas "knowledge" includes at one and the same time the simple act of presenting an object to the mind, whether or not it be thoroughly intelligized (*erkennen, connaître*), and the act of thinking which reaches a complete understanding of this object (*wissen, savoir*). This is the distinction which William James expressed by setting "to know a thing" over against "to know such and such things about a thing."[1] Must we infer from this that the English designa-

---

[1] References are to the Notes at the end of the book.

3

tion is less adequate than the German? We do not think so. We must observe that the term *Wissenssoziologie* did not gain acceptance at once. One of the first contributions to this field by Wilhelm Jerusalem in 1909 was entitled *Die Soziologie des Erkennens*. Moreover — and this is more important — the sociologists of knowledge have not limited their inquiries to scientific knowledge. They have been concerned with virtually any cultural product: political ideologies, philosophy, science and technology, ethical and juridical doctrines.[2] This enumeration gives an idea of the generality of the concept "knowledge" as it is understood here. Any exterior symbolic manifestation of an activity of the mind is what we will express by the term "mental production." It certainly goes beyond what ordinary language — and many philosophers — understand by cognition: a mental representation which claims to convey what objects are. We will see at the end of this study to what degree a broad conception is desirable. But the sociologists of knowledge have turned their attention to a large variety of mental productions, and this is sufficient reason for us to stop at this term.

The sociology of knowledge is not the only science which is concerned with ideas, but it distinguishes itself from the others by its point of view. It considers the relationship between society and mental productions, or more precisely the latter insofar as they are a function of one or another social or cultural factor. It is the "science of the determination of knowledge by social existence." It is the discipline which studies "the existential determination of knowledge," the social and cultural determinants of thinking.[3] The social and the cultural are differentiated in the way ordinarily accepted by American sociologists and anthropologists. By society is meant a group of men who have learned to work together; by culture, the set of particular ways of life of such a group.[4] (In a preliminary definition such as we are establishing here, the analysis of its elements must remain somewhat superficial. That is why we are doing nothing more than indicating this distinction which is not very important at this stage of our study. We shall return to it later.) These social and cultural factors may be extremely diverse: the structure of society, affiliation with a class, membership in a professional group, cultural mentality, generation, etc.

The point of view characteristic of the sociology of knowledge is the consideration of mental productions insofar as they are influenced by social factors.[5] Here again the term "influence" must be taken in a very broad sense. It connotes all the degrees of conditioning which can exist between two variables from simple correspondence up to the most mechanical determinism.

It seems, then, that we may define the sociology of knowledge as the study of mental productions as related to social or cultural factors. This definition is certainly not very precise. Its three elements — mental productions, social factors, and the reference of the first to the second — each one of them entails, as we have just seen, a considerable lack of precision. This indefiniteness is the price of one quality: our definition transcends all the special systems of the sociology of knowledge. These systems vary according to the different replies they give to the following questions: What are the conditioning social factors? What ideas are conditioned? What is the type and degree of this conditioning? Thus the margin of vagueness of the three parts of the definition of the sociology of knowledge permits us to distinguish the various systems in this field. These three questions themselves constitute the principle uniting the different productions of the sociologists of knowledge. It is by virtue of the fact that an author tends to answer these questions that he may be said to deal with the sociology of knowledge and that his system may be compared with others.[6]

The sociology of knowledge has a short history and a long prehistory. We will not trace this evolution, for this task has already been skillfully performed by several others.[7] We will be content to cite several names and to indicate briefly the currents of thought in which our discipline is rooted.

Znaniecki recalls that interest in these questions goes back to the beginning of modern sociology. Comte's "law of the three stages" expressed the idea that there is an interdependence between certain types of philosophy or of knowledge (theology, metaphysics, positive science) and certain forms of social structure.[8] Grünwald looks for the precursors of the sociology of knowledge among the philosophers of the Enlightenment. But we must go much farther back in history if we wish to find the origin of the "discovery" which is the indispensable assumption of our discipline: it is that human knowledge is not solely determined either by its object or by its logical antecedents. This is the indispensable assumption, because if we had not recognized in a general way a certain permeability of knowledge by extra-cognitive factors, nobody would have had the idea of making it the subject of a special study. When the ancient Scholastics put philosophers on guard against "the passion and interest which dim judgment," they did so because they recognized that thought is not determined in a manner purely immanent. In daily life or political discussion, people have not waited for Marx, Freud, and Pareto to qualify the ideas of those with whom they disagreed, as derivations, rationalizations, or defenses of certain interests and desires. Of course, they used other expressions, but the meaning was the same. Politicians notably have always known this. Did Machiavelli not make it his special task to relate the variations in the opinions of men to corresponding variations in their interests?[9]

One further step toward the sociology of knowledge has been taken when, among the irrational roots of thought, the distinction between those which are social and cultural, and those which are not, has been made. Indeed, certain non-theoretical factors which influence thought more or less, may be linked to something besides society — for example, to characteristics which are psychological or biological, individual or general, and even to the physical, geographical, and climatic environment. They may be linked to introversion or extroversion, to being Caucasian or Negroid, to possessing human nature, or to living under the Attic sky or in the fogs of the North. The sociology of knowledge concerns itself only with determinants which are attributable to society.

We can, of course, find in the past indications of this distinction between extra-cognitive factors. But it seems that few thinkers have had their attention attracted to this precise point. Francis Bacon and his theory of the Idola are often cited. Among the sources of error he notes the idols of the tribe, of the cave, of the market and of the theater. But we cannot see clearly whether these "preconceptions" must be attributed to the nature of man, to individual peculiarities, or to tradition.[10] Malebranche, in *De la recherche de la vérité,* is more explicit: "The different ranks, occupations, appointments, and functions, and the adherence to different communities are grounds for the lines of reasoning which start with different principles."[11] Voltaire's theory of the "sacerdotal lie" is also worthy of a place among the early antecedents of the sociology of knowledge.[12]

But if the general idea which is at the base of the sociology of knowledge had been known for a long time, it was not until the beginning of the twentieth century that serious investigations of the field of the social determinants of thought began. This was not by chance. The interest shown in the social determinants of thought was but a manifestation of the awakening of consciousness which had just taken place at this moment, consciousness of the extreme importance of the non-rational in human conduct and in the products of human activity.[13] All that was "discovered" had perhaps been known for a long time, but the interest and the importance granted to these elements was new. In spite of the considerable differences between their tenets, the works of the famous thinkers in the social sciences have brought to light, since about 1860, various aspects of the non-rationality of man. We can cite in history Taine, who interprets literature and art as functions of his famous formula — race, environment, moment; in psychology, Freud; in sociology, Sorel and Pareto; in philosophy, Nietzsche, Blondel, Bergson, etc. Among these creators and representatives of "irrationalist" currents, a special place must be given to Marx, who is perhaps the most immediate and the most important precursor of *Wissenssoziologie*. At least he is at the origin of one of the currents of the sociology of knowledge.[14] It may appear strange to link the herald of dialectical materialism to the "irrationalist" current. It is because of the determining relationship he established between the position of an individual, or rather of a group, with regard to the forces of production and the ability to think correctly. This shows also how near he is to the sociology of knowledge. We will see later on in detail how the Marxist theory of ideology gave birth to Mannheim's system.

Besides the success of the "irrationalist" currents, certain critics of the sociology of knowledge have pointed out another reason which accounts for its emergence and its pertinence to our age. This second reason, related to the one we have just examined, is perhaps more fundamental. Since it explains the birth of a science by social conditions, one may say that it is somewhat *"wissenssoziologisch."*

We have noted above the attitude which consists in interpreting the opinions of others by their origin rather than by their intrinsic value. Instead of asking ourselves whether the arguments in favor of such and such an idea are valid, we look for the possible origin of the idea in a certain individual. This type of interpretation is especially suitable for opinions which seem completely absurd.

We see no reason to take the trouble to discuss the merits of the
idea. It is enough to understand how anyone can *have* such a
curious notion. Now certain social circumstances may spread this
way of interpreting ideas. When the consensus of a special group,
in regard to fundamental values — the conception of the world
and of life — is replaced by universes of thought which are profoundly different and almost without points of contact, most of the
members of the group sharing in one or the other of these systems
of thought become incapable of understanding a *Weltanschauung*
other than their own. The result is that we do not even discuss the
validity of these strange conceptions of life. The only thing which
remains to be done is to explain their origin. Besides, these diverse
conceptions and the organizations supporting and propagating
them are generally avowed antagonists and seek to destroy each
other. In this case, the bearer of different ideas becomes an adversary almost at once. To explain his attitude as determined by
motives unknown to rational arguments seems to be a good weapon.
But the adversary replies in like fashion. Gradually an attitude of
mistrust for ideas develops, and we adopt the habit of neglecting
their face value, so that we no longer consider anything but what
they are supposed to conceal. We may even extend this doubt to
our own ideas: What do they rationalize? Now the state of social
anomie (to use Durkheim's expression), which is at the source of
this attitude, has developed very considerably in the Occident,
especially since the end of the Old Regime. That is why, they say,
it is not accidental that our age has seen the birth of the sociology
of knowledge, which is but an attempt to systematize this attitude.[15]

It is perhaps significant also that the sociology of knowledge
developed after the First World War, in a period when the need
for international understanding was obvious. We can certainly
understand the ideas of other peoples much more completely if we
consider them with regard to their social and cultural bases. Such
an interpretation seems to take account of certain "illogisms"
which an immanent interpretation manages to bring to light very
well but does not succeed in explaining.

Whatever the reasons for the emergence of the sociology of
knowledge, the fact is that the social determinants of knowledge
became the object of methodical research around the year 1910
and especially after the First World War. Among the sociologists
who have made authentic contributions to this new discipline, some

have made them formally under the name of sociology of knowledge, and others have answered its problems while disregarding the name. From this comes a certain vacillation: we can still discover sociologists of knowledge in fact if not in name, and we do not know too well whether such and such an author must be considered as a precursor or as a *Wissenssoziologist*.[16] Several comprehensive bibliographies exist. We will cite here, without claiming to give an exhaustive list, a few names which seem to us particularly important.

In Germany, the article *Die Soziologie des Erkennens* of Wilhelm Jerusalem, who was one of the first if not the first to make use of this term, goes back to 1909. Grünwald cites the period 1921-1924 as the period when *Wissenssoziologie* was definitely established as a science.[17] The most typical authors seem to be Georg Lukács (*Geschichte und Klassenbewusstsein*, 1923), Max Scheler (editor of *Versuche einer Soziologie des Wissens*, 1924; *Die Wissensformen und die Gesellschaft*, 1926) and Karl Mannheim (*Ideologie und Utopie*, 1929). Max Weber did not take any formal interest in the sociology of knowledge, but we find, scattered throughout his work, numerous elements of such a system.[18]

In France, an important part of the work of Durkheim and his school is devoted to the sociology of knowledge, but does not bear the name. The most significant works in this respect are *Les formes élémentaires de la vie religieuse,* by E. Durkheim, *La mentalité primitive,* by Lévy-Bruhl, *Les cadres sociaux de la mémoire,* by Maurice Halbwachs, *La pensée chinoise,* by Marcel Granet.[19]

In the United States, since about 1930-1935, a considerable number of articles, seminar works, doctoral dissertations, and even university courses have been devoted to the sociology of knowledge.[20] These American contributions to *Wissenssoziologie* have drawn their inspiration from European works. It is a curious fact that it is American commentators who have united the German currents within the school of Durkheim, these two tendencies having developed in Europe, not without contacts certainly, but in an extremely independent fashion. Certain currents of thought strictly American might give birth very naturally to a sociology of knowledge. On the one hand, certain aspects of social criticism, such as *The Higher Learning in America* of Thorstein Veblen suggest a study of the influence of academic organization upon the university sciences;[21] on the other hand, the pragmatic philosophy of William

James, C. S. Peirce, and John Dewey, arrives at conclusions on the objectivity of knowledge which are startlingly akin to certain implications of the *Wissenssoziologie*.[22]

The most important works which have been published in the United States are probably those of P. A. Sorokin, *Social and Cultural Dynamics* (Vol. II); of R. K. Merton, *Science, Technology and Society in Seventeenth Century England;* and of Florian Znaniecki, *The Social Role of the Man of Knowledge*. Sorokin and Znaniecki received their formation and started their scientific careers in Europe. However their sociologies of knowledge are independent from the German *Wissenssoziologie* as well as from the Durkheimian school.[23]

II

The sociology of knowledge is a branch of sociology, and the latter claims to be a positive science. The sociology of knowledge, a positive science, has as its ambition a precise description of the way in which certain social factors influence certain mental productions, and to do so follows a strict method of observation. If some generalization is admitted, it will not deviate much from the facts which will always remain the measure of the scientific value of the generalization. Finally, to understand the results obtained in research and to guide further steps, scientific theories will be formulated.[24]

On the other hand, the sociology of knowledge seems to have been impregnated with philosophy, more so, perhaps, than any other sociological discipline. This is due, of course, to the fact that the great majority of works in this field have been written by philosophers. But this fact is not accidental. If these philosophers have shown so much more interest in the sociology of knowledge than in demography, for example, that is because they see a possible or even probable significance in the results obtained by the sociology of knowledge. If our knowledge is dependent, to a very large extent, perhaps, upon extra-cognitive social factors, what may its value be? It seems greatly reduced at least if we measure it in traditional terms of objectivity. (It is, in fact, significant that the first thinkers who noted the action of these non-theoretical factors considered them as causes of error.) From this arises the following question: Can we suppress, or at least neutralize, the influence of these undesirable social factors, or is it impossible to free ourselves from them? In this case, it appears that we are reduced to relativism unless these social determinants can be assimilated to a new concept of objectivity which will define the value of knowledge by something other than our former idea of truth.

If the sociology of knowledge succeeds in showing positively the social determination of ideas — and especially if this determination reaches the fundamental aspects of knowledge — it seems, indeed, that it raises urgent problems for philosophy.

But does it permit us to solve them? That is what some scholars have thought.[25] They have slipped very quickly from the sociology of knowledge to a sociological theory of knowledge, or at least it has seemed to them that philosophical positions were implied in the results of the sociology of knowledge. Thus it has occasionally, or even often, been considered that the sociology of knowledge comprised two parts very closely united: a positive study of the social determinants of thought and a philosophical theory of knowledge which is derived from it. This latter part seemed even more important than the first, and passionate controversies over the sociology of knowledge in Germany as well as in the United States have centered upon relativism and scepticism, the validity of knowledge and the notion of objectivity, rather than upon positive research.[26]

But another group of sociologists and philosophers have forcefully denied that we can give a philosophical significance to the results of the sociology of knowledge. Their main argument is that, in reasoning in such a way, we confuse two questions: that of the origin, and that of the validity of ideas. Let us suppose that Kantianism be proved the product of the interests of the eighteenth century German *bourgeoisie*. This, they say, leaves intact the problem of the truth of Kantianism as a philosophy.[27]

Neither one of these two attitudes seems wholly satisfactory. It is not to be taken for granted, as the first group would wish, that the philosophy of knowledge is a sort of very broad generalization or speculation which is founded upon the sociology of knowledge. Why, indeed, give *Wissenssoziologie,* which is not the only positive discipline having knowledge as its subject, the privileged position of being the base of a philosophy of knowledge?[28] Furthermore — and this seems to have much more weight — a positive science and a philosophical discipline are usually considered very different in their points of departure, their methods, and their aims. These differences have, it seems, been very much emphasized in the domain of the inorganic by the epistemology of the physico-chemical sciences.[29] Naturally, the fact that the philosophy of the material world may not be a generalization of the physico-chemical sciences, is no direct proof of anything in regard to the relationship between *Wissenssoziologie* and the philosophy of knowledge. However, this at least prompts us to ask ourselves if there is not also involved a distinct difference of levels.

Of course, as the second group has pointed out, there is, at least in our tradition of thought, a clear intellectual distinction between origin and validity, but that is not a sufficient reason for treating the two problems separately. For it is necessary that the philosopher who solves the problem of validity be able to think free of all social influence. This seems possible in the question of Kantianism because our thought today is no longer conditioned in any way by the social circumstances which existed in Germany at the end of the eighteenth century. But let us suppose that we have shown that the principle of causality, a fundamental category of our logic, does not exist in Chinese thought and that what is closest to it is a sort of principle of harmony. The question of validity with regard to these two categories claims our attention in these terms: Are there, in reality, relations of causality or rather of harmony? How could the philosopher who would discuss this subsumability of the real in these two categories reject as irrelevant the fact that his own mind has been formed by a tradition in which people are accustomed to see the world in terms either of causality relationships or of harmony relationships?

Besides, even if there were a perfect distinction between questions of genesis and validity, that would not mean that the sociology of knowledge has no philosophical significance. There are in philosophy not only problems of truth, but also those of the nature of knowledge. Now when we seek to explain the results of positive research in the sociology of knowledge, we arrive so easily and so naturally at philosophical conceptions of the nature of knowledge, that it seems, indeed, as if one implies the other.

So then the partisans of the philosophical significance of the sociology of knowledge and those of its philosophical irrelevance do not seem, on either hand, to occupy unassailable positions. In fact, they do not seem to have attempted to solve the central problem of the relations between the sociology of knowledge and the philosophy of knowledge. The first have taken for granted that there was a perfect continuity of the philosophy of knowledge with the results of a positive science of the social determinants of knowledge; the second have been too quick to believe that they have refuted this position by means of the rather superficial distinction between origin and validity. This problem, which has considerable importance in itself, and we think, far-reaching consequences, merits attentive study. The present monograph is an attempt to solve it.[30]

There are two possible methods for its solution. The first consists in making of the relations between the sociology of knowledge and the philosophy of knowledge a simple case of the relations between science and philosophy. It would be sufficient then to see how this question is solved by a very general scheme and to conclude that, since the sociology of knowledge is a positive discipline and the philosophy of knowledge is a philosophical one, they bear the same relation to each other as science in general to philosophy in general.

The dangers of this method appear at once. Either this conception of the relationship between science and philosophy is so abstract that it can provide only a few vague directions for the solution of our special problem, or it is too fixed and defined. This latter is hardly any better, for such precision originates in either an undue generalization or a partisan point of view. Either conception has studied the relationship only between a special type of science and a special philosophical discipline (as in the case cited above of the physico-chemical sciences and the philosophy of inorganic nature), and then affirmed that these special relationships are characteristic of philosophy as such and science as such; or one has considered solely the relationships between science and a particular philosophical system, which gives then only the point of view of a specific philosopher.

To avoid these various deficiencies, we must give this problem a solution which is peculiar to it. That is to say, we must not be satisfied with applying a ready-made formula to the relationship of the sociology of knowledge to the philosophy of knowledge, but we must find this solution through a direct analysis of the sociology of knowledge and of the philosophical implications we draw from it. We will attempt to use this second method without, however, ignoring the valuable suggestions which may be inspired by solutions of analogous problems, especially in the physico-chemical sciences.

There does not yet exist, as the few preceding historical notes indicate, a sociology of knowledge (in the sense of a series of solutions accepted by everyone), but rather disparate *sociologies* of knowledge. To solve our problem, we will study in detail two of these systems — that of Karl Mannheim and that of Pitirim A. Sorokin. Both of these men have formulated a well-developed sociology of knowledge, and have concerned themselves with the philosophical implications of the results which they reached through observation. Furthermore, marked differences separate them. Mannheim is a typical representative of the German *Wissenssoziologie,* while Sorokin develops his system in a totally different, almost antithetical, direction. Mannheim is by formation a philosopher but — although analytical and discerning — little inclined to order; Sorokin is a sociologist and he has constructed, in the grand manner, a vast system of general sociology of which his sociology of knowledge is an integral part. Because differences between the two systems are so marked and profound, they will insure the soundness of our conclusions if the latter prove as correct in regard to one system as in regard to the other.

We will first attempt to determine the significance of the various assertions we encounter in a system of the sociology of knowledge. We find propositions like these: "We observe that such a mental production is determined by such a social factor"; "all ideas of a particular kind are influenced by a particular aspect of society"; "society conditions knowledge"; "such a determination is explained if knowledge is an activity of such a nature"; etc. We immediately realize that these propositions not only have different meanings, but also are of different types and that their criteria of validity do not have to be the same. In a word, they have a different bearing. When we shall have specified the implication of the various stages of a system of *Wissenssoziologie,* we shall see much more readily to what degree a philosophy of knowledge is dependent upon, or independent of, a sociological study of it.

Thus, in spite of the seemingly very restricted character of the central problem of this study — the relationship between the sociology of knowledge and the philosophy of knowledge — the method used to solve it will be the occasion for an exposition of structure and a critical examination of the systems of Mannheim and Sorokin.

One last remark. We do not claim to have undertaken this study with a mind free from all preconceptions. These preconceptions are of two kinds. First come definitions like notions of science, philosophy, epistemology, and gnosiology. We have tried to avoid any dogmatism in adopting these terms in the sense we believe is generally accepted. But these concepts must have one generally accepted meaning — a condition which is not always possible. In such cases, we have chosen one of the meanings and adhered to it consistently. What else could we do?

Preconceptions of another kind are those which Bacon calls *Anticipations of Nature* and without which, as T. H. Huxley has remarked, the positive sciences could not progress.[31] These "anticipations" also seem indispensable to us in the criticism of works of the mind. Ours have special bearing on the structure of a positive science and on the method of philosophical research.

But if definitions are necessary and "anticipations" desirable, it is inexcusable to leave either of these preconceptions unexplained. We hope we have not sinned against this rule and that we have indicated clearly in the course of this work our different assumptions and hypotheses, and their origin.

PART ONE

KARL MANNHEIM

CHAPTER TWO

Mannheim's Sociology of Knowledge

INTRODUCTION

KARL MANNHEIM (1893-1947) is, among the representatives of *Wissenssoziologie,* the one, perhaps, who has provided the most advanced formulation of the sociology of knowledge as such.[1] His theory is rather unsystematic, for he has not attempted to harden into a complete and definitive doctrine the profound perspectives his subtle mind has perceived in the world of ideas.

Born of a Hungarian father and a German mother, Mannheim studied at Budapest, Freiburg, Paris, and Heidelberg. His first interest was the philosophy of knowledge. It was this which furnished him the subject for his doctoral dissertation, *Die Strukturanalyse der Erkenntnistheorie,* 1922. It must be added that he was deeply interested in the social sciences. These two preoccupations gave birth to his sociology of knowledge and account for several of its characteristics.

The intellectual constellation which presided over the birth of his *Wissenssoziologie* might be described in the following way: Marxism (particularly in Karl Marx and Georg Lukàcs), Neo-Kantianism (since Mannheim read Max Weber and took the courses of Heinrich Rickert), and phenomenology (since he was influenced by Max Scheler and was a student of Edmund Husserl). Of these various influences, that of Marx and, through him, Hegel was preponderant; so much so that we may say that Mannheim's sociology of knowledge is principally an elaborated formulation of the theory of ideology. He himself, moreover, presents the sociology of knowledge in this perspective.[2]

19

His doctrine of the sociology of knowledge is found formulated, in its essential points, in a book, *Ideologie und Utopie,* published at Bonn in 1929, and in an article, *Wissenssoziologie,* which appeared in *Handwörterbuch der Soziologie* edited by Alfred Vierkandt at Stuttgart in 1931. The book and the article were translated into English and published in New York in 1936 under the general title *Ideology and Utopia. A Preliminary Approach to the Problem* was written especially for the American edition. This work is a collection of what Mannheim terms scientific essays. This technique was invented, he tells us, in the countries shaken by the repercussions of the intellectual revolution of the Renaissance. "The technique of the thinkers of that period consisted in leaping into any immediate problem which was conveniently at hand and observing it for so long and from so many angles that finally some marginal problem of thought and existence was disclosed and illuminated by means of the accidental individual case."[3]

This form of exposition is particularly well adapted to Mannheim's thought, which operates in a radiating, rather than a linear manner. When Mannheim discovers a central relationship, he follows its consequences in one direction, and then comes back to his point of departure to try another direction. It is not at all astonishing that occasionally the various points of arrival are, or at least appear to be, contradictory. It must be added that Mannheim admits this himself.[4]

But if this technique answers the exigencies of Mannheim's intellectual activity and makes his expositions versatile, varied, and provocative of controversy, it makes his interpretation difficult. We will endeavour to give a systematic account of Mannheim's ideas. When the discrepancies and contradictions spring from two chronologically distinct opinions in juxtaposition, we shall refer to the more recent state of his thought.

After the political events of 1933 which forced him to leave Germany, Mannheim took up his abode in England and became a professor at the University of London. He devoted his intellectual forces to the diagnosis of the crisis of our civilization and to its remedy. He saw the latter in a "planned" society but one in which liberty would be safeguarded. These views are expressed in *Mensch und Gesellschaft im Zeitalter des Umbaus,* 1935 (of which a considerably enlarged English version appeared in 1937) and in *Diagnosis of Our Time,* 1944. We shall indicate the close relationship between the results of the sociology of knowledge and this manner of reforming society.

This first part of our study devoted to Mannheim will be divided according to the distinction he makes between the positive sociology of knowledge and the philosophic consequences of the latter on the plane of the philosophic theory of knowledge.[5] His system of sociology of knowledge will be set forth in the present chapter and will be criticized in the following chapter. Then we shall set about examining his philosophy of knowledge (Chapter Four) and criticizing it (Chapter Five). We will attempt to draw some conclusions from this study in Chapter Six.

ORIGIN OF THE SOCIOLOGY OF KNOWLEDGE

The sociology of knowledge emerged from the theory of ideology. It is closely akin to it, but is increasingly distinguishable from it.

The Marxist ideological analysis was above all a weapon of polemics directed against the dominant groups. When Marx termed the ideas of these groups "ideologies," he meant that they distorted reality, because, instead of showing the situation as it was, they only disguised the interests of these groups. To unmask these hidden interests, by showing how they were linked to certain intellectual conceptions, was the aim of ideological analysis. This method of controversy spread widely among non-Marxists also, who utilized it against Marx himself. Thus Max Weber, Sombart, and Troeltsch did not fail to turn this weapon against the Marxists. The change of attitude resulting from the deliberate application of this method is important. Formerly controversy remained principally upon the plane of ideas. Now, one answers an idea by laying bare the interest it conceals.[6]

Marx, however, scarcely elaborated his notion of ideology and did not draw from his discovery all the theoretical consequences it implied. (We shall see that we may analyze this fact "ideologically.")

Mannheim distinguishes two meanings for the term "ideology": the particular conception and the total conception of ideology. The following is common to the two conceptions: ideas are not taken at their own worth (their "face value," says Mannheim), but are interpreted in the light of the position of the one who expresses them. We do not place our reliance solely on what the adversary *says* to understand the real meaning of his thought and his intent.

This ideological interpretation will be a kind of "transcendental" interpretation, in the sense that it goes beyond what is really expressed. Opposed to this, we find the interpretation which is said to be immanent in the sense that it rests solely upon the expression of thought.[7]

Beside this element common to all ideology, here are the specific traits which distinguish the particular and the total conceptions of ideology from each other. The first considers ideological the particular assertions of the adversary, while the second considers ideological an historico-social group's total conception of the world. In the first case we place ourselves on the psychological plane: we shall say for example that the adversary is lying, that he is concealing or distorting a fact, but we admit, nevertheless, that the two parts have the same criteria of validity in common. The total conception of ideology, on the other hand, takes its stand on a noological plane[8]— that is to say, on the plane of the logical structure of thought. It is not only the content but also the form, the conceptual framework, of a mode of thought which is considered a function of the concrete position of a thinker.

Another difference is that a particular ideology is interpreted mainly as a function of a psychology of interests, such and such interest being the cause of such a lie or deception; while the analysis of total ideology relates different social groups to varied characteristics of the structure of the mind.[9]

A third difference is that the point of reference is always the individual in the interpretation of a particular ideology, and a social group, in the interpretation of a total ideology. Naturally, individual interests will often be expressed in terms of group interests, because each individual shares the point of view of his group in a more or less fragmentary fashion. In this case, reference will nevertheless be made to the individual.[10] Thus, to say that "X affirms such a thing because he is a proletarian" does not mean that we refer to his particular ideology to a social group, but that we refer his assertion to his individual interests insofar as they are identical with those of a group.

Finally, a last difference: The particular ideology, though it may be semi-conscious, is closely akin to falsehood. Total ideology, on the contrary, is completely free from any moral connotation.[11]

The total conception of ideology comes, we see, very close to another concept of Marxist origin: the false consciousness (*falsches*

Bewusstsein)— the totally distorted mind which falsifies everything which comes within its range.[12]

Mannheim will limit the competence of the theory of ideology to the particular conception of ideology, while the total ideologies will constitute the subject matter of the sociology of knowledge. In order to avoid any ambiguity and any moral connotation he replaces the word "ideology" with that of "perspective" (*Aspekstruktur*).

For the sociology of knowledge to emerge from the theory of ideology thus elaborated, there is nothing more to do but to purify it of any trace of its function as an instrument of political struggle. Marx saw total ideology and false consciousness only among his adversaries.[13] The sociology of knowledge will grant no privilege of this type and will endeavor to determine the perspective of any mental production, its own included.

SOME POSITIVE RESEARCH

The sociology of knowledge, as Mannheim has drawn it from the Marxist theory of ideology, might be defined in these terms: research into the relationship there may be between an intellectual perspective and a social group; or again (according to a formula which is more vague but of which Mannheim is fond) a study of the existential determination of knowledge.[14] These formulas are still extremely vague and do not permit us to answer the essential questions raised by any system of a sociology of knowledge: Which are the conditioning social factors, the mental productions conditioned, and the type of reference? It is premature to ask these questions here. We must turn to positive research first in order to see how the principle suggested by the theory of ideology is made clear by reality.[15]

The few examples which follow are explained at length, and occasionally in a rather tortuous fashion, by Mannheim. They have been summarized here and sometimes slightly reinterpreted. They will show in what direction Mannheim's positive research has developed. In the first example, Mannheim studies the different conceptions of history expressed or implied in sundry political doctrines, by putting them in relationship with the social position of the groups which are the vehicles for these various doctrines. These conceptions of history form a part of the utopias of different groups. Thus, we must often refer to these utopias and give some of their traits. "Utopia" means here an idea "situationally transcendent"— that is to say, one which does not correspond to the system of existing personal, economic, or political relationships. It is an image of a better society. We shall return later to this concept, which is very characteristic of Mannheim, and which this definition does not exhaust. It is sufficient for the moment, however.[16]

The liberals (such as Condorcet, Herder, the Girondins) conceive of the objective toward which they are proceeding as an ideal State rationally constructed. It is a formal objective projected into an indeterminate future, from which we are separated by a long, continuously progressing evolution. On the contrary, the anabaptist anarchists, for example (such as Thomas Münzer), are waiting tensely for a complete, mystical revolution which may arrive at any moment and which requires no preparation. In the expectation of another kind of existence into which they hope to be plunged abruptly, historical evolution from the past to the future has no meaning. For them, one may say that history does not exist.

The liberal utopia emanated from groups which were slowly climbing in the social hierarchy. Is it surprising that they optimistically conceived of time as perpetual progress? The extremely rational character of the liberal ideal may be related to two traits of the historico-social position of the *bourgeoisie:* first its secular and rationalist education, which was at the origin of its strength; secondly, the bourgeois classes had been kept from the responsibilities of power for a long time. There was no brush with political reality to limit their rationalist tendencies.[17]

The anabaptist ideas, on the contrary, emanated from the poverty-stricken classes of peasants who were poorly educated and still provided with a medieval mentality. Their poverty demanded a complete, rapid change of condition; their religious faith made them look toward the beyond.[18]

The conservatives do not need a utopia because they are in power. The present state of affairs seems to them a part of the order of the world and so does not raise any theoretical problems. The attacks of the liberals, however, have led them to reflect on their position and to create a utopia of defense. The conservatives (Burke, Moses, v.d. Marwitz, etc.) will turn toward the past, which they consider the creator of values, and will find there "a force working in silence," as Savigny said, the *Volksgeist*. They will be of the opinion that the direction of the State belongs to those whose ancestors, having been the leaders of the people, have had a very special participation in these obscure and unconscious forces in the nation — that is to say, to themselves. For the conservatives, history is an evolution plunging into the past. The present is justified because it is the "flowering" of the past.[19]

The conception of historical evolution integrated in the socialo-communist utopia (we shall not distinguish one from the other) is complex. This character really reflects the position of the proletarian classes which have assumed these doctrines.

A fundamental distinction is established between the immediate future and the distant future. Concerning this latter, unlike the liberals who created a clear image of their objectives, the socialists (at least Marx and Lenin) refuse to outline a plan for the future society. "Communism for us is not a condition that is to be established nor an ideal to which reality must adjust itself. We call communism the actual movement which abolishes present conditions.[20] History unfolds according to an immanent (dialectical) law. Our action has but little influence upon its direction in the far-distant future.

On the contrary, we have a grip upon the immediate future. A political action is then possible. It will be a question of forming the theory of the stage at which we find ourselves and, having rationalized the situation in this way, to act upon the following stage. There we must elaborate a new theory. We must have our minds constantly on the alert, for if our rationalization is not adequate, our action will be ineffectual. Furthermore, it is always possible for the situation to define itself in an unforeseeable constellation of elements.

This mixture of historical determinism and of the possibility of acting upon events, of rationalism and intuitionism, is particularly well adapted to the situation of the proletarian classes. The dialectical march of history gives the assurance of final success to groups upon which an historical mission has devolved. The consciousness of this privileged place in history is necessary for the proletariat, which occupies an inferior situation in the social hierarchy. The vague character of the final objective leaves each one the possibility of imagining it according to his own desires. When a movement wishes to include the proletarians of all countries, it is preferable for each one to be able to color the final goal according to his own particular aspirations. It is easier to unite for the "abolition of present conditions" than to do so for a positive purpose. Finally, a huge class emerging gradually into political consciousness has before it an indeterminate future.

On the other hand, when it is a question of the immediate future, this theory, which is essentially a provisory rationalization of the situation, allows the leader the adaptability necessary for revolutionary action. Ready for the unforeseeable, he will always be on the watch for the opportune moment and will constantly have to redefine the situation with a view to immediate action.

In a word, the rationalist character of this utopia, viewed sociologically, expresses the conditions necessary for cohesion among people who are not near each other locally but simply occupy similar positions in the economico-social system. The precapitalistic groups, like the guilds for example, could be united by common traditions or feelings. But sentimental bonds are effective only in a very limited space, whereas a theoretical *Weltanschauung* has a unifying power across great areas. It is in this sense that we must understand Lenin's phrase, "Without a revolutionary theory there can be no revolutionary movement."[21]

We see thus how the various aspects of the socialist conception of time correspond to the position of a group slowly becoming conscious of its political importance, a group spread internationally and one whose most active elements are ready for revolutionary action.[22]

In the fascist utopia, history is not articulated, and we can recognize no tendency in it. On the contrary, Mussolini held that "anything is possible, even the most impossible and most senseless." Thus, at the origin of fascism at least, they are not building any ideal city in the future and give very little attention to defining aims. "Our program is quite simple: we wish to rule over Italy. People are always asking us about our program. There are too many already. Italy's salvation does not depend on programs but on men and strong wills." For the fascists, history is considered without structure, always susceptible of receiving whatever direction may be given it by a determined minority. "At any rate, history proves that social changes have always been first brought about by minorities, by a mere handful of men."

Sociologically, this doctrine corresponds to the position of an assault group (*putschist*) which wishes to seize power when the occasion presents itself.[23]

The conclusion drawn from this long example is, according to Mannheim, that it is almost possible to establish a sociological correlation between the types of thought of an organized group and a consistent or systematic interpretation of history. Likewise, there exists a profound affinity between groups socially uprooted and loosely integrated and an ahistoric intuitionalism. It is remarkable also that the various utopias evolve as the groups become more stable; they are also more permeable to long-range historical views and an ordered conception of society. Likewise, any group which has come to power and been confronted with the practical problems of government gradually assimilates conservative elements into its utopia.[24]

Another example is furnished by complex concepts like "democracy," "freedom," whose equivocal character is often proclaimed. The various senses of these concepts frequently correspond to the particular perspectives of certain groups. Thus, "freedom" has meant the right for each organized social stratum ("estate" in the sense of the old regime) to live in accordance with its privileges or "liberties." On the other hand, this same term "freedom" has been used to mean the enjoyment, for all men, of fundamentally equal rights (which then implies the destruction of "liberties"). The two meanings of this word bear the mark of their social origin. It is easy to attribute the first sense of freedom to a conservative class seeking to maintain an advantageous historical situation and the second sense to a group aiming to change a non-equalitarian political order.[25]

These first two examples concern the social conditioning of the subject matter of concepts. The fundamental categories of thought may also be related to social groups. Thus we may use morphological or analytical categories in political doctrine. The first do not break down the concrete totality of the facts of experience, but rather seek to preserve their unique character. The analytical approach, on the contrary, breaks each totality down into smaller and more general unities which can then be combined anew.

Now the first of these approaches is characteristic of the conservative writers of the beginning of the nineteenth century in Germany (and also of the beginning the twentieth), while the second is habitual to the parties of the left. Why this correspondence? The things which we are ready to accept, and which fundamentally we do not desire to change, very naturally seem to us indissoluble totalities. On the contrary, the groups which wish to reconstruct the world according to an abstract plan will very naturally dissociate reality into its first elements.[26]

The following example shows that a group by its position in society may even develop certain faculties among its members. Thus the members of certain minority groups — the Jews, for example — generally give evidence of a more abstract and reflexive mind than the representatives of majority groups. That is because a minority, in order to continue to be tolerated, and to adapt itself to the social environment, must ceaselessly reflect on its conduct. The native acts spontaneously, in accordance with the rules of his group. The minority member does not succeed in conducting himself in a way that society expects of him except by a very deliberate action. From this comes his cast of mind.[27]

Finally, the last example presented here explains by sociological reasons why a certain level of abstraction is never exceeded in the Marxist theory of ideology. It is sufficient to elaborate theoretically the discoveries implied in the latter to have the beginnings, at least, of a sociology of knowledge. Now that has never been done. It is due to the fact that "this relationship was perceived only in the thought of the opponent. It was probably due, furthermore, to subconscious reluctance to think out the implications of a concretely formulated insight to a point where the theoretical formulation latent in it would be clear enough to have a disquieting effect on one's own position."[28]

THE THREE ESSENTIAL ELEMENTS IN MANNHEIM'S SYSTEM

Positive research — of which the few examples we have just summarized give an idea — permits us to make a bit more precise the notion of the sociology of knowledge which Mannheim had elaborated from the Marxist theory of ideology.

What is the *social factor* which plays the role of independent variable and which influences thought? It is the *group*. More exactly, it is, on the one hand, the *situation* of a group in society and in history and, on the other, the objectives and necessities of its *collective action*.[29] Thus the socialist conception of historical evolution was put into relationship with the position of the proletariat (an "inferior," international class) and the necessities for its collective action (union, revolution).

The situation of a group in society is defined mainly in terms of political power (to be or not to be in power) and economic power (to be rich or poor). Thus the *bourgeoisie* is said to "climb" in the society of the eighteenth and nineteenth centuries because it gradually captures power and develops the means of production for its own profit. The utopia of the anabaptists corresponds to their lack of political and economic power. However, Mannheim sometimes calls upon the help of factors other than power to define a situation — for example, the secular and rationalist education of the *bourgeoisie,* the mystical mentality of the anabaptists. It is, however, by these relationships of power that a situation is principally characterized.

The "historic" situation is a rather ambiguous expression in Mannheim's vocabulary, one which often means simply that a situation (defined, as above, in terms of power) has been perpetuated during a certain period of the past. To say thus that the historic situation of the nobility corresponds to conservative ideas means that the fact that nobility had governed for generations predisposed it to a conservative conception of the world. This term "historic," however, has also for Mannheim the richer content which was given to it by the German historicist school and then by Marxism. History is a metaphysical reality. Since it is absolute reality, it has a normative value. In this thinking, the historic situation of a group means the position which is assigned to it in the evolution of time and from which the group draws, as it were, its value in regard to absolute reality. Although he never refers explicitly to such a conception, it seems that Mannheim occasionally employs this term in a context which implies such an interpretation. Thus, he writes: "Every theory which arises out of a class position and is based not on unstable masses but on organized *historical groups* must of necessity have a long-range view."[30]

Which are these groups? The manner in which their position is defined (in terms of economic and political power) shows indeed that it is a question of social classes, or at least of groups which are more restricted than a class but which identify themselves with their structure. Mannheim puts it clearly: "By these groups we mean not merely classes, as a dogmatic type of Marxism would have it, but also generations, status groups, sects, occupational groups, schools, etc."[31] We cannot then limit ourselves to classes, for if we do not center our attention upon highly differentiated

social groupings, it will be impossible to find social factors corresponding to the wealth of the types of knowledge and of the
perspectives which have appeared in the course of history. Nevertheless, "we do not intend to deny that of all the above mentioned
social groupings and units, class stratification is the most significant, since in the final analysis all the other social groups arise
from and are transformed as parts of the more basic conditions of
production and domination."[32]

This means that, on the one hand, the notion of undifferentiated
class is not sufficient to play the part of independent variable in a
sociology of knowledge but that, on the other hand, the particular
groupings which are the most qualified to fulfill this function can
be only subdivisions of classes, since the latter express most adequately the relations of production and domination in a society.[33]

The first term of the relationship between social factors and
form of knowledge having been made clear, let us pass to the
second. What are the "mental productions" which correspond thus
to the social group? Mannheim's examples are limited to the field
of political theories (except in the case of the reflexive and abstract
mind of minority-group members, this example being, moreover,
extracted from a work subsequent to his "sociology of knowledge
period"). However, when he indicates what spheres of thought
are socially determined, he extends their limits beyond political
doctrine. Thus he speaks of "social sciences,"[34] "historical knowledge,"[35] of *"Weltanschauungen,"*[36] of "ontology,"[37] even of "the
foundations of the theory of knowledge,"[38] or even more broadly
and vaguely of "practical thought."[39] He excludes mathematics,
because "the assertion (to cite the simplest case) that twice two
equals four gives no clue as to when, where, and by whom it was
formulated." He excludes also the natural sciences, which, especially in their quantitative phases, are largely detachable from the
historico-social perspective of the investigator.[40]

Since the zone of influence has been thus delimited, it remains
to be known what are the socially determined aspects of the qualitative sciences. Here the answer is clear: The influence of the
existential factors is not only peripheral. It extends not only to
the form of ideas and to the evolution of the latter, but also to their
content: the meaning of concepts; the fundamental categories of
political and social thought (in the example of morphological and

analytical thought); the prevailing model of explanation (which is implicitly in the mind of a person when he reflects upon an object, as for example when he wishes to solve the problems of the social sciences upon the model of physics); the level of abstraction of a theory (in the example of the Marxists who have not formulated their doctrines on a more abstract plane); the ontologies subjacent to social theories.[41]

We may then say that the domain of qualitative knowledge (of which the results are not quantifiable) is socially determined in its form, in its content, in all its aspects.

Since the two terms of the relationship have been somewhat clarified, what is the nature of the bond uniting them? Up to the present, we have employed vague terms: thought "corresponds" to social conditions . . .; such a theory "expresses" the position of the proletariat . . .; the social situation "has an effect upon" . . .; or again we have utilized the more precise terms "determination," "conditioning," but indicated that we did not take them in their full sense. The time has come to make them more clear and especially to answer the central question: Is the social or political thought of a group necessarily mechanically determined by its social and historical position? Or is it only a question of a certain influence?

In a note at the foot of a page, Mannheim takes care to warn us that it is only through empirical research that we shall be able to determine the degree of correlation between social factors and thought.[42] Let us refer then to the facts he has analyzed.

The expressions he has used to convey the relationship between knowledge and society are revealing.[43] They are varied and not too precise, but they indicate clearly at least that it cannot be a question of a rigorous determinism. One of them alone, "it is never an accident," seems to imply a necessary relationship. It applies to the case of the Marxism which has not elaborated an abstract theory of ideology. In the exposition of this case, however, Mannheim calls in other terms less clear: "The narrowed focus which a given position imposes . . . *tends* to obstruct the general and theoretical formulation."[44] Besides, whatever this example may imply, it seems that the other expressions imply only a rather loose type of relationships.

If we pass from the very form of the expressions to the examination of the examples themselves, an analogous conclusion is called for. The types of thought really "correspond," are indeed "in harmony," with social situations — but would we dare to say that the latter are the necessary condition for the former? Indeed, it seems not.

In short, even when Mannheim qualifies this relationship without referring to examples, he is very prudent. He warns us that in his preferred formula "existential determination of knowledge," *determination* does not mean a mechanical cause-effect sequence and that the question of its meaning remains open.[45] Elsewhere he simply affirms that thought is bound by the social and vital situation in which it arises; or that "when the social situation changes, the system of norms to which it had previously given birth ceases to be *in harmony* with it"; or that "ideas, forms of thought and psychic energies persist and are transformed *in close conjunction* with social forces";[46] and that "a different mentality *corresponds* to each social structure."[47]

It seems then that we may conclude that Mannheim has not stopped at a single term but that they all indicate a "correspondence" of ideas to the social situation. Such a word insists much more upon harmony among two elements than upon the conditioning of the one by the other. Evidently we know perfectly that it is knowledge which corresponds to society and not the contrary. This influence may be more or less rigid according to the case. May it reach an absolute determination? Perhaps it may, in that Mannheim does not exclude this possibility — but not very probably, in that he does not give any example of it to my knowledge.

It would be useful perhaps to compare this term "correspondence" with Mannheim's philosophy to understand the bearing it had in his eyes. He did not wish to give it explicitly anything but an empirical meaning — the one to which we have given our attention up to the present time; however, he expresses a relationship perhaps more profound than it may appear at first sight. In the Hegelian perspective interpreted by Marx, the gradual development of the world is its last reality. The changes which we perceive around us are, as it were, but manifestations emanating from this fundamental development. Would not the word "correspondence" indicate that, for Mannheim, mental productions and social conditions designate two correlative aspects of the same total reality?[48] Consequently, the priority of social factors over knowledge would not imply that the former are the cause of the latter. It would be a question of priority on the plane of phenomena, while, on the ontological plane, ideas and society are complementary manifestations of the same reality.[49] However this may be, this excursion into metaphysics must be placed in parentheses at the present stage of this study. We do not have to take into consideration here the possible metaphysical repercussions of the expressions used by Mannheim. It seems useful, however, to be conscious of this other dimension of certain of his concepts.

We have attempted to see to what conclusions Mannheim's positive research has led him in the process of defining more accurately the three elements necessary to any sociology of knowledge. The following formula endeavors to summarize the results of this: Qualitative sciences, in their form and content as well as in their structure, correspond more or less rigidly to the social and historical situation of the groups into which social classes are subdivided.

THE EXPLANATION

In order to complete the exposition of Mannheim's sociology of knowledge, we still have to describe the type of explanation employed by him and his method.

It is not enough, in fact, to establish a correlation between thought and social group — one still has to explain it. These two elements — relation and explanation — are often confused. There are two reasons for this. First, the very fact of having established a relationship of a certain kind frequently implies, in an evident manner, the explanation we claim to give of it. Thus, to put in correspondence a social stratification like "the nobility" and a theory like "the conservative idea of freedom which is the right to exercise one's own privileges" does not seem to render necessary the expression of the evident explanation — which is: "The nobility wishes to continue to exercise these privileges and seeks to justify them."

A second reason for confusion is that, in the "order of psychological invention,"[50] the explanation precedes and accompanies the establishment of a relationship. It is because we think that those who enjoy a favorable position wish to maintain it that we have the idea of relating such a conception of liberty to the class for which this conception is advantageous.

The two questions are, however, distinct and appear so in certain examples. Let us suppose that the following correlation has been discovered by chance and then worked out: "The writers who sprang from the German nobility of the beginning of the nineteenth century use morphological categories in their political theories, while those who sprang from the bourgeois classes utilize analytical categories." The explanation of this correspondence is not obvious, for, at first sight, there is a means of accounting for it in several ways. It might be possible that the pedagogical methods used in the education and schooling of the children of noble families favor the morphological approach, while the establishments attended by the bourgeois avail themselves of a different pedagogy. Or again it may be that life in the country, in small, well-organized communities, inspires a synthetic view of things, while, in the large cities where the bourgeois live, the social structure appears less visible than the multitude of individuals. This might give the mind the habit of reducing everything to its first elements. And other explanations could be found.

Mannheim affirms, moreover, that "our task is not only to indicate the fact that we think differently in different social situations, but also to make the causes of this intelligible."[51] However, he does not announce formally his principle of explanation. As the latter is fairly evident from his works, it is not difficult to determine it.

This principle has its origin also in the theory of ideology. It is the Marxist principle of interest, of which we may give this rather crude formulation (for which the Marxists are probably more responsible than Marx himself[52]): "Ideas are but a conscious or unconscious translation of the economic interests of the capitalists."

Mannheim brushes aside the polemical aspect of this idea. Then the way in which he uses this principle implies a distinction which is important insofar as it brings a precision to the principle of interest.

Here is the distinction. An idea may first translate the interests of a group in that it is strategically useful to that group in realizing its collective objectives. Thus the correspondence between the proletarian class and the rationalism of the socialist utopia is explained by the fact that this rationalism makes possible the cohesion of a group of persons who are locally distant, and that the union of the proletarians gives them the strength to create a victorious revolution. Likewise the correlation between the minority group and a high degree of abstract and reflexive thought is explained by the fact that this power of abstraction is the best process for adaptation a minority has at its disposal. It is mainly in this way that "vulgar Marxism" conceives that an idea expresses interests: it is the weapon the dominant class uses to remain in power.

On the other hand, an idea may also be linked to the interests of a group in the sense that it expresses the desires of that group. Thus the correlation between the liberal conception of freedom and the *bourgeoisie* is explained in the sense that this conception is the one the *bourgeoisie* would like to see realized. Again, the anabaptist idea of a time which is a present without past or future is explained because it translates the expectation of a mystical and sudden revolution.

We see that these two senses are clearly distinct: A doctrine may translate the ideal of a group very well without having a strategic value. The unorganized idea of time of the anabaptists was not probably very adequate to produce the revolution for which they were waiting. Vice versa, a conception strategically useful may not express the aspirations of a group. The intuitive character of the socialist doctrine gave it a great revolutionary suppleness, but it is difficult to say whether it translated a desire of the proletariat.

We might formulate Mannheim's explanation in the following manner. The mental productions of a social group correspond to its position because, in its struggle to obtain or retain economic and political power, the group, consciously or unconsciously, utilizes its cognitive productions, whether it be to express its desires, or as a direct means of combat in the pursuit of its collective objectives. That is tantamount to saying that qualitative knowledge is tied to a social perspective because it is a means of adaptation to the conditions of the struggle for domination.

THE METHOD OF RESEARCH

Positive research in the domain of the sociology of knowledge presents problems raised in these terms: A mental production (a political doctrine, a social theory) is given. How are we to put it in correspondence with a social group? Mannheim says that we shall not be able to answer this question of sociological imputation until after having placed the mental production in question in its context on the plane of ideas. In this respect, we will draw our inspiration from the methods employed by the philologic disciplines and the history of art to "date" and "situate" writings or works of art.

This is how Mannheim describes very schematically the method of the sociology of knowledge.[53]

The first stage is located on the intellectual plane (*Sinnegemässe Zurechnung*). Starting with the various isolated mental productions, we reconstruct a complete intellectual system in which these various elements will be co-ordinated around a *Weltanschauung* which they express. Thus, for example, a communist or liberal conception of the world will have been recreated *a priori*.

But "it is quite possible that the investigator will succeed in building up out of fragments of expression the two antithetical, closed systems of conservative thought on the one hand and liberal thought on the other, although the liberals and conservatives of the period might not, in actuality, have thought that way at all."[54]

The question will be then — and it will be the second stage (*Faktizitätszurechnung*)— to examine if historically the conservative and liberal writers really thought in a manner conforming to the hypothetical reconstruction. At the end of this inquiry, we shall know the real history of these two styles of thought in a precise and articulate manner. Instead of having a description of rough aspects, we shall obtain an analysis of the structure of these styles of thought.

Finally, the third stage is that of sociological imputation:

As sociologists we do not attempt to explain the forms and variations in conservative thought, for example, solely by reference to the conservative *Weltanschauung*. On the contrary, we seek to derive them first from the composition of the groups and strata which express themselves in that mode of thought. And secondly, we seek to explain the impulse and the direction of development of conservative thought through the structural situation and the changes it undergoes within a larger, historically conditioned whole (such as Germany, for instance), and through the constantly varying problems raised by the changing structure.[55]

This means that we shall seek the correspondences which exist between, on the one hand, the content and form of conservative thought as it has been realized historically, and, on the other hand, the composition and situation of the group which is the bearer of that thought.

CHAPTER THREE

Evaluation of Mannheim's Sociology of Knowledge

IN THE PRECEDING CHAPTER, we endeavored to explain Mannheim's system without employing any concept foreign to its terminology. In this criticism, we shall introduce a few, especially those which show the various stages of the elaboration of a scientific system. These notions originate in the methodology of the physico-chemical sciences. In the very general acceptation which is given them here, they apply to most of the positive sciences.

We shall distinguish three stages in establishing a scientific system. First, we have research into facts: does a certain mental production of a certain conservative author correspond to his social affiliation? Then we have the expression of the results of this research in a general way. Finally, we have the explanation in the construction of a scientific theory.

This outline, in this very simple form, is rather generally accepted, but it is seldom made explicit in the practice of the social sciences. We do not think that its application to Mannheim will distort his system (we shall see that these categories express it perfectly), but we think it will be productive in that it will underscore the articulations of Mannheim's sociology, and will bring to light its deficiencies.[1]

FIRST STAGE: THE RESEARCH INTO FACTS

The facts with whose observation we are concerned here are complex. Thus we must see, in a particular case, how a certain idea (the concept of freedom, for example), or a certain aspect of

37

an idea (the morphological approach, for instance), may be attributed to such and such a group.

We are acquainted with the method advocated by Mannheim.[2] Its three stages are these: to reconstruct a systematic mentality (liberal, etc.); to see if it is actually realized (did the liberals of a certain epoch actually think like that?); and finally to impute it to certain social groups (the liberal mentality corresponds to the situation of the *bourgeoisie*).

This manner of proceeding, by beginning with a reconstruction *a priori,* seems to offer serious objections. Since it is ultimately a question of performing a historian's work, of seeing what the liberals of a certain epoch were thinking, is it not artificial to elaborate in detail a type of mentality which they should, or might, have had, but which, very probably, they did not have? Is this not putting the cart before the horse?[3]

First, it seems so because it is often impossible to pass judgment on the incompatibility or compatibility of two attitudes of thought. Robert K. Merton gives the example of pacifism and abolitionism (in connection with slavery) in the United States. Among the Quakers, these two attitudes were combined; Garrison and his disciples abandoned non-resistance to make war on slavery. Merton cites also the union, in the Catholic Church, of two seemingly incompatible values: celibacy and fecundity. The contradiction between these two values is largely avoided by linking them to the different social statuses of the ecclesiastical order: linking celibacy to the sacerdotal status, and unrestricted fertility to the married laity.[4] It seems impossible to reconstruct a complete *Weltanschauung* in cases analogous to the latter.

Then, even if we start with a certain number of values and attitudes which are all, shall we say, liberal, there are different means of combining them into systems. Freedom may be inferred from equality, or equality from freedom. These systems will be different according to the pre-eminence we give to one or the other of these values.[5]

It seems then that it is by accident that a conception of the world formulated on a purely intellectual plane corresponds to history. Is it of any use then to create a structure which very probably will have to be abandoned later?

Such a technique seems even to introduce the danger of making the comprehension of the historic mentality more difficult. To be sure, it is impossible to undertake research with the mind free from all anticipation, and this, moreover, is not desirable. To obtain answers, we must ask questions; but to imagine by oneself a complete, very detailed reply (and it is really a question of that here)[6] is to risk reducing our receptivity to the answer of reality.

Mannheim must have raised for himself all these serious objections which immediately present themselves to the mind. What then are the good points of this method which outstrip its grave disadvantages?

These "reconstructions of the style of thought" might very well have been inspired in Mannheim by the famous "ideal types" of Max Weber. In any case, they are closely akin to them. Like the ideal type, the reconstruction *a priori* is a mental image which stylizes a mentality in a manner which seems characteristic to the investigator. Before studying the various historic religions, Max Weber thinks that he may take the liberty of being "unhistorical" and construct ethical religious attitudes which are presented in greater unity than has ever been the case in their actual development.[7] These reconstructions must be highly integrated and completely consistent on the level of the meanings.[8]

What is the utility of these types? They are a technical aid in the sense that they enable the investigator to determine the discrepancy between the historical phenomenon and the theoretically constructed type. Furthermore, they are not so far from the reality because men have always valued very much the logical consistency of an attitude.[9]

These two justifications of the usage of ideal types which Max Weber gives — that they permit us to arrange historical facts by locating them with regard to more abstract images, and that they deviate but little from reality because men have always valued highly the logical consistency of their attitudes — these two justifications might be taken up again by Mannheim. However, it seems that constructions *a priori* have another function for Mannheim, one which he judges more essential. In constructing an attitude, the observer, as it were, lives it intellectually. This is the essential for Mannheim. In like manner, he tells us, suppose that we wish to explain the ethics of primitive Christian communities mainly in terms of the resentment of oppressed social strata, and their completely apolitical view of the world as corresponding to the mentality of classes which did not yet have aspirations to power. For an observer who has not taken a position pro or con in the inferior classes' struggle for ascendancy and who has not discovered the productive aspect of resentment in his own experience, it would be impossible to imagine such an explanation or merely to understand the tension which impregnated the situation of primitive Christianity.[10] In this example, Mannheim seems to say that the observer must have his interests really engaged in the struggle of today's classes in order to analyze the situation of the past in terms of class struggle. This — which goes a bit beyond the point which interests us — shows indeed the very considerable importance which Mannheim grants to inner comprehension. He has taken up again Dilthey's famous opposition between explanation (*Erklärung*) and comprehension (*Verstehen*). Comprehension is the sympathetic intuition which gives us access to, and makes us probe deeply into, the subject. He cites approvingly Max Weber's conception which makes of sociology a discipline of interior comprehension (as opposed to the natural sciences which "explain").[11]

Such seems to me to be the sense of Mannheim's reconstruction *a priori:* it is an effort to recreate a mentality by oneself in order to understand from inside all the articulations. Even if such a reconstruction does not coincide with a historic mentality, the intimacy it implies with the essential themes of a conception of life permits us to grasp it better as a living whole. Without this effort to interiorize a vision of the world, the observer, when in the course of the second stage he is brought face to face with the various elements scattered through a multiplicity of historic documents, risks not seeing any link between them and furnishing but a superficial description instead of an articulated analysis.[12]

If this interpretation of Mannheim's thought is correct, we may ask ourselves what the worth of this technique, closely related to a certain literary technique, may be. But, as the examples given by Mannheim show, it is precisely a question here of studying mentalities and *Weltanschauungen*. Now the relations between the various elements of a conception of the world are not of the same kind as the relations between theorems of a system of geometry, and they cannot be apprehended in the same way. They obey a logic at once less strict and more subtle. In this field, only intuition can furnish deep insights.[13]

This does not introduce any vagary into the sociology of knowledge, for this internal comprehension of a mentality is only a preliminary stage, but one of first importance. Later there will be a question of submitting it to a strict historical control.

This discussion of the method has emphasized a point which is worth being underscored. We saw that Mannheim established correspondences between very particular aspects of thought and the social situation (thus between the morphological form of conservative studies and the desire for things to remain in place; or between the rationalism of the socialist utopia and the fact that the proletarians are spread throughout the world). But we see, through what he says of his method, that these particular points can be studied only as elements of a more comprehensive whole — the conception of the world. In other words, Mannheim begins by relating the liberal *Weltanschauung,* let us say, to the situation and interests of the *bourgeoisie.* Then, in this general relationship of correspondence, he seeks particular correlations between a certain aspect of liberal thought (that which is analytical, for instance) and a certain aspect of their situation (the fact that they desire to reconstruct society by beginning with simple elements, for example).

This method, which appears very satisfactory, unfortunately has not often been brought into play by Mannheim. With the exception of some not very numerous monographs (such as *Das konservative Denken,* 1927, and *Das Problem der Generationen,* 1928) and various examples illustrating his conceptions, he has restricted himself rather to a theoretical work. This is not because he minimized the significance of the "facts" in sociology.

> The most important task of the sociology of knowledge at present, is to demonstrate its capacity in actual research in the historical-sociological realm. It must emerge from the stage where it engages in casual intuitions and gross generalities (such as the crude dichotomy involved in the assertions that here we find bourgeois thinking, there we find proletarian thinking, etc.)[14]

Or again, he affirms that "only empirical investigation will show us how strict is the correlation between life-situation and thought process."[15] If then Mannheim has not studied numerous facts, it is not because he underestimates the importance of empirical research. He thought that a careful analysis of a few cases would assure a sufficient empirical basis for his generalizations. In the following section, we shall see to what extent we may admit that he is right.

The criticism of the first stage of Mannheim's system may be summarized in two points: His method of research into facts is valid. His empirical observation is limited to a small number of cases.

SECOND STAGE: THE RESULTS OF EMPIRICAL OBSERVATION

In the physico-chemical sciences, the results of experiments are synthesized in a general formulation which is usually called a "law." We shall not employ this term to designate the conclusions of empirical observations, because it suggests the repetition of a large number of similar experiments and a strong determinism in the future (all conditions remaining the same, the relationship between two phenomena, as it is expressed by the law, will prove correct in the future as it has in the past). Whether or not such laws can exist in the sociology of knowledge is a question we leave open. In order not to appear to judge its solution beforehand, we shall refrain from applying the word "law" to the syntheses of the results of empirical observations.

The formulation of these results shares with the physico-chemical laws the faculty of expressing the conclusions of positive research in a general way, but a way whose scope does not exceed that of the observations. There is generalization in the sense that we separate from each one of these particular observations an element which is found again in all, and that we disregard their other aspects. On the other hand, we do not exceed these observations in the sense that we express their sum.

As far as we know, there does not exist an accepted term for these "synthetic formulations of the conclusions of empirical observations." To avoid frequent repetition of this periphrasis, we shall express it in one of these terms: synthesis, conclusion, generalization.

In establishing how Mannheim, by means of his observations, makes clear the three essential elements of the sociology of knowledge, a general formula was obtained in the preceding chapter. That formula corresponds exactly to the idea which has just been expressed. It is this proposition which we shall take as the point of departure for our criticism: The qualitative sciences, in their form and content as well as in their structure, correspond more or less strictly to the social and historic situation of the groups into which the social classes are subdivided.

Since such a formula expresses a sum of empirical results, its validity is measured by the observations which permitted its establishment. Criticism will then consist principally in considering whether its scope does not exceed what the observations permitted us to conclude.

THE DEPENDENT VARIABLE: QUALITATIVE SCIENCES

Let us stop at the first words of the formula — "the qualitative sciences." We remember that this idea is defined negatively and includes practically everything that is not physico-chemical or at least quantifiable science. This term has indeed a broad denotation. It covers the social sciences, philosophy, theology, postulates of epistemology, *Weltanschauungen,* etc. Now the positive research on which this generalization is based dealt with a much more restricted field: that of political conceptions as they had crystallized in the Germany of the nineteenth and twentieth centuries. This restricted field most certainly forms a part of the "non-quantitative sciences," but may the relationships which prove correct in political doctrine be extended to the latter? That is to say, is this political domain a good specimen of non-quantitative science, or, on the contrary, must we expect that the relationship affirmed by the law will prove more correct there than elsewhere?

Unfortunately, such is the case. It is in fact very clear that there must be a closer correspondence between political conceptions and social groups than between the latter and conceptions concerning the final nature of the material world. A social group, as Mannheim conceives it, is very conscious of its collective aims. Now the latter are by nature political and social. We may then foresee a strict affinity between this group and its political conceptions. But may we expect as strict an affinity between this group and another sector of knowledge? No. Therefore the first reproach to be aimed at Mannheim's generalization is the following. His positive research dealt with a favorable sector (a sector, that is to say, in which it is very probable that the fundamental relationship expressed by the generalization will be more verifiable than elsewhere); then he extends the scope of the results he has obtained to the whole of qualitative knowledge. This seems unwarranted.

THE INDEPENDENT VARIABLE: SOCIAL GROUPS

Let us consider now the other term of Mannheim's generalization — "the social factor." This means classes and the groups into which classes are subdivided.

Nowhere does Mannheim say what he means by social class. He is so very inexact on this point that some critics have wondered if, in the sociology of knowledge, "class" was not to be considered as a sort of metaphysical being which is endowed with its own conscience, and which appears in the individuals who share in it. It would be an entity of the type of the Nordic race or Gothic man.[16] Undoubtedly, the method for the reconstruction of a mentality resembles this, but it is only the first stage of the imputation, and the third consists in relating ideas and actual social groups. Besides, it seems indispensable to reach finally actual groups.

But all the same it would be necessary to define them. Although Mannheim is in the Marxist tradition from several points of view, it does not seem that it is the part the groups play in the process of production which is the essential element of his conception of class.[17]

The groups he considers — nobility, officials, *bourgeoisie,* proletariat — present two peculiarities to his eyes, it seems: Each one of them is doubled with a team of intellectuals who elaborate the group's social and political doctrines. In addition, each one of these groups generally has a political expression — a party which organizes its collective action.[18] It follows naturally from this that these groups are endowed with a strong class consciousness.

Now all social classes and all social groups are far from enjoying such advantages. We can cite, for example, the peasants, the white-collar workers, the leisure classes (which, however, have had so important a part in the protection and diffusion of the arts and literature). That class consciousness is not a universal phenomenon for all social groups of the type envisaged by Mannheim is well known.[19]

Again, Mannheim has observed cases favorable to his generalization. It is, in fact, much more probable that a clearer correspondence will be found between the social and political ideas and the social position of a group when this group is organized politically and intellectually than when it is not.

This error is further accentuated by the fact that Mannheim sometimes confuses a social stratum with its organized political expression. "It is always possible in the case of a work in the social sciences to say whether it was inspired by the 'historical school,' or 'positivism,' or 'Marxism,' and from what stage in the development of each of these it dates." Now he really seems to consider that to be Marxist or positivist is to belong to a social class, for he continues immediately with these words: "In assertions of this sort, we may speak of an 'infiltration of the social position' of the investigator into the results of his study and of the 'situational-relativity' or the relationship of these assertions to the underlying reality."[20] Now there is no perfect equivalence between the socialist and communist parties and the proletariat. Marx himself recognized that all the members of the proletariat were not Marxists and he had invented a word to designate them, *Lumpenproletariat*. The conceptions of a party sometimes correspond much more to the "social and historic situation" of a little group of the party's bureaucrats than to that of the class of which the party is supposed to be the political expression.

The comparison of Mannheim's positive research with the law he has drawn from it has permitted us to address a serious reproach to him. Twice he has observed cases favorable to his theory, and he has concluded that the relationship which proves correct there exists in other cases of the same order but which appear less verifiable. Thus he extends what he has observed of political doctrines to all qualitative knowledge, and what he has observed of social groups, expressing themselves politically and intellectually, to any social group.

The Relationship of Correspondence

The relationship which is affirmed between two phenomena will be all the more interesting in proportion to its *accuracy*. It is not so important to know that there is a certain indeterminate relationship between A and B, but it is very important to know as exactly as possible what this relationship is. The scientific and practical value of the results of observation is measured by their accuracy.

In this respect, Mannheim's formulation is very unsatisfactory, for the term "correspondence" remains very indeterminate. It cannot be said that it does not teach us anything, for previously, if we suspected an affinity, we did not always know whether it really existed. In the choice of this term, Mannheim scrupulously respected the implications of his positive research. His observations did not permit him to say any more about it.

But if this modest term expresses the relationships which Mannheim has observed in his positive research, may we consider that this term is always suitable for expressing the relationships between *Weltanschauungen* and social classes?

Indeed, it seems not. It happens that the world-views of a social stratum are extended to all the other strata of a society. Thus, in India, it seems that the Brahmins' social conceptions are accepted by all the other castes. The members of an inferior caste judge their own position in the social structure with respect to the same norms as the Brahmins. In the United States, certain sociologists consider the population of many communities to be divided into six classes (three main classes, each one subdivided into two). Now it really seems that the values and the social and political ideas characteristic of the middle class are widely accepted by the other social groups which are located above or below this middle class.[21] Finally, we must note that the following of a political party is not recruited exclusively in the social group which it claims to represent on the political plane.[22]

This criticism of Mannheim's conclusion does not destroy its validity but conspicuously limits its significance.

To what is this due? In the first place, to the small number of Mannheim's positive studies. Since the validity of a synthesis is measured by the results of observations, if the latter are scanty, we cannot express the conclusions in a very general way. As long as a positive examination has not been made of the non-political and non-social sectors of knowledge, among groups less conscious of their collective aims and more poorly organized, and elsewhere than in the Germany of the nineteenth and twentieth centuries, we may draw conclusions of only extremely narrow significance.

Besides, Mannheim would probably have obtained better results by defining more precisely the mental productions and social factors he considered. He takes political and social knowledge as dependent variables without any other specification. Now there was at least one essential distinction to be made between judgments of value and judgments of fact. It was very probable that, in the first case, the relationship between the group and its ideas must be closer than in the second case. We shall see further on that an analogous distinction would also have modified considerably his philosophy of knowledge. Likewise a clear notion of his independent variable (the social classes and their subdivisions), would have avoided his considering together groups of extremely different types.[23]

Mannheim would probably admit the justice of this criticism, but that would not prevent him from continuing to express his synthesis in general terms. For even when he himself has brought all the restrictions we have stated above to his formula, he continues to speak of the "existential determination of knowledge," so that from time to time he forgets that his experimental proofs have not permitted him to establish the "existential determination of knowledge" without more ado.

THIRD STAGE: THE SCIENTIFIC THEORY

We cannot insist too much upon the close relationship between the conclusions drawn from observations and the theories in the social sciences. It is conceivable that in the physico-chemical sciences we seek to determine the exact relationship between two phenomena merely because it has accidentally been discovered that they vary in concomitant fashion, and without understanding the reason for the relationship we are seeking. In the social sciences, this is not theoretically impossible, but since the definition of the phenomena between which we are seeking relationships, includes a human significance (they are not defined solely through a description of exterior properties which can be recorded by an instrument), it is very difficult to study them in a purely statistical way, that is to say by abstracting the significance of the relationship. No sociologist will seek, for example, to determine the relations between Protestantism and capitalism if he has not the slightest idea of the reason for which there might be a relationship between these two phenomena.

In our account, however, we have maintained the distinction between generalization and its explanation because they are definitely different proceedings of the mind. The theory's criteria of validity will emphasize again the difference. In regard to the generalization, we had to ask ourselves whether its significance exceeded the results of positive research, and secondarily whether it was precise. The theory sets up a principle. The generalization must be related to the principle as a consequence of the latter.

The theory by which Mannheim explains his generalization is this: the various groups, social classes and their subdivisions are struggling to obtain political and economic power. The mental productions (such as political and social conceptions) which originate within these groups serve them as means to attain their collective aims.

This theory may be reduced to two principles: first, knowledge has a practical function (and not — or not only — a theoretical or contemplative function). It is a means for the knowing subject to realize his aims. Then, the various groups are constantly under pressure to realize their collective designs for power.

What may be concluded from these two principles? That the mental productions of the various struggling groups will be utilized to attain their collective aims and consequently these mental productions will correspond to the perspectives of these groups. Moreover, these two principles have different roles in the theory. The first — which we may call the principle of practical knowledge — is a general proposition (which might play the part of a major premise in a syllogism) while the second — let us call it the principle of group competition — expresses rather the conditions a situation must realize so that the generalization may be drawn as a consequence of the first principle. Whatever it may be, the union of these two principles well explains the generalization since the latter may be deduced from them. Consequently, we may conclude that this theory is a good explanation.

A theory also has a function as a hypothesis for further research. That is why it must be a principle general enough for us to be able to deduce consequences other than the generalization which is the result of positive research.

The principle of practical knowledge presents a very high generality which permits us to draw multifarious consequences from it. Thus, on the individual plane, we may seek the translation of desires and interests in every individual's ideas.

The principle of the competition of groups is probably very general also. However, it has rather a restrictive function in the sense that we seek conditioned knowledge only in situations which may be defined in terms of group struggle.

However, if we interpret the principle in a broader manner, it really seems that its union with the principle of practical knowledge may produce fruitful hypotheses for research. Thus, for example, we might see how the struggle between two religions to obtain control over a government or to gain the largest possible number of adherents is reflected in their dogmas, or again how the desire of a school of philosophy to secure chairs on a faculty finds expression in its problematics, etc.

We may then admit that Mannheim's theory is not only a good explanation of his generalization, but also a fruitful scientific hypothesis.

This criticism of Mannheim's theory which we have just outlined shows well the pertinence of the distinction between conclusions and their explanation. When it was a question of criticizing the former, we compared them with the results of positive research to see whether they did not extend their scope unduly. A theory, on the contrary, is not measured, at least directly, by empirical results. It is measured by them indirectly in the sense that the consequences which are logically derived from the theory must be confirmed by observation. Thus, if after serious research, we do not succeed in discerning a relationship between the dogmas and the collective interests of a religious group, we must either abandon our theory and formulate a new one (which is often but a clarification of the first), or explain why we are not entitled to pass from our principles to the conclusions we had drawn from them concerning the conditioning of dogmas.

At first sight, it might seem that we have omitted an essential point: that of knowing whether knowledge *in reality* is practical or contemplative by nature, and whether social groups *really* maintain warlike relationships. These questions certainly arise, but not here. Knowing the answer to these questions will not aid us in any respect in criticizing the theory. As a matter of fact, it is not a question of knowing whether or not these propositions are false (in this sense: do they express the real nature of things), but whether or not they are fruitful logical principles. This is tantamount to saying that a good theory may be made from false principles, something which seems rather paradoxical. Later we shall return to this essential question in discussing the epistemological consequences of Mannheim's sociology.[24]

GENERAL SIGNIFICANCE OF MANNHEIM'S SYSTEM

In this criticism we have examined close at hand the research into facts, the generalized conclusion and Mannheim's theory.

Let us consider now his system of sociology of knowledge as a whole. Leaving aside any particular criticism, let us ask ourselves what its general significance may be.

POSSIBILITY OF OTHER SYSTEMS

His system does not identify itself with the sociology of knowledge and cannot claim to do so. It merely affirms the existence of a certain relationship between mental productions and social factors. To deny the possibility of other kinds of conditioning of mental productions by social factors would exceed the scope of Mannheim's system. We do not even have to prove the positive possibility of these other relationships. It suffices to say that the establishing of a relationship between certain facts does not exclude the possibility of other relationships between these facts except insofar as they would contradict that which has been established.

Mannheim would not deny this. However, he practically identifies his system with the sociology of knowledge. At the end of his article on *Wissenssoziologie* in Vierkandt's dictionary (where he explains only his system), he notes: "we did not present it (the sociology of knowledge) in all its variety but only in the form in which the author conceives it."[25] Let us notice, moreover, that, in Mannheim's account, the disproportion between his particular system and the sociology of knowledge is less striking. For the formula which he likes to use, to express what he believes he has established, is extremely general: "the existential determination of knowledge." Since his account has nothing systematic in it, the various qualifications and restrictions which he brings more or less explicitly to this formula throughout the development of his work are often forgotten, and he seems to believe that his "existential determination of knowledge" remains adequate to the result of his research. This may explain his naïveté in reducing the sociology of knowledge to his system.

Besides, he himself, especially in his subsequent works, cites cases of the influence of social factors upon knowledge, cases which cannot be subsumed under his law.

Thus the needs of the social milieu guide the development of a science toward certain problems. Consequently the methods, spirit and structure of a discipline may be somewhat different in environments which have different needs. For example, in Germany, he tells us, the social problem is mainly the tension between classes, and so sociology is centered around this problem of class relationships. It attempts to diagnose the state of society in the present time. It elaborates plans of reform for the social structure, etc. Its subject matter for study will then be a vast totality like culture, society. Its methods and spirit will be adapted to this end. In the United States, on the contrary, where there is more play in the economic field, the central problems are those of social technique and organization. Sociology, instead of dealing with society as a whole, has as its subject matter a series of technical problems of social readjustment, such as the problem of the "gang," of delinquency, of the conflict of different races living in the same area, of the psychic adjustment of immigrants. So sociology is subdivided into a series of special methods proper for solving these particular problems. American sociologists imply in an optimistic way that they do not have to busy themselves with society as a whole, for it will take care of itself.[26]

In the following case, we shall see how, for Mannheim, a function of thought — abstraction — finds its origin in the complexity of the social organization. In a very simple society, without division of labor, individuals consider objects as wholes. They do not need to distinguish their different aspects, for each one of them makes and handles the whole thing. But as the division of labor appears and specialization grows, each individual no longer considers any aspect of a thing but the one corresponding to that part of the collective work which has devolved upon him. The abstraction originates, not in the object, but in the knowing subject's form of activity. When society expands, these personal points of view become objective and are developed into a technique of abstraction which may be utilized by the whole group.

This produces more points of view in a community than each individual really needs. Each one can learn more than is necessary for him to live. This is why the individual, when he contemplates the vast body of abstractions which are at his disposal, has the impression that the categories and processes of thought were given to man when he entered the world.[27]

The following example is even closer to an application of Mannheim's system. However it differs from it, for here a juridical principle is related to a certain organization of society more than to the direct interest of a class. Diverse studies of the sociology of law[28] have confirmed once more that the fundamental principle of formal law, by virtue of which each case must be judged according to general rational principles, which have as few exceptions as possible and are based on a logical foundation, is current only in the liberal competitive phase of capitalism, and not in capitalism in general. The aim of this fundamental principle was to permit capitalistic parties in a contract to calculate the results of a lawsuit in advance. During that earlier period of capitalistic development, the contracting parties appear before the law with approximately equal strength at their disposition. But in a more recent stage of monopolistic capitalism, the partners are unequal in political and economic power and we find an increase of juridical irrationality in the legal forms which leave the decision of the case to the discretion of the judge, freeing him from the old principle of formal law. Clauses like the "consideration of public welfare," the "good faith" or the interests of the enterprise itself give the judge the possibility of neglecting the formal and equalitarian application of the law, and open the door to the influence of those who really possess power in society.[29]

These three examples suffice to show that Mannheim himself has not limited to his system the possible relationships between society and knowledge. In our account of his system, we have not made a place for the formulations which are implicit in these cases and some others, because the incidental way in which they are presented clearly indicates that Mannheim does not consider them applications of his system. Besides, most of them date from the last period of his works which were no longer centered on the sociology of knowledge but on planned society.

POSSIBILITY OF NON-SOCIOLOGICAL INTERPRETATIONS

Another general question arises. To what degree does his system account for the origin of ideas? What is its explanatory value of the genesis of ideas?

Here is how we are going to proceed to answer this question. Mannheim's system is a type of sociological interpretation of ideas. We shall ask ourselves under what conditions a perfect sociological interpretation (that is to say one which has realized its ambitions perfectly) might account for the genesis of ideas. We shall have an "ideal type" by which we can measure the explanatory character of Mannheim's system.

First let us see how Mannheim himself conceives the possible interpretations of ideas and how he judges them. He distinguishes three of them: sociological, psychological and immanent. The first two consist in seeking the genesis of an idea in non-theoretical factors, whether they be social or psychological. All the applications of Mannheim's system we have given are examples of sociological interpretations. A type of psychological interpretation is furnished us in explaining the violent and aggressive ideas of an individual by certain frustrations he endured during his childhood. Or again we account for a man's ideas through his temperament and his life history.[30] The immanent interpretation, on the contrary, is confined to the plane of ideas. The origin of one mental production is sought in another mental production. Thus Thomism is explained as a synthesis of Aristotelianism and traditional Christian thought.

Mannheim does not deny the value of the psychological interpretation. He simply emphasizes its partial character. If, for example, in following Nietzsche, we wish to explain psychologically the transformation of a hierarchy of moral values as it is expressed by the phrase: "the last shall be first," we shall lay stress upon the history of the author; we shall seek to understand this idea of revolt exclusively on the basis of the special events and motivations of the personal history of the author.

Now it is clear that very much can be done with this method for just as the experiences that truly motivate me have their original source and locus in my own life-history, so just is the author's life-history the locus of his experience. But it is also clear that . . . for a mode of behavior of social significance, such as the transvaluation of values which transforms the whole system of life of a society in all its ramifications, preoccupation with the purely individual life-history and its analysis is not sufficient. The transvaluation . . . has its roots basically in a group situation in which hundreds and thousands of persons, each in its own way, participate in the overthrow of the existing society.[31]

For Mannheim, then, a psychological interpretation has to end in a sociological analysis.

In an article published in 1926, Mannheim compares the sociological and the immanent interpretation of ideas and finds them both valid — so one may choose between them.[32] In *Ideologie und Utopie* he does not say the contrary, but insists upon limitations. "The older method of intellectual history, which was oriented towards the *a priori* conception that changes in ideas were to be understood on the level of ideas (immanent intellectual history), blocked recognition of the penetration of the social process into the intellectual sphere."[33]

We might then summarize Mannheim's attitude in respect to the sociological interpretations of ideas in the following way. He tends, like all those who have made a discovery,[34] to underscore the importance and the priority of his method, but he admits the validity of other methods of interpretation. He shows, for example, that the remarkable development of German sociology from 1918 to 1933 is due to the social disintegration and reorganization of that period, but further that the interpretation of this situation and its theoretical formulation were possible only because sociology had already attained a high degree of criticism and perfection.[35] Here is then a meeting of social factors and an immanent development.

But we have not yet answered the question we were asking: what would be the significance of a perfect sociological interpretation? Or, what would amount to the same thing, what are the conditions for the complete explanation of an idea? And can a sociological interpretation claim to realize these conditions?

Let us note that it is a question of taking into account the *origin* of an idea and not the question of its *efficient cause* (mind? nervous system?) or its truth *value*. (This does not mean that there is no relationship between origin, efficient cause and value, but that they are three logically distinct questions.)

Now, the appearance of a phenomenon is completely explained by its necessary and sufficient conditions. For, by definition, "the necessary and sufficient condition is the circumstance in the absence of which a fact cannot take place and whose presence always entails a fact."[36] Let us apply this definition to a sociological interpretation. Let us suppose that an historian of ideas desires to account for the origin of the conception of history in which the latter presents no internal structure, no determination of the future by the past, in which everything remains possible. He wishes to explain this inarticulate conception of history by showing that it responds to a combat group's need for action led by intellectuals who hope to seize power by exploiting crises in transition periods.[37] When can these social factors be considered to give a complete explanation of the origin of this conception of history? When we have been able to show that they are the necessary and sufficient condition of it. Necessary: when the constellation of social circumstances by which we define a fascist group does not exist, the inarticulate conception of history never appears. Sufficient: when the constellation exists, the conception of history appears also. If then all fascist groups and none but they have this conception of history, we have completely explained its origin.

Such then is the relationship a sociological interpretation of an idea must establish if it claims to be a complete explanation of it.

It seems that the theoretical possibility of such an interpretation cannot be denied, at least for certain ideas. But whatever the possibility and probability for the realization of such a program may be, it is useful to become conscious of it. For it furnished us the standard by which we were able to measure the explanatory character of Mannheim's system.

We know that his system does not establish any determination (in a strict sense) of ideas by social factors, but merely a correspondence. Now an affinity is not equivalent to a necessary and sufficient condition. To say that the inarticulate conception of history is coexistent with a fascist group does not imply that all fascist groups and none but they adopt this conception of history. Such a type of relationship cannot lay claim to the complete explanation.

Is this tantamount to saying that Mannheim's explanation has no value? I think not. A correspondence between social circumstances and an idea indicates that these circumstances constitute at least *one of the factors* which explains the origin of the idea. The inarticulate conception of history cannot be accounted for without mentioning a certain constellation of social circumstances. But that is not enough. We must call in other factors.

Then again it seems that a "correspondence" of Mannheim indicates also that an immanent or psychological interpretation cannot give a complete explanation by itself. For, when a relationship can be established between a certain idea and a certain aspect of social reality, we cannot deny that a social factor plays a role in the genesis of this idea.

The explanatory value of Mannheim's system may be characterized thus: it is not complete (in the sense that it does not totally account for the origin of the idea) but it brings to light one of the social elements which, joined with other factors (social, psychological, immanent) gives a genetic explanation of the idea.[38]

POSSIBILITY OF THE INVERSE RELATIONSHIP

Finally, a last general remark: Mannheim's system which seeks to establish how society influences knowledge, does not deny the possibility of an influence of ideas upon social phenomena. The sociology of knowledge is a systematic attempt to clarify the relationship of ideas to society. This does not imply in any way that an effort to bring to light the inverse relationship is invalid or will be unsuccessful.

Mannheim says nothing about this. Probably he would not deny the possibility of this influence. But probably the exclusive interest he has in the existential determination of knowledge would lead him to minimize this influence.

CHAPTER FOUR

Mannheim's Philosophy of Knowledge

INTRODUCTION

THE SHARP DISCUSSIONS which have arisen in regard to Mannheim's ideas, in Germany and the United States have been centered
more upon the philosophical implications[1] which he drew from
the sociology of knowledge than upon the sociology of knowledge
itself.[2] This, it seems, corresponded well with Mannheim's own
views, not only because the first interest of his intellectual career
was the philosophy of knowledge, but especially because of his
constant concern for the interconnection of problems, a concern
which made him condemn the specialization of modern science.[3]
His point of view as a social reformer led him also to insist upon
the gnosiological consequences of his system of the sociology of
knowledge. He saw there the only path which would permit us
"to overcome the vague, illconsidered, and sterile form of relativism (with regard to scientific knowledge) which is increasingly
prevalent today."[4]

In Mannheim's eyes, his philosophic conclusions are very closely
linked to the results of his positive research.[5] Of course, he admits
that we may accept the empirical results without drawing any
gnosiological consequences from them[6]: "it is possible to present
the sociology of knowledge as an empirical theory of the actual
relations of knowledge to the social situation without raising any
epistemological problem."[7] This reserve is even desirable as long
as our aim is simply the analysis of concrete relationships, but it
is "artificial." The fact that the position of the observer influences

57

the results of thought must sooner or later lead us to raise the question of the philosophical meaning of this fact. There is a philosophy of knowledge "already implicit in the very problem of the sociology of knowledge."[8]

THE POINT OF DEPARTURE

The starting point of his philosophy of knowledge is then a reflection bearing upon the results of his sociology of knowledge. The latter, he writes, shows first that the process of knowledge does not develop solely in accordance with immanent laws, but that the emergence and crystallization of actual thought is influenced at numerous crucial points by extra-theoretical factors of a social nature, and then that the influence of these factors is more than peripheral; "they are relevant not only to the genesis of ideas, but penetrate into their forms and content and . . . furthermore, they decisively determine the scope and the intensity of our experience and observation."[9] The result of this is that our knowledge is linked to a perspective (*Aspekstruktur*). When we think, we think from the point of view of the interests and aspirations of our group. But if this is true, what validity can this knowledge have?

A form of thought in which everybody recognizes a "perspective" character is propaganda. Is it not sufficient to term a mental production propaganda to deny it any value as truth? For Marx also, ideology, the ancestor of perspective thought, did not have any value. In other words, perspective really appears to be synonymous with distortion of reality.

At this stage of the development of his theory of knowledge, Mannheim does not define what he means by knowledge which is not "valid." It is clear that he more or less equates validity with "conformity with reality,"[10] but what is this reality? We may understand by that, the object. This is the current conception of truth: conformity of the representation with the object. It is in this sense that Mannheim employs reality most often.[11] The reality to which thought must conform may also be an ideal reality, a sort of Platonic world. Mannheim, who claims that this is the older conception of truth, more infrequently (but occasionally nevertheless) means truth as commensurate with the Idea.[12] In this account, unless we specify the contrary, we mean conformity in the first sense.

The problem may then be stated in these terms: what can knowledge produced by a thought linked to a point of view teach us about reality? Or again, how are we to utilize so poor an instrument as perspective thought to have an undistorted knowledge of reality?

FIRST SOLUTION

The first solution which naturally presents itself to the mind would consist "of discovering and analyzing the 'social equation' present in every historical-political view"; then of "disentangling from every concretely existing bit of 'knowledge' the evaluative and interest-bound element." Having eliminated it as a source of error, we shall arrive "at a non-evaluative, supra-social, supra-historical realm of objectively valid truth."[13]

This process, Mannheim concedes, is justified, for there are without any doubt realms of politico-historical knowledge in which is to be found an autonomous regularity which may be formulated, in large measure, independently of any social equation.[14] Demography, it seems, might be given as an example, but outside of this quantifiable sociology, it is doubtful that this procedure produces results. For social conditioning reaches not merely the superficial aspects of knowledge, which would be easily separable from it, but the very structure of a mentality, its fundamental categories and its essential concepts. How are we to dissociate a perspective which so deeply permeates a mental production, from the mental production itself? What objective residue would we obtain after such a dissociation? The idea "purified" in such a manner would greatly risk vanishing.

The comparison Mannheim establishes between perspective thought and visual perception[15] expresses clearly the direction of his thought. Our visual image of an object depends upon the point of view from which we perceive it. If, in order to have an image of the object by itself, we wish to suppress the perspective, what will remain of our vision? Nothing. It is not possible to see the thing otherwise than from a point of view.

We must then forego obtaining valid knowledge by separating the point of view from the idea. However, the fact of having established a relationship between an assertion and a situation can teach us something about the validity of the former, but the procedure is rather the opposite. Instead of attempting to separate perspective and idea, we have to enter perspective as an element in the description of the idea. By doing this, we immediately "particularize" the validity of the idea, that is to say that its claim to the expression of reality, which was first absolute, is reduced to a limited significance.

We must then first become conscious of perspective, something which cannot be done directly. Mannheim shows by a very simple example what one of the processes is. Let us imagine

the son of a peasant who has grown up within the narrow confines of his village and spends his whole life in the place of his birth. (For him) the mode of thinking and speaking characteristic of that village is something that he takes entirely for granted. But for the country lad who goes to the city and adapts himself gradually to city life, the rural mode of living and thinking ceases to be something to be taken for granted. He has won a certain detachment from it, and he distinguishes now, perhaps quite consciously, between "rural" and "urban" modes of thought and ideas.[16]

Thus we become conscious of our perspectives whether it be in leaving our social group (for instance, through emigration, or by climbing or descending the class ladder); or if the basis of existence for a whole group changes in respect to its traditional norms and its institutions; or if in a society several socially determined modes of interpretation are opposed to each other and, by mutual criticism, render themselves transparent to each other and establish each other's perspectives.[17] This is tantamount to saying that you cannot become conscious of your own point of view until you have reached another, or when adversaries do you the service of "unmasking" the relationship between your social situation and your ideas.

This being so, we shall replace the assertion of the type "that is such" by another of the type "that is such in a certain perspective," which implies at least the suspicion that this affirmation represents but a partial view. An elaborate analysis of the trend toward certain meanings and values inherent in a determined social position will permit us to specify their scope and their degree of connotation. Mannheim hopes that "with the growing methodological refinements in the sociology of knowledge, the determination of the particularity of a perspective becomes a cultural and intellectual index of the position of the group in question."[18] Finally, by defining the scope and limits of the perspective implicit in the given assertions, this analysis reaches a point where it also becomes a criticism.

This method of particularization, even if it proves as fruitful as Mannheim hopes, is far from answering the question raised above:

what is the validity of perspective knowledge? To become conscious that I have a certain idea because I am a bourgeois will induce me to cast doubts upon its complete objectivity. But to what degree does this perspective falsify reality? Is there any better perspective and how are we to know it?

The particularization is a preliminary to the solution of the problem of validity rather than its solution. As a matter of fact, Mannheim admits this explicitly: it is a preparatory step. "The mere delimitation of the perspectives is, by no means, a substitute for the immediate and direct discussion between the divergent points of view or for the direct examination of the facts." [19]

RELATIVISM

But how are we to proceed to a "direct examination of the facts" by means of a thought linked to a perspective? Two replies are possible, says Mannheim: relativism and relationism. The first denies the possibility of a valid science, the second affirms it.

The relativist position was born of the encounter of an aged theory of knowledge with the recent discovery of the real way in which thought operates. [20]

What is this "aged" theory of knowledge which Mannheim terms idealistic? It is that which was organized under the double influence of the natural sciences and a certain philosophic ideal of the contemplative life. This theory of knowledge was elaborated at the time when the natural sciences dominated intellectual life and, very spontaneously, the ideal to which all science must aspire was seen in the type of objectivity which they represent. The results of these positive sciences are largely detachable from the historico-social perspective of the investigator. From this came the conception that all knowledge, to be worthy of the designation "scientific," had to be impersonal in this fashion. Since it is almost impossible to obtain a knowledge devoid of all subjectivity, when one aims at understanding qualities, it has been decreed that such knowledge is inferior by nature. If assertions of the type of two and two are four are examined, it is very clear that they have a value of their own, are totally independent of the knowing subject, and that their genesis has no relation to their validity. From this, we conclude that the origin of any proposition is, under no circumstances, pertinent to its truth. [21]

Moreover, there has existed since the origins of philosophy, a current which sees an ideal life in contemplation. This esteem for what is considered the highest form of activity is not the result of the observation of the operation of thought, but stems from a hierarchy of values based upon a certain philosophy of life. From this comes the idea that knowledge is pure only insofar as it is a "theoretical" activity, that is to say that knowledge is pure passivity. Accordingly, any cognitive activity more or less linked to action will be considered an impure form of knowledge.[22]

A sort of sphere of truth by itself has been conceived, a sphere which corresponds, on the plane of knowledge, to the "other world" of spiritualist metaphysics. Just as in ontology, a transcendental sphere of perfection has been postulated, with respect to which all the events and realities of this world are shown to be finite and incomplete, so a sphere of truth by itself has been created. Then it has been forgotten that this ideal, by which human knowledge is measured, is but a construction emanating from a conception of the world. It has been taken for an essential fact and a condition for the interpretation of the phenomenon of thought.[23]

When such a theory of knowledge is confronted with the fact of the perspective character of our thought, the only possible result is relativism. For if there is no valid knowledge but that freed of all subjectivity, if the truth of an assertion must be timeless, ahistoric, asocial — then knowledge, which is socially conditioned in its very structure, cannot be valid. We must forego then a knowledge of the world.

RELATIONISM

To escape relativism, we must then either elaborate another philosophy of knowledge or deny the results of the sociology of knowledge. Since the latter seem solidly established in Mannheim's opinion, only the first part of the alternative remains. This new theory of knowledge is relationism.

But on what conditions is it legitimate to modify a gnosiology? Its function is to lay the foundations for, and to justify the validity of, knowledge. Does not this confer a certain intangibility upon it? Of course, Mannheim replies, a philosophy of knowledge is fundamental in respect to various sciences, but that does not give it the right to develop independently of these sciences. Since a gnosiology may draw its conception of the nature of knowledge only from particular existing sciences, it is then at one and the same time the basis of the special sciences and their consequence. "This peculiar situation is characteristic of all theoretical, philosophic disciplines. Its structure is most clearly perceivable in the philosophy of law which presumes to be the judge and critic of positive law, but which is actually, in most cases, no more than a *post facto* formulation and justification of the principles of positive law."[24]

Besides, we have seen clearly that the idealistic theory of knowledge is in fact determined by the model of a certain type of science, predominant at that period. Consequently, when new forms of knowledge emerge, they do not have to be first legitimized by a theory of knowledge. They cannot be condemned in the name of a certain conception of objectivity which claims to be the same for all science, when it but reflects the ideal of a particular science. We must, on the contrary, elaborate a new theory of knowledge by reflecting upon the perspective linked to thought — a perspective which the sociology of knowledge has made us discover. "The problem lies not in trying to hide these perspectives or in apologizing for them, but in inquiring into the question of how, granted these perspectives, knowledge and objectivity are still possible."[25]

Relationism begins then by affirming that spheres of thought exist where there cannot be absolute truth, independently of the values and position of the subject, and without relation to the social context. It is not then a weakness of our minds which prevents us from finding the truth; "even a god could not formulate a proposition on historical subjects like $2 \times 2 = 4$, for what is intelligible in history can be formulated only with reference to problems and conceptual constructions which themselves arise in the flux of historical experience."[26]

In this sphere of qualitative knowledge, we discover two new aspects of thought. The first discovery is this: alongside purely contemplative thought, there exists a thought linked to action. In other words, thought is also an instrument placed at the disposition of a certain kind of being to enable it to solve problems of action in concrete circumstances. "The conception of knowledge as an intellectual act, which is only then complete when it no longer bears the traces of its human derivation, . . . is misleading . . . and tends to obscure fundamental phenomena in those broader realms of the knowable where, if the human historical element is overlooked, the results of thought are completely denatured."[27]

There are then two possible theories of knowledge: the idealistic and the activistic. For the moment, they must be kept separate, and the differences between them must be emphasized rather than minimized. It is only by a method of trial and error that we may determine whether this is the type of knowledge detached from the social situation which must be taken as the point of departure, while the situationally conditioned type is secondary, or the contrary.[28]

The second discovery which we can make, in becoming conscious of the essentially rational structure of human mind, is that, for certain types of ideas, validity is relative to the genesis. That is to say, the thesis, according to which the origin of a proposition has no bearing upon its validity, is too broad. Again, it is justified in the domain of the exact sciences where objectivity is attained by suppressing the "personal equation" of the investigator, but in a domain where perspective is inseparable from the idea, the validity of the latter depends necessarily upon the point of view, that is to say upon the genesis. Recourse to the comparison with visual perception allows us to grasp this point. To pass judgment upon the value of the visual image, we do not attempt to separate the image from the point of view, but, on the contrary, we suppose that the validity of the image depends upon the point of view. It is taken for granted that certain perspectives permit us to obtain better images.[29]

We may then summarize relationism in the following manner: a type of knowledge exists in which thought manifests itself as an instrument of action. This type of knowledge is socially conditioned and its validity is linked to this social perspective.[30]

THE CRITERIA OF TRUTH

The problem is now to see how, in terms of this conception of knowledge, we may identify the "socially conditioned mental productions" which are valid from those which are not. What are the criteria to be utilized in this new sphere of truth?

Mannheim's various replies to this question have such slender links between each other that the existence of a systematic answer may sometimes be questioned. Two possible approaches are offered to us: to attempt to follow or rather to reconstruct the train of his thoughts or, on the contrary, to distinguish clearly several criteria without attempting to record their complex relations. The second solution offers the advantage of clarity while the first gives us a more faithful image of our author's thought. We have decided in favor of a compromise between the two methods. We shall endeavor first to follow his thought step by step; after which we shall summarize his criteria by noting their distinction. We shall start with a very brief account of the criteria of objectivity given by Mannheim in his article *Wissenssoziologie* in Vierkandt's dictionary, which is the last stage of his thought on this subject. We shall make this summary explicit by having recourse to his previous works.

EXPOSITION OF THE CRITERIA

In the case of situationally conditioned thought, objectivity comes to mean . . . first of all the fact that insofar as different observers are immersed in the same system, they will, on the basis of the identity of their conceptual and categorical apparatus and through the common universe of discourse thereby created, arrive at similar results, and be in a position to eradicate as an error everything that deviates from this unanimity.[31]

This criterion of unanimity appears to resolve a problem preliminary to that of the validity of perspective ideas. Here it is a question of determining, among several ideas conditioned by the same social situation, the one which corresponds best to this situation, that is to say which is the thing we really see when we are placed in this point of view. The process used is a means of suppressing the personal equation. It is supposed that what will be seen by all observers sharing the same point of view, really exists in the thing considered in such a social perspective. This criterion tends then but to establish "authentic" socially conditioned knowledge, and to purify it of any subjectivism on the part of the different observers.

Let us pass now to the essential question. There are several views of the same thing emanating from different perspectives; what will be the criterion of objectivity? Mannheim answers this capital question with two solutions. First, he shows how we attain a certain objectivity by comparing different perspective ideas; then he attempts to determine the criterion of the best point of view.

The synthesis of the perspectives

When observers have different perspectives, "objectivity" is attainable only in a more roundabout fashion. In such a case, what has been correctly but differently perceived by the two perspectives must be understood in the light of the differences in structure of these varied modes of perception. An effort must be made to find a formula for translating the results of one into those of the other and to discover a common denominator for these varying perspective insights. Once such a common denominator has been found, it is possible to separate the necessary differences of the two views from the arbitrarily conceived and mistaken elements, which here too should be considered as errors.[32]

Thus first comes the question of "particularizing" our point of view[33]: of becoming conscious that its limitation cannot lay claim to absolute knowledge; then of finding a common denominator by the translation of one perspective into the terms of another. Will objective knowledge be reduced to a sort of residue (what can be seen from any point of view), or, on the contrary, does it imply the creation of a new, larger perspective which will synthesize the previous ones?

In *Ideologie und Utopie,* published a few years before the passage we have just cited, Mannheim expresses himself in a somewhat more explicit manner on this subject. He wonders whether the notion of "scientific politics" is not contradictory, whether it is possible to elaborate a veritable science of politics. We see that this is but a particular application of the problem of the criteria of validity of perspective knowledge. He answers this by tracing two possible lines of development. The first of these lines is that elaborating a complete *Weltanschauung* in the perspective of a party, of constructing a coherent image of the world from the point of view of the party;[34] the second, that of integrating the points of view of the different parties in a dynamic synthesis. It is this second possibility which interests us at the moment.

Here is an approximation of Mannheim's reasoning. Since the various political doctrines are not the product of an arbitrary will, but correspond to various social situations, they are complementary. Each social group having a political expression (doctrinal at least), all these theories cover the whole of the political field. "The present structure of society makes possible a political science which will not be merely a party science, but a science of the whole" (that is of all the parties).[35]

This synthesis is never definitively established. "In a realm in which everything is in the process of becoming, the only adequate synthesis would be a dynamic one, which is reformulated from time to time."[36] As a matter of fact, Mannheim conceives this dynamic synthesis in a Hegelian manner: a series of syntheses linked to each other, each one arriving at a broader perspective than the preceding one, and incorporating the results of all the preceding syntheses. In that sense, we may conceive a certain progress "towards an absolute synthesis in the utopian sense."

The following example gives an idea of what Mannheim has in view. He attempts to show how the role assigned to rational thinking by different political doctrines is in accordance with the particular perspective of the different social groups.

For the official, especially of the Prussian state, the essential activity consists in applying laws which he has not elaborated himself. His social situation makes him see the world and any event as essentially subsumable under rulings, and the particular order prescribed by concrete law as identical to the order in general. Thus the world is rational for bureaucratic conservatism. Its vision is restricted to the stabilized part of the life of the State — the administration.

For the nobles, the heirs of a feudal tradition, having no experience in administration, but having been the leaders for generations, the political sphere is, on the contrary, mainly the domain of the unforeseeable and the irrational. The only rational activity possible consists in deciphering the growing tendencies of the silently working *Volksgeist*.

We see that these two social situations, that of the officials and that of the aristocrats, lead them to exaggerate the significance of their experience. However, the perspective of each one of these groups has brought to light an aspect which could not be perceived except from its own point of view. Bourgeois liberalism effected a synthesis between the political rationalism of the officials and the political irrationalism of the aristocracy. It admits that the political world presents incoherence, disorder, and struggle, but it believes that it is possible to channel this irrationalism into institutions like Parliament, and later the League of Nations, and that finally through free discussion, the world will be completely directed by reason. Thus the perspective of the bourgeois permitted it to synthesize two partial views in a broader conception.

This broader view was, however, still partial. The bourgeois mind had a social interest to hide the limits of its own rationalism. But socialism, for which it was advantageous to unmask exactly what was left in the shade, showed that politics does not consist purely in parliamentary discussions, but that the latter are but the superficial expressions of more profound economic and social situations. This discovery of the social and economic conditioning of political thought produced a new invasion of the irrational into the political domain which had been put in good order by liberalism. But Marxism also endeavored to reduce this inflow of non-rational factors by adding its conception of historical determinism — progressing dialectically — which reconciles "the liberal generalizing tendency with Hegelian historicism, itself also of conservative origin."[37] The social perspective of the Marxist thinkers has permitted them to perceive a new dimension in political reality, and thus, little by little, the picture is completed.

Finally, fascism showed that this rigid construction of historical development had exaggerated the purely structural foundation of politics. It insisted upon the critical situations "in which class forces become disjointed and confused," and in which men of action and their assault troops can dominate the situation, but it gave too big a part to this amorphism, this disorder.

Thus, Mannheim concludes, "at different times, different elementary social interests emerge and accordingly different objects of attention in the total structure are illuminated and viewed as if they were the only ones that existed."[38]

In the explanation of this example, Mannheim endeavors to follow Hegelian dialectics.[39] This clearly shows what he means by objectivity resulting from the comparison of perspectives. It is not a sort of residue, but the reconciliation of two points of view, operating on a higher plane which has been discovered in a broader perspective. "A true synthesis is not an arithmetic average of all the diverse aspirations of the existing groups in society. . . . The principle of the *juste milieu* . . . is rather a caricature of a true synthesis than a solution of it which can only be a dynamic one."[40]

Now, since each perspective is linked to a social situation, we may ask ourselves who will make the synthesis, that is to say, what group will be in a position to transcend the two points of view in conflict, in order to make a broader perspective. There is little chance that it may be the groups whose interests are in conflict who will attain this new, more comprehensive point of view. Mannheim thinks that a class occupying a middle position will simply tend to stabilize the status quo and protect its advantages from the attacks of the Right and the Left. The group from which we may expect a progressive synthesis will be rather a social stratum which is not too firmly situated in the social order. This is the "socially unattached intelligentsia" (*freischweibende Intelligenz*).

What unites the intellectuals is their common education. Now, "modern education is . . . a replica, on a small scale, of the conflicting purposes and tendencies which rage in society at large."[41] This gives the intellectual the suppleness of mind which allows him to understand the different perspectives. To be sure, he is also affiliated with an economic-social class; he emanates from a bourgeois, proletarian, or aristocratic milieu; he has a liberal profession, he is an official or a capitalist. However, his sensitivity to various currents of political thought will make of him a being less clearly linked to, and identified with, the interests of a group than those who participate only in economic progresses. Thus, when the latter, but for rare exceptions, are incapable of going beyond the limits of their class point of view, the intellectuals alone are in a position to choose their affiliation.

As a matter of fact, we find them in all camps in the course of history. They furnished theorists to the conservatives, who, because of their own social stability, had little inclination to theorize their situation; to the proletarians who lacked the necessary formation to fight in the modern political conflict; to the liberals especially, "the capitalist and educated class." Along with these intellectuals who are "engaged," others try to realize the social detachment possible for the intelligentsia — and the mission implicit in it — by attempting to transcend particular points of view with a more comprehensive perspective that will permit a dynamic synthesis. Even the intellectuals who have chosen their "engagement" aid, unconsciously perhaps, the construction of the synthesis, for they are not content to dress up crude interests in ideas. Their comprehension of other points of view incites them to integrate certain of these elements with their own perspective, that is to say, to enlarge it.[42]

After this development concerning dynamic synthesis and the function of intellectuals, let us return to the question which was its point of departure: what will be the criterion of objectivity when we are confronted with different perspectives? Mannheim gave two replies, of which the first was the comparison of different, opposing points of view which may be complementary in a synthesis. The latter will be more "objective." The second is to find out what is the best point of view. Let us now stop at this question.

The best perspective

It is natural that here we must ask which of the various points of view is the best. And for this too there is a criterion. As in the case of visual perspective, where certain positions have the advantage of revealing the decisive features of the object, so here pre-eminence is given to that perspective which gives evidence of the greatest comprehensiveness and the greatest fruitfulness in dealing with empirical materials.[43]

The best point of view will then be the broadest and the most fruitful. We know already what the broadest perspective is: it is the one which, going beyond oppositions, permits a synthesis. The fecundity of the point of view is a very interesting idea and we will be concerned with it for quite some time.

Just what is this "point of view fruitful for action in empirical matters?" It is the one which allows a perfect adjustment of the action to the objective we wish to obtain. If I desire to buy a fir-plantation to make an investment, the good point of view will be that of the businessman and not that of the artist. On this plane, the idea of adjustment to reality presents no difficulty, but this does not always happen. Let us take a more complex case: the antinomy ideology-utopia in which this criterion of efficiency plays a part.

Ideology has been described previously. It is the name given by the Marxists to an idea which masks interests, and by Mannheim to a perspective idea. But since in the duality ideology-utopia the sense of the first term is a bit different, we are going to define the two terms of this famous antinomy which gave its name to the collection of essays by Mannheim.

Ideologies and utopias are ideas which are "situationally transcendent." They are unreal with respect to the existing order, something which must be understood, not in a metaphysical sense of existence by itself, but in terms of the economic-social structure, the political organization and culture actually existing at a certain moment of history. Thus we may say that the fraternal love of Christians situationally transcends a society founded upon slavery.

But utopias, at the same time that they are directed towards objects which do not exist in the present situation, have a destructive power upon the actual order and finally succeed in transforming the existing historical reality into another more in accord with their conceptions. Thus in the absolutist France of the eighteenth century, the bourgeois idea of political freedom did not correspond to the situation, but was a powerful ferment in the dissolution of that society, and prepared a new order conforming more to the idea of political freedom.[44]

Ideologies, on the contrary, do not succeed in realizing a society more in conformity with themselves. Instead of destroying the existing order, their meaning is rather warped by it. Thus Christian asceticism, in contemporary materialistic society, not only does not succeed in destroying materialism, but is often disfigured when it inspires individual conduct — because it is almost impossible to live in a manner consistent with that of an ascetic in a world based on materialism.[45]

The criterion of distinction between ideology and utopia is still efficiency, but this time it has to do with a very complex adjustment. Since, by definition, utopia is situationally transcendent, it is necessarily poorly adjusted to the existing economic, social, and cultural order, but it is adapted to the future order. This criterion is not too difficult to manipulate in regard to the past. Among the ideas which were not adapted to the situation of the seventeenth century, for example, we may easily distinguish the utopias from the ideologies: the first were realized later and the second were not. But for the present, how are we to know what is going to be realized in the future? Mannheim also admits this difficulty.[46]

Besides, Mannheim extends his concept of ideology still further. Ideology will be not only the idea which will not be realized, but also the one which was realized in the past but which no longer corresponds to a later social situation and which, by this very fact, prevents a good adjustment.

The history of the taboo against interest on loans may serve as an example of the development of an antiquated ethical norm into an ideology. The rule that lending be carried on without interest could be put into practice only in a society which economically and socially was based upon intimate and neighborly relations. In such a social world "lending without interest" is a usage that commands observance without difficulty, because it is a form of behavior corresponding fundamentally to the social structure. Arising in a world of intimate and neighborly relations this precept was assimilated and formalized by the Church in its ethical system. The more the real structure of society changed, the more this ethical precept took on an ideological character, and became virtually incapable of practical acceptance. Its arbitrariness and its unworldliness became even more evident in the period of rising capitalism when, having changed its function, it could be used as a weapon in the hands of the Church against the emergent economic force of capitalism. In the course of the complete emergence of capitalism, the ideological nature of this norm, which expressed itself in the fact that it could be only circumvented but not obeyed, became so patent that even the Church discarded it.[47]

It seems then that an idea may be said to be efficient when it allows conduct adapted to the situation in which it develops or at least when it permits the effective preparation of a future social order. In this last case, it may be said to be adapted to the existing social order, like a pickaxe may be said to be well adapted to the house it destroys. "A theory then is wrong if, in a given practical situation, it uses concepts and categories which, if taken seriously, would prevent man from adjusting himself at that historical stage."[48]

Thus the best perspective is the one which, at a given moment of history, gives the possibility for the broadest synthesis, and permits the best adaptation to the situation.

Summary of the Criteria

We have endeavored to explain the criteria of objectivity for perspective ideas according to relationism. We have attempted to reconstitute the process of Mannheim's thought. As was announced, we are now going to separate and characterize Mannheim's different criteria for guaranteeing the validity of ideas.

It seems that the different criteria of Mannheim which we encountered in the preceding account can be reduced to two distinct types: Some aim at reaching the real object indirectly; we might speak of criterias of objectivity in the strict sense. The others guarantee the validity of ideas by their efficiency.

The criteria of objectivity in the strict sense

When Mannheim defines as an error that which deviates from the unanimity of various observers plunged in the same perspective, he merely endeavors, in this indirect fashion, to attain knowledge which, very probably, corresponds to the object seen from the social perspective. The value of this method rests, in fact, upon the supposition that what all the observers see is more probably in conformity with reality than what a single one sees.

The comparison between the various points of view in order to obtain a synthesis is also an indirect means of approaching reality. Why is a more comprehensive view worth more than a partial one?

This question seems ridiculous the answer is so evident: the synthetic view gives more than one aspect of reality — consequently it is a better image of it.

The same criterion of objectivity is the basis for the high role Mannheim assigns to the intellectuals. We remember the considerable importance Mannheim grants to the socially unattached intelligentsia in the construction of the synthesis. So much so that it has been suggested that, for Mannheim, the validity of an idea was guaranteed when it emanated from a group of intellectuals. Mannheim's intelligentsia, wrote Professor Merton, has a function very similar to that of Hegel's "absolute Geist" and Marx's proletariat. It possesses in itself the justification for the validity of its mental productions.[49] We shall not follow this interpretation because Mannheim never admits, even implicitly, conferring a sort of infallibility on a group, but it is interesting to note the reason why he values the role of the intelligentsia so much. That is because it enjoys to some degree a non-situationally conditioned vision. The world-view of the intellectuals (at least of those who do not seek only success and who understand their mission in regard to synthesis) can then conform to reality since they escape the limiting point of view of the other classes. It is again the criterion of objectivity which is brought into play.

The criteria of efficiency

To affirm that a certain idea is valid because it permits efficacious action is very different from affirming its validity because the object to which it corresponds in reality is really such. The conception of "history without structure" is valid according to the criterion of objectivity if, in fact, historical unfolding is amorphous. According to the criterion of efficiency, this conception will be valid if it gave the fascists the conviction that their action would succeed, and if it discouraged the resistance of their adversaries. We see that the validity of an idea is somewhat different according to whether we attain it by one or the other of these criteria. This does not deny that there may be relations between the two, that finally if an idea is fruitful in action, it is because it corresponds in a certain fashion to reality. But however the relations between efficiency and objectivity may be, these criteria answer two distinct questions and cannot be confused.

GENERAL CONSEQUENCES

Nothing more remains but to end this account of Mannheim's theory of knowledge by indicating in a word the happy consequences Mannheim hopes to obtain from it.

On the intellectual level, the sort of vague, discouraging and sterile relativism emanating from science can be surmounted by this theory of knowledge.[50]

On the level of individual action, there is a possibility for more freedom and responsibility. A better knowledge of the determining factors which enter into the formation of our ideas does not diminish our free-will. On the contrary, "it is the one who is ignorant of the significant determining factors and who acts under the immediate pressure of determinants unknown to him who is least free and more thoroughly predetermined in his conduct."[51] Each time we become conscious of a determinant which has dominated us, we draw it from the realm of unconscious motivation to that of control. Gradually we succeed in dominating what formerly dominated us.

Finally, on the level of political and other controversies, Mannheim hopes that, if each one is conscious of the linking of his conceptions to an economic and social point of view, and if, besides, each one attempts to transcend his point of view and to find a broader perspective and a common language, we can expect less numerous and less bitter conflicts.[52]

CHAPTER FIVE

Evaluation of Mannheim's
Philosophy of Knowledge

INTRODUCTION: EPISTEMOLOGY AND GNOSIOLOGY

IN THE WRITINGS we have analyzed, Mannheim ignores the distinction between epistemology and the philosophical theory of knowledge. For him all the general implications of the sociology of knowledge fall into the category *Erkenntnistheorie* (gnosiology, philosophy of knowledge) and, as far as I know, he does not utilize the word *Wissenschaftslehre* (epistemology).[1] That is why, in attempting to give an accurate explanation of Mannheim's thought, we have not distinguished in his conceptions what appears to us strictly gnosiological from what is epistemological. Now that we have to criticize Mannheim's conceptions, it seems useful to introduce these two concepts.

The meaning of these two terms — gnosiology and epistemology — is very far from being generally accepted. The articles which are devoted to them in the philosophical dictionaries reveal this confusion well. Even within a philosophic current which, like Neo-Thomism, rests upon a long tradition of thought, things are scarcely better determined.[2] This obliges us to define the meanings by which we shall understand these two terms.

Epistemology is understood here in the sense of the study "of the conditions, value and limits of human knowledge."[3] It is a critical study of "the principles, results and hypotheses of the various sciences, intended to determine their logical origin, their value and their objective significance."[4] It is the critique of the cognitive claim of certain assertive mental states and the assessment of their validity.[5] This conception approaches what certain authors call methodology. Thus Professor Parsons means by this, not techniques of research (like statistics, the monograph, the interview, etc.) but a sort of border-line terrain between science and philosophy, which has for its object the consideration of the general foundations of the validity of propositions and scientific systems.[6] For Dr. Mandelbaum, methodology examines the materials and methods of the particular sciences in order to estimate just how far these methods permit the investigator to apprehend the object he is seeking to attain.[7] Those who hold this conception of epistemology often admit also that this discipline may have a bearing either upon knowledge in general or the various types of knowledge realized in the different special sciences.[8]

Besides, this problem of the value of knowledge is resolved by epistemology on a purely critical plane and not in terms of a system of philosophy, of an ontology. An attempt is made merely to determine what kind of cognitive result may be attained by the methods of such a science.[9] Thus we enter the realm of epistemology when we ask ourselves what political knowledge, linked to a social perspective, can teach about the subject on which it has bearing, and when we reply that this teaches us this political knowledge is incomplete.

The theory of knowledge (or gnosiology), on the contrary, has as its objective the determination of the ontological meaning of knowledge.[10] It is an integral part of a philosophic system. If it is admitted that a philosophy tends to give a general explanation of reality, it must also interpret human knowledge in terms of its essential theses. Thus, Professor Noël clearly distinguishes the critical (epistemological) question from the ontological one. The first precedes all philosophic systematization. The second is a chapter of the special ontology which has for its subject matter a certain level of being: man.[11]

The gnosiological problem is stated in the following way: what is the nature of knowledge? The reply will be situated also on the ontological or noumenal plane. These last terms do not necessarily refer to a spiritualistic philosophy which locates the last reality beyond this phenomenal world. They simply mean that knowledge will be envisaged with respect to what is considered the real nature of things. We shall say, for example, that it is a form of activity by which a being extends beyond itself and participates in the nature of another. In this perspective, ontological conditions will be established under which one being can become another without ceasing to be itself.

Such is the variety of considerations which may be found in a philosophic theory of knowledge. This shows that it concerns itself with the place of knowledge in the philosophical structure of the real. Here is another example pointing out how gnosiology is dependent upon the ontological nature ascribed to the knower and the tangible world. If, according to Descartes and Locke, the knowing subject is conceived as a mental substance and the tangible object as only a material substance, we have to explain how two entities ontologically completely different can be united in the act of knowing. If, according to Aristotle and St. Thomas Aquinas, every being (the knower as well as the known object) is a union of matter and form, the problem of the possibility of a communication between subject and object will be raised and resolved quite differently. Thus gnosiology is closely dependent upon general ontology.[12]

We see that epistemology and gnosiology are opposed to each other from two points of view. The former has as its objects the value of knowledge; the latter, the nature of knowledge. Then epistemology is limited to a critical plane, while the theory of knowledge, on the contrary, is located on the philosophical plane of the internal structure of reality.

Their relationship, however, is close. First, both of them have the same subject matter: knowledge; second, the finality of knowledge may be deduced from its nature. Thus, in the Aristotelian current, from the proposition that knowledge is a participation in the outer world by means of mental representations, we conclude that it is contemplative and that, to be perfect, it must be adequate to the object.[13] Now the ideal finality assigned to knowledge by such and such a philosophic system may often be utilized by epistemology as a datum which will serve as a standard of measure. In this sense, epistemology will determine whether such and such a variety of knowledge realizes this ideal type, and to what degree. This may be expressed as follows: *if* it is admitted that knowledge has a certain finality (to make the thing known objectively, for instance), a certain type of knowledge (mathematics, for example) attains this objective to such and such a degree.

But this does not imply that a gnosiology must always precede an epistemology; first, because there is a vulgar notion — not so vulgar perhaps[14]— of the finality of knowledge which can be taken as a standard; then, because epistemology can forego a standard. The direct study of the methods of a science permits the discovery of its scope and its limits without our having to establish an ideal type as a point of comparison.

Let us see how these categories may help us to clarify a bit the philosophic implications Mannheim draws from his sociology of knowledge. The problem Mannheim attempts to solve and of which he never loses sight is that of the *value of perspective knowledge*. In this sense, it may be said that the clue of his thought is epistemological and that his principal interest remains epistemological.

He is then going to attempt to determine what the value of knowledge linked to perspective is. He will measure this value in terms of "conformity to reality." As it has already been noted above, this notion of "reality" is a bit ambiguous. It means now the object, now a sort of subsistent Platonic idea.[15] However, his reference mark more frequently is that of the general conception of the finality of knowledge: representation in conformity with the reality of the object. Here Mannheim remains upon a purely epistemological plane. This conception of the finality of knowledge is accepted as a datum.

But the reply Mannheim can give the epistemological question: knowledge is valid in perspective — does not satisfy him. He estimates that this failure arises from the poorly chosen standard. Passing then onto the plane of gnosiology, he is going to attempt to criticize the conception of the nature of knowledge which is subjacent to the idea of objectivity and to replace it with another idea of the nature of knowledge: activistic knowledge. Thus, to answer the epistemological question (value of knowledge), he is led to raise the gnosiological problem (nature of knowledge).

Mannheim claims to solve the gnosiological problem without having recourse to metaphysics, but by remaining upon empirical grounds. In criticizing relativism, he expounds his views on what a good theory of knowledge must be. It cannot be founded upon a certain philosophy of life like, for example, the one which makes of contemplation the highest human activity.[16] Its basis will be the actual types of knowledge we can observe.[17] It is then by an empirical method that Mannheim wishes to construct his conception of the nature of our knowledge.

We will criticize him first from that point of view. We shall ask ourselves whether he has really succeeded in constructing a solid conception of what the nature of knowledge is through implications of his observations of the sociology of knowledge, or whether, on the contrary, his theory of knowledge is consistent only in terms of a philosophy, an ontology which implicitly and yet unavowedly underlies his system.

DIRECT CRITICISM

Is the Problem Correctly Stated?

Let us recall in what terms Mannheim raises it. What truth value can perspective knowledge have? That is to say: can it correspond to reality?

As we have indicated above, the conclusions he draws from his positive researches go a bit beyond what he had a right to conclude from them. He has not proved that all qualitative science is perspective, but merely that a certain political and social knowledge has been so. This does not vitiate his point of departure but greatly limits the scope of this question. It is well to remember this.

What is even more serious is that, within this political and social realm, Mannheim makes no distinction between concepts and judgments, fundamental categories and models of thought, levels of abstraction and *Weltanschauungen*. These various elements are doubtless "knowledge linked to perspectives," but, *independently* of that, the validity of each one of them cannot be measured by the same yardstick. To say that a *"Weltanschauung* is valid" or that "a concept is valid" has a sense, but validity does not mean the same thing in the two cases. Now, when confronted with elements so different, he asks himself the same question: in what do they correspond to reality?[18]

If we consider only judgments (generally recognized as being more directly related to the question of truth than concepts), it seems that affirmations of value or judgments "of strategy" must not be measured by the same standard.

"Democracy is the ideal regime." When confronted with judgments of value of this variety, Mannheim asks himself: is that true? According to his ambiguous criterion, this may mean: "does this assertion correspond to a real object?" or "does this affirmation correspond to an absolute idea?" We do not really see the sense these two questions might have. This affirmation will be valid if it can be linked to a fundamental value (for example, "democracy is better because it respects the dignity of man"). The latter is justified only philosophically (for example, "the superior dignity of man with respect to other beings is based upon the fact that he alone has a spiritual destiny"). There is, if you wish, conformity with reality, in the sense that the affirmation of the value of democracy may be said to be more or less consistent logically with a certain philosophic interpretation of the world, and that the latter generally claims to be but a faithful image of reality. The least we may say is that this conformity of the value assertion with reality is very complex and indirect.

As for the judgments we term "strategic," like: "such a reform must be obtained through parliamentary action and not through revolution," these judgments are also ill-suited to questions of truth such as Mannheim raises. Their validity rests upon their fruitfulness: is parliamentary action a means which will permit us to obtain the desired reform?

Now the political sphere is organized mainly upon such judgments of value and strategy. The question of their validity raised in Mannheim's terms applies to this very poorly. It is more pertinent when it is a question of judgments of fact.

Mannheim has found out that these criteria of validity were leading him to a deadlock, but he has thrown the fault back upon the perspective character of knowledge. He has not seen that the result would not have been better, independently of all social conditioning. He has failed simply because he raised the problem of the value of knowledge in an unsuitable way, and not because knowledge was perspective. This is a bad beginning.

IS THE SOCIAL EQUATION UNDISSOCIABLE FROM THE MENTAL PRODUCTION?

It appears necessary to Mannheim to elaborate a new theory of knowledge for two reasons. The first of these is that the criteria of truth, which spring from the aged philosophical theory of knowledge appear to him to deny perspective knowledge any value at all; the second, that the perspective character permeates mental productions so deeply that it cannot be dissociated from them without at the same time suppressing the mental production itself.

We have just seen that if the "aged" criteria of validity give negative results when they are applied to perspective knowledge, it is not because the latter is perspective, but because the majority of mental productions in the political field are judgments of value or means to which these criteria are not applicable. Let us see if the second foundation of Mannheim's theory of knowledge is more substantial.

His argument is serious.[19] Social conditioning reaches as far as the framework of thought: fundamental categories, models of thought, levels of abstraction. To isolate the social equation from it appears impossible, and this is certainly so if we wish to obtain it by direct means. However, it really seems that several of Mannheim's criteria of validity tend to, and succeed in, disengaging the observer more or less from his perspective.

Here, it seems, are what would be the principal stages of these indirect tactics.

First, to become aware of one's perspective, when one changes surroundings, when one is criticized by one's adversaries. These procedures are not infallible. In particular, polemics may serve rather to crystallize the point of view. One may also object that in changing surroundings, for example, one replaces one perspective by another. Of course these processes do not have a mechanical action but they provide the possibility of realizing the influence of our social affiliations upon our ideas. It is possible to be attentive to the criticisms of adversaries; it is possible, when one has acquired a new perspective, to go back intellectually to the former, in order to judge the new one from the former point of view.

Then comes *particularization*,[20] which consists in realizing that a point of view is not a total view. This principle of particularization is very fruitful but not very original.[21] It is but the application of the universally admitted idea that, from the fact that a proposition is true under certain conditions, we cannot deduce that it is true without any qualification. Mannheim's originality lies in the discovery of the important bearing social affiliation can have upon ideas. But once it has been admitted that it constitutes a perspective, it follows from this that it particularizes the validity of the mental production.

We might add a third stage, a very radical one. Since perspective originates in the identification of an individual with the interests and collective aims of his group, the individual must attempt to *dissociate himself from his group* in spirit or even in fact. This is, in a sense, perfectly in Mannheim's line. This kind of renunciation corresponds to what he expects from his pure intellectuals. In another sense, this conception departs from his idea of "partisan" knowledge: we must take sides in order to understand certain things.[22] This latent contradiction exists in Mannheim himself, however.

We might object that the intellectual, according to Mannheim, does not escape perspectives, but merely has the perspective corresponding to his situation. We may, of course, express things in this manner, and Mannheim does it sometimes. But this does not mean that the intelligentsia, as a social group, has collective interests which determine its vision of the world. It means that, being "socially unattached," it is not linked to any perspective.[23]

It seems that this shows the possibility of non-perspective mental productions. Even in the political field, it is possible to free ourselves from the social equation. The result is that this liberation of the group point of view is a problem which must be treated on the plane of conditions preliminary to a valid knowledge. It has been admitted generally that one could not be judge and party at the same time. That is to say that disinterestedness and serenity were preliminary conditions to be realized before devoting oneself to intellectual activity. It seems that it is somewhat the same with the social equation. Since it is unconscious and deeply integrated with our knowledge, it is probably difficult to eliminate. This problem however has to be raised and solved on the level of the preconditions to judicative activity.

But, we might say, Mannheim's intellectuals have as their principal mission the construction of ever more comprehensive dynamic syntheses. Is that not somewhat different from, and more constructive than, a view freed from a perspective?

It is useful to introduce here the distinction we have made between the various cognitive elements of the political sphere.

When, by the three stages we have just described, we succeed in detaching ourselves from all social perspective, we have good conditions for undertaking the intellectual exploration of the political sphere and, concerning each cognitive element — concept, judgment, etc. — to ask ourselves the question of validity in terms adequate to each one. Thus, when it is a question of judgments of fact, we may measure their objectivity. In the case of judgments of value, we shall apply complex criteria to them, criteria we believe suit them.

Mannheim's dynamic synthesis intervenes only to resolve the problems of validity on the plane of complete political doctrines (like liberalism, Marxism and fascism). We imagine the complication and difficulty of such problems. We might conceive as an approach to the solution of these problems an analysis which would reduce these impressive systems to their simplest elements, and then would try to criticize them separately. Mannheim prefers transcending the opposition between two doctrines and reconciling them on a higher plane, to this method. It seems difficult to take account of this preference solely and even principally by positive and empirical reasons. We shall see later where we must seek the reason for Mannheim's predilection for this method of synthesis.

Is Relationism Not Relativist and Contradictory?

If the two criticisms which have just been expounded are valid, Mannheim can no longer place his reliance upon the discoveries of the sociology of knowledge to affirm that it is necessary to postulate a new theory of knowledge. We might then stop our commentary here upon the gnosiological implications of Mannheim's system. We shall not do so, for there are still several elements which are very interesting from the point of view of our central problem of the relations between the sociology of knowledge and the philosophy of knowledge.

Mannheim has sharply opposed his relationism to relativism. However, several of his critics have made no difference between the two and have reproached him merely for his relativism.[24] Might he have escaped relativism only in a verbal manner?

Let us now recall briefly the development of his thought. The point of departure is that a certain type of knowledge is necessarily linked to a perspective. Mannheim raises the question about its value in terms of conformity with reality. He replies that it gives a partial view of reality, but that it is impossible to determine in what measure. It is a deadlock. To get out of it, the criterion of objectivity which was used is questioned. Since this criterion depended on a contemplative conception of the nature of knowledge, he affirms that alongside the sphere of knowledge which has a theoretical function, there is another which has a pragmatic or activistic function. It follows logically from this that a different criterion of validity will correspond to each sphere: objectivity will be limited to theoretical thought; efficiency to practical thought.

This means that we define the validity of thought linked to a perspective essentially by a criterion of efficacity, and that we deny its theoretical value. Now it really seems that to say that our knowledge is relative, has this meaning: it is an instrument useful for permitting us to live, but it does not give us an undistorted view of reality.[25]

It is true that Mannheim lets one sphere of theoretical knowledge exist, but it is reduced to very little: to the sciences which are quantifiable. All the rest of our knowledge, from philosophy and qualitative science right up to daily knowledge, has a practical validity.

From this has come the classic reproach for Mannheim, that of the circle.[26] The arguments by which he proves relativism, belong themselves to mental productions tainted with relativism, and consequently his affirmations on the nature of activistic knowledge do not, themselves, have any theoretical value.

But there is more. It happens that Mannheim, after having clearly distinguished between the two spheres of thought and having assigned a different function and nature to each one, reintroduces criteria of objectivity in the sphere of activistic thought where they are misplaced. We remember, as a matter of fact, that his criteria of perspective thought could have been classed under two headings: criteria of efficiency and criteria of objectivity, the last being: the unanimity of observers in the one same perspective (aiming to suppress the individual equation) and the broader point of view of the synthesis.[27]

So that we reproach Mannheim's relationism as being but a form of relativism, and moreover of a relativism which does not remain coherent with itself, since it reintroduces criteria of objectivity in the domain of perspective thought after having excluded them from it. These criticisms seem deserved, but it is worth while to attempt to understand why such a subtle mind has rendered itself guilty of such obvious faults. To do this, we shall examine later on his theses in the light of his philosophy.

THE BEARING OF THE GENESIS OF AN IDEA UPON ITS VALIDITY

A conception dear to Mannheim and one from which he has made an important element of his relationism is that the validity of an idea may be relative to its genesis.

> The dogmatic exponents of classical logic and philosophy are accustomed to maintain that the genesis of an idea has nothing to say concerning its validity or meaning. . . . I believe that from the standpoint of strict interpretation, we are infinitely enriched when we attempt to understand the biblical sentence, "The last shall be first," as the psychic expression of the revolt of oppressed strata.[28]

By genesis, Mannheim means social affiliation.[29] The question arises then in these terms: when I know that a certain idea corresponds to a certain social group, what does that teach me about the meaning and validity of that idea?

It certainly teaches me a great deal concerning the *meaning* of the idea. To know the manner in which it was born historically, to know what the social stratifications are which have been the bearers of this idea, is certainly of first importance for correctly understanding an idea in its nuances. It is probable that few "dogmatic logicians" would deny, even if they have not practised this method in reality, that knowing the psychological, social and historic context of an idea aids us in understanding its meaning.

Nor is the genesis of an idea indifferent to its *validity,* but seems rather to concern it "exteriorly," in the sense that it draws the attention to a certain probable distortion. To know that a certain idea emanates from a certain class teaches us first that it is partial and second the direction of that partiality. To know that it emanates, on the contrary, from a certain group of "pure intellectuals" makes a presumption of greater validity. But these are only exterior tokens. This question of validity will be decided finally by direct discussion. There can be no substitute for this direct examination.[30]

Mannheim has exaggerated a bit the bearing of genesis upon validity because of his conviction of the relational character of our knowledge. In this line, it follows logically that if the point of view is good, the idea will be valid (or at least that it will not be invalid because the point of view is bad; it may be so for other reasons).

It was useful to note this point, for an important consequence follows from it, the consequence that an idea cannot be refuted solely by laying bare its genesis. Once the interests have been unmasked, it still remains for us to refute it directly.

IMPLICIT METAPHYSICS

Mannheim claims that his conception of knowledge is founded upon some implications of his positive observations of the sociology of knowledge. That is why our criticism of his propositions has remained on a positive plane up to the present. We have attempted to see whether its implications were really postulated by the results of his research. We have concluded that the positive research does not make the construction of a new philosophy of knowledge necessary; also, that his relationism does not completely escape the reproach of contradiction; and finally, that his choice of certain methods, such as synthesis, remains unexplained.

Now it seems that a metaphysics is subjacent to Mannheim's conception of knowledge, and that, if we consider this conception in the light of this metaphysics, many things are explained, contradictions disappear and the reasons for certain preferences become clear. Finally, his system gains in consistency.

But how do we become acquainted with this metaphysics? We find a few of its scarce fragments scattered in his writings. Since Mannheim did not have as his aim the expounding of his philosophy and since he even disclaims being influenced by it, these tokens are neither very numerous nor very extensive. To interpret them, we know the predominant philosophic influences he has undergone: they are those of Hegel and Marx.[31] It would be impossible, on such a basis, to reconstruct an elaborate and refined philosophy which would have any chance of really being Mannheim's. We shall be content then to indicate very modestly the essential themes we may attribute to him with sufficient certainty. It will rather be a philosophic climate than a system.

CENTRAL THESES OF MANNHEIM'S METAPHYSICS

The central point of Mannheim's metaphysics is what Engels calls "the great basic thought" of Hegelianism: the reality is Becoming, "the world is not to be comprehended as a complex of ready-made things, but as a complex of *processes*."[32] This affirmation is repeated in several places in Mannheim's work. The concept of reality is dynamic. [33] "The reality . . . is in constant flux,[34] (it) is in a constant process of change."[35] This total becoming is the last reality of the world and does not need any ulterior explanation. It is the absolute to which all the rest refers. This central idea had been generally admitted by the German intellectuals since the time of Hegel. It has "so thoroughly permeated ordinary consciousness that . . . it is scarcely ever contradicted,"[36] remarks Engels again.

This becoming of the world is the world itself, and does not transcend it in any way. With Marx, the motor factor in world affairs took the form of an economic determinism.[37] Mannheim does not seem to accept the fact that the ultimate reality is to be found in the economic field.[38] Wherever the ultimate reality may be found, if Mannheim is not a materialist in the sense of the *Vulgärmarxismus,* he denies any "dualistic world-view which, alongside of our world of concrete immediate events, creates a second world by adding another dimension of being." This transcendental ontology "postulates a sphere of perfection which does not bear the scars of its origins and, measured by which, all events and processes are shown to be finite and incomplete."[39]

The idea that the becoming of the world is immanent, is expressed by the dialectical conception of reality or of history (these terms being synonymous). History, in its autonomous unfolding, realizes a meaning.[40] As Hegel said, the historical development has been a rational process[41]; History is the realization of the Idea.[42] The dialectical evolution will be developed according to a scheme of progress Mannheim terms Hegelian. Each historic period contains in itself the germs of the following one and consequently its own disintegration.[43] Here are the terms in which Hegel expresses himself:

The principle of development involves also the existence of latent germ of being — a capacity or potentiality striving to realize itself.[44] The dialectical nature of the Idea (means) that it is self-determined, that it assumes successive forms which it successively transcends; and by this very process of transcending its earlier stages, gains an affirmative, and, in fact, a richer and more concrete shape.[45]

Man is also inserted in this becoming and is himself becoming. His faculties were gradually developed in the course of historical unfolding. According to Marxist philosophy, human consciousness originates in an elementary faculty of representation whose primitive function was to adapt man to his moving environment by permitting him to master it.[46] Even when he had reached the stage of speculative reason, this faculty preserved its character as an adjustive function.

The question whether objective truth can be attributed to human thinking is not a question of theory but is a practical question. In practice man must prove the truth, i.e., the reality and power, the "this-sidedness" of his thinking. The dispute over the reality or non-reality of thinking which is isolated from practice is a purely scholastic question, wrote Marx.[47]

It really seems that Mannheim shares this view, although he does not express himself formally on this point. Dr. Mandelbaum, who studied Mannheim from another point of view than ours, arrives at a similar conclusion. For him, a metaphysical conception is implicit in Mannheim's thought: this is that human nature, including its rationality, emerges from an interaction between man as an organism and the exterior world.[48]

MANNHEIM'S CONCEPTION OF KNOWLEDGE IN TERMS OF HIS METAPHYSICS

These few theses — ontological dynamism, dialectical historicism, the materialistic, or rather non-transcendental, conception of the world — constitute the philosophic background of Mannheim's system, and confer upon the latter a coherence it does not seem to enjoy at first sight.

The affirmation of the activistic character of human thought is placed here, no longer as a necessary implication of positive observations, but as a consequence of the nature of man in a world "without a second dimension of being" and in the process of development.

But does this activistic conception of knowledge take away all sense from the notion of truth defined as "conformity with reality?" It seems not. Does a mental production not permit a better adaptation to the becoming of the world just by its adequateness to this becoming? Let us look a little closer.

The opposition between objectivity and efficiency may be placed on different planes. Objectivity taken in its most simple form means that various observers "see the object as it is" since they have a similar perception. Likewise, the fruitfulness of knowledge means simply its immediate utility. But the duality objectivity-efficiency takes all its meaning in Mannheim's opposition of more complex concepts: on the one hand, the dynamic synthesis resulting from the conciliation of several points of view and, on the other, the fruitfulness of a political conception which permits adjustment to a given economic-social situation.

In terms of a materialistic dynamism, the best political theory, the most efficient, will be the one which is the best adapted to the present economic-social situation, or which prepares somewhat the following stage of the unfolding of reality by foreseeing it and destroying its obstacles. On the other hand, this efficient political theory is efficient because it is adequate to reality. It conforms with it to the degree in which it is the changing image of changing reality, that is to say to the degree to which it is adapted to its object, which is political and social evolution. Thus the fruitfulness of a political theory is measured by its degree of conformity with the unfolding of history. Efficiency and objectivity find their common origin in the historicity of the political view, that is to say in the fact that its meaning is inserted in the profound orientation of history.

Since the clear distinction between objectivity and efficiency grows blurred when it is considered in relation to this philosophy, the result is that we cannot reproach Mannheim for contradicting himself by introducing criteria of objectivity in the sphere of perspective knowledge. We must greatly temper the accusation of relativism which was brought against relationism.

This philosophic background also gives us the key to Mannheim's preference for the synthesis as a means of obtaining an authentic view of reality. Because reality is dialectical, that is to say evolves according to a certain scheme, it is by an intellectual process which endeavors to reproduce this outline that we shall remain closest to it. This is the profound reason for which the "truest" social and political doctrine will be expressed in the form of a synthesis.

Any social and political doctrine includes an image of the future society which is desirable for it to realize. This image is by definition inadequate to the present situation. But present reality is not all reality, it is but a stage of a development directed by an immanent law. Consequently the criterion of reality may be employed to distinguish, among these "inadequate images," those which are completely unreal (with respect to present and future historical evolution) and those which, although they are inadequate to the present situation, conform to the following historical stage. Thus we find again the notions of ideology and utopia and their criterion of differentiation, which seem rather strange outside of this philosophic context.[49] The importance of utopia is capital because of its dialectical function. It is the germ of destruction which the existing order carries in itself and which prepares the coming of the following stage. "The existing order gives birth to utopias which in turn break the bonds of the existing order, leaving it free to develop in the direction of the next order of existence."[50]

This conception of history explains also why, when Mannheim speaks about mental productions, he thinks above all of political and social doctrines (like liberalism, Marxism, etc.). That is because these systems are the real unities of the political and social field if we consider the field in the perspective of dialectical unfolding.

MANNHEIM'S SOCIOLOGY OF KNOWLEDGE IN TERMS OF HIS PHILOSOPHY

It is not only Mannheim's conception of knowledge which is elucidated by his implicit philosophy, but also his system of the sociology of knowledge. We have noted above the profound philosophic sense which certain of his concepts conceal beneath their empirical meanings; thus, the term "historic" and the term "correspondence."[51] But there is more.

In Mannheim's philosophy, knowledge has as its function the adaptation of man to his environment. This environment has taken various forms in the course of history, but always it has presented itself, if not as hostility, at least as resistance to human action. It was necessary to master natural forces in order to survive, it was also necessary to fight against other men in order to dominate or at least not to be dominated by them. This means that the adjustive role of knowledge very often aimed at helping the fighting man. Hence, it may be expected that mental productions reflect this preoccupation with struggle.

In modern times, this adjustment to a hostile environment has taken the form of the struggle of the classes for political and economic power. In this crude competition, mental productions will furnish the different groups with arms that will permit them to attain their collective objectives, and express their group desires. Thus thought will translate collective interests, and will be linked to a class point of view.

Mannheim's metaphysics does more than underlie his theory of knowledge and his sociology of knowledge. Starting with these few central, philosophic propositions, we can deduce the essential points of his system right up to the general formulation of the results of his positive research: knowledge is perspective.

The possibility of the deduction of the gnosiological and sociological system of Mannheim is evidently not a guarantee of its validity. For validity to be guaranteed, it would be necessary for the theses of his metaphysics to be proven true and for the deduction to be perfectly rigorous (that is to say for no element not derived from the principles, to intervene). We leave these questions open, for Mannheim, in fact, clearly refuses to base his sociology of knowledge and his conception of the nature of knowledge upon anything but empirical observation. We can only criticize him then from this point of view. It is very clear that Mannheim has not given himself over to a work of deduction in order to attempt to find his conclusions again by induction starting with empirical observation. But it is very probable that this ontology was, more or less consciously, the clue to Mannheim's positive research. It is this ontology which directed his research towards perspectivism and which induced him, from time to time, to establish, on weak, empirical bases, conclusions conforming with what he believed in other respects.

CHAPTER SIX

Conclusions Drawn from the Study of Mannheim

THE CLARIFICATION OF THE RELATIONS between the sociology of knowledge and the philosophy of knowledge is the essential object of the present work. The method—the critical analysis of two systems — which has been adopted to solve this problem has given rise to a second concern: the determination of the degree to which these systems contribute to the establishing of our young discipline. It seems desirable to retain this duality of interests. Thus, our conclusions comprise two parts. We shall ask ourselves, first, what can be concluded from Mannheim's system in regard to the relations between the sociology of knowledge and gnosiology; and, second, what are Mannheim's contributions to the establishment of the sociology of knowledge.

PHILOSOPHIC SIGNIFICANCE OF A SYSTEM OF THE SOCIOLOGY OF KNOWLEDGE

Mannheim's system really seems to give the lie to those who assert that the sociology and the philosophy of knowledge move on completely separate planes. Indeed, by starting with empirical observations, Mannheim has arrived at an implication of a philosophic theory of the nature and the finality of knowledge. In another connection, by starting with an ontology of the world and of man, it is possible to deduce from it the conclusions of Mannheim's observations (thought linked to a social perspective). It would seem then, that instead of an absolute separation, there is rather an unbroken continuity from the facts of observation to the principles of metaphysics.[1]

Unfortunately, as we have attempted to show, Mannheim, starting with his positive sociology, did not succeed in implying validly a new philosophic conception of the nature of knowledge. His attempt, since it failed, cannot then convince us that there is continuity between sociology and philosophy. But we cannot, on the other hand, deduce the contrary from it. The reason we cannot do so is that, from the point of view of our problem, the meaning of this failure depends upon the causes of it. Those which were noted above were particular errors, irrelevant in this respect. Let us see now if there is not a more fundamental reason for this failure.

Ambivalence of the Principle of Activistic Knowledge

We remember that, in Mannheim's positive sociology, his scientific theory (or explanation of the conclusions of positive research) consisted in the combination of two principles: that of the pragmatic character of knowledge and, secondarily, that of the struggle of groups.[2] Now these same two principles are essential elements of Mannheim's philosophy.[3] Thus we can find out exactly where the meeting point of the philosophic sphere and the sphere of positive sociology is. It is in these two principles and particularly in that of activistic knowledge. The other has the rather negative role of expressing the conditions of application of the first, and its philosophic significance is less clear.[4]

The principle of activistic knowledge is ambivalent. It is scientific theory and philosophic conclusion at one and the same time. This means that it has two very different statuses. As scientific theory, it is propounded by the mind simply as a logical principle from which can be logically deduced the relation between two phenomena as observation has established it (explanatory function), and from which can be deduced other relations which observation must verify (function of guiding new researches). We expect a scientific theory only to fulfill these two functions correctly.

As philosophic affirmation, the principle of activistic knowledge is supposed to express the profound nature and finality of knowledge in correlation with an ontological conception of the world and of man. We expect a philosophic affirmation to be true, to actually express the ultimate nature of things.

Mannheim does not seem to have realized clearly the ambivalent nature of his principle of activistic knowledge. As a matter of fact, he has reached it in the way a scientific theory is obtained: by starting with observations, by looking for what the principle implied by them is — that is to say, the principle explaining them.[5] Then, once he had attained the principle, he considered it as being an affirmation of philosophic significance which actually expressed the nature of human knowledge. This transition is all the more explainable, since, on the strength of the Marxist philosophy to whose influence he was profoundly subjected, he was convinced that knowledge is a function of adaptation. It is not astonishing that he believed he had rediscovered this "truth" through empirical channels.

EXPLANATORY THEORIES OF A REAL TYPE

It is because of the ambivalence of the explanatory proposition that there is no clear-cut distinction between philosophy and science in Mannheim's system. Is this accidental? Or can we expect to find the same phenomenon again elsewhere? This is tantamount to asking ourselves the reason for this ambivalence, which does not seem to appear in other scientific fields — as in physics, for example.

This ambivalence results from the type of explanation: it is real. This is to say that we seek to deduce the results of research from a proposition expressing the *nature* of knowledge. It follows from this that any explanatory proposition of this kind always has a possible philosophical meaning. To pass from scientific theory to philosophic assertion, it is sufficient (if we may express ourselves in this way) to change the coefficient of reality. Instead of saying, "*If* knowledge is activistic, we can deduce from this that it is socially conditioned," we say, "Knowledge is activistic; we can deduce from this that it is socially conditioned." Ambivalence is not then an anomaly peculiar to Mannheim's system, for there will be ambivalence each time the explanations of generalizations are of a real type.

Is this avoidable? Let us see what has taken place in the physico-chemical sciences. In this field, the distinction between physical theories and the philosophy of matter appears very clear today,[6] but it has not always been like this. When the physicists of the Middle Ages, in order to explain the circular movement of the stars, propounded the hypothesis that they were perfect bodies and therefore could move only according to a perfect and hence circular trajectory, their theory was a real explanation which had also a possible philosophic significance. Descartes explained the invariability of the quantity of movement in the physical world by the fact that God is immutable in his designs. Therefore he maintains in the world the quantity of movement he assigned to it at the time of creation. These ancient physical theories were of a real type. The principle of perfect bodies and divine immutability were susceptible of a philosophic sense. Moreover, in the eyes of the physicists who enunciated them, they were evidently more than logical principles from which experimental results can be deduced. They really claimed to express the real nature of things. The modern physical theory is no longer a real explanation, but "a system of mathematical propositions deduced from a small number of principles, which have as their aim to give a representation as simple, complete and exact as possible of a set of experimental laws."[7] Such a mathematical explanation[8] is not ambivalent, is not susceptible of being affected by a coefficient of reality.

But there can be deduced from "a small number of mathematical principles" only other mathematical propositions; consequently the results of positive research themselves must be expressed also in mathematical form, "in the form of variable and qualified numbers,"[9] if we wish to deduce them from mathematical principles.

Would such a mathematization of the sociology of knowledge be possible? To be sure, certain of its results can be translated into numbers, but it is doubtful whether our discipline can be content with retaining from experiment only facts expressible mathematically.

Real explanation and mathematical explanation are not the only two possibilities. The theoretical principle may be of a phenomenal type — that is to say, expressing not an assertion concerning the intimate nature of reality, but certain phenomenal aspects more general than the one we wish to explain. In the sociology of knowledge, such a phenomenal explanation is often psychological[10] — that is to say, the results of positive research will be deduced from a general affirmation bearing upon human psychology. Thus the principle of group struggle might be interpreted psychologically. In Mannheim's system, however, it has rather a philosophic meaning.

THE PRINCIPLE OF PROBABLE CONFORMITY

Whatever these possibilities may be, Mannheim's explanation is real. In this case, what are the relations of the sociology of knowledge and gnosiology?

At the beginning of this section, we mentioned the two extreme positions: complete separation and unbroken continuity. We saw that continuity is but an illusion due to the ambivalence of certain propositions which may be reached as implications of the results of positive research and as deductions from a metaphysics. There would be continuity if scientific theory and philosophic assertion had the same status. They do not, however. The same proposition has two different values. They are not identical. Hence there is a break.

This seems to have to lead us back to the other extreme conception: that of the absence of relations. However, two considerations claim our attention. Let us stop first at the following fact, which is somewhat disturbing. It is exactly the same proposition which is scientific theory and philosophic conclusion: "knowledge is activistic." The result of this is the following paradoxical situation: this principle can be a good theory and a false philosophy at one and the same time. This means: "The observations we have made are explained if we suppose that reality is such, but, as a matter of fact, reality is different." Or, vice versa, a true philosophy may be a poor theory; which is tantamount to saying: "Reality is such, but we must suppose it to be other than it is in order to take account of our observations."

Then let us suppose that, starting with empirical observations, we imply a real explanation by a necessary inference — that is to say that this explanation of the facts observed is the only one logically possible. In this case, we cannot deny that the philosophic explanatory principle is not only good, but true, without denying, by this very fact, the validity of the necessary inference, which is one of the essential logical tools of the traditional Occidental philosophic method. It may happen, as a matter of fact, that no case of necessary inference occurs in the sociology of knowledge. However, the mere possibility of such a necessary inference shows the close relationship between real explanation in sociology and philosophic inferences.

These two considerations lead us to reject the radical position which denies any relationship between positive sociology and philosophy. Now that the two extreme solutions have been rejected, it remains for us to clarify the intermediate solution which seems to us valid.

On the one hand, it is certain that the attitude of the sociology of knowledge and that of the philosophy of knowledge are clearly distinct. The first seeks to clarify the manner in which social factors influence mental productions. It seeks facts and a scientific theory which will permit explaining them and which will suggest fruitful directions for its subsequent research. The second is interested in what the profound nature of knowledge is, in the place of this activity in its conception of the nature of man and the world. These different aims are pursued by different methods: on the one hand, conclusions based upon observation, and the construction of theories; on the other, deduction from general metaphysical theories, and the necessary implications from experience. The result of this is the possibility of the paradoxical situations of which we have just spoken.

On the other hand, however, it does not seem that such situations have to be the rule. We have no reason to admit that things generally happen in a manner not in conformity with their nature. When a philosopher claims, let us say, that the nature of knowledge is such that its finality is purely theoretical, and that, on the other hand, our observations are explained perfectly by supposing that the nature of knowledge is practical, the situation is abnormal. This is tantamount to saying that there is a probable conformity between good theory and true philosophy — that is to say, a greater probability of agreement than of disagreement. Denying this principle of conformity amounts to questioning the pertinence of the philosophic effort, for if, when I know that reality is such, there is no chance for things to occur in conformity with — rather than contrary to — their nature, it seems that the subsumability of the real under our intellectual categories becomes somewhat doubtful.

In short, there is a contact between philosophy and sociology of knowledge when a philosophic principle serves as an explanatory theory for the results observed. That this principle may be satisfactory in its function as a theory is an indication, but not a proof, of its philosophic validity. Reciprocally, the philosophic truth of a principle of explanation is an indication, but not a proof, of its value as a scientific theory. The result of this is that when a good theory is a false philosophy, and vice versa, the situation is abnormal, and consequently we must take account of this.

COROLLARY: A HYPOTHESIS OF CRITICISM

This conception of the relationships between philosophy and positive science in the domain of the sociology of knowledge suggests, it seems, a profitable direction for criticism. Many authors, like Mannheim, who utilize scientific explanations of a real type, are not fully conscious of the ambivalence of their principles. They tend to consider that a scientific theory which is good is a proven philosophy, and they unduly link a philosophic position to their systems.

This is what prompts certain critics to admit this intimate relationship and to consider these systems as philosophico-scientific wholes. Because the philosophic affirmations appear unacceptable to them, they attempt to deny the value of the conclusions of positive research which are, they think, "the empirical basis" for these affirmations. On the contrary, it seems preferable to bring to light the ambivalence of explanatory principles. This permits the discernment of the valid elements from the others. In this case, the critic has not to reject the first because of the second.

We might formulate this hypothesis of criticism in the following way: In the systems of sociology of knowledge which utilize explanations of a real type, the principal point of criticism will consist in the exact determination of the ambivalent significance of explanatory principles. Starting with this fundamental distinction, the significance of the various stages of the system will become apparent.

CONTRIBUTION OF MANNHEIM'S SYSTEM TO THE
SOCIOLOGY OF KNOWLEDGE

MANNHEIM'S SCIENTIFIC THEORY IS FRUITFUL

We have noted several of Mannheim's contributions in the course of our criticism: his monographs on certain concrete relations between social factors and knowledge; his method of analysis by the reconstruction of a type of mentality; the various elements with which we may elaborate a process permitting us to transcend the social perspective; and so on. In this conclusion, we shall stop at what appears to us to be his essential contribution to the sociology of knowledge: his scientific theory. We mean his working hypothesis which combines the principle of knowledge as a function of adaptation with that of the competition of groups. Let us note that, from the point of view of the "science to be created"— a point of view particularly important in a young discipline which has defined its field of action rather than explored it — the fruitful working hypotheses are the most precious. Mannheim's system then furnishes the sociology of knowledge with a very important element.

We have already indicated above that his theory is a good explanation and, what is more important, a source of fruitful hypotheses. On the one hand, it is sufficiently precise to permit foreseeing a certain relationship in special cases. Thus it is possible to verify the existence of these relationships without losing ourselves in interminable fact-finding processes. On the other hand, it is sufficiently general and flexible to be able to suggest numerous relationships when it is confronted with determined historical situations.

This praise must not make us lose sight of the limited scope of this theory. Thus, in no way is the sociology of knowledge identified with the system of relationships which may be synthesized by this principle. We cannot insist too much upon this fact, for Mannheim seems to overlook any variety of sociology of knowledge which is not his own. It is sufficient to recall the name of Durkheim to evoke an influence of society upon human knowledge which would not be "explicable" by Mannheim's theory. We expounded above several similar cases drawn from Mannheim's own works.[11]

THE PARADOX OF THE "GOOD" EXPLANATION AND THE "FALSE" PHILOSOPHY

One last problem arises. This theory, being an explanation of a real type, also has a philosophic significance. Since its explanatory value is considerable, it follows from this, according to the principle of probable conformity, that the philosophy it expresses is very probably true.

According to this philosophy, man is conceived as strongly determined by the group to which he belongs. The almost exclusive motivation of his activity is his group's pursuit of political and economic power. Knowledge is an aspect of this activity. It is not a faculty of contemplation but an instrument which serves man in acting upon his environment, and which is, to a very large degree, determined in fact by the present situation of his group in the struggle of the classes for power. As we saw above, this conception of man is perfectly in line with an ontology for which reality is a dialectical, non-transcendental becoming.

In the present monograph, we evidently do not have to give our attention to the truth or falsity of such a philosophic proposition, but simply to its relations with sociological theory. The fact that this philosophy permits the explanation in a satisfactory fashion of the results obtained through observation is an indication, but not a proof, of its truth.

Consequently, for the one who has adopted for other reasons such a materialistic philosophy (in the broad sense) of man and of the world, the scientific theory by which Mannheim explains the results of his research will contribute a new argument of probability to his philosophic views.

On the other hand, the philosopher who conceives of man as provided with a spiritual nature manifesting itself especially through the theoretical faculty of the true and through the possibility of transcending economic and social determinism — this philosopher must take account of the curious fact that a certain human behavior, observed by the sociologist, is explained better by a materialistic conception of man (which this philosopher judges false) than by a spiritualistic conception (which he judges true). He cannot be content to state this anomaly, but he must explain it.[12] Let us see how our spiritualistic philosopher might solve this paradox.

THE CULTURAL PERSONALITY TYPES

Among the philosophies which endeavor to construct a spiritualistic conception of man, some base their explanations and their arguments upon the exterior observation of "characteristics common to all men"; others are based above all upon a very profound inner experience. Both, however, claim to attain a universal human nature. Since the latter must be verified by all men of all times, it will be expressed either in terms of a high abstraction (for the first) or in terms of a profound interiority (for the second). In both cases, this human nature, even if it is really identified with the profound and universal essence of man, will coincide only very partially with man in his phenomenal totality — that is to say, the individual bearer of all his particular determinations (to have had a certain history, to belong to a certain environment, to practice a certain profession, etc.).

But between these two extremes, human nature and the individual, there is a place for less extensive and more comprehensive abstractions than the man of the metaphysicians. They are what we might call personality types. Their psychological equipment is made up not only of raw elements which may be found in any *homo sapiens,* but these elements are particularized and combined in such a way that they form a determined psychological structure. Such psychological structures are common to a certain number of individuals living under the same conditions. These conditions may be geographic, climatic, occupational, social, or cultural. These various conditions, however, do not have the same importance. It seems certain indeed that if geography, climate, occupation, can give rise to certain psychological *traits,* different types of personality can correspond to scarcely anything but the social and cultural environment. The reason for it is that social organization, cultural institutions and practices rule very important domains of human activity. "It is actually a commonplace that collective life explains almost all of man."[13]

It seems indeed that, in the Occidental world, the passage from the precapitalistic economy to the capitalistic economy, and the subsequent development of the latter (with the concomitant phenomena of technical progress and industrialization), have created such changes in social organization and interpersonal relations that we may speak of a capitalistic culture which, starting in commercial and financial milieus, has gradually invaded, although in unequal fashion, the various social strata of Western Europe and North America.[14] This culture has gradually molded a type of personality which has been described more than once by psychologists and sociologists.[15] Now most of these descriptions insist upon two elements which are particularly important from our point of view.

For the man of the capitalistic age, the earning of money is not an activity limited by the satisfaction of his needs as they are defined by the society in which he lives. Profits are not limited by any principle. They obey only the law of "always more."[16] All things will be seen by the eyes of a merchant for whom a tree is not a tree but a beam.[17]

This extreme valuation of profit as such has had as its effect that of making economic activity dynamic and competitive. Since each one wishes to earn in an unlimited way, and since neither natural resources, nor manpower, nor the market are indefinitely elastic (in a limited period of time), he must ceaselessly measure himself against others and attempt to outstrip them. This competition is not limited to individuals, or to the strictly economic sphere.

Now our spiritualistic philosopher will say men's concrete actions do not manifest only the intimate reality of their ontological nature. Many of them have their origin at the less profound level of the type of cultural personality they realize. To make use of mental productions as justifications for keeping or obtaining economic and political power for one's group corresponds not to the essentially spiritual nature of man but really to the human type which has been molded by the dominant culture in the countries of the West during the last centuries.

Thus the man of the capitalistic culture will utilize his thought for practical purposes (even if he is endowed with a faculty of the "true") and will pursue his interests ardently (even if his spiritual essence permits him to transcend them). This enables us to take account of the paradox: a certain human behavior seems to be explained more easily by a false philosophic conception than by a true one.

Naturally we do not say that *all* individuals living in the capitalistic age realize the corresponding human type, or that those who realize it manifest it in *all* their actions. But the number of "children of this world" is statistically sufficient and their behavior consistent enough for the hypothesis to remain sound.[18]

This reduction of the theory's paradox brings to light another limitation of the Mannheim hypothesis. When the human type of the capitalistic period does not exist, the hypothesis will lose its value, as is shown by the following case which stimulated Max Weber to conduct research on the relations between Calvinism and capitalism. An attempt was made to introduce piece-wages in regions where traditional conceptions prevailed. The result was that the Catholic workers, in certain places where the new principle of limitless increase of profits had not yet been realized, used to stop working as soon as they had earned the sum necessary to assure them their customary level of subsistence.[19] Consequently, to take as a working hypothesis the struggle between groups for economic power is to limit one's research to epochs of capitalistic culture.

MANNHEIM'S SYSTEM AND THE RECONSTRUCTION OF SOCIETY

We said that Mannheim's last interest during the years he spent in London was the reform of our society. We would like to indicate in a few words two points of contact between this problem and the sociology of knowledge.

The thinkers who, having diagnosed a crisis of civilization, are concerned with finding a remedy, are stopped by the following question. Can improvement be brought about by reforms in institutions, in the social structure? On the contrary, is not the solution solely in the reform of man?

It seems that the sociology of knowledge furnishes at least one element for the solution of this problem. Indeed, its fundamental affirmation of the social conditioning of knowledge implies that, in this domain at least, by changing certain factors of the social structure we may act upon one human activity. Is this not an indication of the possible efficacy of the social reforms which are only social (in opposition to moral reforms)? In any case, Mannheim believed in the efficacy of social changes. He saw the remedy for the crisis in a planning of society — that is to say, in the deliberate organization of social conditions with a view to acting upon man in different ways.[20]

The second contact is more direct. Mannheim expected that his system of sociology of knowledge would have a pacifying effect upon the conflicts which divide men deeply.[21]

If political adversaries and others made the effort we have described above[22] to realize good conditions of discussion, there is no doubt that many conflicts would be avoided or softened. But is it not probable that one would merely "unmask" and be "unmasked"? That is to say that conflicts of ideas will be reduced to conflicts of interests. A commentator of Mannheim wonders if that is not a doubtful advantage.[23]

It seems, on the contrary, to be very appreciable. In fact, it often happens that, when two groups are in conflict, only the interests of a few individuals in each of the groups are truly opposed. These minorities present, consciously or not, their own interests as linked to ideas which appear sacred to the other members of the group. Thus they gain others' support for a merciless struggle.

Then, in the case where the authentic interests of two groups are truly opposed to each other, the travesty of this conflict of interests as a conflict of ideas will have as its effect the rendering of a more difficult, or even impossible, compromise.

This does not mean evidently that all conflicts of ideas are reducible to conflicts of interests; but when an ideological opposition is merely disguising an economic opposition, the fact that the adversaries are fully conscious of it is very favorable for peace.

PART TWO

PITIRIM A. SOROKIN

General Framework of Sorokin's Sociology of Knowledge

INTRODUCTION:
THE SCIENTIFIC CAREER OF PROFESSOR SOROKIN

THE SCIENTIFIC WORK of Professor Sorokin is of considerable magnitude from several points of view. First of all, from the time of his first publications[1] till the present, he has written an imposing number of articles, essays, monographs and treatises. Moreover, this output covers not only special fields such as criminal law, the sociology of revolution, rural sociology, but also general areas such as structural and dynamic sociology. Finally, his encyclopedic knowledge of the various social sciences and especially of sociological theories have allowed him to construct syntheses whose extent exceeds that which one mind can generally master.

Pitirim Alexandrovitch Sorokin was born in 1889 at Touria, Northern Russia, of a poor peasant family. His father was a Great Russian and his mother of Ugro-Finnish origin. During his childhood and adolescence he shared his father's rough life.[2] The latter, a travelling workman, plied the trade of icon gilder. At the age of fourteen, the son entered the teacher's school of the province of Kostroma. He remained there for three years. It is there that he had his first skirmish with the czarist police: he was arrested for revolutionary activities. On leaving prison, he went to Petrograd where he attended a night school, then the Psycho-neurological Institute and the University. The latter conferred on him in 1915 the degree of Magistrat of Penal Law.[3]

During this formative period perhaps the strongest influence was Ivan Pavlov, who trained him in behavioristic psychology. Although Sorokin was never a strict behaviorist in the Watsonian sense, part of his works are strongly tainted with behaviorism. In his first works especially,[4] he applies to sociology a method inspired by the psychology of Pavlov. Here is the way in which it may be characterized, according to Sorokin himself. One concentrates one's attention on phenomena which repeat themselves in time and space. Whenever possible, one studies them experimentally and quantitatively. One neglects, at least at the beginning of the study, the verbal reactions and the ideas of the subjects, because they are of little importance in human conduct and may often be misleading. One avoids any value judgment in a scientific study. Finally, one realizes that not everything can be studied by this method and consequently one does not apply it to everything.[5]

This scientific output was far from exhausting the activity of Sorokin. This sociologist was not merely a spectator to the deep social upheavals through which his country was passing. In 1917, he was Privatdocent (lecturer) at the Psycho-neurological Institute and at the University of Petrograd. At the outset of the Revolution, he was editing a newspaper with socialistic leanings, *The Free People*. In the Provisional Government, he was secretary to Prime Minister Kerensky. He was frankly anti-bolshevist. Although elected a member of the Constituent Assembly, he was arrested on the unfounded charge of having made an attempt on Lenin's life. Freed, he fought against Bolshevism by publishing a newspaper, *Regeneration*. Arrested in the attempted counter-revolution of Archangel, he was condemned to death. An article in *Pravda,* signed by Lenin, in favor of the intellectuals who participated in the Revolution, and in favor of Sorokin in particular, won him his freedom.[6] He then became a professor, and later President of the Department of Sociology at the University of Petrograd until his final banishment from the Soviet Union in 1922. During this lively period, he had published, besides the books cited above, *Elements of Sociology* (1919) and *General Theory of Law* (1920). After a short stay in Berlin and Prague, he became a professor at the University of Minnesota in 1924. He remained there until 1930, at which time he was called to Harvard University, where he founded the Sociology Department (1931).

This story of Sorokin's political activity in Russia is important from the point of view of his ideas. It is there, in fact, that we find the psychological basis for his conception of socio-cultural changes as he expounds it at length in his four volumes of *Social and Cultural Dynamics* (1937-1941). Social thought, at the beginning of the twentieth century, was dominated by a belief in continuous progress, "in revolution, in socialism, in democracy, and in scientific positivism." The first World War, the Russian Revolution, and all that followed were very disturbing facts, scarcely explicable to Sorokin, who was waiting with confidence for a betterment of society and progress towards peace, tolerance, and humanitarianism. "What are the reasons, the cause, the significance of these surprises?"[7] Little by little, the idea emerged that the development of history must be conceived not according to a law of constant progress, but rather as a series of fluctuations in which one can discern the recurrence of three essential phases.

Sorokin's thought did not evolve only from the point of view of what one might call his philosophy of history. His first books published in the United States still betray some behaviorist influences. *The Sociology of Revolution* (1925) is a description of the effects of revolutions on various aspects of human conduct and social life. He there makes abundant use of the categories of conditioned and unconditioned reflexes.[8] *Social Mobility* (1927) belongs to the same trend.[9] Sorokin writes in that work that speculative sociology is beginning to be left behind. An objective sociology, behaviorist and quantitative, is successfully replacing it. That is why one must avoid grounding one's conclusions exclusively on verbal reactions.[10] This point of view is especially reflected in his examination of the physical differences between individuals belonging to various social classes; of the differences in their vitality, measured chiefly by their longevity; of the differentiations in their intelligence and other mental characteristics.[11] These various studies are founded on a considerable amount of quantitative material.

Time Budgets of Human Behavior (in collaboration with Clarence Q. Berger), although much more recent (1939), still belongs partially to this trend. It is a study of the average time allotted each day to various psychological, economic, social, religious, and intellectual activities. This monographic study is based on extremely detailed notes (the unit of time being the minute) taken for four weeks by some one hundred people. They were as a rule employees living in Boston or its vicinity. We say that this study is only partially behaviorist because the authors have also tried to determine the motivation behind these different activities.[12]

Sorokin, in fact, has broken away from his mild behaviorism on several essential points. In the first place, in sociology, behaviorism is a type of psychological theory in that it interprets social phenomena as derivatives or manifestations of psychological variables.[13] On the contrary, Sorokin's present system may be characterized as "sociologistic," one might say, in that it does not give psychology priority with regard to sociology. Social regularities are different and cannot be reduced to the psychological sphere.[14] For Sorokin, as we shall see better later on, sociocultural phenomena constitute a category irreducible to any other kind of phenomena.[15] Sociology has its own method and frame of reference. Thus Sorokin has formed concepts of *social time, social space, social causality*. His book *Sociocultural Causality, Time and Space* (1943) is devoted to this question.[16]

Next, he has clearly taken a stand against behaviorism on another essential point. To study external conduct and to abstract its significance is nonsense, and furthermore, impossible. Human phenomena are such only because they have a meaning. If one neglects the latter, one must give up designating the studied phenomena by such terms as robbery, religion, communism, etc. But then there remain only purely physical or biological phenomena: taking an object, making a series of gestures, etc. These are already studied by physics or biology. The sociocultural phenomenon has thus an aspect of significance, it is not merely trans-subjective.[17]

On the other hand, Sorokin has preserved several elements which he considers of behaviorist inspiration: sociology will concern itself with phenomena which repeat themselves.[18] And as much as possible, they will be studied quantitatively.[19] Professor Sorokin has used this method in several monographs[20] and in his three main works on general sociology: *Social and Cultural Dynamics* (1937-1941), *Sociocultural Causality, Time, and Space* (1943), and *Society, Culture, and Personality* (1947).[21]

Moreover, Professor Sorokin, since about 1940, has concerned himself with using his sociological science for social action. First of all, by a cry of alarm — by showing the depth of the crisis of our civilization. For that, he has published works meant for a non-specialized public, in which he summarizes his conception of the sociocultural fluctuations in the course of history. This enables him to situate our present crisis in a very broad framework. These books are *The Crisis of Our Age*, 1941; *Man and Society in Calamity*, 1942; *Russia and the United States*, 1944; *The Reconstruction of Humanity*, 1948.

But he is not content to diagnose the crisis of our time. His conception of history allows us to foresee a better future. The fact that our civilization in undergoing a crisis does not mean that it is about to die. It is simply passing from one stage to another. If this stage seems to be coming anyway, it is up to men to prepare for it and make the transition less painful.[22] Therefore Professor Sorokin, with several other sociologists, has undertaken the study of the factors of social solidarity in order to determine the techniques which will allow an increase in their intensity.[23]

Thus the works of Professor Sorokin, especially those published in the United States since about 1930, present themselves in the form of a vast system. *Society, Culture and Personality* is an ample systematization of his previous research. He has succeeded, starting from several fundamental concepts, in establishing a complete system of structural and dynamic sociology. His sociology of knowledge is integrated in this system. That is why we think it advisable to sketch the latter in order to assign a place to the former.

OUTLINE OF SOROKIN'S SYSTEM OF GENERAL SOCIOLOGY

THE SOCIAL SCIENCES

One may distinguish the inorganic realm which is studied by the physical sciences, the organic realm studied by biology, and the superorganic realm. The latter is distinct from the living world because it brings it a new determination — the mind. Superorganic are the vital phenomena in which a spirituality shows itself by scientific, philosophic, religious, ethical or artistic creations, by technical and social institutions. The superorganic is studied by the social sciences.[24]

Why call "social" the sciences of the superorganic? One readily conceives that history and the juridical disciplines should be social sciences. But, one might object to Sorokin, it is less evident, for example, in the case of philosophy or mathematics. He would probably answer that they, too, are social sciences, first because they were created and enriched by the interacting activities of innumerable human generations. Moreover, human personality, which is at the basis of these sciences, is a product of sociocultural forces. "At birth (man) is not yet a human personality or an agent of the superorganic life. . . . His scientific ideas, religious beliefs, aesthetic tastes, moral convictions and manners and mores; his occupation, economic position, and social status; his destiny and life career — none of these are yet determined."[25] Thus all sciences of man may be said to be social sciences. All superorganic phenomena are sociocultural.

What are the essential elements which are common to any object of the social sciences? Sorokin answers this question by describing the structure and the composition of the generic sociocultural phenomenon. Each sociocultural phenomenon is always a meaningful human interaction. *Interaction* means any situation in which one party influences in a tangible way the external actions or the state of mind of another.[26] By *meaningful,* one must understand that which, for the intellect, is the indication of something more than the mere physical properties of the interaction.[27] Finally, the idea of *human* reminds us that the superorganic is identical to the human world. No doubt a biosociology studying the biological interactions of animal and vegetable organisms is possible,[28] but it would be a science relating rather to biology than to sociology as the latter is conceived by Sorokin. Thus a sociocultural phenomenon is any interaction where the influence exerted by one party on the other has a meaning or a value superimposed on the purely physical or biological properties of the respective actions. If the interaction is stripped of this human element, it would not be a social phenomenon, but rather physical or biological.

The generic sociocultural phenomenon having been defined, Sorokin seeks to specify its components. They are three, each capable of being determined later on by many other factors. The first comprises meanings, norms, and values. These are immaterial elements, without spacial or temporal determinations. Then there are the vehicles of these norms and values: physicochemical and biological phenomena (second component). Finally — third component — there are the human agents, subjects of the interaction, who bear and use the meanings with the aid of the material vehicles.[29]

The *subjects of the interaction* are either individuals or organized human groups. The biological and psychological properties of human beings will not be studied for most of them are presupposed. They are assumed in the sense that *homo sapiens,* subject of the interaction, is considered possessed of a well-developed nervous system, the ability to accomplish a great number of external actions, a mind — that is to say, sensations, perceptions, ideas, imagination, memory, feelings and will; biological and psychological heterogeneity as regards race, sex, age, intelligence, etc.[30]

All phenomena of human interaction become simply physical or biological if they are deprived of their *human meaning.* Sexual intercourse between married or unmarried persons is physiologically similar. It is only its meaning which will make of it a diverse human act. The national flag is physically only a piece of wood and a piece of cloth. Physically, Beethoven's *Missa Solemnis* is only a compound of sounds or vibrations of air.[31]

The vehicles too are essential because without them the norms and values, which are immaterial, cannot be transmitted directly from one mind to another. The same vehicle may convey a very great number of meanings. The same gesture, that of holding out a bank note, may signify the payment of a debt, a salary, expression of gratitude, a bribe, or the price of a murder. In certain cases, however, a sort of crystallization will take place and the same vehicle will always be linked to the same meaning; this will give birth to the phenomenon of fetishism.[32]

These three components are indispensable. One can nevertheless say that meaning is more important than the vehicle in the sense that, even though a vehicle is always needed, the particular type of vehicle is of little importance. On the other hand, Sorokin underlines the fact that vehicles have a retroactive effect on values.[33] From the point of view of the sociology of knowledge, it is interesting to note that Sorokin admits that the vehicles and the human agents can strongly influence the meaning. A radical change in these two components can bring about great modifications in the meanings. Thus a great increase and considerable enrichment of the "vehicles" of Christianism has had important repercussions on its doctrine.

Parallel with an increase of its wealth in the centuries from the first to the ninth, when it became the richest landowner, several doctrines of the Church concerning private property, wealth, secular power, and other principles changed notably in the direction of a weakening of the "communist" trends of early Christianity to a more and more positive attitude toward wealth and property and secular power, to a less and less apocalyptic interpretation of the end of the world.[34]

Here is an incipient sociology of knowledge. But, as we shall see, Sorokin will develop his in another direction.

Thus sociocultural phenomena, subject matter of the social sciences, can be schematically defined by the formula: "meaningful human interactions."

SOCIOLOGY AMONG THE SOCIAL SCIENCES

Among the social sciences, what will be the place of sociology? It is a generalizing science It studies the properties of the superorganic which repeat themselves in time and space. It differentiates itself from the other generalizing sciences — economics for instance — in that it does not limit itself to only one compartment of the superorganic. And in that its fundamental presuppositions concerning the nature of man and the interrelations of social phenomena are different. Thus in economics, they postulate the *homo economicus,* a purely economic being, motivated by economic egoism and rational utilitarianism, to the exclusion of religious and moral beliefs, of altruism, of artistic values, of passions, and of irrational mores. In conformity with this postulate on the nature of man, economic phenomena are supposed to be entirely isolated from other sociocultural phenomena and insensible to religious, legal, political, artistic, moral or instinctivistic forces. On the contrary, the *homo socius* of sociology is in fact *the man,* with no limiting qualifications, at the same time inseparably economic, political, religious, ethical, artistic, partly rational and utilitarian, partly non-rational or even irrational. Consequently, each class of sociocultural phenomena is considered by sociology in its relation to all other classes, inasmuch as it affects and is affected by the rest of the cultural universe.[35]

But although a generalizing science, sociology is, according to Sorokin, a special science. It is not a sort of encyclopedic summary of all the social sciences. It seems — Sorokin is not very explicit on this point — that sociology is the point of view from which one considers the sociocultural phenomena that make its specificity. And this point of view, as we have just shown, is to consider these phenomena in *every* aspect, except the physical and the biological.[36]

One might perhaps summarize this conception by saying that

sociology is the science of the sociocultural phenomenon insofar as it repeats itself.

The Divisions of Sociology

Sorokin effects three divisions in sociology. The first follows the trilogy: society, culture, and personality; the second is the rather usual distinction between structure and dynamism; the third, between general and special sociology.

The three aspects of the generic sociocultural phenomenon: personality, society, and culture, are never separated in reality. There is no personality without the interaction of other human beings transmitting by appropriate vehicles meanings, values, and norms. There is no society without people having relationships on the superorganic level. Finally, there is no set of values objectified in vehicles (culture) without personalities interacting to create and communicate them. Although these three aspects are complementary, and involve each other, one can study them separately.[87] This is the reason why sociology will divide itself along three lines: study of the social universe; study of culture, and study of personality.

The second division is classic and does not require any commentary. The *statique sociale,* to use Comte's expression, will show what is the internal constitution, the structure of the society, of the culture, and of the personality. The dynamic study will have as its subject matter the change of these three aspects of any sociocultural phenomenon.

General structure sociology studies from a static point of view the generic sociocultural phenomenon (we have just given a summary of this analysis); the principal structural types of the groups or institutions into which the population is differentiated, and their relations; the structure of the principal cultural types and their relations; the composition of the types of personality which are integrated in the social groups and in the cultural systems.

General dynamic sociology studies the social processes which are repeated, such as contact, interaction, socialization, conflict, domination, subordination, adaptation, amalgamation, migration, mobility, etc. It also shows how social systems are born, acquire and lose their members, how the latter are distributed within the system, how the systems organize and disorganize themselves, and how all these processes affect the personality. It also studies cultural processes: invention, diffusion, integration and disintegration, conversion and accumulation of cultural traits and the influence they may have on individuals. It is also concerned with rhythms, regular recurrences, trends and fluctuations in the social and cultural processes together with the general problem of the evolution of society and culture. Finally, it describes the sociocultural changes as they affect people and looks for the how and the why of these changes.

The special sociologies raise the same questions and try to answer them, but merely in relation to a particular class of phenomena selected for an intensive study. Among the special sociologies existing today, Sorokin cites the sociology of knowledge.[38]

THE CULTURAL REALM

Mental productions are sociocultural phenomena. They have the threefold aspect we have described above. Let us take an example. Kant's philosophy is composed of a set of meanings (the Kantian system of categories, reasoning, etc.) objectified as vehicles (oral teaching, books, etc.) created and diffused by people (Kant, his disciples, his readers) acting one upon the other (for as long as Kant lived, at least, there was mutual action). Obviously, when one is concerned with philosophy, of these three elements it is the system of meanings which is the most important. That is why Sorokin will locate his sociology of knowledge at the level of a study of the cultural world.[39] In this very sketchy outline of the fundamental categories of Sorokin's sociological system, we shall leave out what concerns the social universe and the person.[40]

Cultural phenomena are of varying complexity. Some consist of very simple meanings, for example, a proposition such as "A is B" or "two and two make four"; others are very complicated, such as a religious doctrine, a philosophy, Euclidian geometry, or a Bach invention.

This raises the questions of the relations between those different meanings, values, and norms. To resolve it, Sorokin introduces the categories of integration, non-integration, and contradiction. Cultural phenomena will be said to be *integrated* when they are logically or, for artistic phenomena, aesthetically consistent. Here is the way in which systems are constituted: three propositions such as: "All men are mortal"; "Socrates is a man"; and "Socrates is mortal" constitute a system. A symphony is also composed of more simple elements which are aesthetically consistent. The relation of integration exists not only between simple meanings but also between systems which are themselves integrated. Thus they will be able to sustain among themselves a relation of integration either by subordination (geometry being a system subordinated to another larger one, mathematics), or by coordination (Faust written by Goethe; the Faust music of Gounod; a series of pictorial illustrations of the history of Faust constitute three aesthetically coordinated systems).

Cultural phenomena will be termed *contradictory* when they are logically or aesthetically inconsistent. For example: "A is non-A." Or again "All men are mortal"; "Socrates is a man"; "Socrates is immortal." Or a piece of jazz combined with Gregorian music.

Finally, cultural phenomena will be neutral or *non-integrated* when they are without aesthetic or logical relations. The meanings of words like "apple, Hitler, auto, rain, triangle, fish" have no mutual relationship. Michelangelo's "Last Judgment" and a monument in Teotihuacan are aesthetically non-integrated.[41]

These relations exist not only in the ideological culture, but also in the behavioral and material culture of an individual and of a group. Thus a person who would act now according to Christian ethics, now according to hedonist ethics, would have a contradictory behavioral culture. An example of contradictory material culture could be furnished by a book reproducing a text preaching asceticism and illustrated by pornographic drawings.

Finally, one can also define in terms of integration, non-integration, and contradiction, the relations between the various levels of culture of a person or a group. One person may have a moral culture well integrated on the ideological level, but a behavior which does not correspond to it.[42]

The cultural ideological systems are innumerable (each syllogism is one of them!), but certain ones have an especially considerable importance. These are notably the most vast ones. Thus the *scientific disciplines* (mathematics, chemistry, biology, philology, economics, etc.) constitute for the most part integrated systems of meanings. Most of their principal propositions are mutually consistent and logically interdependent to the extent that when one of the principal propositions is changed, many others must also be changed in order to harmonize them once more. Each of these disciplines certainly has here and there series of propositions which are not linked to the rest or which are even contradictory to other propositions. One of the reasons for these inconsistencies is the perpetual change in the scientific disciplines. The new discoveries claim adjustment to the older parts of the science, and this adjustment can only be made with a certain time lag. However that may be, the bulk of the propositions which constitute a science is generally integrated. One may say the same thing of the great systems of *philosophy*, of the doctrines of the important *religions*, of the codes of *law*, of *moral doctrines*, of great *artistic creations*, and of *languages*, especially in their grammars.

Besides these vast systems, there are others which combine their elements according to another formula. Thus, for example, an institution such as the monogamous family is a center around which is constituted a system formed by historical and sociological studies on this type of family; moral rules concerning it; religious precepts recommending it and making of it a "way of life"; laws protecting it; philosophical systems proving that it is the only family organization compatible with "human nature"; artistic creations being inspired by it.[43]

Another type of vast system is furnished by the culture of a nation at a given epoch. Or, more exactly, it happens that among all the cultural elements of such a group, a certain number are integrated around a few values. Thus according to Professor F. S. C. Northrop, an important part of the culture of colonial Mexico was systematized around the values of Spanish Catholicism: such as religion, education, morals, juridical organization, baroque architecture, hierarchic and monarchist political organization, painting, music, etc.[44]

These various examples show that the terms *consistency* and *integration* should not be taken in the narrow sense that a treatise on logic would attribute to them. They also show that these vast systems are still very numerous. Accordingly, many sociologists have attempted to find even more vast cultural unities. Thus there exists quite a number of dichotomous theories which divide cultural phenomena into two classes inside of which they are united. They make a distinction either between material and non-material culture (Marx, W. Ogburn, etc.); or between technological and ideological culture (A. Coste, L. Weber, etc.); or between civilization and culture (Bacon, A. Weber, R. McIver, etc.). Sorokin submits these theories to a sharp criticism. We do not have to dwell on this point. We will simply point out that this definition of the sociocultural phenomenon opposes a division which would separate into two fundamental classes two complementary aspects of these phenomena: the meaning would be in the non-material class and the vehicle of this meaning in the material class.[45]

Sorokin proposes to unite the ideological cultural systems into three great systems, "the most vast known." He refers to these as supersystems. Their foundation rests upon the three answers which can be given to the essential question: what is the ultimate nature of reality and consequently the supreme value? One may answer either that the ultimate reality is the world of our sensory experience and that there is nothing beyond what we can perceive with our senses. Or that the true reality is, on the contrary, above and beyond this world (one will call it God or Tao, or Soul of the World, or Brahman). It is supra-sensory and supra-rational, and this world is illusory. Or that it is partly perceptible and rational, partly supra-sensory and supra-rational. These three propositions are the premises of the three great cultural systems which Sorokin calls respectively ideational, sensate and idealistic.[46]

Around these three cultural premises, complex cultures organize themselves. In other words, we will be able to regroup a certain number of other systems (sciences, ethics, laws, arts, etc.) or subsystems under these three categories. This means that there will be certain artistic schools, certain scientific currents, which are logically or aesthetically consistent with the idea that "the ultimate reality is sensory," whereas other ethics will be consistent with the idea that "the supreme value is beyond this world."

Sorokin gives a detailed and methodical description of the psychological mentalities corresponding to these three cultures. Here are a few of their characteristics. For the ideational man, reality being fundamentally transcendental and eternal, his needs will be mainly spiritual. Consequently his attitude towards the external world will be negative and passive. He will not deny its importance but he will be concerned more with adapting himself to it than changing it. Such is the extreme ideational type as it has been more or less realized by the Indian ascetics and the Christian hermits. Even if conduct conforming completely with this mentality is rare, vast human groups nevertheless have had and still have this mentality. Thus the Hindus (Brahmanists), the

Buddhists, the Jainists, the Taoists, the Sufites, the first Christians. At the other extreme, the sensate personality is completely plunged in this changing world. His desires are not spiritual but material. The adaptation will be conceived as a modification of the environment in order to make it serve man. Among historical individuals characteristic of this tendency, Sorokin cites Caesar and Lenin. Our contemporary Western civilization (Euro-American) belongs to this type.[47]

Between these two extremes, there are several mixed types, but in each of them one of the two fundamental tendencies is dominant, except the idealistic type which is a harmonious balance of the two tendencies. For the idealistic person, the world of the senses and the transcendental world are both real. Neither is illusory. He will ask at the same time for both worldly and spiritual satisfaction. Finally, the idealistic personality will try to have an effect upon the world and, at the same time, transform himself. Such was the Confucianist attitude and that of the ancient Egyptians.[48] But the two most characteristic periods of this mentality are the century of Pericles and the Parthenon, and that of Saint Thomas Aquinas and the Cathedrals.

The choice of such an ontological principle of division is rather unexpected. Why has Sorokin taken as the basis of the most vast cultural systems the different attitudes towards the ultimate reality of the world? He will answer that, this problem being "the ultimate and most general,"[49] it furnishes the final principle of division of the cultural world. We will come back later to this point. Let us note right away, however, that these considerations are principally justifications, whereas the origin of this discovery is found in an intuitive view of the general evolution of history. We have indicated above the psychological conditions of this intuition. Sorokin, finding that the idea of a continuous progress conceived as a law of history does not take into account the march of events of the recent decades, has sought something else. The conception of these three great cultural systems is the intuition around which he will integrate his system of general sociology.[50]

The structure of the cultural world is thus composed of meanings, values, and norms (the ideological level) which are objectified and manifested by the conduct of human agents (the behavioral level) and by vehicles (the material level). At these three levels, relations of integration, of non-integration, and of contradiction determine the constitution of more or less vast cultural systems. Finally, almost all these systems are subsumable under one of the three premises: ideational, sensate, or idealistic, and thus comprise the three supersystems which divide the cultural universe.

There only remains, before passing to Sorokin's sociology of knowledge, to say a word of the dynamics of the cultural universe and of Sorokin's method.

THE DYNAMICS OF THE CULTURAL WORLD

This field is broad. Sorokin devotes two hundred pages to it in *Culture, Society, and Personality* alone. We will just briefly indicate those aspects which seem the most important for the sociology of knowledge.

How are cultural systems born? All cultural systems pass through three phases. The *conception* of two or more meanings, values, or norms in order to constitute a consistent system; the *objectification* of the ideological system in the vehicles and the *socialization* — that is to say, the propagation of the meanings among human beings. When the cultural system is born, it evolves, develops, changes, and often perishes.[51] We shall neglect what concerns the small and medium systems in order to consider only the three great cultural systems.

One can conceive differently the manner in which these supersystems are realized historically. It could be that they coexist simply in a rather static manner, being linked to stable groups. This would be the case for example if Mongoloid stock were ideational, Caucasian stock idealistic, and the Negroid sensate. Or again one could imagine that they could constitute three stages in the life of a people or of humanity, somewhat like the three stages of Comte. For example, humanity would pass through the ideational age, then the idealistic, then the sensate.

According to Sorokin, the three supersystems must be considered as three recurrent forms or three phases of a rhythm. In the course of the unfolding of the history of the Graeco-Roman and Occidental worlds since the twelfth century B.C. till the end of the Middle Ages, the three phases are twice repeated; since the fifteenth century A.D. the sensate phase has appeared for the third time and is probably for the moment on the decline.[52] Here is approximately (we will give below the reason for this "approximately") how things happened, according to Sorokin's conception.

In the Greek world, from the twelfth to the ninth century B.C., there is a sensate period; from the ninth to the sixth B.C., the dominant culture is ideational; it will be idealistic during the fifth century. Next, in the Graeco-Roman world, a long sensate period stretches from the fourth century B.C. till about the fourth and fifth centuries A.D. It is followed by an ideational period which dominates the Occidental world until about the twelfth century. There is a short idealistic period in from the twelfth to the thirteenth centuries. From the fourteenth till the present there has developed a culture which is predominantly sensate.[53]

Thus each of the three cultural supersystems appears, becomes dominant and is replaced by another which itself disappears. Finally the first comes back again. This rhythm of three phases has already been produced twice in the Western world.

THE METHOD OF SOROKIN'S GENERAL SOCIOLOGY

In the preceding outline, the empirical nature of Sorokin's method has been very little apparent. Till now, we have dealt only with the intuitional and rational aspects of Sorokin's account. We have been confronted with a few essential intuitions (such as that of the three premises of culture and of their recurrence), and with an elaborate rationale which has brought order and defined the complexity of the sociocultural world. The point now is to show that not only can cultural phenomena be logically assembled into vast supersystems, but that they actually have so existed.

How are we to prove it? Let us take, for example, the field of art. We must first deduce *a priori* from the ideational cultural premise ("the ultimate reality and the supreme value are beyond this world of senses which is only an illusory appearance"), what an ideational art can be. Thus it seems that we can say *a priori* that the subject matter of such an art will be primarily religious (religious events, superhuman beings). The emotional tone will not be sensual. One will avoid the nude or it will not be erotic. The artist being turned towards the eternal world, there will be few landscapes, individual portraits, or caricatures. It will delight in symbolism (for example the use of the dove among the early Christians). It will be static, will utilize simple means. The appreciation of art will be done primarily from a moral and non-aesthetic point of view.[54]

When a notion of ideational art has been constructed, the

sociologist will have to see if, in ideational periods, the art which really existed answers to the *a priori* description. If the result of the survey is positive and if such correlations during the sensate and idealistic periods exist, and if moreover one cannot discover any correlation between the form of ideational art and the sensate and idealistic periods, then we will be able to conclude that the logical and aesthetic consistency between the forms of art and the cultural premises exists *in fact,* and that each type of art really forms a system with the corresponding cultural premise.

The empirical method will then have a considerable place in Sorokin's sociological system.

One can say that Sorokin's method admits of three aspects: intuitive, rational and empiric. He himself emphasizes the importance of the second aspect which he calls the logico-meaningful method. This means that when studying phenomena, they will be considered as meaningful. Consequently the investigator will look for the intelligible relationships which may exist between their meanings. Sorokin insists strongly on this method against that of certain sociologists too desirous of conforming to procedures which have succeeded so well in the physico-chemical sciences. They seek to study sociocultural phenomena solely by factorial analyses. They try to find out the relations between human phenomena (whose meaning they neglect) only by means of statistical correlations. The relations obtained in that way are called by Sorokin causal or functional. It is the relation which exists between two variables A and B if each time A appears, B appears, and each time A varies, B varies.[55]

We will analyze these methods below in their application to the sociology of knowledge. The brief outline which we have just given finishes the exposition of Sorokin's general sociology, the framework into which his sociology of knowledge will integrate itself.

CHAPTER EIGHT

Sorokin's Sociology of Knowledge

THE THREE TRUTHS

DEDUCTION OF THE THREE CRITERIA OF TRUTH

What Sorokin himself calls his treatise on *Wissenssoziologie* is a part of his study of cultural fluctuations. His purpose is to find out if the realm of knowledge — which he defines as covering philosophic, scientific, and religious thought — is logically and actually consistent with his cultural premises. This amounts to saying: can the various scientific, philosophic, and religious productions be integrated into supersystems organized around propositions concerning the nature of the ultimate reality? Or again, can these metaphysical premises be considered as independent variables in the fluctuations in the realm of knowledge?[1]

One of the most fundamental points in that realm is the concept of truth which one adopts.[2] Therefore we are going to see, first, whether there are three ways — ideational, idealistic and sensate — by which one can and does say that "such a knowledge is true."

This question must be asked and solved on two planes. First, on the plane of logic. That is to say: is there a meaningful relationship between each cultural premise and a concept of truth? Then, on the plane of reality: has this logical relationship actually arisen in the course of history?

Let us begin with the level of logic or of meanings. For the ideational mentality turned completely toward the invisible and eternal world, denying that the world of the senses can have an authentic reality, the evidence of the senses and even that of reason will not have great value since they cannot put us in touch with more than a mere semblance of what is truly real. The criterion of truth will have to be supra-sensory and even metalogical. It will be religious revelation, mystical experience, or even magic. This is what Sorokin calls the criteria of truth of faith. When one believes that reality is transcendental, valid or true knowledge will be that which conforms to it. Since neither the senses nor reason can attain this authentic reality, true knowledge will be attainable only by intuition. On the contrary, for the sensate mentality, as there is nothing beyond this tangible world, it will be the senses (and their extensions: telescopes and microscopes) that will put us in contact with authentic reality by means of knowledge. The idealistic mentality will have an intermediate criterion. This will be human reason and logic whose foundations are found in the laws of the mind itself, considered as a source independent of the sense organs. The truth of the senses and of faith will be acknowledged subsidiarily only insofar as they are reconcilable with human reason.[3]

It seems then that we can say *a priori* that to each one of the ontological positions which the cultural premises are, there corresponds, or rather ought to correspond, an epistemological position which makes of either the senses, or reason, or intuition, the source and ultimate criterion of truth. Now, we must pass to the factual plane to see if these concepts of truth have existed in history in correlation with the three cultural premises upon which they seem logically dependent. This point will hold our attention longer.

CONFIRMATION BY FACTS

Qualitative and quantitative study

These are the two ways in which we can verify the actual realization of the systems of truth throughout history. A qualitative study of the whole of knowledge from the point of view which occupies our attention will consist in considering a few authors from each period in a more or less thorough way in order to find out which system of truth they adopt and why. A method of this sort is frequently used, but Sorokin does not find it reliable enough, as subjectivism appears not only in the interpretation of the authors, but in the choice of them. How many theorists consider their theory confirmed by facts when they have merely shown that it applies in a few cases! To avoid these disadvantages, there remains, thinks Sorokin, only quantitative study, the mass study which encompasses not merely several works of a few thinkers of each epoch, but one which has as an ideal the consideration of all the works of all thinkers. Sorokin utilizes the two methods, but gives more importance to the second.[4]

We could be content to give the results of positive research obtained by quantitative study on the problems of systems of truth. It seems, however, that the interest of this question justifies our making a long digression to describe this method more closely. Actually, this type of study is not common and is very important from the point of view of the sociology of knowledge, which necessarily has to trace the trends of ideas through history and to gauge their respective importance.

Digression on the quantitative study of the trends of thought

The problem is: how is one to measure adequately the fluctuations of the currents of thought through history? The question is not the fluctuation of the ideas themselves (to know, for example, how such and such a doctrine of Saint Thomas was modified by Cajetanus) but of their influence.

Any kind of history, especially that of ideas or of philosophy, includes affirmations of this type: "the Neoplatonic trend grew weak at such a period and disappeared in the following one"; or again: "the positivism dominant in the nineteenth century lost a great deal of influence during the first years of the twentieth." If one asks the historian on what he founds such assertions, he would answer that the number of important authors inspired by positivism was less in the twentieth than in the nineteenth century. Thus he takes into account two considerations in his evaluations: a number of writers and their value. By value is meant not only, nor even principally, the intrinsic value of the work, but the recognition by contemporaries and other thinkers of an author's importance. It would be more exact to say "recognized value," a notion which implies both the idea of influence and of value. Let us point out that these criteria allow only very indirect evaluation of what one actually wants to evaluate: the diffusion of positivism in a social group. But this is absolutely impossible to know, at least inasmuch as the past is concerned, for then they did not care to gauge public opinion. Moreover, it is probable that many people have no opinion whatsoever on a good many philosophic ideas.

Sorokin also grounds his measurement of the currents of thought upon these two elements: the number and what he calls the *weight* of the eminent thinkers who share in the trend which is studied. By eminent thinkers is meant those whose memory history has kept alive. Actually one may suppose, especially for the more distant periods, that the mere fact of having left traces in history is proof of the high esteem of one's contemporaries.[5] The only difference between Sorokin's method and that of the historians of ideas is that he has endeavored to base his evaluations of the influence of trends of thought upon the examination of *all* the thinkers of a period and upon a more *precise* determination of their recognized value.

The first stage of the work will consist in drawing up a list of *all* the thinkers who have brought a contribution to the field which one wants to study. This is no mean enterprise when one intends to cover Graeco-Roman and Occidental civilization during two and a half millenaries (specifically, from 580 B.C. to 1920 A.D.). These twenty-five centuries are divided into twenty-year periods. Specialists in the history of philosophy[6] have drawn up the lists which locate each thinker in one or several of the 125 twenty-year periods. The bibliography of specialized works which have been used to formulate these lists is indicated in the second volume of the *Dynamics*.[7] At the end of the first stage, we shall have the list of all the thinkers who have interested themselves, for example, in the problem of universalia.

The second phase of the research will consist in dividing the thinkers among the various currents. Thus one will classify the philosophers who have dealt with the question of universalia as realists, conceptualists, or nominalists. The value of such a classification will depend largely upon the validity of the definitions of the various trends.

The third stage — most difficult — consists in measuring the influence of each one of the thinkers. It will be done by assigning each of them an index, a value from one to twelve. One could obviously choose another scale of more or less than twelve degrees. Sorokin has chosen the scale of 12 mainly for the following reasons: if the number of degrees were very great, say 1 to 1000, one would arrive at a point where one system of thought, represented by only one person, might appear more powerful than the systems represented by all the other thinkers of the period. Now this paradoxical situation would distort reality, for if one thinker is the only representative of a current, this means that he did not influence the other thinkers and therefore his influence is not so preponderant as it seems. On the other hand, the fact that an outstanding thinker with a considerable influence, such as Plato or Aristotle, has only 12 as an index, does not minimize the importance of the current he represents, for his influence is conveyed not only by this value 12, but by the indices of all his disciples.[8]

A series of eight criteria have been established according to which an index will be assigned to each thinker. These criteria insist upon objective elements. They do not, however, eliminate all subjectivity. The latter will appear primarily in the combination of the criteria which is not made mechanically.[9]

It really seems that the ascription of an index can have value for a thinker only in respect to a single problem. It is conceivable that the same person could rate a 10 on the question of universalia but only a 1 as a moralist. Sorokin does not mention this point. In practice, Sorokin and his collaborators cite certain thinkers in connection with one field of thought but not with the others.[10] But on the other hand, when the name of a thinker appears in connection with several problems, the same value, it seems to me, is always ascribed to him by Sorokin.[11]

The fourth stage will consist in adding the indices of all the philosophers who have been classified in one group. The sums thus obtained interpreted in percentages will indicate the relative strength of each current in each period and will allow us to follow the fluctuations in importance of each current through the different periods during twenty-five centuries.

Application of the quantitative method to the problem of gnosiological systems

Let us return to our problem. The point is to see whether the three concepts of truth (of the senses, of reason, of faith) which correspond deductively to the three cultural premises, have really existed, as may be expected, during the ideational, sensate, and idealistic epochs.

For a reason which is not mentioned very explicitly — "the nature of the relevant material"[12] Sorokin studies instead of the rise and fall of the three gnosiological concepts, the fluctuations of six main trends: empiricism, rationalism, mysticism, criticism, skepticism, fideism. Then he transposes these six trends into the three gnosiological currents so that the fluctuations of the former can be understood in terms of the latter.

First let us examine the definitions of these six trends. "Since we plan to attack the problem quantitatively, we shall have to leave out many shadings and delicate details."[13] For *empiricism*, the source of knowledge is the sensory perception of single objects separated in time and space. The principles of logic are pure associations of the repeated experiences. *Rationalism* presents itself in two distinctly different forms: religious (or ideational) rationalism, and idealistic rationalism. For the first, the source of truth is revelation. Reason plays a subordinate role but one which can nevertheless be important. (Sorokin is probably thinking here of the rational systematizing of the content of revelation.)

Idealistic rationalism gives priority to reason, to the intellect and its categories. It admits, but in a subordinate position, sensory and revealed knowledge. It seems very strange to claim that a truth is revealed and to give it secondary rank. To this objection Sorokin answers that nominally one declares the supremacy of revelation but that actually one gives it only a subordinate role. "Like a constitutional monarch, it (the revelation) nominally reigns, but does not rule; the real ruler . . . is the logic of the human mind, its laws, categories and concepts."[14] *Mysticism* recognizes only the truth of faith. It differs from religious rationalism in that it condemns rational knowledge as illusory; it tends towards esotericism. *Skepticism* is a systematic and methodical doubt of the possibility of valid knowledge. *Fideism* agrees with skepticism in saying that the truth of the most important principles cannot be obtained by a mere empiric and rational knowledge but that it may be attained by an act of the will. It is a desperate form of the truth of faith. Finally, *criticism* (or agnosticism) affirms that only the world of phenomena is accessible to our knowledge, whereas the transcendental or ultimate reality is inaccessible and cannot be known and even is perhaps non-existent.[15]

Under these six definitions are classified the names and the indices of the philosophers who have professed these six doctrines.[16] By adding these figures and expressing them in percentages, a series of tables and graphs is obtained which shows the fluctuations in these six currents in the course of twenty-five centuries.[17]

Knowing the fluctuations of these variables, it is still necessary to relate them to the three systems of truth, for it is the fluctuations of the three conceptions of truth which we seek to establish. Empiricism is equivalent to the system of the truth of the senses. Religious rationalism, mysticism and fideism manifest the truth of faith. Idealistic rationalism belongs to the current of the truth of reason. Skepticism and agnosticism are not tied in by Sorokin with any of the three gnosiological systems.[18]

Sorokin devotes his attention to a detailed commentary on the fluctuations by twenty-year periods. It is not within the scope of this work to follow such a commentary step by step. In order to give a complete account of Sorokin's methods, it seems, however, advisable to give a succinct outline of it.

Before the fifth century B.C. religious rationalism is clearly dominant. Empiricism is evident only as a minor trend (about 20%). No one of the other currents, even idealistic rationalism, exists.

The fifth and fourth centuries are distinguished by the dominance of the truth of reason which accounts for about 40%. The truth of faith is still existent in the form of Plato's "divine folly" and Aristotle's theology. Empiricism is quite strong. It is a period in which the three gnosiologies are present and in which the rational system dominates.

During the three following centuries (third, second, first), empiricism grows and becomes as strong as rationalism; negative and desperate doctrines also become important. This is the sign of an intellectually disorganized period.

From the first century B.C. until the beginning of the third A.D., the Romans and the Christians come into action. An analysis of the gnosiological mentality of this period presents itself in the following manner. (The numbers were counted separately for the heathens and the Christians. They are not given in *Dynamics*.) Among the pagans: decline of the sensory concept of truth and increase in skepticism, mysticism and fideism whereas empiricism and rationalism are on the decline. Among the Christians, only two trends can be found: mysticism and religious rationalism, the latter being only half as strong as the former (the indices are 32 and 61).

During the third and fourth centuries, fideism and skepticism disappear whereas empiricism and mysticism increase, the former especially among the pagans and the latter especially among the Christians.

From the fifth to the eleventh centuries, empiricism disappears completely as do fideism and skepticism. The system of the truth of faith reigns alone in two forms: mysticism and religious rationalism. The former is less important. Here are the figures for these two trends: in the sixth, 25.8% as against 72.6%; in the seventh, 35% as against 65%; in the eighth, complete victory for religious rationalism: 100%; in the ninth, 32.3% as against 67.7%; in the tenth, 25% as against 75%.

Empiricism makes a modest reappearance in the eleventh century (7.7%), grows in the twelfth (14.3%) and is stabilized in the thirteenth (12.8%) and the fourteenth centuries (17.2%). Mysticism representing the truth of faith is important while independent rationalism is the most important of the movements of thought. The gnosiological situation presents itself once more as a harmonious synthesis under the direction of reason. This reminds us of the Greek fifth and fourth centuries B.C.

In the fifteenth century, the equilibrium is already disrupted and mysticism prevails (47.6%). In the sixteenth and seventeenth, it will diminish (33.6% and 23.3%) whereas empiricism will increase from 7.2% (fifteenth) to 29.6% (seventeenth) and to 37.5% (eighteenth). Rationalism still solidly holds its own especially in the seventeenth where it stands at 40.1%. Nevertheless, during the eighteenth and nineteenth centuries, empiricism is dominant. It attains figures which it has never reached during the preceding centuries: 37.5% (eighteenth) and 42.6% (nineteenth). The period 1900-1920 gives the record of 53%. Besides this, criticism and skepticism during these twenty years reach a very high total of 19%.[19]

The final stage of the quantitative study of epistemological systems consists in comparing the movements of the three gnosiological systems with the fluctuations of the three cultures: ideational, idealistic, and sensate. These cultures, we remember, are defined by the three premises concerning the nature of ultimate reality.

The flunctuations of these three cultures can be schematized approximately as follows: before the fifth century B.C., Greece is primarily ideational. It will be idealistic on the contrary during the fifth and fourth. The subsequent centuries are primarily sensate. From the beginning of the Christian era up to the end of the fourth, there is a period of transition. Ideational culture dominates once again from the fifth to the twelfth centuries — idealistic from the twelfth to the fourteenth, and sensate from the sixteenth to the twentieth.[20]

This indicates that the two evolutions show a general agreement between the three gnosiological systems and the three cultures. One can summarize it in the following manner.

Period	Dominant Culture	Dominant System of Truth
Before 5th B.C.	ideational	religious rationalism
5th and 4th	idealistic	all 3 under the dominance of rational gnosiology
3d-1st B.C.	sensate	empiricism grows; negative doctrines.
1st-4th A.D.	transition	decline of empiricism and rationalism (pagans); emergence of truth of faith
5th-12th	ideational	mysticism and religious rationalism
13th-14th	idealistic	all 3 under the dominance of reason
15th-20th	sensate	mysticism, transition (15th); empiricism grows (16th-20th)

Sorokin concludes that since quantitative study shows that the gnosiological systems vary in a manner parallel with the dominant culture, one may say that the three concepts of truth are integrated in the supersystems organized around attitudes concerning the final reality and the ultimate value.

In *Dynamics,* this quantitative proof is followed by a qualitative study. He analyzes the doctrines of the principal authors of the several periods by explaining the relationship between their gnosiological attitudes and the cultural premises which they accept. We only mention this study which arrives at the same results as the quantitative study and by means more habitually used.[21]

Such is the first correlation established by Sorokin between the cultural premises and a fundamental element of the realm of knowledge: the systems of truth. We have expounded this question in a relatively extensive fashion in order to give a rather complete insight into the manner in which Sorokin treats this type of problem. Let us pass now to a more systematic analysis of Sorokin's sociology of knowledge. This means that we shall attempt to determine how it answers the three essential questions which constitute, as we have seen above, the necessary framework for any sociology of knowledge. What is that independent variable of a social nature which influences mental productions? What are the mental productions which are subject to this influence? Exactly what is the type and the extent of the influence exercised by the independent variable upon mental production?

THE INDEPENDENT VARIABLE

Sorokin does not like the term "independent variable" very much. It is borrowed from the methods which seek to establish causal or functional rather than logical or meaningful relationships between sociocultural phenomena.[22] The acceptance of this term as it is used here does not mean the rejection of the logico-meaningful method of research. It simply designates the social element to which mental productions (as, for example, the concepts of truth) may be connected, whether causally or meaningfully. Moreover Sorokin himself occasionally utilizes these concepts. "What appears to be true and what is not, what appears to be scientific and what is not, what is a valid criterion of truth and what is not, are, in the statistico-mathematical language, to a considerable degree a 'function' of the sociocultural variable."[23]

The case of the systems of truth has clearly shown that this variable is, for Sorokin, the cultural premise. This means, to repeat it once more, the conception adopted as to the ultimate reality of the world and consequently that of the supreme value. This conception is expressed in one of the three following ways: "The world which we can attain through our senses is real and there is nothing but illusion beyond this world," "that which is beyond our senses is real and this world is but an illusory appearance," and finally "that which we can attain through our senses is real, but all reality is not limited therein; that which is beyond is also real."

It seems evident that the independent variable is such. And it has been understood in this way by critics.[24] One could, nevertheless, oppose to this interpretation a note from *Sociocultural Causality, Time and Space* where Sorokin says that the fundamental principle explaining a sociology of knowledge must be the following: "the essential character of the . . . system of each prominent thinker is largely a function of two variables: of the system of truth and reality assumed by the thinker; and of the totality of his existential, especially sociocultural, conditions."[25] To this we reply that the sociology of knowledge expounded in *Dynamics* deals only with one variable: the cultural premise. Also that, even in the former text, Sorokin gives more importance to the cultural variable. Indeed, he adds that if different thinkers have the same cultural premise, even if they belong to societies far distant in time and space, their theories will show essential similarities. If, on the contrary, the existential conditions are similar and the cultural premises different, the theories will show a series of similarities on secondary points. (The existential conditions meant here are facts of this type: living in the same period, in the same social group, etc.).

The text which has just been quoted is subsequent to the sociology of knowledge of *Dynamics* and its principal objective is to criticize Mannheim's *Ideology and Utopia*. Therefore it cannot be interpreted as a change in Sorokin's theory. It merely expresses incidentally a limit to the explanation of mental productions by cultural premises, a limit whose principle Sorokin had already pointed out in *Dynamics*.[26]

Moreover, the three cultural premises occupy this preponderant role of independent variable not only in the realm of knowledge, but also in the artistic and literary realms. They also hold an important place — although less so[27]— in the types of interaction among men (familial, contractual, and compulsory types) and in social troubles such as war and revolution.[28] Thus, for example, Sorokin shows that the periods of transition from the sensate phase to the ideational or vice versa are periods of a notable increase in the number and importance of wars.[29]

But which premise will play this part of independent variable? This question must be raised because there are three of them. Sorokin answers clearly: it is the premise dominant at the moment in question. "The volume (AJ) attempts to demonstrate that what a given society regards as true or false, scientific or unscientific, right or wrong, lawful or unlawful, beautiful or ugly, is conditioned fundamentally by the nature of the dominant culture."[30] On the other hand, we know that the dominant culture is not exclusive: two or even three frequently coexist. It seems that this must result in the fact that the premise of the dominant culture will not be the only independent variable in the mental productions of a period. It seems more accurate to say that the dominant premise will tend to be the independent variable for the whole knowledge of a period, but that, probably, it will not succeed. At the present stage of our research, it is impossible to be more precise.

Finally, it must also be pointed out that in the realm of knowledge, Sorokin will often express his variables in terms of "systems of truth" rather than in terms of "premises of culture."[31] This does not imply a new theory but simply his conviction of the complete, logical, and causal relationship between the cultural premises and the corresponding gnosiological systems.

Since Sorokin's independent variable is the intellectual position in regard to ultimate reality and ultimate value, his sociology will have a very idealistic character (in the current sense of the word, as it is used, for instance, in Comte's sentence "ideas rule the world") which will distinguish it and even radically oppose it to that of Mannheim.

THE DEPENDENT VARIABLES

The study of the other pole of the fundamental relationship which characterizes the sociology of knowledge will require a somewhat more extensive survey. The question to be solved is the following: what are the sectors in the realm of knowledge and what are the aspects of these sectors Sorokin considers influenced by his independent variables? To answer this question, we shall review a certain number of mental productions which have been the subject of positive studies by Sorokin. We have already shown how the systems of truth are connected with the cultural premises. Let us begin by seeing how the fundamental categories of the human mind are influenced by the cultural premises.

THE FUNDAMENTAL CATEGORIES: CAUSALITY, TIME, SPACE AND NUMBER

Without any doubt, Sorokin writes, certain fundamental categories are prerequisite to all coherent thought and all knowledge of facts. This does not preclude the possibility of their meaning or content being different.

Let us consider the category of *causality*. For a sensate mind as well as for an ideational one, each phenomenon has a cause or reason for being. But we may expect that it will be sought in the world of the senses or in the world beyond the senses according to whether or not one shares the sensate or ideational belief. Moreover a sensate mentality will probably conceive that "the same causes are followed by the same effects." For if one refers to the senses in order to discover causal relationships, cause A always has to be followed by the same effect B, or else (if A was followed once by B, another time by C, etc.) it would be impossible to distinguish a causal relationship from a simple accidental sequence. The same does not apply to the ideational mentality. The supra-sensory nature of cause makes of it a creative and free spiritual being (God, Brahma, Providence, Satan, etc.). It is therefore unnecessary to affirm that the same cause is followed by the same effects. "The will of God is inscrutable."[32]

The proof that these two conceptions of causality have actually existed and that there has been a factual correlation between the conceptions of causality and the types of culture to which they logically correspond, is given by a qualitative study of which we will summarize only a few points.

Among primitive peoples, the two conceptions seem to have existed. Durkheim, Lévy-Bruhl and Brunschvicg have shown that the primitive mentality was not satisfied to stay on the level of sensory experience but sought to establish a connection between the visible effect and the invisible cause.[33] Thus death by the bite of a poisonous snake is generally considered due to the fact that the snake was under the influence of a wizard.[34] Or again, the Australian aborigines do not connect the fact of birth with sexual intercourse but think that each conception is due to a sort of mystic fecundation.[35] On the other hand, the critics of the theory of the alogical mentality and of Levy-Bruhl's law of participation have shown that along with this ideational conception of causality, the primitives had another applied to many daily experiences and one in which the connection between phenomena is experimentally explained as being a result of the natural properties of the phenomena.

Chinese civilization presents, for Sorokin, the two mentalities: Taoist (ideational) and Confucianist (partly idealistic and partly sensate). Now, according to the great scholar on China, Marcel Granet, it seems that this mixed character is found in the Chinese conception of causality. First, here is the ideational concept. The interest of this quotation from Granet excuses its length, we hope.

Mythical thought . . . is penetrated by a belief that the realities are raised up by symbols . . . Viewing Tao as the principle of order that rules mental activity as well as the life of the world, it is admitted uniformly that the changes in the course of the realities are identical with the substitutions of symbols in the course of thought. This axiom once admitted, neither the principles of causality nor that of contradiction can be invoked to take the role of the directive principles. This is not because Chinese thought enjoys confusion, but, on the contrary, because the idea of Order — and of the order that is efficacious and totalitarian — dominates it, engulfing in itself the notion of causality and of class. . . . Instead of registering the succession of the phenomena, they register the alternations of aspects. If two aspects appear to them related, it is not a relation of cause and effect; they appear to them to be like the two sides of cloth . . . or sound and echo; or shadow and light. What they like to notice are not the causes and effects but (the order of the apparition being unimportant) the singular manifestations that are offshoots of the same root. Equally symptomatic, these manifestations appear to substitute for one another. River that dries up; mountain that slides down; man that changes into woman — these announce the approaching end of a dynasty. Here we have four aspects of the same phenomenon: an order destined to disappear, giving place to a new order. Each aspect deserves to be noted as the premonitory sign or a confirmation of a sign (or of a series of signs), but nothing invites us to seek for an efficient cause. . . . The most useful premonitory signs are those that are the most singular, most delicate, most rare, and most furtive. A bird that destroys its own nest furnishes a physical and moral indicator of the destruction of the Empire; its gravity is extreme, because the sentiment of familial piety is lacking *even* among the humblest animals. The slightest symptoms (appearances) thus deserve to be catalogued, and the most peculiar are more valuable than the most normal. The catalogues are not intended to discover the *sequences* but to disclose the *solidarities*. . . . The Chinese see in the sensible realities but a mass of concrete signs.

This conception is ideational in the sense that it accounts for the changes in symbols and realities by means of Tao, a supra-sensory principle.

On the other hand, sensate causality is not unknown in China.

These dispositions of their thought have not hindered the ancient Chinese from manifesting their great mechanical aptitudes. . . . The perfection of their arcs and their carriages is an evidence of that. . . . Their thought is animated by a passion for empiricism that predisposes it to the minutest observation of the concrete and has led it to such fruitful results (discoveries in pharmacopeia, chemistry, agriculture, etc.) [36]

In Graeco-Roman and Western thought, the fluctuations in the two types of causality correspond to the fluctuations in the dominant cultures. Thus (and we cite only a few characteristics), the great philosophers of *the idealistic period,* Plato and Aristotle, acknowledge the two forms of causality. In *Phaedo,* for example, we have an explanation of why man grows: Because, by food, flesh is added to flesh, bone to bone, etc. Elsewhere in the same dialogue, Plato shows that an explanation of this type is not completely satisfactory. Aristotle's theory of the four causes is also an idealistic synthesis. The material cause and frequently the efficient cause belong to the sensory world, whereas the final and the formal, at least in part, belong to the supra-sensory world.[37]

During the *ideational period* from the beginning of the fifth to the end of the twelfth century A.D., the Christian conception of causality is ideational. The sole cause of all things is God, ever present in his creation which he maintains in existence.[38] This omnipotence of God partially eliminates the contrast between the natural and the miraculous. Of course, God can establish an order in the world of phenomena but he can replace it with other relationships if he so desires. The principle that "the same causes produce the same effects" is much less important in this perspective and is always subordinate to a condition: if it pleases God to establish such uniformities. Sorokin claims to find this conception in Boethius, Isidore of Seville, Bede, Rhabanus Maurus, the pseudo-Dionysius, and others up to John Scotus Erigena.[39]

From the fifteenth to the twentieth centuries, a *sensate period,* the concept of causality is entirely different. Since Osiander's famous preface to Copernicus' *De Revolutionibus Orbium Celestium,* the idea of the empirical causality of phenomena has taken on more and more importance. In thinkers such as Francis Bacon, Montaigne, Thomas Hobbes and David Hume, the problem of the ultimate cause has been accorded less attention. Other thinkers such as Descartes, Malebranche, Spinoza, Leibnitz, Berkeley, acknowledge the transcendental causes, but what is really important in their system is the causality derived either from experience or from pure reason. Even within the sensate conception of causality, there are several important differences whose evolution is very significant. Let us consider the two following points. First, the *nature* of the causal link has been represented very differently. For some, such as the Cartesians, it is a mechanical link which ensures a continuity of movement. For others, such as Leibnitz, the causal link is dynamic. It implies the existence of forces. Still others, such as Bernoulli, Maxwell, K. Pearson and most of the statisticians consider it purely functionally or mathematically. It is a relationship which may be expressed in the form of a differential equation or some other mathematical formula of probability. Contrary to the dynamic and mechanical concepts, this last concept no longer implies any question of what is beyond pure quantitative uniformity.

The second point concerns the *necessity* for the causal relationship. For many thinkers (Descartes, Newton, Leibnitz, etc.), to be a causal relationship, the association between two variables had to be not only stable but necessary. This necessity stems either from the "nature of things" (Montesquieu) or from the automatic and mechanical functioning of the universe (Descartes). Others reject the idea of necessity because it is not provided by sensory experience. Remaining on the plane of probability, they simply distinguish uniformities which have a high or a low degree of probability which is expressed by the value of the coefficient of correlation on a scale of 0 to 1 — 1 being the highest probability and zero the sign of a complete lack of any association between the variables.[40]

Now, from the seventeenth to the twentieth centuries, we have gone farther and farther away from the mechanical or dynamic link toward the purely functional link and we have abandoned more and more the idea of necessity as indispensable to the concept of causality.[41]

The category of *time* also presents ideational and sensate forms, whose comparative influence has fluctuated as expected. Sorokin takes up Pierre Duhem's fundamental division on the subject of theories concerning time. Some of them deal with an absolute time in a world different from the world of our sensory perceptions. Others make of time a phenomenon relative to the movements of the tangible world.[42] From these two fundamental differences, many others follow. We are going to cite a few of them and illustrate them by examples.

Since ideational time is an emanation or a manifestation of transcendental reality, its unit will be determined by the "pulsations" of this reality. Thus the Hindu time units will be Brahma's day and night, his dematerialization and his materialization. Similarly for the Pythagoreans, the unit of time is the movement of the Soul of the world.

These units of ideational time are not generally divisible as are the units of sensate time and they are generally very long (when measured in terms of sensate time). Thus for the Hindus, each period of the world consists of 4,320,000 mortal years. The "great year" of the Pythagoreans was also extremely long. The ideational temporal sequence is often quite confused. Present, past, future are considered as simultaneous in eternity.

Sorokin proves the correlation of these concepts of time with the cultural phases by a qualitative analysis. We shall point out only a few of its aspects. The Aristotelian concept is idealistic, indeed. On the one hand, Aristotle defines time in relation to the movement of things which change and, on the other, he makes time the yardstick of the motion of the primary sphere, which has a metaphysical relevance. During another idealistic period, the great Scholastics will take up the Aristotelian ideas in their categories of *aeternitas,* an ideational and transcendental time; *tempus,* a sensate time linked to sensory phenomena; and *aevum,* an intermediary notion.[43]

During the sensate period from the sixteenth to the twentieth century, ideationalism gradually disappears from the notion of time. It is no longer anything but a pure derivative of the motion or the evolution of empirical bodies. Newton's absolute time is neither empirical nor transcendental; it is mathematical. But even this absolute time has been declared useless.[44] Time has become a symbol t. In the twentieth century, a reaction against this tendency appears in Bergson's qualitative time.[45]

The question of *space* is treated more briefly by Sorokin. Sensate space is the three-dimensional space or even any form of multi-dimensional space. Ideational space is that where realities surpassing the senses, such as God, the soul, the mind, may be located. This appears to be a very strange space. We may clarify this notion if we connect it with the category of sociocultural space which Sorokin elaborates in a later work. The space in which sociocultural phenomena are located consists of three planes: that of meanings, that of vehicles and that of human agents. Being located on the plane of meanings is to have one's place in a system of meanings which is itself located in a larger one, and so on until one arrives at the most vast systems. It is, moreover, in this manner that this procedure has always been carried out in practice. Ideational space must be conceived in a similar way. It is above all a frame of reference in which are located, each in relation to the other, supra-sensory realities.[46]

Besides, ideational space, in opposition to sensate space, will not be homogeneous, but often composed of sectors which are qualitatively different. Thus, according to Marcel Granet, "none of the Chinese philosophers have found an interest in considering space as a simple extension resulting from the juxtaposition of homogeneous elements or as an extension all of whose parts are superposable. All prefer to view space as a complex of the domains, climates and horizons."[47] Sorokin might have added, as an example of non-homogeneous space, the concept of the Australian aborigines who, according to Durkheim, organize space into qualitatively different districts corresponding to the division of the tribes into clans.[48]

The category of *number* is susceptible of taking on either an ideational or a sensate tinge. The sensate number is linked to the idea of quantity. The comparative size of two numbers appears to be determined only by their quantitative value. If one wants to compare the numbers eight and four, the only point which one will take into consideration is their quantitative value: eight comprises more units than four.

The ideational conception of number is, on the contrary, plainly qualitative. In this light, it is not inconceivable that the number eight could be smaller than four. Thus, in China, the "idea of quantity does not play any role in the philosophical speculations of the Chinese. Numbers, however, passionately interest the sages of the ancient China."[49] Here is a significant example. It is a debate of a council of war: should we attack the enemy?

The Chief is inclined to the idea of attack, but it is necessary that he should engage the responsibility of his subordinates and take their advice. Twelve generals, including himself, participate in the Council. The opinions are divided. Three generals refuse to engage in the battle; eight want to go to it. These eight are thus the *majority* and they proclaim it. However, the opinion that unites 8 votes does not carry the opinion that unites 3 votes: 3 is (for the Chinese) almost *unanimity*, which is quite a different thing from a mere *majority*. The Chief will not fight. He changes his opinion. The opinion to which he adds his *unique* vote becomes the *unanimous* opinion.[50]

Thus the number four may be greater than the number eight because it is qualitatively greater; relative to twelve, it represents unanimity whereas eight represents the majority.

This ideational conception is found in Greece in Hesiod's Calendar, which indicates lucky and unlucky days. Thus the sixth day of each month is an unpropitious day for the birth of a girl, the thirteenth for sowing, the sixteenth for planting.[51] These examples will suffice to remind one of the existence of sacred numbers in several religions.

Such is the manner in which Sorokin shows that his independent variable, the premises of culture, influence the essential categories of the mind.[52] They do not create them, but they confer very different meanings on them. Since these categories are fundamental, many of our mental productions depend on them, and thus, in some way, a large number of our ideas, of our concepts are profoundly influenced by the cultural premises. Of course the role of the latter is not limited to this function. Another area of knowledge which Sorokin relates to his premises is that of the first principles.

THE FIRST PRINCIPLES

Sorokin does not use this expression according to its usual meaning. He understands by it the fundamental ideas which, implicitly or explicitly, underlie any philosophy or science. It is these attitudes which are at the basis of what is generally called *Weltanschauung*. Each scientist, more or less consciously, takes some position relative to these few fundamental questions.[53]

The method will be similar to that used in connection with the gnosiological theories. First, the different first principles are to be defined and logically related to the premises of culture. Then their evolution has to be retraced throughout Graeco-Roman and Western civilization in order to see if their fluctuations and those of the cultural premises are correlated.

We shall review four groups of principles: idealism and materialism; eternalism and temporalism; realism, conceptualism and nominalism; determinism and indeterminism. We shall dwell briefly on the notions of these various principles and on their relations to the cultural premises rather than on the quantitative study of their fluctuations. This study follows exactly the method expounded above. The graph of the total results may be found on page 154.

Idealism and materialism

For idealism, the ultimate reality is spiritual, be it God, the Platonic ideas, a spirit or a psychic reality. The several varieties of idealism may be reduced to two fundamental classes: monism and pluralism. For the former, all individuals and the separate systems of immaterial realities are only temporary manifestations of the same principle. For idealistic pluralism, it is a multitude of spiritual entities which constitute the ultimate reality.

Materialism asserts that the ultimate reality is matter and that the so-called immaterial phenomena are but a manifestation or the result of movements of particles of matter. Materialism is hylozoistic when it assigns a sort of life to matter. It will be endowed with sensation, and to a certain degree, with conscience. It is especially emphasized that the spirit cannot exist without matter. The mechanistic variety of materialism is more radical: immaterial phenomena, if they exist, are but a purely passive product of matter.[54]

The logical relationships between these two currents: materialism and idealism, and the sensate and ideational premises are so evident that the difficulty is rather in distinguishing materialism from the sensate premise. . . . As for the idealistic premise which occupies an intermediary position, it would probably be put in relationship with a middle position such as hylozoism.

The curves inform us that things actually happen in this way. The intermediate position seems rather to correspond to monist idealism. The correlation is evident for the great fluctuations, less for the lesser changes.[55]

Eternalism and temporalism

Is reality being or becoming? One of the possible answers to this question is *eternalism:* reality is eternal and immutable. Change is denied, or it is deduced from being in one way or another. But eternalism, in its radical form, is hard to retain. Therefore, often the becoming which one had wanted to dismiss will be reintroduced. The notion of being can only be understood in relation to becoming; change, even qualified as illusory, has a certain reality. Therefore it is opportune to classify the eternalists into two groups: the radicals, few in number, and the moderates, who in maintaining the primacy of being, accord, however, a certain inferior value to change.

A similar division may be traced among the *temporalists*. Radicals maintain that only the becoming is real. What appears stable is only becoming viewed statically. But one will often have to reintroduce being, if only as a point of reference to affirm becoming.

Finally, a third class: the solutions which recognize the reality of the two categories. Certain ones, such as Leucippus and Democritus unite being and becoming by an atomic theory: atoms do not change, they represent being; their combinations are always changing, this is the becoming. Or again some juxtapose *aeternitas. tempus* and *aevum,* like most of the medieval thinkers. Or it is affirmed that concrete things change but that the relations between them are constant and immutable. This idea dominates, for instance, in the nineteenth century concept of evolution. Still others will reconcile being and becoming by the distinction between the constant "form" of a class of phenomena and their ever-changing "content." One can also find similar conciliations in the duality of changing positive law and immutable natural law.

This triple division corresponds logically to the three types of culture. The sensate mentality which sees nothing beyond the changing world of our experience will lean towards temporalism; the ideational mentality for which reality is beyond sensible appearances will admit eternalism, whereas the idealists who admit the real character of this world and the other will seek a conciliation between being and becoming.

An analysis of the five trends (radical and moderate temporalism, radical and moderate eternalism, and intermediate solutions) by the usual quantitative method confirms this hypothesis at least insofar as the general direction and the importance of the movements are concerned.[56]

Realism, conceptualism, nominalism

Is this group of first principles well chosen? Does it not seem that this problem of *universalia* is raised only in reference to a scholastic framework? No, replies Sorokin. The problem existed before the Middle Ages and it still exists today. Its formulation alone is linked with scholasticism. When a contemporary physicist, chemist or sociologist creates his definitions, he cannot help giving explicitly or implicitly, consciously or not, an answer to this problem.

Logico-ontological *realism* is a system of thought which asserts that in all the single objects of the same class which exist at different points in space. there is, beside their individual differences. some element common to all which composes their essence. For the radical realists, this essence is both transcendental (existing *ante rem,* for example, in the divine intelligence) and immanent (existing *in re,* as Aristotle's form). It is, moreover, the principle of our knowledge (existing *post rem,* being abstracted from the thing). But all realists do not profess this doctrine. Certain ones simply affirm the reality of universals *in rem,* others, *ante rem.* From another point of view, some consider them substances (Clarenbaud, Bernard of Chartres, etc.); others as characteristics (Walter of Montagne, Gualterus of Mauretania). Despite all these important shadings, all the realists will be classed in the same category. Their common feature is that, for them, universalia have a trans-subjective existence.

Conceptualism denies that there exists in the trans-subjective world anything more than single individuals. The knowing subject perceives only these singularities but transforms them into general concepts. *Universalia sunt in mente.*

Finally, *nominalism* holds that there are no universalia either beyond the mind or within the mind. The concept is only an illusion due to the association of concrete impressions with the same word.

What is the relationship between the cultural premises and these three trends? Sorokin explains that the system of the truth of faith is logically linked to realism. Indeed, eternal reality sought by faith in the supra-sensory coincides with the universalia of realism and, even in this world, the general essences are more important for the truth of faith, than single empirical phenomenon. Similarly, empiricism and nominalism are twin brothers. If the senses are the only criteria of reality, they cannot attain eventual trans-subjective universalia nor even can they verify eventual concepts. All the human mind can do is combine single images by means of a word. Finally, as rationalism is a mixture of the two extreme systems of truth and since conceptualism also occupies an intermediary position between nominalism and realism, an association of the two may be expected.

The method is quantitative analysis. It indicates that the logical relationships are corroborated by the facts, for that which concerns the parallelism of the curves of ideational gnosiology and realism, sensate gnosiology and nominalism, and, to a lesser degree, idealistic culture with conceptualism.[57]

Determinism and indeterminism

The *determinist* thinkers admit that everything in the world — man, his mind and his actions included — is causally conditioned. More specifically, they claim that no free will whatsoever exists as a factor in human conduct. *Indeterminism* denies in a general way the existence of an invariable causal relationship between phenomena. It admits the possibility of variations, either by the will of God or because different effects may result from the same cause. As far as man is concerned, it affirms either the existence of free will or at least the possibility of various ways of governing one's conduct.

Each of these two currents presents an extreme variety of concrete forms and of shadings. Often the same thinker presents a complex doctrine in this respect. Kant, for example, maintains that human conduct in the world of phenomena is absolutely determined and that if we knew all the circumstances, we could predict it as accurately as an eclipse of the sun; but, man as a noumenal being is perfectly free from all exterior conditioning. This shows the difficulties of classification: certain authors have had to be placed in two classes or in a mixed class.

We have seen above[58] that the sensate premise led to the admission of an invariable relationship between cause and effect while a belief in active supra-sensory beings leads to the introduction of more indetermination into the world. The tables and curves confirm this correlation when one considers the general profile, leaving aside many secondary fluctuations.[59]

SCIENTIFIC AND PHILOSOPHIC THEORIES

Not only vast currents of thought, such as those we have just examined, may be connected to the three cultural mentalities, but more determined mental productions are also subject to the influence of these premises. Such are philosophic and scientific theories. We are going to examine a few of them briefly.

Sociological universalism and singularism

The problem is the kind of reality society is. Is it an entity distinct from the mere aggregate of its members and if so, in what respect? Which is the supreme value, the individual or society? One can see that this problem is closely linked to the question of realism-conceptualism-nominalism.

The answers to this problem fall into five categories. *Radical sociological singularism* is a nominalistic position: the individual alone is an ontological reality, society is but the aggregate of its members. Moreover, the individual is the supreme value. *More moderate forms* of singularism, while admitting the ontological superiority of the individual, do not make him the supreme moral law. Its forms vary from moral liberalism, which takes into account the rights of other individuals, to totalitarianism, which sacrifices the individual to the society while admitting theoretically that the latter has no ontological reality. Singularism is logically consistent with the sensate premise.

For *radical universalism,* reality and value are social. Only by participating in society, the individual has his being and value. *Moderate universalism* will admit that the individual has a certain reality and a certain value in himself, but subordinated to society which has rights even to the life of the individual. This universalist trend will be linked to an ideational culture in the sense that the absolute principles which it propounds minimize individual rights and liberty.

Finally, *integralism* will try to harmonize the two trends: both the individual and the society are real. The individual is a concrete incarnation of the social reality; the realization of individual values is obtained by collaboration with society.[60]

Quantitative analysis leads to the conclusion that the expected correlations are verified at least in their main fluctuations.[61]

The theories of the juridical personality

These, too, are an application, on the juridical level, of the three currents: realism-conceptualism-nominalism. The juridical personality is defined as: anybody consisting of one or more individuals treated by the law as a unit and usually endowed with the right to succeed and to act in justice. This juridical personality will be conceived of either as real, or as a fiction created by the law, or as an intermediate reality. As this question is very closely related to the theory of singularism-universalism, we shall not develop it further.[62]

Various conceptions of the cosmic, biological, and sociocultural processes

These conceptions may be classed in three groups: the linear processes, the cyclical, and the mixed. Darwin's biological evolution, Comte's and Spencer's social progress, are examples of the first. Nietzsche's famous "eternal return" is a cyclical process. The mixed processes combine the two schemes. This was, for example, the case in the thirteenth and fourteenth centuries. On one hand, Christianity provided a rather linear conception of the history of mankind, unfolding itself from the Creation up to the End of the World. On the other hand, certain regular recurrences and cycles were recognized within that history; they were caused by the influence of the celestial bodies and of their conjunctions.

Now the fluctuations of these concepts are, to a great extent, logically dependent on the various types of culture. An idea of linear progress tends to arise parallel with a sensate culture. A cyclical conception whose fluctuations are not mechanical, but rather the manifestations of interior transformations in the ultimate spiritual reality (Providence, Brahma, Tao, etc.), may be expected during ideational periods. Finally, mixed concepts will exist during idealistic periods.

Sorokin's factual proof is provided by a long qualitative study in which he examines not only the Western civilization, but also the Indian, Chinese, and Babylonian civilizations.[63]

Atomistic theories

It seems that atomistic theories must be linked to materialism, and since the latter is associated with the sensate premise, we may assume that the success of these theories corresponds to the most sensate periods, and their lack of success to the most ideational periods. A brief qualitative history of these theories confirms this assumption. Atomism, indeed, appeared during the idealistic periods (fifth B.C. and thirteenth A.D.), grew during the sensate periods (third century B.C. — Epicurus — and first and second centuries A.D., then from the sixteenth to the twentieth), and disappeared almost completely during the periods of dominance of an ideational culture (before the fifth century B.C. and from the fourth up to the twelfth century A.D.).[64]

Mechanism and vitalism in biology

The essential distinction between these two types of theories is that the first asserts that the phenomena of life are reduced to material phenomena, so that an organism is a pure dynamic structure subject to physico-chemical forces. There is no element among living beings which cannot be the subject of a physical or chemical study. For the vitalists, on the contrary, the living body is not subject exclusively to physico-chemical forces.

The history of the fluctuations in these theories may be summarized thus: mechanism appears during the fifth century B.C. It grows during the following centuries to reach its peak during the third century B.C. for the Greeks and the first century B.C. for the Romans. It weakens from the first century A.D. on and gradually disappears till the thirteenth. Then it becomes stronger and stronger till it dominates from the seventeenth up to the nineteenth, with temporary reverses. It begins to weaken in the twentieth. There is indeed a general parallelism with the trends of culture.[65]

SCIENTIFIC AND TECHNOLOGICAL PROGRESS

Normally this progress must be different in the three cultures. When there is more interest in the supra-sensory world than in that of our experience, men tend especially toward spiritual progress and prefer to adapt their needs to what the exterior world can offer them. Consequently few investigators will devote themselves to the pursuit of progress in the positive sciences and their application. On the contrary, in a milieu where the sensate mentality is dominant, the means of increasing man's mastery over his material environment will be very highly valued, for they will allow for an unceasing increase in the possibilities of sensory enjoyment. One may then assume that scientific progress will be more rapid while a sensate mentality is dominant.

Sorokin will attempt, by a long qualitative analysis, to check this correlation. Such an enterprise is not easy. It is necessary first to determine the criterion of scientific progress which permits us to determine at which moment the concept of it has been most important. Till now, the best thermometer of the comparative progress of science is founded upon the number of scientific discoveries and technological inventions made during each of the periods under consideration.[66]

Such a list must be interpreted with different restrictions in mind. First, it would be necessary to consider not only the number, but also the value of the discoveries. One ought to be able to allot an index of importance to each. This has not yet been possible. This deficiency, however, does not take all the value away from a curve constructed solely upon the number of inventions. We have seen above that curves expressing the movement of inventions in the Arab world from 700 to 1300 A.D. are different only in amplitude when one is founded on an equal evaluation of single cases and the other on a differential evaluation.[67] The reason for this is that an important discovery is usually a fruitful one which leads to a series of other discoveries and that these usually follow at a relatively small interval. A period in which there are many discoveries is then normally a period of great discoveries.

Then it is to be remembered that the more we move through history from the present toward a distant past, the less complete is the list of discoveries. The interpretation of the results are therefore to be corrected by increasing the figures of the distant past and by diminishing those of the recent past. It is the same for space. Western historians even now tend to exaggerate the importance of inventions and discoveries occurring in their civilization in respect to those which take place in the East.[68]

When interpreted with these reservations in mind, the tables and graphs show that the curve of the inventions of the positive sciences (we are dealing with physics, chemistry, astronomy, mathematics, geology, geography, biology and medicine) confirms the predictions. The curve of discoveries has two peaks in the Graeco-Roman world: a rise from the sixth to the fourth century, a decline in the third and the second. In Rome, the maximum is attained in the first century A.D. From the seventh to the ninth century, the curve remains very low. From the twelfth, it rises until it attains an unequaled peak in the twentieth century. It may be said, therefore, that, on the whole, scientific progress and sensate culture are linked together positively.[69]

MORAL PHILOSOPHY

For the person who accepts the *ideational premise,* the ultimate aim of human activity will be participation, union, or even unity with the supreme spiritual reality. The latter being the final and absolute value, the moral principles which lay down the rules which men must follow in order to attain it, will also be absolute. Hence the ethical ideational systems are called: the systems of absolute principles. Often they will be considered as emanating from the divinity. Generally it will be added that happiness hinges on living a life conforming to these principles. Happiness will not be considered an objective to be attained, but rather a consequence. There are several ethics founded on absolute principles; one of the most important is the ethics of love in which the supreme value is the love of God and of men. Jesus and St. Francis of Assisi are its most typical representatives.

For the *sensate mentality,* on the other hand, only the sensible values count. Happiness in this world will be man's aim. This happiness will, moreover, be considered quite differently. For some it will be a harmonious life in which the total of agreeable things will outweigh, if one may say so, the total of painful things (eudaemonism). For others, the ideal will be a life of pleasure (hedonism). Or again, some will dwell on the means of obtaining happiness (utilitarianism). From another point of view some of these doctrines will be individualistic (seeking happiness for the individual no matter what its effects are on others), others will be social (seeking above all the happiness of the group).

Finally, the *idealistic mentality* claims an absolute ethical value, but insists on the happy life which leads to it.[70]

The quantitative study of these various moral currents throughout the Graeco-Roman and Western worlds is made on the basis of a classification of the ethics of happiness, of love, and of absolute principles. The tables, the graphs and the list of authors do not mention the mixed idealistic ethics. Thus these quantitative results require a long commentary. The conclusion is that the curve of the ethics of happiness is rather similar to that of the sensate culture (this ethical current disappears completely from 400 up to 1440). The two ideational ethics show quite a definite decline since the sixteenth century.[71]

CRIMINAL LAW

The chapter which Sorokin devotes to this subject matter is very long and detailed (Sorokin's first specialization having been penal law), and goes much farther than the examination of the influences of the cultural premises on penal law.[72] His method of comparative law is the following. First of all it establishes a list of the actions

which, from the fall of the Roman Empire until the twentieth
century, have been considered as criminal at one period or another
in one of the following countries: France, Germany, Austria, Italy
and Russia. This list consists of 103 "crimes" classified in the usual
manner: crimes against the physical person, against property, etc.
On this basis, the several codes are compared: What are, among
these actions, those which have been integrated with the law at
certain periods and in certain countries? and those which have
been "decriminalized" and why? This permits the establishment
of the fluctuations of authoritarian, democratic, liberal, anti-
humanitarian trends, etc.[73] From the point of view of our independent variables, as one might expect, the medieval penal law
sanctioned many purely religious crimes which were not sanctioned
under the barbarian law. These crimes occupy the central position
not only in canon law but also in the secular laws. They were,
moreover, severely punished. In the fifteenth and sixteenth centuries, the number of crimes against religion decreases. This process
has continued up to the present time and reached its acme in the
Soviet Code of 1926. A slight movement of return toward ideational
values appears in certain articles of the Fascist Code of 1930[74]
and of the National Socialist Code of 1935.[75] Thus criminal law
practically follows the curve of the cultural mentality.[76]

We thus have ended the summary exposition of the dependent
variables of Sorokin's sociology of knowledge. One sees that the
influence of the cultural premises encompasses an extremely vast
realm, actually one might say *the whole of knowledge.* Thus Sorokin does not exclude from the influence of his variables the positive
sciences, as Marx or Mannheim do.[77]

But even though knowledge is influenced, it is not totally influenced. It is conditioned *at a certain level* only, the level of the
vast trends of philosophic thought. By this is meant very general
positions always concerned rather closely with the nature of the
world, the meaning of human life, etc. Thus the physical and biological sciences are considered in their most general and philosophical aspect: atomism inasmuch as it is linked to materialism; vitalism
and mechanism as related to the philosophic structure of living
beings.

On the other hand, it is the *content* of mental productions which
is considered as more dependent than their structure or their origin.

This is particularly apparent in the fundamental categories of causality, time, space, number. Sorokin says explicitly that only the particularized meanings which these categories may take on are linked to the premises of culture. But thinking according to these categories (no matter what their content) is considered an assumption. "They have to be present in the mind in order that the mind can grasp and know anything."[78] It is important to emphasize this point in order not to misunderstand the scope of Granet's texts which have been cited. Granet insists on the point that the Chinese do not think according to our logical categories. "This axiom once admitted (that the realities are raised up by symbols), neither the principle of causality, nor that of contradiction, can be invoked to take the role of the directive principles."[79] Sorokin uses these texts merely to show the ideational character of the Chinese concept of causality. On this point, the aim of Sorokin's analysis of the categories is very different from that which Durkheim attributed to his analysis: the aim being to show that the idea of causality has a social origin, no matter what particularized content is given to it, whether the cause is sought in the world of our experience or in the other.[80] This does not mean that Sorokin does not admit the social origin of categories, but simply that this question is not considered in his sociology of knowledge.

The premises of culture thus influence the content of all the mental productions at the level of their philosophic meaning.

This account has not merely enumerated the dependent variables but has indicated briefly for each how Sorokin proves the existence of the relation which he affirms. The two graphs on page 154 make an approximate summary of the quantitative proofs concerning the actual correlation between the dependent variables.[81]

THE TYPE OF RELATIONSHIPS

How is one to state precisely the kind of influence the cultural premises have upon these mental productions?

Let us remind ourselves of the way by which Sorokin arrived at the cultural premises. He was looking for the relationships which could exist between cultural phenomena on the level of meanings. They could be integrated, contradictory or neutral. Integrated cultural phenomena constituted systems, some as simple as syllogisms, others as complicated as a treatise on geometry, or a scientific discipline. The principles concerning the nature of the ultimate

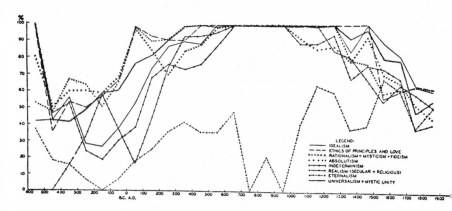

MOVEMENT OF EIGHT IDEATIONAL VARIABLES

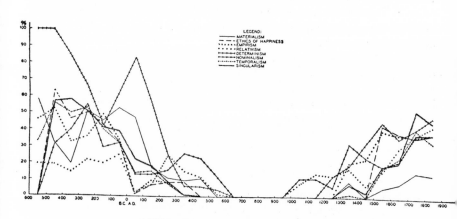

MOVEMENT OF EIGHT SENSATE VARIABLES

reality were to play the part of the premises of the most vast systems. The relationship which unites our independent variables with mental productions is a *relationship of cultural integration.* In other words, it is that one which links the fundamental principle of a well-integrated culture to its various parts.

Let us insist upon this consideration of cultural integration. On the level of ideological culture, Sorokin conceives of only one true form of cultural integration: logical consistency.[82] The independent variables rightly bear the name of "premises." The integrated ideological cultural system is thus a group of propositions coherent among themselves because they may be logically deduced from a principle concerning the nature of the ultimate reality.

The foregoing account shows clearly that Sorokin has been faithful to the method which he advocates. He always follows the same development: If such a premise of culture is admitted, it follows logically that there must be such an ethic, such a concept of truth, of causality, and such and such position as regards certain biological and physical theories. But a view of Sorokin's positive research also allows us to answer a question which his theoretical account of cultural integration does not permit us to solve.

There are sever.' kinds of logical consistency, or rather different degrees of strictness in this logical consistency. There is first the reasoning whose conclusions necessarily follow premises. Thus: "The ultimate reality is supra-sensory. Now the supreme value is the same as the ultimate reality. Therefore the supreme value is supra-sensory." There is also a reasoning in which the conclusion which is drawn from the principle is only one of the possible conclusions. Thus: "The true reality is beyond visible things, from which it follows that the aim of human action is union with this authentic reality." Perhaps. But one could also reason in this manner: "The true reality is beyond visible things, from which it follows that it is beyond men's reach." As a matter of fact, in neither of these two cases is there a complete reasoning. In the first sequence, one implies that human action must have a supreme goal, that this supreme goal is nothing but true reality, and that man is capable of entering into relations with that which surpasses the tangible. In the second sequence, one implies that man is only a sensory being.

The logical ties between the cultural premises and the dependent variables almost always belong to this second type. Thus we cannot

pass rigorously and directly from the ideational premises to indeterminism. We may indeed think both that the ultimate reality is
supra-sensory and that the order of things is determined. Nevertheless, one can easily see that determinism is more in the sensate
line. Similarly we are told that when we accept the ideational
premise, we seek the cause — and not only the ultimate cause —
of phenomena in the supra-sensible world. It seems that one may
perfectly well think that the ultimate reality is immaterial and at
the same time that there are regular sequences among the sensory
phenomena even if they are ultimately nothing but illusions. But,
on the other hand, we perfectly well feel that the tendency to seek
supra-sensory causes for all phenomena conforms more nearly to
the ideational belief. The logic which is used here is a sort of logic
without rigor which is not afraid to skip the intermediate phases of
reasoning. It is that which is used in everyday life and in the personal *Weltanschauungen.*

It is nevertheless a true logic: Any conclusion cannot be drawn
from anything, but proceeds by very simple reasoning which jumps
the minor premises and which is especially sensitive to a sort of
similarity between the principle and the conclusion. Thus the
sensate number, it is said, will be quantitative and the ideational
number, qualitative. One immediately perceives a coherence, an
affinity between the idea that the real is material and the idea of a
quantitative number. The same holds for "immaterial" and "qualitative number." Certainly it would be hardly consistent to believe
that there is only the visible world and at the same time attribute
qualities to numbers. Similarly, one may believe that the world
is illusory without admitting the existence of universalia having a
trans-subjective reality. But we conceive that it is quite right that
an ideational mentality should be realistic and that, moreover, it
would be contradictory to be simultaneously sensate and realistic.

This interpretation seems to be corroborated by the way in
which Sorokin expresses himself on the subject of integrated cultural realities.

The properly trained mind apprehends, *feels, perceives, senses,* and
understands the supreme unity of Euclid's or Lobachevski's geometry of
perfect mathematical deduction; of Platonic metaphysics; of Phidias'
Athena; or a suite or concerto by Bach; of a Shakespeare drama; of
the architecture of the Parthenon or the Cathedral of Chartres. Such a
mind comprehends their sublime unity *internally, intimately;* often
feels it immediately and directly, *senses* it without any experimental

or statistical manipulations and without indirect reasoning. . . . If by chance the torso of the Venus of Milo were found in one place and its head in another, when they were brought together their belonging to each other would be self-evident; while if to the head of the Venus were added, say, the body of Bernini's St. Teresa, their heterogeneity would also appear at once.[83]

This text in which Sorokin talks of a logical unity being felt both as regards Euclid and Bach is expressive of the kind of logical relationships which he seeks not only in the field of esthetics but also in that of knowledge. Thus the terms "logical consistency" which define the relationships between the dependent and independent variables must be understood as designating a flexible, felt, non-critical logic but one which is in no way devoid of value.[84]

In certain cases, the logical link is much more loose. It results merely from a similarity in the position of an independent variable and a dependent variable. Thus, after the logical consistency between realism and the truth of faith and between nominalism and the truth of the senses has been shown, it is added that inasmuch as rationalism is a mixture of the two systems of truth, and as conceptualism occupies a middle position between nominalism and realism, an association of the two may be expected.[85] A similar manner of reasoning is used in connection with the mixed concepts of historical processes (partly cyclical and partly linear) which must exist during idealistic periods.[86]

We may thus conclude that the relationship which unites the independent variables to the dependent ones is that which exists between principles and consequences in a flexible logic.

Now that we have determined how Sorokin's sociology of knowledge specifies the three essential points of any sociology of knowledge, we may summarize this triple answer in a formula: "The content of mental productions, in their fundamental aspect, is logically consistent with the premise — ideational, sensate or idealistic — dominant during a certain period of the Graeco-Roman or Occidental world." It seems to us that this formula presents quite exactly, in a general form, the various results which Sorokin believes to be proven by his positive research.

THE EXPLANATION

To be content to affirm a proposition because it is proven empirically is insufficient for Sorokin.[87] It is also necessary to understand the reason for which things happen in such and such a way. He prefaces a chapter of *Dynamics* with a quotation from Aristotle: "Since we never reckon that we understand a thing till we can give an account of its 'how and why' . . ."[88] We are then perfectly in line with Sorokin if we are not satisfied with the formula which has just been established, but if we ask ourselves this question: "Why are mental productions in their content and their fundamental aspect logically consistent with the dominant premise?"

We do not find this question raised in these terms nor solved explicitly by Sorokin. This is explainable, for his dominant preoccupation is to show that the sociocultural world changes recurrently in its fundamental aspects. Thus, after having proved these points empirically, his explanation will endeavor to determine their reason.[89] Our question is, on the contrary, more precise (being concerned with the sector of knowledge and not all sociocultural phenomena) and is primarily, but not exclusively, on a static level. Nevertheless, it will not be hard to adapt the Sorokin explanations to our problem.

EXPLANATION OF THE STRUCTURE OF THE FUNDAMENTAL RELATIONSHIP OF SOROKIN'S SOCIOLOGY OF KNOWLEDGE

We may divide our interrogation into two subquestions. First, why has the problem of the ultimate reality been answered by the three propositions (which act as cultural premises) and why have these three solutions been maintained so consistently throughout history despite their temporary eclipses? Next, why do they act as independent variables with respect to the fundamental aspects of our mental productions?

Why are the three propositions so stable?

When one wonders what the nature of the ultimate reality is, the number of possible answers is very limited. We can hardly imagine logically more than five possibilities: (a) the nature of the reality is supra-sensory; (b) it is sensory; (c) it is inseparably sensory and supra-sensory; (d) it is entirely unknown and unknowable (skepticism); (e) it is known in its phenomenal aspect, whereas its transcendental aspect, if it exists, is unknowable (agnosticism). All the other solutions, says Sorokin, lead to these in one way or another. And the last two are purely negative.[90] Sorokin could have added also that these solutions are not answers to the question of the nature of reality. They are justifications for refusing to answer. Thus the possible answers are limited to three.

How is it that these attitudes show such a stability? Indeed, despite the fluctuations in their importance, the lessening of their influence, and even their disappearance at certain periods, they have known rebirths and periods of dominance. Moreover, if one evaluates the three trends quantitatively, it seems that, for the twenty-five centuries, there are no extreme inequalities in their influence.[91]

The fact that none of the three answers to the question of the nature of reality has succeeded in eliminating the other two, is explained by the partial validity of each one of them. Actually, if one of the three answers were completely true, it would give an adequate knowledge of reality — it would allow the best adaptation to reality.[92] It would be incomprehensible that such an attitude would not eliminate the other two. If, on the other hand, one of the attitudes were entirely false, its total inadequateness to reality would prevent it from surviving long. But if we admit that each one of these attitudes is partly true and partly false, we understand why they have been able to maintain themselves without ever eliminating each other.[93]

Why are mental productions logically consistent with these philosophic attitudes?

Or why are philosophic attitudes independent variables? The answer lies in the idea which one adopts about the human mind. Sorokin asserts that "a human being is neither perfectly logical and rational, nor entirely illogical and irrational."[94] But he certainly tends to be logical. For most men, logical consistency is an important value. Experimental studies have shown, Sorokin reminds us, the tendency of individuals and groups toward logical integration.[95] To say to someone that he is contradicting himself is certainly one of the most serious reproaches which can be made. The considerable amount of intellectual effort which man devotes to rationalizing his actions is another proof of the high esteem in which he regards logical consistency.

If we assume that the human mind is logical, or at least that, strongly appreciating logical consistency, it tends to realize it, we can understand that the concept of ultimate reality which is adopted, acts as an independent variable for other mental productions. This philosophical question will actually be an excellent point of reference around which one will be able to build a culture. First because it is really fundamental and because the criterion around which the logical consistency of other attitudes will be built, must be an essential element. Moreover many mental productions have a philosophic aspect (what we have named the fundamental aspect). In taking a philosophical problem as a criterion, one has a sort of common language which will permit the comparison of a great number of, if not all, mental productions from this point of reference.

Of course, we must not imagine that these different steps are taken in a perfectly premeditated fashion. This explanation means simply this. In a given place, at a given moment, one of the three attitudes toward the fundamental reality dominates. The intellectual, artistic, etc., productions, which emerge from this cultural milieu, will make their fundamental aspects conform more or less explicitly and with more or less success to the dominant attitude.

To sum up, if we suppose that the human mind tends toward logical consistency, it becomes understandable that the various mental productions should be logically linked to an essential principle and particularly to the fundamental philosophic problem of the nature of reality. If we admit, besides, that the only three possible answers to this problem are neither entirely false, nor entirely true, but partially adequate, it becomes comprehensible that these three solutions as well as the three cultures they permeate should have survived.

EXPLANATION OF THE DYNAMISM OF THE FUNDAMENTAL RELATIONSHIP

We know why the three cultural systems have never disappeared. But why has their influence known so many fluctuations? Why, instead of coexisting in a parallel direction, if one may say so, have they, each in turn, dominated? This question is, from the point of view of the sociology of knowledge, less important than the explanation of the structure of the relationship between independent variables and mental productions. For Sorokin, who puts the emphasis on sociocultural changes, this question is really of prime importance.

He answers it by combining two principles which he calls *principle of immanent change* and *principle of limits* (one of whose forms we have already encountered). The principle of immanent change is a stand against all the types of explanations of sociocultural phenomena by an exterior factor. Many of the contemporary sociologists who study the fluctuations of a social phenomenon, for example, the family, seem to conceive of this phenomenon as essentially passive. It seems to them that it is necessary to seek the reason for its changes outside of the phenomenon. Thus it is said, for example, that the changes in the family institution in the United States during the past century are due to industrialization, even if industrialization is explained by another factor, such as, for instance, the increase in the density of the population.[96] The principle of immanent change claims that the changes in any sociocultural system are due principally to the system itself. If all the exterior conditions had remained constant, the American familial institution would nevertheless evolve, simply because it is a system functioning unceasingly, a "going concern."

Sorokin utilizes the analogy of the living organism to make his principle understood. Even if the exterior conditions were such as to remain always constant, one could not prevent a man from changing as the years go by.[97] This naturally does not prevent the acknowledgment of the role of exterior forces in the changes in the sociocultural systems. Their interaction with the immanent principle accentuates the tendency toward change.[98]

Our cultural systems integrated around their premises also change. But it will be necessary to interpret this principle of immanent changes in such a way that it means that cultural systems are in themselves the causes, not only of their own changes, but of their own destruction. We know that the three cultural premises are inadequate to reality. This inadequacy is their internal reason for destruction. As a system develops and becomes dominant, it tends to accentuate this lack of adaptation to reality. Thus it prepares its own downfall. One may repeat the opinion of Toynbee and Spengler that a culture perishes not by murder but by suicide.[99]

The principle of immanent change thus explains that a cultural system may disappear. By what will it be replaced? Here, the principle of limits intervenes. We already know that there are only three answers to the question of the ultimate nature of reality. It follows from this that when one of the three premises — with the whole culture which it permeates — has disappeared, one of the two others must replace it. And the same story starts all over again with one of the premises.[100]

In summary, if we admit that the three sociocultural systems have within themselves the reasons for their evolution and for their decline (principle of immanent change), and that, when one system has disappeared, there are only two other possibilities (principle of limits), their recurrent dynamics become comprehensible.

This view of Sorokin's *Wissenssoziologie* shows that within the framework of his general sociology, he has created an authentic and complete sociology of knowledge. Although, in the works of Sorokin, it is not presented as detached from the rest of his system, and although its development has been limited to the place which it should fill in this system, it possesses the essentials which define any sociology of knowledge: A determination of the three elements (independent variable, dependent variable, and relationship between the two) based upon abundant material from positive research and an elaborate explanation of the conclusions drawn from this research. Let us now pass on to a positive criticism of the various parts of this sociology of knowledge.

CHAPTER NINE

Evaluation of Sorokin's Sociology of Knowledge

THE POINT OF VIEW adopted in this part is that of positive criticism. We shall ask ourselves to what degree Sorokin's sociology of knowledge provides a better understanding of the influence of social factors upon human knowledge. More precisely, we shall ask ourselves whether research conducted along the lines he has laid down promises to be productive of results.

This criticism will bear only upon the sociology of knowledge. In spite of all the interest there might be in discussing certain points of Sorokin's general sociology (as, for example, his extremely broad conception of sociology which makes of it almost the science of man) we shall not examine it except insofar as certain of its aspects play an essential role in the sociology of knowledge.

We shall begin in this chapter with an examination of each one of the parts of Sorokin's *Wissenssoziologie*: the method of positive research; the generalized conclusions; the theory.[1] Then, in Chapter 10, we shall pass to a more general criticism (bearing upon his sociology of knowledge as a whole), and a more fundamental one (questioning his very conception of this discipline).

CRITICISM OF THE METHOD OF POSITIVE RESEARCH

MEANINGFUL AND CAUSAL RELATIONSHIPS

Any positive research in the sociology of knowledge as well as in any other social science has for its objective the outlining of the relationships between sociocultural phenomena. The first point of the method then will concern the kind of relations which we must seek. Several types of relationships between phenomena may be conceived, from simple spacial contiguity to the profound unity of phenomena linked functionally and logically at one and the same time.[2] In fact, the choice of the sociologist is limited, for obvious reasons, to two types of relationships: causal (or functional) and meaningful (or logical).[3] Let us recall that the first merely affirms that two phenomena always appear simultaneously or according to a certain sequence: "Each time that A appears, B appears." These are the relations on which the physico-chemical sciences focus their attention. Logico-meaningful relationships, on the contrary, affirm that the meanings of two phenomena appear to be linked logically.

What type of relations are we to seek between sociocultural phenomena? One of the three components of any sociocultural system is meaning.[4] It follows from this that logical relations are possible between two such phenomena. Furthermore, the meaning component is, might we say, the most important of the three, for it differentiates the sociocultural phenomena from the physical or biological phenomenon. It seems that the result of this must be that strictly sociocultural relations will be logical. In another connection, we know what difficulties research into causal or functional relationships encounters in its application to the social field (isolating two variables, making them vary separately, making experiments, repeating them). All this induces Sorokin to conclude that sociology must seek logical relationships.

However, we must not on this account reject the study of functional relationships. They seem to me to play a double role for Sorokin. First, when we cannot discover logical relations between two phenomena,[5] we may find it useful to know their degree of association.[6] Then, and this is much more important, the establishment of causal relationships is the confirmation of the existence of meaningful relationships.[7]

The sociologist then will seek first logical relationships between sociocultural phenomena, but he will seek also functional relationships. He will devote his attention then to relationships which are meaningful and functional at one and the same time ("meaningful-causal relationship").[8]

It seems that this principle is perfectly balanced and that the considerations upon which Sorokin grounds it are valid. It is certain that sociocultural phenomena are human and cannot be reduced to pure physical or biological phenomena, and that meaning is the former's most important element. This suffices to establish the possibility of links of a logical order between these phenomena.[9]

However, there are two points on which it appears advisable to insist. First, we can establish functional links between human phenomena without ignoring their meaningful nature. Seeking to see whether B be considered the consequent of A does not imply that A and B must be defined in purely physical and biological terms. Sorokin does not deny this point. The confirming role he assigns to the functional relationship even implies this possibility. In his positive research, he constantly establishes functional relationships between sociocultural phenomena. It does not seem useless, however, to make this precision explicit.

Then — and here it seems that Sorokin underestimates this very point in practice — the relationship between two significant phenomena can, in certain cases, be said to be logical only in a very broad fashion, or more accurately, we must clearly distinguish between *logical* and *rational*. In fact, meaningful human phenomena will often be linked to each other by relations which are themselves meaningful, although they are emotional or psychological or even unconscious rather than rational. However, such relationships may be said to be *logical* in the sense in which we speak of a logic of sentiments or emotions. This simply means that we expect, that we *understand* certain emotional sequences. Such being the case, if we are told that there are many more suicides during an economic depression than during prosperous years,[10] this increase will appear comprehensible to us. It is not rational, however. Suicide is not a rational solution for the problems raised by economic depression. However, this correlation is comprehensible in the sense that a profound economic crisis produces a large number of individual ruins, that an important personal catastrophe has grave repercussions upon the nervous system and emotional stability. It entails, for example, a state of despair, and we consider suicide as one of the reactions we may expect from a desperate man. We may in a very broad sense call *logical* this sequence uniting two phenomena which have a human meaning: an economic crisis and a suicide.

Another example. A positive correlation has been noted between low economic indices and the lynching of Negroes in the Southern United States. There is evidently no rational means for the whites of the South to attribute the responsibility for the lack of rain — which was the cause of the poor cotton crop — to the lynched Negroes. However, this typically irrational behavior becomes comprehensible if we accept the frustration-aggression sequence. In this sense it can be said that the relation between the two phenomena: economic difficulty and lynching, is a logical relation.[11]

Now it seems that Sorokin's "logico-meaningful relationship" tends to be considered as rational (or logical in the strict sense of that term), rather than meaningful (or logical in the broad sense we suggest). Words have little importance, but it seems essential to explicitly enlarge the extent of the logical relationship to make it embrace, besides rational logic, all the other kinds of conscious and subconscious meaningful sequences by which human phenomena are linked. The reason for this is simple: to limit the sociologist to seeking purely rational relationships between phenomena will force him to ignore or to study in a functional way probably a very considerable number of human phenomena.[12]

Let us note that this broad interpretation of the notion of logical relationship really makes factual proof necessary (whether the latter is qualitative or quantitative), and even extends its role. For these different "logics" of emotions and feelings are characterized by their lack of rigor (in the following sense: their consequences are not compulsory, necessary with respect to the premises). After all, the whites of the South might have found other forms of aggressiveness than the lynching of Negroes to follow up their economic frustration. Let us suppose, for example, that they have interiorized their aggressiveness and have turned it into an inferiority complex. Since this reaction to frustration is also frequent, we might have said that the relationship between a poor crop and an inferiority complex was "logical." Likewise, there are other reactions just as normal as suicide to the loss of one's possessions. The result of this is that knowing the premise of a certain "logic" does not necessarily lead us to know its consequence.[13] It follows from this that it is indispensable to seek relationships which are actually realized between phenomena. This procedure alone will permit us to decide which, among the logical relationships which can unite phenomenon A to phenomena B, C, or D, is the one that is actually realized.

This is also true even if we consider only rational relationships between phenomena, for, except in the case of an absolutely rigorous logic moving in necessary matter, there will often be several ways of reasoning starting from one and the same premise. Sorokin gives a very good example of this in a criticism of Max Weber. Weber claims that the doctrine of predestination is at the origin of the spirit of profit because success in trade was considered a sign of divine election. Sorokin remarks very justly that the doctrine of predestination can just as well lead to passivity and inactivity. Since it is unnecessary to act in order to be saved, is it not natural not to struggle at all?[14] This example shows that, starting from the same principle, we may very well arrive at two opposing conclusions. Sorokin adds indeed that quietism is a more "natural" conclusion than the spirit of profit, but this is only a very moderate estimation which does not destroy the other reasoning. Now the rational relationships between the meanings of cultural phenomena will generally be of this type of logic which we described above as a flexible, non-critical and valid logic.[15] Hence, even if we mean by meaningful (or logical) relationships merely rational relationships between meanings of cultural phenomena, an objective study of what has actually taken place will be indispensable, in order to know what type of reasoning was actually practiced: the one which makes us conclude economic effort, or passivity from predestination. No more than he can be content to establish causal relationships between human phenomena, can the sociologist stop at the logical relationships *possible* between these phenomena. These two relationships are complementary in sociological research.

To this first problem of method — what kind of relationships must we seek between sociocultural phenomena — Sorokin replies in a complete and seemingly valid way. We would have liked him, however, to broaden and make explicit the notion of logical relationship in order to make it cover all types of relationships which unite human phenomena according to an intellectual, emotional or even subconscious "logic."

QUALITATIVE AND QUANTITATIVE PROOF

The second question of method which arises is: how are we to prove that such and such a relationship exists between two phenomena? There are two possibilities: qualitative study (or monographic) and quantitative study (or statistical). These two procedures are sufficiently well known to allow us to characterize them briefly.[16] Sorokin means these terms in their ordinary sense, it seems. Qualitative study will consider in detail a certain number of cases in which it is estimated that a certain relationship is realized between phenomena. By the analysis of Aristotle's philosophy, for instance, it will be shown that it really presents idealistic characteristics. Quantitative study, on the contrary, aims to translate mathematically the aspects of sociocultural phenomena between which we may wish to establish a relationship. The degree of association between these phenomena may also be translated mathematically and graphically.

To avoid all confusion, let us see first how this question of qualitative or quantitative proof is distinguished from the problem of logical and functional relationships which we have just discussed. One would be tempted to say that qualitative study is the proof of logical relationships and quantitative study, the proof of causal relationships. This is not so simple. If, by proofs, we mean confirmations by the facts ("things really take place in that fashion in reality"), the proof of logical relationships may be made either qualitatively or quantitatively. On the other hand, it cannot be said that the proof of causal relationships is quantitative. On the contrary, the causal relationship is the result of a quantitative study. It cannot be conceived that we lay down a causal relationship and then undertake to prove it, since the only basis for the causal relationship is the *actual* association between the variables. We lay down a logical relationship and then see whether it is causal also.

Thus the questions treated in the two parts of this section on method are partially interlocked, or more exactly, we approach the problem of method by two routes: that of the type of relationship and that of the factual proof. We can indicate the connection between the two points of view in the following way:

Logical relationship can be proven
either qualitatively
or quantitatively (in this case, the logical relationship is also causal).

Sorokin adopts the two methods of proof and insists, it seems, equally upon both, in practice as well as in theory. He has been reproached, however, for having an ambivalent attitude in respect to quantitative study.[17] On the one hand, it is said, he makes abundant use of statistics, graphs, etc.; on the other, he violently condemns the sensate sociologists of our time for whom the co-efficients of correlation are "the Law and the Prophets."[18]

There does not seem to be any contradiction. As he indicates in his outline of an integralist sociology (this qualifier is significant), quantitative empirical methods must be employed also.[19] More clearly still, he writes that the fundamental technique of the causal analysis employed by his integralist method is necessarily statistical.[20] What Sorokin condemns is the exclusive use of the statistical study which completely ignores meaningful relationships between sociocultural phenomena. However, in the ardor of polemics, his expression of this idea has not always been very felicitous, as when he approves of one of his critics saying that the statistics of the Dynamics are a concession to the contemporary dominant mentality and system of truth.[21]

The advantages and disadvantages of the two types of proof are known. Qualitative study permits us to describe phenomena in a nuanced fashion but can be applied practically only to a reduced number of cases, and it includes a large amount of subjectivity. Quantitative study can envisage a very large number of individual cases. It seems more objective, but it simplifies its subject matter and is often very difficult to apply.

We have to turn our attention to these two types of proof only as long as they concern Sorokin's sociology of knowledge. Let us ask ourselves first whether it is not sufficient to prove logical relationships qualitatively, then whether it is not absurd to wish to study currents of thought quantitatively.

The qualitative method, in spite of its disadvantages of subjectivity, may probably suffice for the proof of certain relationships between social factors and knowledge when it is a question of the connections between certain special phenomena well-defined in time and space. Such are Mannheim's studies on the influence of social affiliation upon the writings of German conservatives in the nineteenth century. In fact, it does not seem impossible to know accurately both the social status of all the conservative and liberal political writers in Germany in the nineteenth century and, on the other hand, the whole of their works. In this case, subjectivity will be reduced to interpretation. In another connection, such a subject calls for a detailed and refined analysis, which may be attained very well by the qualitative method. But the conclusions of such a study may not be generalized except with a great deal of prudence, and to a very limited degree. On the other hand, when we wish to prove the existence of relationships between currents of thought extending through twenty-five centuries, the qualitative method alone seems insufficient. This is true first, because to the subjectivity inherent in any interpretation is added the subjectivity in the selection of thinkers who are considered representatives of the epoch or the current. This subjectivity is extremely dangerous. The author, perhaps not very consciously, will select the facts which best suit his theory. Instead of proofs, we shall have merely a series of illustrations. The abuses in this field allow us to term this method "the plague of sociology."[22] Then, even if to avoid this disadvantage, we devote ourselves to an exhaustive study, of the ethics of happiness during twenty-five centuries, for example, it will be necessary, in order to utilize the results, to translate them in a manner which will permit us to apprehend them in a single view and to compare them. How are we to do this without figures or curves?[23]

But if a qualitative proof is insufficient for a sociology of knowledge having a bearing, like that of Sorokin, upon vast movements of thought, this does not mean that a quantitative study is possible. It seems at first sight that metaphysical and moral conceptions, *Weltanschauungen,* are indeed the last things to reduce to figures. Furthermore, it seems that we cannot repeat nor even realize a single time, experiments with variables of this sort.

Such considerations show well that it is vain to discuss this question in a general way. We must not ask ourselves "whether mental productions can be analyzed quantitatively" but "whether the quantitative methods of analysis utilized by Sorokin are justified."[24]

One remembers that the question was to measure the strength of influence of various currents of thought in the course of history. Sorokin's quantitative translation rests upon the number of thinkers belonging to the current and the influential value of each of them. This procedure is legitimate, Sorokin will say, because it is but an attempt to make the estimations of the strength of the intellectual currents more precise, estimations which are common in any historical work, and which, besides, are generally based upon the same two criteria. The only difference is that, from the point of view of the number of the participants in a current of thought, instead of employing vague terms like "the Aristotelians, at the beginning of the twelfth century, were more numerous or much more numerous than the Platonists," we shall say, for instance, that "from 1100 to 1120, there were 85 Aristotelians as compared with 53 Platonists," which indicates the relationship between the forces more precisely. Likewise, from the point of view of the influential value of each individual, instead of saying, for example, that Malebranche rationalism had a bit less influence upon his contemporaries than Newton empiricism, we shall say that, from 1680 to 1700, the influence of the first was measured by 7 and that of the second by 9. Furthermore, Sorokin will add, the criteria upon which his numerical estimate rests are explicitly indicated and are made as objective as possible.[25]

This way of giving values to all the thinkers appears very curious and somewhat sacrilegious, but the legitimacy of such a procedure cannot be judged by reactions of intellectual sensitivity. Sorokin's fundamental argument seems pertinent: If it is admitted that we speak of *more or less* important currents and *more or less* influential thinkers, we cannot object to the replacement of these vague estimates founded upon implicit and rather subjective criteria, by precise estimates based upon explicit and rather objective criteria.

To this it might be objected that it is useless and even false to wish to give a precise definition of vague phenomena.[26] The influence of a current of thought or of an individual philosopher is a multiform, subtle and imponderable phenomenon. Consequently, it is more accurate to estimate it in vague terms than in precise terms. Such accuracy is but apparent.

This objection certainly raises an important problem. It seems, however, that concepts like *influence* may be considered in a manner analogous to the experimental concepts of the physico-chemical sciences. The latter are defined only by their procedures of measurement.[27] Sorokin defines *influence* by the procedure by which he attributes values to each thinker. This seems legitimate provided he indicates clearly how he measures influence. Evidently this empirical definition of influence will be somewhat different and less rich perhaps than the current notion, just as the concept of *heat* is richer than, and different from, the *heat* which is defined solely by a thermometer.[28] The problem raised is this: how are we to avoid employing terms, whose sense has been defined empirically, in a vocabulary whose other terms have preserved their primitive and current sense? So long as a complete set of empirical notions has not been established, we always risk replacing surreptitiously, for instance, "influence in the ordinary sense" by "influence in the empirical sense" in a context where "influence in the ordinary sense" alone is suitable. Of course, this danger is very real and even difficult to avoid. It does not seem, however, that the objection is conclusive.

In another connection, it is accurate that we cannot make sociocultural phenomena of this kind undergo laboratory experiments, but it is not a question of that here. If we cannot cause repeated appearances of variable A in order to verify its degree of association with variable B, we can find, however, in the course of history a certain number of appearances of variable A and so verify more or less the degree of association between the variables. Naturally, history will never furnish a satisfactory substitute for laboratory experimentation.

This quantitative method is not, however, deprived of other grave dangers. Especially, the attribution of an author to a current of thought is not always clear. If philosophers like Abelard and William Ockham cannot be easily classified with respect to conceptualistic, realistic, or nominalistic currents, we imagine that many authors who did not focus their attention upon these problems will be even more difficult to classify. Furthermore, especially for the ancient periods, not all the thinkers are known. If the indices of materialism and other sensate currents fall to zero in the Middle Ages, it is perhaps because these currents did not have complete freedom of expression. Besides, in the valuation 1-12, there is, in spite of the objective criteria, a bit of subjectivity which enters into the estimation of the relative value of these systems. . . . This enumeration might be multiplied. The result is that figures and curves cannot be considered, it seems, as an adequate translation of historic situations.

However, quantitative study offers us two remedies for this situation. First, the very fact that it is a question of a quantitative study, or a mass study. When a meaningful relationship is confirmed by only a few cases, the error in interpretation may completely vitiate the proof. On the contrary, the larger the mass of cases envisaged is, the less considerable is the significance of an error in interpretation.[29] For the curves, in their general direction, to completely distort reality, we must have a rather large number of errors in the same sense, which is at least partially avoidable by having various investigators work independently and without their knowing the final objective of their studies.

A second remedy is the interpretation of quantitative results in terms of a qualitative study.[30] We cannot take figures at their face value without risking the worst mishaps. For example, in the study of idealistic and materialistic currents, the period 580-560 B.C. is, according to the tables, 100% materialistic, while that from 1880 to 1900 A.D. is but 17.9% materialistic. This seems rather unexpected. To interpret these figures correctly, we must go back to the realities they express. We see first that this period 580-560 B.C. is represented by a single thinker, Thales, while the other (1880-1900) is represented by 255 thinkers.[31]   Furthermore, Thales' materialism is hylozoistic (that is to say he attributes life to the ultimate material reality), while the 17.9% of materialism from 1880 to 1900 is 12.2% hylozoistic and 5.7% mechanistic. Furthermore, Thales' index of influence is 4 while the sum of the influence indices of the materialistic thinkers from 1880 to 1900 is 140 (95 for the hylozoists and 45 for the mechanists).[32] This shows that a good interpretation of quantitative results leads to the conclusion that an epoch of 17.9% of materialism was probably scarcely less materialistic than another in which the proportion of materialism is 100%. This is an extreme case, but one which well illustrates the necessity for an interpretation of quantitative results in terms of the quantitative realities they represent.

In short, it seems that Sorokin is right to say that the quantitative proof of meaningful relationships between sociocultural phenomena is more certain than a simple qualitative proof on condition that it be interpreted in terms of a qualitative knowledge of the phenomena we wish to represent.

Thus, for Sorokin, the sociologist of knowledge will seek rational relationships between social factors and knowledge. He will verify whether these logical relationships are actually realized, by attempting to establish functional relationships between them. The results will be interpreted in terms of a qualitative study. This method as it has just been explained seems to us to withstand any criticism of principle, which, naturally, does not mean that all the positive results obtained by Sorokin are also protected from all criticism. We are now going to examine this question.

CRITICISM OF THE CONCLUSIONS OF SOROKIN'S POSITIVE RESEARCH

Sorokin's positive research tends to determine to what degree we may make out of the cultural premises, variables of which the Sociocultural phenomena and especially the mental productions depend. The results of positive research are expressed in particular terms such as "the coefficient of correlation between rationalism and idealism, from 580 B.C. to 20 B.C. is .796,"[33] or "the Scholastics had an idealistic conception of time." When these various special results are numerous and present constant tendencies, they may be expressed in a general form, which is a conclusion proceeding directly from research. Since they do nothing but express a sum of empirical results and add nothing to it, except perhaps a certain expectation that, all conditions remaining equal, things in the future will continue to take place in the manner they have taken place in the past, these general formulas are supposed proven if they realize two conditions: first, if the particular results of positive research are valid; then, if the general formula scrupulously summarizes these results without extending them.

The sentence "the content of mental production in their fundamental aspect is logically consistent with the premise dominant at such a period in the Graeco-Roman and Occidental world" answers exactly this concluding notion of positive research.

Is this generalization valid? Our criticism will be made along two lines, as we have just indicated. Are the particular results of positive research valid? Do the formulas not generalize them unduly?

VALIDITY OF THE PARTICULAR RESULTS OF POSITIVE RESEARCH

In the preceding section concerning the method of positive research, this question has already been partly answered. It has been seen that a research into meaningful relationships between phenomena and the proof of these relationships by a quantitative method were good. To obtain valid results, a good method is not enough, it must also be applied suitably.

It is of course beyond our possibilities to criticize in detail the interpretation Sorokin gives of the principal intellectual currents during twenty-five centuries. Fortunately, such a step does not seem indispensable to the realization of the objective we are pursuing, one which is above all a theoretical study. Besides, Sorokin's general formula does not require that there be no error in order to be proven. Simply, the broad lines of the cultural history of Western civilization must not be distorted by Sorokin's positive research. Now we may verify this without an exhaustive criticism.

A reproach which often returns under the pen of various critics of Sorokin is the following: In his application of the "logico-meaningful method," his frame of reference is too broad — he unites in the same categories very different facts which are torn from their historical content, and then disfigures historical reality by imposing his categories upon it.[34]

This criticism does not seem devoid of a basis. There is a certain danger in tracing currents of thought through twenty-five centuries. Thales' materialism was probably very different from that of William Ockham, Diderot and Espinas. However, they are all arranged under the category of hylozoism and, if we may say so, they share in the same curve. The two idealistic periods are very different from each other: Saint Louis and Pericles do not seem very congenial.[35] Of course, all this is true. Sorokin does not claim to deny the differences which can exist between two materialists separated by a period of twenty centuries, and between the classical fifth century and the Christian thirteenth century. It is nonetheless true that the two materialists share the same belief on what the ultimate nature of things is. Likewise, there is an essential similarity between many intellectual currents of the Greek fifth century and those of the Occidental thirteenth. Sorokin has never claimed, much to the contrary, that *all* the culture of an epoch depended *only* upon the cultural premise and that consequently two periods that have the same premise are identical.[36] Sorokin simply utilizes the abstraction, which is a method employed by any historian. This position seems to be justified, except for a nominalist. However, we concede that it may be dangerous when the level of abstraction is very high. Thus it is certainly audacious to unite in the same ideational category Brahmanism, Buddhism, Taoism, the Greeks before the sixth century and the occidental Christians from the fifth to the twelfth century A.D. But, after all, do we not employ concepts as abstract in the history of ideas and of philosophy? It is not Sorokin who invented the concepts: materialism, spiritualism, realism, etc. Why should he not be allowed to employ them? Let one think about the categories such as "group," "religion," "state," etc., which are utilized in sociology. It does not seem that we are forbidden to use very broad categories, on condition that we define them clearly. Sorokin's works do not appear to me to reveal serious transgressions against this principle.

A few criticisms of points of detail will give an idea of the errors which can be found in Sorokin. It happens occasionally that the logical relationship between the premise of culture and such and such an aspect of mental productions is indicated vaguely. In such a fashion, the sociological universalism (reality and value are social and not individual) is linked to the ideational premise because ideational ethics is an ethics of absolute principles. For that reason, absolute principles are called in — religious, moral, philosophic and other principles — to subordinate the individual to the group.[37] We do not see why an ethics with absolute principles must require the submission of the individual to society. It even seems that if this ethics has God as its end, it will be said that one must obey God rather than society. The situation becomes more complicated when the third current in this domain, integralism (affirming the reality of man and of society), is not considered idealistic but ideational.[38] It happens also that logical relationships which are expected are not realized. Thus Sorokin explains how an idealistic ethics may be established, but neither the tables nor the list of names indicate any idealistic ethics which has ever existed.[39]

In the statistical field,[40] there are several defects of which probably the most important is to be found in the quantitative proof of the fluctuations of epistemological currents. The point is to see how the three systems of truth have evolved. Instead of classifying the thinkers directly into three categories: those for whom the criterion of truth is respectively, faith, reason, and the senses, they are classed into six categories: empiricism, rationalism, mysticism, criticism, skepticism, and fideism. It would be all right if each one of these six categories could be related to a single one of the three systems of truth. Unfortunately, rationalism insofar as it is religious is related to the truth of faith, and insofar as it is idealistic, to the truth of reason. Now the figures and graphs are aggregate for rationalism. It is then impossible to make a clear statistical distinction between the three systems of truth. The qualitative interpretation can partially palliate these difficulties. Thus for Sorokin, rationalism before the fifth century B.C. and of the

third to the twelfth A.D. will be considered religious. In opposition
to this, from the fifth century B.C. to the second century A.D., it will
be considered non-religious because it was mainly logico-dialectical
during these periods.[41]

These few points of detail we have just cited appear to us the
gravest special criticisms which can be made of Sorokin's positive
research. There are certainly other points where one might quarrel
with him. No doubt all the historians of philosophy would not
agree with all the classifications nor with all the indices of influence
he assigns to thinkers. Sorokin is very conscious of this, but, as
Dr. Rashevsky points out, it is not because Sorokin's data are crude
that they are unreliable.[42] One must remember that this work,
according to Sorokin's own expression, aims to define a continent
and not a province and that what, on the scale map of the continent,
is a straight line, is changed into a curved and wavy line on the
scale of the province.[43] Besides, we do not have to be concerned
here with the exactitude of all Sorokin's researches, but merely with
that which proves his conclusions in the field of sociology of knowledge. Now it seems that the errors and inaccuracies of detail are
not numerous and serious to the point of questioning the value of
the research as a whole, the research which serves as a basis for his
generalization concerning the relationships between mental productions and premises of culture.

IS THERE NOT UNDUE GENERALIZATION?

In other words, the particular results being valid, can we say that
the general formulation of these results does not extend their scope
illegitimately. This generalization affirming the logical consistency
of mental productions with the dominant premise was obtained by
attempting to clarify the three elements — independent variable,
dependent variable and the relationship between the two — in terms
of Sorokin's research. The criticism of this formula, which is not
due to Sorokin himself, was made above, along with its elaboration.
We have endeavored to express accurately a summary of Sorokin's
positive research while at the same time respecting its limitations.

CRITICISM OF THE THEORY

Let us now review the three explanatory principles. Sorokin
does not use the word "scientific theory," but his explanation constitutes one. It is, in fact, made of a few principles from which we

can logically deduce the conclusions of positive research, and which, by this very fact, render the conclusions intelligible.

Logical consistency is an essential value for the human mind. This means that it will endeavor to harmonize its mental productions so that at least they will not contradict each other either directly or in their implications. It means, besides, that it will attempt to link them, at least in certain aspects, to fundamental intellectual positions. Among the latter, the most fundamental is probably the question of the nature of reality. It is then very understandable that any important mental production may be situated with respect to the different replies that can be given to this question. These replies can be but one of the following three: The true reality is limited to the sensory world, or, on the contrary, is beyond this world, or it is in this world and in the other at one and the same time. From this comes the possibility that, with respect to this fundamental question, mental productions as a whole may be divided into three categories according to the consistency of each production with one of the three replies. As, on the other hand, each one of these replies is true, but only to a certain degree, no one can prevail definitively over the other two. Finally, each one of these premises — and the whole of the culture which is molded by it — will dominate in turn in the same tradition of civilization, because any sociocultural system is submitted to the rule of immanent change wherein it will destroy itself. At this moment, one of the two other systems will emerge.

This theory can be reduced to three or four explanatory principles: the tendency of the human mind toward rationality, from which it is deduced that mental productions as a whole will have to be integrated logically with respect to a fundamental principle; the partial truth of each one of these premises of culture from which is deduced its soundness (because it is true) and its weakness (it cannot supplant definitively the others because it is partially false); finally, the principle of immanent change explaining the recurrence of the three systems. We can, if we wish, add a fourth principle, which is that of the number of answers possible for the question of the nature of reality, a number limited to three. It is the logical aspect of what Sorokin names the principle of limitation. That is why we shall consider it in connection with our principles of logical consistency rather than as a separate principle.

These propositions (the human mind has a tendency toward logical consistency — the three possible replies to the question of authentic reality are partly inadequate — any system possesses in itself its own law of destruction and development) will be considered here merely as constituting a scientific theory, that is to say independently of the value they may have by themselves. These propositions are susceptible of having a philosophic or a psychological sense. They will be considered here merely insofar as they are good explanations and good guides for further research. Their psychological or philosophic truth will be left between parentheses here and will be considered only as hypothetical.

CRITICISM OF THE PRINCIPLE OF LOGICAL CONSISTENCY

If we admit that the human mind has a tendency toward logical consistency, it follows indeed, that it will aim at cultural integration and that, besides, it will seek to harmonize the different mental productions logically with respect to a fundamental question.

This sequence: "logical consistency of the human mind, cultural integration, fundamental criterion of harmony" appears very satisfactory. Once you have logical consistency, the rest follows. But it is still necessary to make it more precise or, if you prefer, to continue the sequence until we arrive at these other consequents: the fundamental question will be the ontological problem; it will be enunciated in terms of sensate—non-sensate; there are but three possible answers.

It may be considered that the ontological problem, that of the nature of ultimate reality, is truly the most fundamental problem: we do not see that a further question is raised for the human mind.

But what are we to think of the expression Sorokin gives of it: "Is reality sensate or non-sensate?" The subject of this proposition is taken in two senses. It means either ultimate reality or true reality. Sorokin seems to make scarcely any difference between the two.[44] However, there is such a distinction. Thus, for Christians, ultimate reality is supersensory, but the world of the senses is a true reality although dependent upon ultimate reality. As for the predicate of the proposition, it is certain that Sorokin's formulation is not necessary. The ontological problem can be raised and has been raised in many other terms. Is ultimate reality a becoming? Is the world contingent? Does a God creator exist? Sorokin's formula is not the necessary expression of the ontological problem, but it seems a satisfactory expression of it because it attains the center of it. For it appears linked to the other formulations of the philosophic problem and covers them at least partly. If the ultimate reality is sensate, it is, it seems, a becoming, there is no transcendental God, the material world as a whole is absolute, etc. Sorokin himself seems to assimilate the sensate affirmation with the philosophy of becoming.[45] Or again, he will say that in ideational culture, "reality is perceived as non-sensate and non-material, everlasting Being."[46] Moreover, the term "sensate" itself is not clear. From time to time it is taken in the strict sense, meaning what is sensory;[47] occasionally it includes the idea of "rational" at least in the sense of inductive reasoning.[48]

Hence, the formulation of the ontological question by Sorokin would have gained, it seems to us, if he had made the distinction between ultimate reality and true reality. Besides, it might have been raised in other terms than those Sorokin chose, but it seems that his choice has not been unfortunate, for its formulation appears to reach the center of the problem.[49] Finally, it seems right that there are logically but three possible answers to this question. Either the true reality is sensate, or it is not, or it is sensate and non-sensate at the same time. We do not see any other possibility.

CRITICISM OF THE PRINCIPLE OF INCOMPLETE TRUTH

We reason in the following manner. Let us suppose that each one of the three solutions is partly true. It will follow that the human agents of these forms of culture will be able to adapt themselves to their cosmic, organic and social environment in a partly successful fashion. That explains the solidity of these systems. But, being partly false, men will not be able to adapt themselves to it in a perfectly successful manner. Thus no system will be able to supplant the others definitively.[50]

We do not have to ask ourselves here if the premises of culture are partly true or not, but we must merely see whether this hypothesis of their partial validity explains the relative soundness of the two cultures. Sorokin's ingenious reasoning rests upon two assumptions: first upon the assumption that the premises of culture have a cognitive purpose and that their validity is measured in terms of truth, that is to say, in terms of adequateness to reality; then, upon the assumption that a good adaptation to reality is based upon a valid knowledge of the latter.

That cultural premises are of a cognitive nature is a datum. It follows then that we may speak of truth in connection with them and, according to the traditional conception, of adequateness to the object. The second assumption appears valid. It seems sure that a good adaptation to reality requires, for men at least, a satisfactory knowledge of the latter and that, the truer his knowledge is, the better the adaptation will be. For this to be applied to the premises of culture, we must naturally mean adaptation in a very high sense, in the sense in which we shall say, for instance, that a hedonistic ethics is not adapted to human nature.

CRITICISM OF THE PRINCIPLE OF IMMANENT CHANGE

This must take account of the fluctuations of dominant cultural systems. The first meaning of this principle can be summarized thus: "the reason or cause of a change of any sociocultural system is in the system itself, and need not be looked for anywhere else."[51]

This principle, at first sight, annoyingly recalls the "vis medicatrix naturae" or a "vis dormitiva." It would be astonishing, however, for Sorokin, who has himself criticized the principle of equilibrium from this point of view,[52] to have succumbed to this error. Let us look more closely.

Sorokin opposes this principle to research into the causes of the changes outside of the system. Such an attitude implies, he says, that the system is considered essentially inert. Now this is false. Even if all the conditions exterior to a system remain constant, it would change nevertheless because it is a dynamic entity.[53]

From this principle, understood in this way, we may deduce that cultures integrated around their premises are dynamic entities which hold in themselves the reason for their changes, and hence *will* fluctuate even if they *were* not submitted to any exterior influence. But we certainly cannot deduce from this that these systems have in themselves the reason for their growth, development, maturity and destruction. The very example given by Sorokin, the family institution,[54] does not seem to carry in itself the source of its own destruction. Its forms can change. That is not the same thing. Now it is exactly the dominance and decline of the three forms of culture which must be explained.

Sorokin makes explicit a few of the corollaries of his principle of immanent change. "As soon as a sociocultural system emerges, its essential . . . course of existence, the forms, the phases, the activities of its life career are determined mainly by the system itself."[55] Exterior circumstances act principally by retarding or accelerating the development of the immanent potentialities of the system. The example is taken from Aristotle: an acorn bears in itself only the potentiality of becoming an oak. Another corollary will lead us nearer to the conception of the destruction as a law inherent in the system. The system, by its activity, engenders consequences incessantly, which must be imputed to it. This means that any action of the sociocultural system changes the system itself and also changes its environment. It follows from this that the following action of the system will be different from the first because it will emanate from a different system and will be realized in a different environment.[56] Now certain of these consequences can be bad for the system itself. It is this point which is particularly interesting for us.

Already in his *Systematic Source Book in Rural Sociology,* Sorokin explains that the differentiation between rural society and urban society, once it has attained a certain point, creates the seeds of its own decline.[57] Another example, a more classic one, is that of the capitalistic system. It is based upon contractual relationships which require, among other conditions, an equal freedom to contract or not to contract. Now, in the inevitable phases of depression and unemployment, either the workers will have to accept working under conditions they would not accept if they enjoyed the same freedom as their employers, or state organizations will furnish them with work or doles which will not be based upon a contract. In any hypothesis, the contractual basis of the capitalistic system disappears.[58] As for what concerns the destruction of a culture because of the consequences it itself engenders, we may give the following example. In an ideational culture, ascetic and religious personalities scorning power and riches will be particularly appreciated. Because of this, they will be placed at the top of the social scale and, even if they do not seek them, riches, honors and political power will come into their hands. Let us think of the monasteries of the Middle Ages. It will follow from this that extremely spiritualistic persons will have to devote a notable part of their energies in busying themselves with values they judge inferior. This will gradually diminish their aversion for these values. Besides, persons much more interested in sensate values will try to appear very ascetic in order to enter the elite and occupy situations for the control of power. Thus an ideational society comes little by little to comprise a sensate elite which, in its turn, will influence the dominant spirit and make it more sensate.[59]

But these examples, as convincing as they may be, merely show that a system *can* engender consequences which are finally prejudicial to it. But must it necessarily be so?

When Sorokin applies explicitly his principle of immanent change to the three cultural supersystems, he again interposes the idea of the inadequateness of the cultural premises to reality. "When such a system of truth and reality ascends, grows, and becomes more and more monopolistically dominant, its false part tends to grow, while its valid part tends to decrease."[60] It is very possible that things take place in this fashion but we do not see why. It does not seem contradictory to say that a dominant system will gradually have a tendency to adapt itself better to reality and hence to diminish its partial validity. Do we not say frequently that a set of laws which do not respect "reality" must gradually adapt themselves to it rather than go further away from it?

Hence it really seems that we shall not be able to explain the recurrences of three supersystems by the principle of immanent change unless it means something else than "the change of sociocultural systems has its reason in them and not outside of them." This is the sense Sorokin gives to his explanatory principle in the chapter he devotes to it[61] and in the application of this principle to the Occidental cultural supersystems.[62] The principle of immanent change must be interpreted in either an organistic sense or in a dialectical sense.

The organistic interpretation means that we must consider sociocultural systems in general, and supersystems in particular, analogous to living beings which are born, develop, reach their maturity, then decline and die. Certain comparisons and certain affirmations would suggest an organic interpretation.[63] We reject this interpretation, however, because it does not seem to us that there are other clues of organicism than these few illustrative passages and these few not very felicitous sentences. Moreover, Sorokin has criticized organicism very strongly. It is not because we recognize in a group a reality *sui generis* and different from that of its components that we have "to place the concrete where it does not exist" and assimilate the social system to an organism.[64]

By dialectical interpretation of the principle of immanent change, we mean that in its inner law, any sociocultural system contains its contradiction in itself, that gradually the latter is realized and thus suppresses the system itself. If the principle of immanent change is understood in this manner, it is intelligible that each system disappears in turn. This dialectical conception corresponds well with Sorokin's profound thought. Thus, he writes:

John Scotus Erigena, Nicolas of Cusa, and Hegel, in their dialectical method, claimed that any idea contains in itself implicitly its own denial, any thesis, its antithesis; therefore no thesis can remain static, but must incessantly change until its implicit contradiction is made explicit. . . . One is not obliged to become a Hegelian in order to perceive the immanent dynamism of ideas, norms and values.[65]

In short, Sorokin does not seem to have perceived clearly that the affirmation of the principle of immanent change (in the sense he ordinarily gives to it) does not permit us to infer the auto-destruction of the system. However, since as elsewhere, Sorokin admits a dialectical logic, we can conclude that in his books are to be found all the elements which permit us to interpret this principle in such a manner that it may be a good explanatory principle for the disappearance of systems of culture.

Conclusions of This Triple Criticism

We have just seen, in rather detailed fashion, how we were able to deduce the conclusions of Sorokin's positive research from each one of the three principles. Thus we have been able to take account of the explanatory value of these principles. The conclusion is that, from this point of view, Sorokin's scientific theory is a good explanation. However, the logical connection between principles and conclusions is of a variable closeness in the three cases. The deduction of the destruction of the system starting with the principle of immanent change interpreted dialectically seems perfect. The partial validity of the premises of culture explains well the soundness and relative success of each system if we mean adequateness to truth in a high sense. Finally, the rational consistency of the human mind renders meaningful the integration of mental productions and the choice of the ontological problem as an essential premise. But it cannot be said that we may, *a priori,* deduce from it in detail the formulation of this ontological problem and the terms in which Sorokin expresses his solutions.

THE GUIDING FUNCTION OF THE THEORY

Do our three explanatory principles furnish new directions for research? They really seem to be sufficiently broad and deep at the same time to suggest different paths than those followed by Sorokin in his positive research. The sociologist of knowledge who seeks to make precise the relationships between social factors and mental productions, at such an epoch, in such a country or in such a science, will find in these three principles, either using one of them or combining them in some other way than Sorokin's, numerous suggestions which may guide him in his work. For example, the investigator could attempt to find out how the "inadequateness of ideas to reality" changes them either by accentuating the inadequateness or by diminishing it. Or again, instead of taking the three fundamental ontological attitudes as independent variables, he could study how the tendency toward logical consistency works in a more restricted group in regard to a philosophic position more elaborate than the Sorokin premises. This is what Professor Northrop realized in *The Meeting of East and West*. He characterized cultures by their *philosophic presuppositions*. The latter are expressed in historic philosophic systems. The cultural unities to which these philosophies correspond have a narrower extent than the Sorokin cultures. Thus the philosophy of Locke is considered as the presupposition of the free culture of the United States[66] and the philosophy of Hegel as the presupposition of German culture.[67] The value of Northrop's work is a proof of the fruitfulness of hypotheses based upon a fundamental theory similar to that of Sorokin.

CHAPTER TEN

Significance of Sorokin's Sociology of Knowledge

OUR CRITICAL EXAMINATION of the essential articulations of a sociology of knowledge (methods of research, generalizations of positive studies, explanatory theory) ended with the conclusion that Sorokin's sociology of knowledge is valid. This means, among other things, that the content of mental productions in their fundamental aspect is really logically consistent with the premise dominant during a certain period in the Graeco-Roman and Occidental world. But criticism cannot stop at this point. It may appear strange at first sight that there is another question beyond that of validity. However, it is indeed so. There remains for us to determine the relevance of a proposition or a system; to see to what degree this proposition or this system answers the problems concerning the conditioning of social factors by knowledge. It is seen that validity and relevance are different. A proposition can be valid and not have any relevance with respect to a given problem for which we are seeking the solution.

A question of "relevance" is solved by the determination of limits. We shall examine two kinds of limitations of Sorokin's system. First, we shall study its external limitations, if we may say so. These are certain factors which have an influence upon knowledge and which he deliberately omits considering: existential determinants, on the one hand, and the law of immanent development of mental productions, on the other. Then we shall study the limitations inside the relationship between cultural premises and mental productions. There are three of these limits: the philosophic plane, the rational relationship, the macroscopic point of view.

Before passing to this examination, we have to solve a preliminary question. Is this sociology of knowledge really a sociology of knowledge?

IS IT A REAL *WISSENSSOZIOLOGIE?*

After having concluded that Sorokin's system is a valid *Wissenssoziologie,* it may seem paradoxical to raise this question. It arises, however.

In fact, the sociology of knowledge, as we have considered it up to the present, is essentially a research into the influence of social factors upon mental productions. It has been emphasized that the originality of this point of view consisted in inserting non-theoretical elements into the history of ideas, the latter elements being either psychological or social; and that the sociology of knowledge was concerned with these last. Now, for Sorokin, the independent variable is itself a mental production. The three premises of culture are nothing else but philosophic positions.

There is more. The principle of immanent change means that the reason for the changes in systems is found in themselves. It has as a corollary that the system, at the time of its emergence, has the history of its development already inscribed in itself, if one may say so. Now is the sociology of knowledge not mainly a research into "external factors" which influence thought?

Can one speak, then, of a Sorokin sociology of knowledge? Would it not be more proper to speak of the negation of the possibility of a *Wissenssoziologie* and of a return to what Mannheim calls an immanent history of ideas, the evolution of mental productions being explained by a succession of antecedents which are all in the domain of thought? The sociology of knowledge presented itself up to the present in a rather revolutionary manner. It owed to its Marxist origin[1] the faculty of clearly underlining the existential bases of ideas. Does Sorokin not tend to put ideas back into a pure heaven where they are submitted only to the action of the other ideas, and, in his general sociology, does he not go as far as making of philosophic ideas the independent variable of the whole of sociocultural phenomena and not only of mental productions?

This comment does not lack pertinence. It seems, however, that the Sorokin *Wissenssoziologie* is truly an authentic sociology of knowledge although of a type very different from what might be called, if this discipline were not so young, the "traditional" type.

It is right that the premises of culture are not non-theoretical factors. However, they are social factors, or more accurately sociocultural in the sense in which any idea expressed is a phenomena impossible without society.

Moreover — and this is more important — these cultural premises, although being ideas, are, however, external factors with respect to the various fields of thought. If, for example, our conception of the juridical personality is influenced by the idea we have concerning the ultimate reality, it can be said that the juridical field is conditioned by an external factor. Or, further, if sensate premises influence scientific productivity and technology, it can be said that these premises are factors exterior to scientific progress.

If the principle of immanent change meant that the evolution of physics, for instance, were due solely to discoveries of physical order and to reasonings about the latter, there would evidently no longer be any place for a sociology of knowledge. For Sorokin, physics as a system is under the control of immanent laws, but as part of the cultural supersystem, it is influenced by the premise of culture which is exterior to it.

Thus, because the independent variable is sociocultural and especially because it is exterior to each particular field of knowledge, we can speak with good reason, it seems, of Sorokin *Wissenssoziologie*. However, this system of Sorokin is set in a very different direction, almost in an inverse sense, from that which the Marxist origin of the sociology of knowledge had impressed upon it. Sorokin approaches the immanent conception of intellectual history inasmuch as he admits that ideas must be interpreted above all in terms of antecedents of an intellectual nature. This aspect is one of the most important of Sorokin's system, for it will permit us to see to what degree it is possible to minimize the "revolution" of the sociology of knowledge which consisted in emphasizing the importance of the non-theoretical social determinants of knowledge.

EXTERNAL LIMITATIONS FOR SOROKIN'S SYSTEM OF *WISSENSSOZIOLOGIE*

The Existential Factors

Sorokin does not claim that his independent variables determine mental productions to the exclusion of existential factors. Concerning Mannheim's *Ideology and Utopia,* he writes that the essential characteristic of the mental productions of a thinker is "largely a function of two variables: of the system of truth and reality assumed by the thinker; and of the totality of his existential, especially socio-cultural, conditions." Furthermore, Sorokin indicates clearly that existential determination is secondary. "If the existential conditions (in which there are several thinkers) are similar, the theories will display a series of similarities, at least in secondary points, in spite of the dissimilarity of their major premise."[2]

This importance — but secondary importance — of external factors is affirmed again in other places in his work. Thus, "the endorsement of the immanent principle of change does not hinder a recognition of the role of the external forces in the change of the sociocultural sphere."[3] Or again, an "additional reason for change of a system is its milieu."[4] Elsewhere he notes the influence of the profession upon the philosophy of life; of the type of family upon ideas, norms and values; of the sociocultural influence upon mental development.[5]

Besides these affirmations of the role of the existential, non-theoretical factors, we find two points in Sorokin's general sociology in which the importance of these factors is particularly emphasized and from which a sociology of knowledge of a "traditional" tendency could be originated.

The first support for a *Wissenssoziologie* other than the one which has been effectively developed by Sorokin could be found in Sorokin's conception of the generic sociocultural phenomenon. It is remembered that the latter was made up of three components: (a) meanings, values and norms; (b) vehicles (physico-chemical and biological phenomena) which objectify these meanings; (c) interacting human agents. Now the vehicles are not merely passive carriers of meanings; they have an influence upon the latter also. A good example of this retroactive influence is given by Durkheim. An identical juridical rule expressed in written law and in non-written law acquires a double meaning after a certain time, or, more accurately, the original rule disappears and is replaced by two new rules which are different from each other.[6] These changes and this differentiation in meanings are due to the fact that the same meaning was conveyed by two different vehicles.

A different phenomenon, but one somewhat similar to the preceding one, is worthy of notice here. The existing vehicles influence the creation of new vehicles and hence influence meanings indirectly. Spencer relates that the English green-grocers of his time used to shorten *artichokes* to *chokes* and to change *asparagus* into *asparagrass, sparrowgrass* and finally *grass.* Now this appearance of new verbal vehicles is due to the general characteristics of the sounds of the English language which, as it were, left hardly any other possibilities of simplification than the ones cited. But these "new" words already existed and had a meaning by themselves (*choke* means suffocation and *grass,* the common herbage of the field). Whence comes the fact that these abbreviations, by evoking former meanings, will change the meaning of these concepts somewhat. As Spencer points out, some day philologists will probably explain that the word *choke* given to a food must refer to some effect which comes from swallowing it, and that the word *grass* applied to asparagus comes from an erroneous classification of this plant among herbage in general.[7]

This is not yet *Wissenssoziologie,* but Sorokin's idea that vehicles have a direct or indirect modifying action upon the meanings they objectify[8] is a sound basis upon which might be developed a sociology of knowledge which would look for the non-theoretical factors that influence our knowledge.

The second possible point of support for a "traditional" sociology of knowledge is found in the Sorokin theory of the structure of personality. This theory offers, moreover, a great interest in itself.[9]

Sorokin distinguishes four levels in the personality. First, there is that of the supra-sensory and transcendental self; then, the conscious, sociocultural level; third, the conscious biological level; finally, the unconscious biological level composed of drives, reflexes and instincts. Sorokin, in his treatise on sociology, does not turn his attention to the supra-empirical self. It belongs, he says, to metaphysics and religion. He pays scarcely any more attention to the third and the fourth level of personality. They merely express consciously and unconsciously the biological composition of the

human organism and its physical needs. There is no reason to introduce a unique and mysterious Freudian "id." There is no mystery
in being impelled to eat when we are hungry, in trying to avoid
pain when we are suffering and in satisfying our sexual impulse
when it is intense. Furthermore, there is not a unique principle
like the libido or the death instinct. It would be more exact to
speak of a plurality of biological egos, each one corresponding to
an instinct, a tendency or a need at this level. The proof of this
multiplicity is that two biological egos can be in conflict: a soldier
is impelled by hunger to forage in enemy territory and is curbed
by his biological need of preserving life.[10]

Above this biological level is the domain of the sociocultural
ego. This distinction is nothing else but the very ancient idea of
human dualism. The ancients used to speak of the conflict between
the flesh and the spirit or of egoism and altruism, of pleasure and
duty. Just as on the biological level, there is, on this sociocultural
plane, plurality of egos, as William James has demonstrated very
well.[11] Sorokin — and this is very important from the point of
view of the sociology of knowledge — links these different egos to
the different social groups to which the same physical individuality
belongs. These different egos may appear confused because of
the integrating functions of a single nervous system. In reality, an
individual possesses a family ego in terms of which he behaves in a
certain way toward his relatives, a professional self which plays
the dominant role when the individual is at the place where he
works. This self gives place to a religious self when attending
church or to a self of diversion when one is at the theater or at a
concert.[12]

The origin of these different *egos* or *roles* (Sorokin occasionally
employs this last term also) lies in the fact that each individual
in a very differentiated and stratified society like ours belongs to a
multiplicity of organized groups, each one claiming certain pre-
stations and conferring certain rights. One must have a professional
self if one wishes to continue to carry on one's professional activity. If one does not have the ideas, the beliefs and aspirations
required by the group, if one does not accomplish what it expects,
one cannot remain a member of it. Finally, the possible lack of
harmony between the expectations of the various groups to which
the individual belongs, explains the contrasts and even the contradictions in the conduct of the same individual. "Not infrequently

they are as great as those between Dr. Jekyll and Mr. Hyde. There is little in common between Robespierre tenderly weeping in his apartment over the sentimental novels of Bernardin de Saint Pierre and the pitiless Robespierre in the Convention."[13]

Considering the personality on the sociocultural plane as composed of several egos which each correspond to a role in a social group, is a conception that brings us near the *Wissenssoziologie* of Marxist origin. "Voluntary or involuntary membership in any organized group, whether it is the family, the church, the state, political party, club, or association, quite definitely influences our ideas and beliefs, our values, standards, and emotions, our volitions and overt actions."[14] This is different from Mannheim's system. More especially, it is not a question of collective struggle for economic or political power, but it is a formal recognition of the influence of social affiliation upon ideas.

Let us note another aspect of this conception of personality which has its importance from the point of view of a more "traditional" sociology of knowledge. *Wissenssoziologie,* from its origin, has placed considerable insistence upon the part irrationality plays in man. If man were considered a completely rational being, we cannot see how non-theoretical social factors would be able to act upon his knowledge. Now one of the consequences of Sorokin's doctrine on the structure of personality is that he seems to recognize in man a greater margin of irrationality than when he speaks of cultural integration.

In fact, if the lack of harmony between the requirements of various groups of which the same individual forms a part is translated into conflict and contradiction between his various social egos, we may expect a rather large number of inconsistencies.

This explains also why not only the plain citizen but even the most prominent thinkers and leaders display so many contradictions in their speeches, writing and actions. . . . When Hegel acts as a member of humanity and as a participant of the World Geist, he talks of the world-court as a supreme judge of all states and governments. When he speaks as a member of the Prussian State, he makes the Prussian State the supreme and final goal of universal history. When Karl Marx speaks in terms of humanity, he talks of the movement from unfreedom to freedom, of classless society, and so on. When he functions as a member of the proletarian class, he appears the ardent ideologist of the dictatorship of the proletariat.[15]

In order not to give an inaccurate impression of the share of inconsistency which Sorokin recognizes in man, let us note that the sociocultural personality of an individual is not only a pure juxtaposition of all his social roles. No individual can absorb all the cultural elements of his milieu. In one fashion or another, he must choose some of them and reject the rest. This selection can be made in an active way: by comparison or even creation.[16] In this selective activity, there is a possibility for the individual to make his tendency toward logical consistency play a part.

We may conclude that this conception of the structure of personality, admitting a plurality of egos corresponding to social affiliations, is also a point of Sorokin's general sociology starting with which a *Wissenssoziologie* somewhat akin to that of Mannheim might be elaborated.

Such is the first limitation of Sorokin's system of sociology of knowledge. Existential conditions play an important although secondary role along with cultural premises. Besides, his general sociology offers two supports for an inquiry into the existential conditioning of knowledge.

THE LAWS OF IMMANENT DEVELOPMENT

These laws constitute the second limit to the conditioning of mental productions by the premises of culture. The progress of biology, for example, will not be determined solely by, first, the premise of culture, and then, by existential social factors (such as the social affiliation of the biologists, the place of this discipline in the academic organization, or the needs of society). Besides these two factors recognized by Sorokin, he admits a third one which is the internal law of the development of biology (such a discovery gives rise to such a theory which itself directs research toward such and such a sector, etc.). This is but the application of the principle of immanent change, no longer on the level of the cultural supersystem, but on that of a scientific discipline which is also a cultural system.

As soon as we admit the existence of systems, we must recognize immanent laws in them. This is the case for Professor Znaniecki's *closed systems*. They are relatively isolated from external influences thanks to their structure. Their changes are due mainly but not exclusively to internal influences.[17] Likewise, for Professor Kluckhohn, a culture, because it is a going concern, manifests some independence from the external forces with which it is in interaction.[18]

The principle of immanent change has a value for any system and applies more perfectly the better integrated the system is.[19] Among the integrated systems — that is to say those whose parts are interdependent to such a degree that the elimination of one of the parts tangibly influences the remainder of the whole[20]— philosophic disciplines, scientific doctrines, juridical constructions, ethical systems, etc., occupy a choice position.[21] The result is then that they enjoy a large degree of autonomy or of auto-determination with respect to existential factors and premises of culture at the same time. This last point is clearly admitted by Sorokin.

Many (scientific theories) can fluctuate independently of our main variables, within their limited sphere of autonomy and the immediate mental atmosphere of their compartment.[22] Due to the principle of autonomy of any really integrated system, each of the integrated currents of culture mentality studied should be expected to have some margin . . . of an independent movement not completely related to the other currents and compartments of culture.[23]

In his positive studies, Sorokin also underlines this autonomy which may be very broad in certain cases. Thus, for instance, he notes that the fluctuations of cosmogonic theories concerning the center of the world (heliocentrism and geocentrism) have been independent to a very large degree of the fluctuations of cultural supersystems. The oscillations in this field show at the very most a slight tendency toward the domination of the heliocentric system in periods of sensate culture, and a preponderance of the geocentric system in periods of ideational culture.[24] Even when it is a question of mental productions whose fluctuations are more closely linked to cultural premises, Sorokin indicates that if the curves show the same general tendencies, the secondary fluctuations of lesser amplitude are independent.[25] Concerning the set of sensate and ideational variables he has studied in the field of knowledge, he points out that their principal movements indicate a tangible parallelism. "This association is imperfect, however, due first to the principle of the margin of autonomy and internal self-regulation possessed by any integrated system; and also to interference of other (cosmic and biological) forces that may decrease or break the logically expected association."[26]

We see in what sense existential factors and laws of immanent change are external limitations for Sorokin's system of sociology: mental productions are not conditioned solely by the premises of culture, but also by these two other kinds of factors. Sorokin does not give his attention to studying the latter experimentally. He is content to call attention to them. He attempts to bring to light only cultural premises. This position is perfectly legitimate. A system of sociology of knowledge does not have to claim to be a *complete explanation* of the origin of mental productions, but such a system must simply try to determine accurately the degree of influence social factors have upon mental productions. A system of sociology of knowledge does not have to claim either to be a *complete sociological explanation* of the origin of ideas, that is to say, to consider that social factors *alone* take account of the origin of ideas.[27]

INTERNAL LIMITATIONS FOR SOROKIN'S SYSTEM OF *WISSENSSOZIOLOGIE*

Let us turn now to the factor examined by Sorokin: cultural premises. The whole of Sorokin's dynamic sociology is an explanation of the fluctuations of sociocultural phenomena by the changes in philosophic attitudes. This is an idealistic conception (in the sense of the colloquial expression: "ideas lead the world"). Sorokin attempts to make precise and to extend as far as possible the sphere of the conditioning of social phenomena by philosophic ideas. It is extremely interesting to see the results of this attempt in the field of mental productions: to what degree do philosophic ideas lead the world of knowledge? We know already that they are not the only determining factors. Let us see now more directly *which* of the mental productions the cultural premises condition.

THE PHILOSOPHIC ASPECT OF MENTAL PRODUCTIONS

As has been observed above,[28] the influence of the cultural premises is exerted at a certain level: that of the philosophic meaning of the various mental productions. In other words, when confronted with a biological or juridical theory, or any mental production whatsoever, we ask ourselves: can it convey a philosophic sense? Can it imply a position with respect to the fundamental questions (nature of man, of the world, etc.)? If the answer is yes, it is located with respect to the ontological question (of the ultimate nature of reality). In such a case, the logical relationships between dependent and independent variables are *relationships between philosophic ideas*. Let one cast a glance at the list of mental productions influenced by the premises of culture. Not only do all have a philosophic meaning, but many are themselves philosophic tendencies: idealism-materialism; eternalism-temporalism; realism-conceptualism-nominalism; determinism-indeterminism; conceptions of truth, etc. When the mental production is not susceptible of being interpreted philosophically, it is not conditioned by the cultural premise. That is the reason why the influence of cultural premises upon the fluctuations of heliocentrism and geocentrism is so slight.[29] This system of sociology of knowledge remains within a philosophy.

This is the reason for the reproach of tautology which was pronounced against this system, especially by Professor Merton.[30] He gives the following example of this: Sorokin begins his *Wissenssoziologie* by showing that a different gnosiological system corresponds to each culture: "In a sensate society and culture, the sensate system of truth based upon the testimony of the organs of senses has to be dominant."[31] Now in the definition of the sensate mentality, it has been said that the sensate mentality views reality as only that which is presented to the sense organs.[32]

This accusation of tautology can be rejected. In the indicated passage from the first book of the *Dynamics* (AI), Sorokin gives a general description of the whole of sensate culture. Then, in the second book (AJ), he demonstrates that the various sensate traits of the description are truly realized. In a certain sense, the establishment by the facts of a meaningful relationship may always be said to be tautological. In fact, if it is meaningful for A to be linked to B, it is because, in a certain fashion, B is logically contained in A. Thus, when a correlation has been shown between the curves of the sensate culture and of the system of the truth of the senses,[33] it may always be said that the system of the truth of the senses was comprised in the sensate premises and hence that the discovery claimed is tautological. But then we must admit that only the discoveries of inexplicable relationships (in regard to the present state of the theoretical elaboration of a science) are not tautological. In this case, the reproach of tautology would include, besides Sorokin, almost all the social scientists.

If the Sorokin system gives rise to the reproach of tautology more than others, it is because, in the field of knowledge, its dependent and independent variables are located on the philosophic plane. Besides, their meanings are sometimes very close. Let us take, for instance, the correlation between ideational culture and idealism, sensate culture and materialism.[34] There is, certainly, a difference between saying that the ultimate reality is sensate and saying that it is material. But nobody will be astonished to learn that the curves expressing the fluctuations of the sensate premise and of materialism are parallel. The contrary rather would be surprising.

The fact that dependent and independent variables may be philosophic is not a defect of Sorokin's system, but it constitutes a limit restricting the significance of his sociology of knowledge. In fact, it will never be able to explain anything but the philosophic aspect of mental productions. Probably a good number of mental productions have a philosophic aspect and this aspect is more fundamental and more extensive than we usually think. It is no slight credit for Sorokin's work to have brought to light this level implicit in physical and biological theories, but, as a matter of fact, everything does not have a philosophic aspect and the mental productions which have this aspect have other ones too.

RATIONAL RELATIONSHIPS BETWEEN VARIABLES

Within this limitation, a second one may be outlined, which narrows the bearing of the Sorokin system. It has to do with "logico-meaningful" relationships.

We said above that these logical relationships are not relationships of a rigorous and critical logic moving from principles to necessary consequences, but rather of a logic which passes from the principle to one of the possible consequences.

On the other hand, we stressed the fact that Sorokin really meant by his "logico-meaningful" method to establish rational relationships between the meanings of sociocultural phenomena and not only meaningful relationships in terms of emotional or unconscious "logic" like the frustration-aggression sequence. He wants to establish relationships which are valid from the point of view of reason.[35]

Thus, in reality, each one of the three forms of culture constitutes a philosophic system: the principle is the independent variable; the consequences are the various dependent variables and the relationships between both of these are rational, since they are valid for any mind independently of circumstances of time and space.[36]

One might object that this is not a second limitation. Can one conceive — between variables susceptible of a philosophic sense — of relationships which cannot be perceived by any mind? It seems so. Historical circumstances can establish intelligible relationships between meanings which do not have any such relationships, from the point of view of a mind claiming to transcend time and space. In other words, a mind participating in such a culture can perceive a logical connection between two ideas although, for a mind sharing in another culture, there is none.

Here is an example. Sorokin concludes from the study of the fluctuations of heliocentrism and geocentrism that they reveal scarcely any correlation with the fluctuations of cultural premises. There is indeed a slight tendency toward the domination of heliocentrism during sensate periods and of geocentrism during ideational periods. However, he adds, it would be incorrect to affirm the reality of this association, for the facts are not decisive and for *the correlation does not follow logically from the cultural premises* (the emphasis is ours).[37] Of course, from a purely rational point of view, ideationalism does not imply that the center of the material universe is the sun rather than the earth. However, when the sacred books of a religion locate the most important event in the history of the world on the earth, a geocentric cosmology becomes logically consistent with that ideational religion. For an occidental mind of the tenth century, there was probably an evident connection between the ideational Christian premise of his culture and geocentrism.

Another example is furnished by the fluctuations of a biological theory, that of the spontaneous generation of life (abiogenesis). Sorokin outlines briefly the fluctuations from Anaximander to Pasteur. In the course of this history, the idea of spontaneous generation knows periods of success and abandonment. These oscillations appear completely independent of the dominant cultural premises. Sorokin is not surprised by this. On the contrary, he says, "the very nature of this theory is such that logically it can be associated with any of the three systems of truth and, on the other side, it is not associated definitively with any of them."[38] In fact, he continues, the spontaneous generation of life can be considered as a miracle accomplished regularly by mysterious supra-sensory forces, something which is very suitable to ideational culture. In another connection, to hold that the living can be born only from the living seems also to be the admission of a miracle. Of course purely rationally, we can reason in this way, but this is no longer true when ideas are placed in a historical context. Thus, in Occidental Catholic countries at the end of the last century and at the beginning of this one, popular opinion saw a logical connection between materialism and abiogenesis, on the one hand, and between faith and the negation of spontaneous generation, on the other.

Our conclusion will again be that it is perfectly legitimate to consider only rational relationships between variables. Only this has as its result the bringing of a limitation as to what such a sociology of knowledge may attain, for between various meanings susceptible of a philosophic sense, there are other logical or intelligible relationships than rational relationships.

The Macroscopic Point of View

Sorokin studies the cultural pulsations of twenty-five centuries. Such a study cannot be made with the microscope. Therefore, his unities cover several centuries of a whole as vast as Graeco-Roman, then occidental civilization. It could not be otherwise. If the sociologist of knowledge envisages making his research bear upon objects covering millennia and continents, very large categories will be necessary for him. If, on the contrary, he seeks to clarify the relations between society and knowledge in a sphere less vast, Sorokin's conceptual tools will have to be adjusted. Left as they are, they could let too many elements escape. It is in this sense that it can be said that Sorokin's macroscopic point of view is a limitation of the relevance of his *Wissenssoziologie*.

First, some differences which are significant from a microscopic point of view are neglected. Thus communism, capitalism, fascism are subsumable under the same category of sensate culture. In the field of art, impressionism and certain reactions to impressionism, such as cubism, futurism, dadaism, etc., are seen as manifestations of the decline of sensate culture and the announcement of a change.[39]

When things are considered from a sufficient distance, it really is thus. But if the object of the study is located within a sensate culture (which can mean, for example, that of the sixteenth to the twentieth century in Europe and America), the use of conceptual tools like the three premises of culture will let a rather large number of differences very important in regard to a narrower frame of reference, escape. This does not mean that Sorokin's categories lose any relevance at this level. For instance, research may very well be done on how the sensate premise is reflected in the mental productions of the French eighteenth century. But if we wish to compare the French eighteenth with the French nineteenth or with the English eighteenth century, it seems that it will be better to define the cultural premises more precisely. This, as we have already noted, is what is realized in Northrop's *Meeting of East and West*. We may indicate by utilizing a more precise philosophic principle how these shorter periods are not only more or less sensate, but are sensate in a different way.

In the same connection, it may be worthy to note that the concept of dominant culture is fully valid only from a macroscopic point of view. When, in summer, we fly over a forest, it seems to be of a uniform green. When we wander through it on foot, we distinguish a scale of very different greens and a fairly large number of other tones besides: the brown of the ground, the gray of the road, the yellow of a clearing, the red or the blue of flowers. At a certain distance, the dominant color drowns all these differences.

It is somewhat the same with Sorokin's sociology of history. The dominant mentalities tend to absorb the differences. These differences exist, however. Even in our hypersensate period, there exist a certain number of mental productions which are not logically subsumable under the sensate premise, but, on the contrary, under the idealistic or ideational premise.

This fact is recognized by Sorokin and his figures bear witness to it. Thus, from 1800 to 1900, the average figure for empiricism (which represents the sensate gnosiological system of the truth of the senses) represents 42.6% of the whole of the epistemological currents. In 1900-1920, it rises to 53%.[40] To a critic[41] pointing out that this figure is astonishingly low to permit the characterization of a period, Sorokin answers[42] that what matters is the increasing development of empiricism passing from 2% in 1400-1420 to 53% in 1900-1920. This increase is very significant, no doubt. However, the figure 53% itself is significant, for it indicates important minority cultures alongside the majority culture.

In 1460-1480, materialism (hylozoistic and mechanistic) has an index of 0%, idealism (pluralist and monist) has an index of

100%, and mixed systems: 0%, of course. From 1900 to 1920, the indices of these three currents are 23.3% for materialism, 40.3% for idealism and 36.4% for mixed systems.[43] Again the increase of materialistic and mixed currents at the expense of the idealistic current is remarkable. However, it is significant also that our sensate period indicates only 23.3% for a variable typically sensate.

For eternalism, the 1900-1920 index is 38% against 49% for temporalism and 13% for the mixed current.[44] Another sensate variable, singularism, indicates 55% from 1900 to 1920 as against 45% for universalism during the same period.[45] These few figures indicate that even in a period which may be styled sensate because the sensate variables are gaining ground, the two other cultural types remain so important as to maintain extremely high percentages, since, with respect to certain variables, they are sometimes superior to the percentages of the dominant culture.

Let us repeat that Sorokin's macroscopic point of view — a point of view which is translated into his very extensive concepts and into his notion of dominant culture — is not only legitimate but required by the nature of the subject matter of his study. But the sociologist who would wish to study the relationships between cultural premises and mental productions in less wide space and time, must remember, to take up Sorokin's comparison again,[46] that the straight lines of a map on a continental scale are wavy on a lesser scale and that, to take a walk in the neighboring countryside, it is not enough to provide oneself with a map of the continent. As we have indicated above, this does not prevent the Sorokin scientific theory from being able to furnish fruitful hypotheses for research on a reduced scale. On the other hand, his quantitative and logico-meaningful method is applicable to microscopic as well as to macroscopic studies.

CONCLUSION: WHAT IS THE MOST IMPORTANT FACTOR?

The cultural premises do not claim to be the only factors which condition mental productions. At least two other factors play a role: the autonomous laws of the particular system (of the scientific discipline, for instance) and the existential conditions. Of these three factors, which is the most important?

For Sorokin, it is certain that the existential factor is the least important. He indicates clearly that the similarity of existential conditions in which two thinkers are located can give rise only to superficial resemblances in their doctrines.[47]

Which one of the other two factors has priority? The degree of autonomy of a system depends upon a fairly large number of elements: the number of human agents who are carriers of the system, their qualities, the efficiency of organization, etc. But the most important of these elements, from the point of view of ideo-logical systems such as those we are considering here, is the degree of integration.[48] Now we know that Sorokin's supersystems are very well integrated. Besides, they are the most extensive we can find. All this gives us grounds for thinking that he considers that the premises of culture are really the most important factors for the determination of mental productions. This seems confirmed by the texts in which Sorokin notes that the degree of autonomy of each compartment takes account of the secondary movements of the curves rather than of the general fluctuations.[49]

Can this order of importance — cultural premise, immanent law of the particular system and existential factors — which corre-sponds well, it seems, with Sorokin's opinion, be proven empiri-cally?

The *Dynamics* suggest an indirect method of measuring, in regard to each current of thought, the comparative importance of the premise of culture, on the one hand, and the whole of the other factors, on the other. When, logically, the correlation between the variables ought to be perfect (that is to say, when the coefficient of correlation ought to be equal to unity) and when, in reality, the coefficient of correlation is only .7 or .5, the difference between these coefficients and unity is an approximate measure of the in-fluence of the factors other than the cultural premise, upon such and such a current of thought.

According to this indirect approach, can one draw general con-clusions concerning the order of importance of the determinants of thought? Since the fluctuations of the diverse variables usually present a high degree of correlation,[50] we can say that in reality the cultural premise truly exercises a predominant influence.

This conclusion is proven, of course, only for the research made by Sorokin. Consequently, it must be interpreted by taking account of the internal limitations of Sorokin's *Wissenssoziologie,* and especially by considering that its dependent variables are either philosophic currents or philosophic aspects of mental productions. Within these limits, the facts justify the preponderant place given by Sorokin to cultural premises.

As to what concerns the other factors, we do not have empirical means of determining, even approximately, their respective influence. They are indistinctly joined in a residual category with respect to cultural premises.

CHAPTER ELEVEN

Sorokin's Philosophy of Knowledge

INTRODUCTION: SOROKIN'S POSITION IN REGARD TO PHILOSOPHIC IMPLICATIONS

THIS PART, devoted to the philosophic meaning of the Sorokin *Wissenssoziologie,* will be shorter than the one concerning Mannheim's philosophic theory of knowledge. This is accidental in the sense that this difference is not due to a difference in the fundamental position of our two authors regarding the relevance a sociology of knowledge may have to a philosophic theory of knowledge, and regarding the philosophic sense which must be attributed to an explanation of the results of positive research. The difference is simply that Mannheim has a greater interest in epistemology and gnosiology than in positive sociology. Sorokin, on the contrary, is more interested in constructing a strong, positive sociology of knowledge, and does nothing but point out the philosophy which may be drawn from it. Let us indicate what Sorokin's fundamental position in regard to this question is.

"What is a valid criterion of truth and what is not is, . . . in a considerable degree, a function of the sociocultural variable. If this be found valid, then the sociologist should have his say also in the problems of epistemology and logic."[1] Hence, for Sorokin, the fact of having proved that mental productions and especially concepts of truth are logically coherent with cultural premises has a philosophic significance.

It is remembered that we interpreted Sorokin's explanation as a scientific theory. In our criticism, we have asked ourselves merely to what degree the conclusions of positive research can be deduced from these principles and we have left the eventual intrinsic validity of his principles in parentheses. But, like Mannheim, Sorokin does not make this distinction between a hypothetical and a real explanation. He indicates more than once that he does not like constructions of the type "as if." "When scientists declare that they are not concerned with reality and make their schemes 'as if they were corresponding to the reality' they turn reality, science and truth into mere fiction, into a mere *als ob,* a mere expedient and arbitrary 'construct.' If science is not concerned with the reality, then what is it concerned with?"[2]

This rather polemical passage condemns a science which would be entirely hypothetical rather than scientific hypotheses themselves. We cite it simply to show that Sorokin has no inclination toward any kind of "as if" construction. He then very naturally intends, like Mannheim, that his explanation be taken for something else than a convenient explanatory principle.

Now if we take Sorokin's three explanatory principles at their face value (saying that positive research gives such results because reality *is* like that), they include a good share of philosophy. The principle of the logical consistency of the human mind, when it is considered as expressing reality, is located on the psychological rather than the philosophic plane. Philosophic conclusions can, of course, be drawn from it, but by itself it does not express what the nature of the human mind is, but rather a phenomenal characteristic of human psychology.

The affirmation of the partial validity of cultural systems (comprising metaphysical premises and the various concepts of truth) has philosophic significance when it is not considered hypothetical. We shall have occasion to return to this point subsequently. Finally, the principle of immanent and dialectical change is not considered a mere logical principle,[3] since it regulates the evolution of sociocultural phenomena. The connection established by Sorokin between this principle and the "gigantic, impersonal, spontaneous forces"[4] of the historical process, and, on the other hand, the high esteem in which he holds Hegelianism, which he considers one of the most perfect theories of immanent change,[5] suggest that this explanatory principle has a philosophic significance also, when the question of intrinsic value is not set aside.

Since Sorokin asserts that his sociology of knowledge can have a philosophic meaning, we are going to try to determine what its epistemological and gnosiological implications are.[6]

HOW THE PROBLEM OF TRUTH ARISES

Positive research has permitted the conclusion that mental productions, in their philosophic aspect, present different characteristics in the three types of culture. Among these mental productions, the concepts and criteria of truth are especially interesting for the epistemologist and the philosopher of knowledge.

In the course of the history of the Western world, three notions of truth dominate in turn. All three have this in common: they consider truth as an adequation between a thing and an idea, but they are differentiated from each other with regard to the criteria of validity. For some, it is the senses which must judge this conformity, which, of course, reduces reality to matter. For others, it is intuition which must judge conformity and, in this case, reality will be supra-sensory and an object of revelation. Finally, others confer upon reason the mission of determining whether the idea is adequate to reality. The latter will be then considered as subsumable under logical categories.[7]

No one of these conceptions is thoroughly all-embracing in the sense that no one of them generally denies any value to other criteria than its own, but, nevertheless, they are contradictory in the sense that each one insists upon the last word for its criterion. It is that which is important, for when there is a conflict between what is in conformity with reality according to one criterion and not in conformity according to another, each culture will decide the truth differently. But this raises the inescapable question: which of these conceptions of truth is right?

FIRST REPLY: INTEGRALISM

Sorokin affirms that all three systems of truth are valid, at least in part.

The criterion utilized by Sorokin to justify this affirmation is, we remember, the degree of adaptation which each system permits its human agents to realize. It is a satisfactory adaptation since society survives, but imperfect because we feel the need of change from time to time. This very pragmatic way of judging the truth of a concept might furnish, it seems, the criterion which would permit us to choose, from among the three concepts of reality, the one which is really the best.

We must note first that Sorokin does not at all like to have truth grounded upon pragmatic criteria.

When these dominant currents declare that scientific propositions are mere "conventions," and of several different conventions that which under the circumstances is most convenient, or most "economical" or expedient, or more useful, or more "operational" for you or me is most true, they obliterate the boundary between the true and the false, undermine truth and knowledge itself.[8]

Then — and this is most important — this criterion of adaptation merely means that each one of the systems of truth is partly qualified to assure the preservation of the society which adopted it, since, in reality, sensate, ideational and idealistic societies have maintained themselves for a long time. This criterion shows us simply that no one of these three cultures is "anti-natural" to the point of preventing the preservation of society except during the decadence of these cultures. But this is not enough to constitute an ultimate criterion, for it does not seem possible to determine precisely which of the three cultures permits the best adaptation. Thus Sorokin writes that the predominance of the total indices of idealism over materialism "may perhaps be interpreted as an indication that, all in all, a certain predominance of idealism over materialism is necessary for the continued existence of human culture and society."[9]

The affirmation of the validity of the three concepts of truth is expressed by the term integralism. Sorokin means by this an epistemological position asserting that there are three types of truth, each one corresponding to a system and to a criterion.

He expresses this integralism in various ways, for instance in a concrete form taken from a novel of Anatole France in which it is said (it is the devil speaking!) that the whole truth is white. This means that it is composed of all colors of the spectrum.[10]

On the plane of sociology, Sorokin speaks also of "integral sociology." In the *Sociocultural Causality, Space, Time,* he traces an outline of the principles of such a sociology[11] but his best account of it is found in the *Dynamics.*[12] He means to show that there are three valid sources of truth: the sense organs, reason and intuition. The value of the first two sources is generally admitted. Intuition and the truth of faith which is derived from it is much less accepted. Such being the case, Sorokin devotes several pages to showing its importance and value.

He takes up the definition of K. W. Wild to express what is

common to, and fundamental in, any intuition: the immediate awareness by the knower of some reality without the intervention of the senses or reason to account for that awareness.[13] Now, Sorokin says, such an intuitive view is found at the very origin of rational activity, for the acceptance of the first principles rests solely upon an immediate consciousness of their value. In the second place, intuitive views have been at the point of departure of an enormous number of the most important scientific, philosophic and mathematical discoveries. He cites the testimony, among others, of Meyerson and Newton, and he recounts the story of the discovery of the fuchsian functions by Henri Poincaré. Besides, religious and mystical intuitions have been at the origin of artistic, religious and ethical systems.[14]

Such is Sorokin's epistemological integralism. It affirms the validity of the three systems of truth and especially of their sources. However, the difficulty remains: the three systems are contradictorily opposed to each other in the sense that each one of them claims to retain the decisive and ultimate value for its criterion. Integralism does not solve this problem. It makes it more difficult rather by clearly affirming the three competing positions.

SECOND REPLY: RELATIVISM

When one is confronted with such a situation, it seems that there is place only for relativism. Each one of the three systems ought to be legitimately considered ultimate when it is a question of judging mental productions belonging to the same culture. We should have then to judge the various elements of a culture in terms of its own conception of truth. A Marxist critic of Sorokin estimates that his system taken seriously must lead to the admission that each type of mentality has a point of view which is legitimate in its own frame of reference.[15] Another critic estimates that Sorokin has not escaped relativism any more than Mannheim has.[16]

Certain texts of the *Dynamics* suggest this sense without any doubt. Sorokin points out more than once that the condemnations of the mental productions of an epoch stem from the fact that they are judged in terms of the criteria of truth of another.[17] He emphasizes especially that the lack of understanding in our era of other conceptions of truth than the sensate conception leads it to deny any value to different mental productions. Our contemporaries persist in wanting to judge everything from their point of view, which they naively assimilate with the truth.[18] For instance, he expresses in a note an hypothesis concerning a difference of sensitivity in the nervous system of ideational and sensate individuals (the first would have a lesser sensitivity of the exteroceptive organs and the second would have a less well-developed interoceptive system). Now he indicates that this hypothesis is made from a purely sensate point of view,[19] which gives us to understand that its validity could not be taken into consideration in an idealistic or ideational perspective.

It is certain that admitting a plurality of contradictory and partly valid criteria would easily lead to relativism. However, in spite of the few clues we have just noted, Sorokin is not relativistic. He affirms that the fluctuations of systems of truth do not lead in any manner to a relativistic or skeptical position.[20] In fact, the idea of the relative value of each principle with respect to its culture is utilized mainly against the participants in the sensate culture in order to defend the value of the mental productions of the two other cultures. There is certainly a potential relativism in Sorokin's sociology of knowledge, but it is not actualized.

But to reject relativism does not solve the problem of truth in any respect. We are again at integralism: the three conceptions are valid. But we still have to resolve their opposition.

THE DOUBLE PRINCIPLE OF SOROKIN'S SOLUTION

Relativism being out of the question, Sorokin offers us a solution which really combines two solutions in a more or less felicitous manner. We are going to explain them separately.

METARATIONALISM

To express what we mean by this rather inelegant term, let us begin with a summary of Sorokin's metaphysical position.

If we ask him the essential question he himself has addressed to so many thinkers: "what is the ultimate reality?", he will answer that it is an infinite and inexhaustible manifoldness. The absolute is, he says, for all the great thinkers regardless to what school they belong, an inexhaustible infinite. Moreover, this idea of the unsoundable richness of the real moves him to enthusiasm.[21]

This infinite reality is beyond all we can say about it. It is metalogical and metarational. He likes to cite mystical writers like the pseudo-Dionysius, Gregory Nazianzen, Master Eckhart and especially John Scotus Erigena and Nicolas of Cusa. He judges that one of the best notions of divinity is expressed by the formula of Nicolas of Cusa: *coincidentia oppositorum. Deus est supra nihil et aliquid.*

> The Absolute is the End ending all things, the End whereof there is no end, and thus an end without end, or infinite. This eludeth all reason because it implies a contradiction. Thus, when I assert the existence of an end, I admit darkness to be light, ignorance to be knowledge and the impossible to be a necessity. . . . Thus we admit the coincidence of contradictions, above which is the infinite.[22]

Thus the ultimate reality embraces, unites and reconciles in itself the rational and the irrational, the law of identity and of contradiction. No category of our thought (laws, logics, space, time, substance, causality, etc.) is applicable to it. It is beyond any specification and definition. It is the reason for the famous phrase of Erigena: *Deus itaque nescit se, quid est, quia non est quid.* Since any specification and definition is a limitation, no limitation is applicable to the infinite and the unlimited.[23]

These quotations show Sorokin's insistence upon the inability to know the ultimate reality because it is infinite while our knowledge is finite. Of course, as he says, many philosophers have affirmed our incapacity to have an adequate knowledge of the infinite reality. But only the philosophers belonging to a mystical tradition have insisted — as Sorokin does — upon the fact that we cannot know anything about this infinite reality because it transcends the principles and laws of our knowledge. Thus Sorokin's metarationalism is in line with that of the great mystics who, at the same time that they affirm the existence of an Absolute, conceive of it as completely unknowable by our reason.[24]

But, it could be said, how can this metarationalism solve our problem of the agreement of the three contradictory criteria of truth? At first sight, we don't see how it can.

Sorokin does not seem to limit to God this characteristic of being the coincidence of contradictories. We have noted above that he does not distinguish between ultimate reality and true reality. This leads him very naturally to extend the characteristics of the ultimate reality to any true reality. Thus he will cite as a testimony of the inexhaustibleness of reality the words of Sir Isaac Newton concerning the limitation of scientific knowledge.[25] After having explained the fluctuations of physical and biological theories, he concludes his chapter by noting that his insistence upon the fluctuations does not imply any skepticism on his part, but simply that the whole and complete truth is "white" and can be accessible only to the divine mind. He continues as follows:

These eternal oscillations . . . mean that we are almost always in close touch with the ultimate reality, in spite of our inability to grasp it fully. . . . The whole truth is infinite in its aspects and unfathomable in its depth. It is more worth our while to be in partial possession of such an infinite value that to be in complete possession of something which is . . . limited and finite.[26]

The following quotation shows also that it is not only a question of divine reality, but of any reality. "The reality given by the integral three-dimensional truth, with its sources of intuition, reason and the senses, is a nearer approach to the infinite metalogical reality of the *coincidentia oppositorum* than the purely sensory, or purely rational, or purely intuitional reality, given by one of the systems of truth and reality."[27]

We see how Sorokin passes from the inexpressible characteristic of the ultimate reality of the metaphysicians and the mystics to the inexpressible characteristic of the reality studied by the sciences. It seems to be in the same line to assert that valid pieces of knowledge bearing on this reality may be contradictory since any authentic reality is inexpressible and of an unsoundable depth. Just as contradictory assertions concerning the divine nature can be harmonized in this nature which is *coincidentia oppositorum,* so the three sources of truth providing man as a knower with contradictory elements of knowledge can be harmonized in the reality they express, for the latter is also an infinite diversity.

It is not perhaps inopportune to note here a certain affinity between this idea of the possibility of contradictory assertions concerning the authentic reality and another explanatory principle of Sorokin: that of immanent change. Taken dialectically, it means, on the logical plane, that any concept contains its own negation. But it is also a law of reality, since historically the cultural supersystems obey it. Reality itself also contains its own negation. Is this not a confirmation of the fact that reality can be the object of contradictory affirmations? Sorokin himself puts the principle of immanent change together with the name of Erigena and Nicolas of Cusa. For them, it must be noted, any concept is also a *coincidentia oppositorum.*[28]

Let us note that Sorokin does not assert that his integralist conception of three valid and contradictory truths is explained by a metarationalism which locates the final reduction of the oppositions in the infinitely diverse reality. This is an interpretation. As we have already noted, Sorokin pays scarcely any attention to expressing in an elaborate fashion the consequences of his sociological system for the philosophy of knowledge, and the little he says about it is not exempt from a certain lack of precision. In such circumstances, an interpretation must necessarily make explicit what is implicit, and pass from certain principles to their consequences. We must not be astonished then by the fact that it says more than what it interprets. We believe, however, that it does not falsify what it claims to explain.

SOVEREIGN COMPETENCE OF EACH CRITERION IN ITS SPHERE

This second solution offered to the opposition of the contradictory and valid criteria of truth is much more classic. It consists in distinguishing different fields of knowledge and in assigning to each system of truth its own dominant field. So we have three fields of knowledge and in each one of the three, one of the criteria will have the last word.

At the beginning of his *Wissenssoziologie,* Sorokin had said that he was not starting with the distinction between religious, philosophic and scientific thought, because the difference between the three systems of truth is the only fundamental one. If the system of truth utilized in religion, philosophy and science is the same, there will be no logical distinction between these three realms. If, on the contrary, each one of these disciplines corresponds to one of the systems of truth, their distinction will have a logical foundation.[29]

At the end of the last volume of the *Dynamics,* Sorokin gives a reply to this question. The empirico-sensory aspect of reality is given by the truth of the senses; the rational aspect, by the truth of reason and the supra-rational aspect, by the truth of faith.[30] This is tantamount to relating the three systems of truth to three fields which are customarily termed scientific, philosophic and religious.

This attribution to each one of the three criteria of truth of a sphere of competence in which it is dominant permits us to solve the paradox of valid and contradictory truths, at least to a certain degree. For certain scientific truths contradict or seem to contradict certain philosophies or revealed truths. But by setting aside these conflicts which perhaps are but pseudo-conflicts, most of the oppositions disappear in this separation of fields.

In spite of the importance of this solution, Sorokin does not emphasize it. He does nothing but mention it. This is to be explained partly by the fact that he does not pay very much attention in general to the epistemological consequences of his sociology. Since he hardly emphasizes the problem of the opposition of contradictory and valid criteria, it is normal for him to scarcely emphasize its solution. However, he insists more upon certain other aspects of his philosophy, such as his metarationalism, for instance. Besides, he points out what unites the different fields, and this tends to minimize the significance of the solution. Each one of the systems of truth, if it is separated from the others, becomes less valid, even in the specific field of its competence. The sense organs unchecked by reason and intuition can only give us a chaotic mass of impressions, of sensations. . . . They become very limited instruments of knowledge even of the sensory aspect of reality. Likewise, pure dialectics can give us an impeccable syllogism or a mathematical deduction, but such a syllogism or such a deduction will be empirically valid only if the premises are empirically valid, something which cannot be known by the truth of reason.[31] Finally, intuition unchecked by reason and the senses deviates very easily. Whence the necessity for using the three sources of knowledge and, as much as possible, checking one by the others.[32]

Sorokin has sketched this solution in so discreet a way that it seems to have escaped certain of his critics who have seen a contradiction between the value he bestows upon intuition and the manner in which he himself practices science. Hence Dr. Merton is astonished by the fact that, after having affirmed an integralist conception of truth which seeks to assimilate intuition and mystical experience as well as empirical and logical criteria, Sorokin himself adopts the sensate scientific position.[33] Sorokin, he says, asserts that his constructions must be proven in the same manner as any scientific law. First, the principle must be logical by nature. Then, it must emerge triumphant from the proof of facts, that is to say it must fit and represent them. Sorokin even says formally that he will follow the empirical system of truth in his study.[34]

According to the perspective we have just indicated, there is nothing contradictory. Sorokin's work is located in the scientific field, that is to say where the ultimate criterion of truth is that of the senses. Intuition has a role in Sorokin's sociology, but it is that of a source, not a criterion; reason has a very important place in the "logico-meaningful" method. But finally, it must be checked if the logical relationship foreseen by reason actually exists. Thus it is the sensate criterion which decides in the last resort. Sorokin does not then contradict himself in any respect by following a sensate method in sociology since he admits that each one of the three criteria is sovereign in its own field.[35]

Thus the division of the competences of the three truths permits us to solve the paradox of integralism: three valid and contradictory criteria of truth. Let us add, however, that metarationalism accounts for integralism perhaps better than the division of competences. It explains, indeed, why any knowledge will always remain partly valid: because it is finite and reality is infinite. A certain necessary margin of error exists thus in any knowledge, while the division of spheres of competence in which each criterion is sovereign seems to imply that knowledge can be perfectly adequate.

CONCLUSIONS

Such are the implications concerning the problem of truth which Sorokin draws from his sociology of knowledge. Let us repeat once more that, being above all a sociologist, Sorokin does not turn his attention to elaborating a philosophy of knowledge in detail. We must not be astonished then at certain lacks of precision like, for instance, the defect of distinguishing clearly between source of knowledge and criterion of knowledge; between the subordinate real (not the ultimate) and the unreal or the illusory.[36]

The main lines of this theory can be summarized in a few words. It is an integralist conception of knowledge, that is to say one which admits that the three types of truth are valid. The paradox of contradictory truths is solved in two different ways which are not perfectly synthesized.[37] They are, on the one hand, mystical metarationalism founded upon the infinite manifoldness of the real and the finiteness of our knowledge, and, on the other, the attribution of a sovereign field of competence to each one of the criteria of truth.

CHAPTER TWELVE

Evaluation of Sorokin's Philosophy of Knowledge

INTRODUCTION: REMINDER OF THE HYPOTHESIS OF CRITICISM

IN STUDYING Mannheim's gnosiological theories, we have stated a hypothesis of criticism. When a system of sociology of knowledge is closely linked to an epistemology and to a gnosiology, the first question to be examined is the possible ambivalence of the explanatory principles. If this ambivalence is discovered, it will generally be fruitful to center the examination on this point.

An ambivalence is possible because the facts observed and synthesized in a general formula can be deduced from propositions expressed not in mathematical or psychological terms, but in ontological terms, that is to say assertions which set forth principles concerning the profound nature of things. In this case, the proposition, besides its relevance as a scientific theory (being a principle from which scientific laws can be logically deduced), has also a philosophic relevance.

The difference between the two values is not expressed in any way in the content of the principle which remains materially the same. The only difference is in the coefficient of reality which is attached to the principle in question. This explains how easily one can neglect this ambivalence and pass unknowingly from one value to the other.

We know already that such an ambivalence exists in Sorokin's system of sociology of knowledge. Indeed, his explanation is susceptible of philosophic significance,[1] because it concerns the

215

very notion of truth. Besides, we know that Sorokin takes his explanatory principles at their face value, which suggests that he tends to minimize or neglect their ambivalent character. Up to the present time, however, we have not put this scheme of analysis into effect. Let us see if its application will permit us to understand Sorokin's philosophy of knowledge better and to criticize it.

HOW IS INTEGRALISM AMBIVALENT?

Sorokin's arguments in favor of integralism appear to be reduced to two: its conformity with the facts observed and its harmony with his metaphysics. Or, more accurately, integralism may be seen from two points of view: in the perspective of the conclusions of positive research or in the perspective of the metaphysics of infinite Manifoldness.

Sorokin insists upon the explanatory value of integralism The recurrence of three cultural supersystems "seems to be possible only under the condition that each of the three main systems of truth — and the corresponding form of culture — is partly true and partly false, partly adequate and partly inadequate."[2]

It is only because each of them contains a valid part that it gives to its human agents the possibility of adapting themselves to their cosmic, organic and social milieu; that it gives them a minimum of real experience to provide for their wants and that it serves as a foundation for their social and cultural life. But because each one of the three systems is also partly invalid, each one diverts its human agents from reality, at least partly, gives them a pseudo-knowledge in place of a real knowledge and partly prevents the satisfaction of their social and cultural needs.

Hence the reason for the relative stability (each form of culture lasts several centuries) and the recurrence of the three cultural supersystems, is their partial truth. This partial truth or validity is measured in terms of adjustment to reality. "If each of these systems of reality and truth were wholly false, it could not dominate for centuries without leading to the perdition of all its bearers. Still less could each of these systems re-emerge and become dominant again and again."[3]

Let us now consider integralism in the perspective of Sorokin's metaphysics. Reality is infinite. This infinity is not simple. It is, on the contrary, a multiplicity of innumerable aspects. It is probably accessible in its entirety only to the Divine Mind.[4] Human knowledge which is limited and finite will necessarily be inadequate. But, on the other hand, the infinite richness of the aspects of the real suggests that all the means which man possesses of entering into contact with the internal and the external world will attain something real. Reality is of such an inexhaustibleness that each one of our three sources of knowledge could not help reaching something.

We do not claim that integralism can be rigorously deduced from the metaphysical affirmation of the infinite Manifoldness of the real. We simply wish to show that conceiving of numerous and very different means of validly attaining the real presents a considerable connaturality with Sorokin's metaphysics. We perceive their affinity when we consider this epistemological position in Sorokin's metaphysical perspective.

This argument is strengthened still further when one remembers the role of metarationalism in the reduction of the paradox of the systems of truth simultaneously contradictory and valid. Because the real is incommensurate in its Manifoldness, because it is *coincidentia oppositorum,* the opposing pretensions of the criteria are reconciled in the real itself.

Thus we discover two avenues of approach to integralism, one considering it as explaining the facts observed, the other seeing it in the perspective of a metaphysics. The integralism attained by the first route is a scientific theory; that attained by the second, an epistemological or rather a gnosiological position. But in regard to their content, scientific theory and gnosiology are identical: There is but one integralism. Hence, as for Mannheim, there is a continuity from positive science to philosophy. Of course, there are stages on this line, but there is no break. The point of contact where the two fields meet and overlap is integralism. For there to be unbroken continuity, integralism must be considered as one. This is what Sorokin does. To what extent is it possible to separate the two aspects? This is to say: Is it possible to admit Sorokin's sociology of knowledge and not his gnosiology?

SEPARABILITY OF THE TWO ASPECTS

The meeting point being integralism, the question to be solved is: Can one admit integralism as a scientific theory and reject it as a gnosiology? In other words, the facts observed permit us to assert that there are three different conceptions of truth which dominate for long periods of time and repeat themselves. This is explained very well if it is supposed that each one of these concepts of truth is partly valid. We admit integralism then as a hypothesis. Can we reject it as a gnosiology? This means: Things take place as if integralism were an exact philosophic theory of knowledge when in reality it is not.

It is easy to give a theoretical reply which we have already encountered in connection with Mannheim. Since one demands a validity of different order from a scientific theory and from a philosophical doctrine, it is perfectly justifiable to admit a proposition as a theory and to reject it as a philosophy. In fact, integralism will be a good theory if the empirical law can be deduced from it, but it will be a true philosophy only if it expresses the authentic criteria of true knowledge. A theory can be "good" without being "true."

But the "good" theory ought to be "true," because it is more probable that things take place in a manner conforming to their nature rather than not. Since we cannot underestimate this conformity, it requires us to explain, to take account of the fact, that a good theory is not a true philosophy.

The explanation of this fact can be given directly by showing that for one reason or another integralism is a false philosophy; or indirectly, by merely showing that gnosiological positions opposed to integralism are compatible with Sorokin's sociology of knowledge. We are going to follow this second method. The criticism of philosophic doctrines goes beyond the limits of this monograph.

Let us grant a philosopher who defends a positivistic gnosiology. He denies any sort of cognitive value to an intuitive knowledge of the transcendental. Let us suppose, besides, that he admits Sorokin's sociology of knowledge. How may he harmonize his philosophy of knowledge with Sorokin's integralistic explanation? We can imagine that he will give some justification like the following one.

The adaptation of a society to the conditions in which it must live can be made successfully, as Sorokin says, only with a minimum of adequate knowledge of the milieu. "If human beings do not know what is eatable and what is not; if they try mistakenly to eat uneatables and do not eat eatables, and display similar folly in regard to other necessities and phenomena, they very quickly perish, and with them, their society and culture."[5] If they take an enemy for a friend, if they are ignorant of weather signs, they will quickly perish.[6] A minimum of valid knowledge is necessary for everybody to exist for some time. A great deal of it is required for a culture to exist for centuries. But this knowledge which permits survival, our positivist will add, is furnished exactly by what Sorokin calls the sensate conception of truth. However, it does not follow that this adaptation is possible only during periods in which a sensate culture dominates because, actually, even under other cultures, the criterion of the senses (and of empirical reason) continues to function, as Sorokin often recognizes, at least sufficiently to assure the preservation of the social group.[7] If the other two cultures can, however, dominate for a certain length of time and come back into vogue after having disappeared, or at least after having been reduced to a minimum, this is due to the fact that they answer certain rather permanent tendencies in humanity like the need for security or certain social necessities like that of supporting social rules by an inner sanction. The reason why a sensate culture dominates at a certain epoch and an ideational one at another can be sought in an ensemble of factors of all kinds: history, social and economic organization, etc.

But, whatever solutions may be given to these questions, the important point is that it is not the adaptation to the external world which brings success to each system. Thus, we can at one and the same time admit the recurring dominance of each of the three systems and affirm that only the sensate system of knowledge is adequate.

Let us see now how an ideational thinker might harmonize an epistemology which sees the ultimate criterion of truth in conformity with a revelation and Sorokin's system of sociology of knowledge.

His solution will be closely related to that of the positivist, but more radical. He will probably say, Only conformity with the ultimate reality can provide a true knowledge, and in this sense, this knowledge alone permits the ultimate adaptation to the real. But the success of this adaptation will be located on a very high plane. It will be, for example, an adaptation in the sense that a Christian society would be said to be better than a Moslem society in furnishing its members with the opportunity of realizing their destinies.

Success in this domain will then be either union with divinity or peace of mind or salvation in the hereafter. At this level, we shall be able to judge the tree by its fruits and the fruits of ideational conception will be incomparably more numerous than those of the two other conceptions of the world. Unfortunately, this better adaptation will not be easily discernible. This explains why the sensate culture has been able to maintain its domination for such a long time: it answers certain human tendencies, it is "easier" and the ultimate lack of adaptation it engenders is never completely visible.

But there is an adaptation based on another plane: the one which is required to provide for the material survival of the group. This plane is assured, whatever the dominant culture may be, because it little matters whether the world of the senses is the only real one, or whether it is illusory or whether it presents a dependent reality. One acts in the same way in one's relations with it. Even the primeval men in the "prelogical" stage in which they tended to give a magical explanation of all phenomena knew many sequences of cause and effect such as "eating such a type of fruit" and "dying." They knew also the characteristics of the animal species. "Animals of certain species are unable to climb trees. Hence trees are good refuges in respect to them."

Thus our ideational thinker may also simultaneously admit Sorokin's positive sociology and affirm that only the ideational theory of knowledge is true.

These two attempts at conciliating non-integralistic gnosiologies with Sorokin's sociology of knowledge show how scientific theory and philosophy can be dissociated in the case at hand.

Two levels of adaptation must be clearly distinguished. The first is that of adaptation to the ultimate, ontological reality. It is at this level that one may speak of a success in the adaptation which would guarantee the validity of the ideational, idealistic and sensate positions. Only we do not see very well how it is possible practically to measure the success of adaptations of this kind. How shall we know whether or not the ideational Indian civilization allows its bearers a better adjustment to ultimate reality than the sensate Euro-American civilization if one does not *previously* have a conception of what human perfection and hence the ultimate reality is?

Then there is the level of adaptation to the environment. This adjustment is required to assure the preservation of the group. Here, one can easily check the success of this adjustment. But it does not seem to be closely related to the plane on which the cultural systems are located. We must avoid reviving the *baculi argumentum*. "Thrash an idealistic philosopher with blows of a club, certain ones said. Thus he will feel the reality of the external world." This argument misses the point entirely. The question is not to know whether or not this world has any physical reality but whether or not the fundamental reality upon which it depends is thought or being. One would fall into a very similar error if one imagined that the Indian ascetic for whom the world is a dream must, in order to be consistent in regard to this philosophy, behave as if the sensory world surrounding him were made of an evanescent material. He can perfectly well recognize cause and effect in this world, sequences presenting a certain stability, and hence act in consequence, that is to say like the one who believes that there is nothing beyond these appearances, and at the same time affirm that the world is but an illusion in respect to the supreme reality.[8]

In conclusion the success of the adaptation of the social groups under the three cultures does not imply that the philosophic positions proclaimed by these cultures are partly true. This shows that these three philosophic positions have no discernible influence upon the success in adjustment, at least the minimum success which permits the preservation of the group.

This distinction between the two levels of adaptation permits one, it seems to us, to dissociate Sorokin's sociology of knowledge from its gnosiological implications and to take account of that dissociation.

It could be objected that this distinction does not reject only integralism as a philosophy but even as a scientific history since it denies that the facts observed can be deduced from the partial truth of the three cultural supersystems. Is this not tantamount to saying that integralism is not a good principle of explanation?

We do not think so. The reasoning of Sorokin's scientific theory can be schematized in the following syllogism:

A philosophic concept of reality and of truth can maintain itself for a long time and revive only if it is partly adapted and partly unadapted to reality.

Now the three systems of truth and reality have maintained

themselves for a long time and have revived more than once. Hence the three systems of truth are partly adapted and partly unadapted to reality.

This is the basis of Sorokin's explanation. It subsists and is valid. The distinction has merely made it clear that when we are dealing with philosophic systems, the adaptation to the external world which permits the preservation of the group is not significant, but rather the adaptation to the ultimate reality, an adaptation which, unfortunately, is not easily measured.

REMARKS AND CONCLUSION

This criticism is not directed in any way against the validity of an integralist epistemology. We have not attempted to show that integralism, a "good" theory, is a "false" philosophy. We have simply affirmed that admitting integralism as a scientific explanation did not imply that it is admitted as a philosophic theory of knowledge, and we have tried to show how this dissociation could be made. The result is that Sorokin's sociology of knowledge is not sufficient to establish integralism as gnosiology. Hence, if one wishes to prove integralism, other arguments must be employed.

This question completely extends beyond the aim of this work. Our criticism, indeed, does not claim to judge the validity of the philosophic conceptions of the authors we are studying. We are not concerned with the problem of knowing whether or not Sorokin's metarationalism or Mannheim's metaphysics of becoming are true. We try simply to determine to what degree their positive systems of sociology of knowledge imply the epistemological and gnosiological positions they are defending: Sorokin's integralism and Mannheim's relationism. Consequently it is not because we dissociate Sorokin's integralism from his *Wissenssoziologie* that integralism is a false conception of knowledge.

Does Sorokin's conception of knowledge constitute an epistemology or a gnosiology?

The question raised by Sorokin is epistemological. It is asked to what degree each one of the systems of truth attains what it claims to attain: authentic reality. The means by which Sorokin solves this epistemological question is partly epistemological and partly gnosiological. It is partly epistemological, that is to say without relations with a complete philosophic system — with an ontology. Indeed, he attempts to attain integralism as an implication of positive research. It is partly gnosiological because integralism and its complement (not necessary), metarationalism, are related to the conception for which the ultimate reality is an infinite manifoldness.[9]

Thus it can be said that Sorokin's philosophic doctrine concerning knowledge is simultaneously epistemological and gnosiological.[10]

In conclusion, we may say that our hypothesis of criticism centered upon the ambivalence of the theory seems to have manifested its fruitfulness in its application to Sorokin's sociology of knowledge.

It has shown first that the ensemble constituted by the positive *Wissenssoziologie,* the conception of knowledge and Sorokin's ontology manifested much more unity than appeared at first sight, and really made up a whole of great consistency.

Then, it has shown that Sorokin, by ignoring the double significance of his integralism — simultaneously scientific theory and gnosiology — has based his theory of knowledge upon arguments which do not present sufficient solidity.

Finally, by putting in relief the exact import of each element of Sorokin's sociology of knowledge, our method of criticism has permitted us to state precisely each of their respective meanings. By making a distinction between two levels of adaptation to reality, our critical method in this particular case has illuminated the division between scientific and philosophic domains.

CHAPTER THIRTEEN

Conclusions Drawn from the
Study of Sorokin

SOROKIN'S CONTRIBUTION TO THE SOCIOLOGY OF KNOWLEDGE

SOROKIN, unlike Mannheim, has not focused his research upon the sociology of knowledge. The latter has been for him but a chapter, one might almost say, of his study of sociocultural changes. However, his contributions in this field are important. They are of two sorts. Sorokin has, we think, elucidated definitely certain relationships. On the other hand, he has opened new avenues for the sociology of knowledge. Let us consider first what we might call his pioneering contribution.

AVENUES OPENED UP

Quantitative study of mental productions

The insufficiencies and dangers of this method of proof were emphasized above.[1] However, for studies of vast currents of thought, stretching across centuries and continents, it appears indispensable. It alone permits us to avoid the error to which the qualitative method of proof almost inevitably leads and which consists in replacing proofs with a few illustrations corroborating the author's thesis. Now Sorokin is one of the first sociologists to have boldly applied the quantitative method to such a degree in the examination of the movements of ideas. He and his collaborators have not recoiled before the considerable and unusual work which consisted in appraising thousands of thinkers and in deter-

224

mining the currents of ideas in which they have participated. It seems that such a method is of very great intellectual honesty.

But it is above all a pioneering contribution. We mean by this that the lines traced are more important than the results obtained and that if the quantitative study of mental productions is an essential method, the application of this method by Sorokin is not necessarily perfect. We pointed out some of its defects above.[2] Whatever these defects may be, Sorokin has shown the sociologists of knowledge how to utilize the statistical tool in the study of currents of thought. These sociologists know by Sorokin's experiments how to improve it and how to adapt it to the objectives of the particular studies they are pursuing.[3]

The "idealistic" point of view

Sorokin has enlarged the boundaries of the sociology of knowledge by showing that it was possible to construct a system of *Wissenssoziologie* in an "idealistic" perspective — that is to say, to take a mental production as an independent variable. Sorokin's originality, in this respect, consists in having avoided simultaneously what we have called the "traditional" point of view of *Wissenssoziologie* and the immanent interpretation of the former history of ideas. Preceding this awareness that the milieu in which ideas develop is more than a framework, the origin of mental productions used to be sought only in ideal antecedents belonging to the same discipline (taken in the strict sense).[4]

On the other hand, thinkers who turn their attention to analyzing mental productions in relation to things other than immanent antecedents — these thinkers even when they are not Marxists — like Durkheim and Max Scheler, for instance — generally turn their attention to existential conditions.

Sorokin's cultural premises occupy a middle position between these two tendencies, for the premises are simultaneously philosophic *ideas* and factors *exterior* to the systems certain of whose mental productions they condition.[5]

This does not mean that Sorokin's idealistic approach can replace the research into the existential conditioning of mental productions. We have seen that Sorokin himself recognizes a place for this type of sociology of knowledge.[6] We think rather that these two approaches to the conditioning of ideas, far from suppressing each other, complement each other. We shall return to this question later. However this question may be settled, this new type of independent variable offers the sociology of knowledge a new perspective.

Logical relationships

These relationships play a considerable part in Sorokin's sociology. First, from the heuristic point of view: The investigator begins by establishing a logical relationship between the meanings of two sociocultural phenomena. Thus, from among thousands of phenomena, he chooses two because of the meaningful relationship they sustain. He will then see if they have an actual correlation. Without this logico-meaningful method, the sociologist would be completely lost in an ocean of phenomena without having the slightest possibility of finding any correlations except by chance.

Then, from the point of view of cultural integration: Sorokin is one of the few sociologists to have envisaged in such a complete way the problem of the nature and extent of cultural integration and to have given a clear notion of the logical consistency between the different parts of a culture.

It will be said perhaps that Sorokin is not the first to have seen meaning in social phenomena and to have attempted to establish logical relationships between them. This is true. But a fairly large number of sociologists have tried to adopt a purely behaviorist point of view. Others have believed they were applying this point of view even when, in their positive research, they continued to be attentive to meanings. Sorokin's worth in this respect is that of having made the impossibility of the purely behaviorist point of view very explicit.

We are not, of course, forbidden to modify and improve the tools Sorokin has forged. Thus, as has been suggested above,[7] it seems that the "logico-meaningful" relationships would be rendered more fruitful if the notion of "logical" were enlarged to "intelligible," something which would permit taking emotional and unconscious sequences into consideration. The logico-meaningful relationships would also prove more fruitful if, on the other hand, one substituted for the rational point of view, that of a mind engaged in the historical conditions of a particular, given culture.

Sorokin has not been a pioneer solely in respect to these three points. We must also cite, among other things, his conceptions of the generic sociocultural phenomenon. But the three contributions we have just mentioned seem the most significant from the point of view of the development of the sociology of knowledge.

DEFINITIVE CONTRIBUTIONS

The Sorokin sociology of knowledge has not only opened up new perspectives. It brings a definite contribution to the problem of the social conditioning of thought. A large part of the present work has been devoted to specifying the definite results obtained by Sorokin in this field. To summarize the essential point of this work in a sentence, it might be said that Sorokin has proved the existence of a logical relationship between the fundamental and philosophic aspect of the ensemble of a culture's mental productions, and the position concerning the nature of reality adopted by that culture.

This relationship — which the summarized formulation you have just read considerably impoverishes — has been established, within the limits indicated in the course of our analysis, in a manner which renders it definitive.

RELATIONSHIP BETWEEN THE SOCIOLOGY OF KNOWLEDGE AND THE PHILOSOPHY OF KNOWLEDGE

In this respect, the study of Sorokin's system confirms what the analysis of Mannheim's system had taught us concerning the relations between science and philosophy on the plane of *Wissenssoziologie*. Just as in Mannheim's sociology, we have found in that of Sorokin a close relationship between the positive results of his research and the philosophic implications he draws from them. We have attempted to show by the notion of the ambivalent character of the scientific theory that there is a real distinction between the two realms, but that, on the other hand, there is not an unbridgeable chasm. We may rightly expect a harmony between the two.

One might object that Sorokin — just like Mannheim — does not make this distinction between the philosophic significance and the explanatory significance of his scientific theory, and that the distinction is made by the critic. Does the latter not draw confirmation of his theory from the fact that he finds a distinction in Sorokin's sociology which he himself, and not Sorokin, has placed there?

We reply that the attitude of the sociologist and that of the critic (that is to say the one who makes an epistemological study of sociology) are different and that what is very important for the second can be implicit in, or even neglected by, the first. For a very long time, physicists have worked out physics, and good physics, without worrying about the exact significance of their affirmations in relation to the neighboring philosophic compartment: that of the philosophy of nature. A fairly large number of them, even the greatest, tended to exaggerate this significance — Descartes for instance.[8] Can it be said that today all the physicists agree on the philosophic bearings of their research? When a conception of the exact significance of the different stages of physical research and of the connections between physics and philosophic cosmology is easily applied and even makes more comprehensible the results obtained by physicists who do not turn their attention to these problems, the soundness of the critical conception becomes greater.

For the same reason, it seems that a certain notion of the different significance of the various stages of the sociology of knowledge, and especially of what it may legitimately imply on the philosophic plane, is confirmed when systems of *Wissenssoziologie* are adapted to it, although their authors had no intention whatsoever of constructing their science according to this scheme.

PART THREE

GENERAL CONCLUSIONS

This study has been undertaken for the purpose of clarifying the relations between a relatively young discipline, the sociology of knowledge, and, on the other hand, the philosophy of knowledge. To accomplish this purpose, it has appeared indispensable to consider in a rather detailed way two systems of sociology of knowledge representing two different currents, a current of Marxist inspiration and one of idealistic inspiration.

The result of this examination has been to furnish an answer to the question which we raised at the point of departure: What are the relations between science and philosophy in this particular area? A second result has been to provide a better knowledge of the value which these systems of sociology of knowledge have in themselves independently of the philosophical implications which may be drawn from them. Although this is rather an incidental product of our research, it has appeared to us sufficiently important not to neglect it.

We are now going to endeavor to synthesize the conclusions which have been reached in regard to these two centers of interest in the course of the development of this work. Since the elements which will be synthesized here are not new, this chapter will include some repetition.

CHAPTER FOURTEEN

The Sociology of Knowledge and the Philosophy of Knowledge

THE RELATION BETWEEN these two fields closely allied in their subject matter depends upon the structure of the two disciplines and the scope of the sociological and philosophic affirmations concerning knowledge. The clarification of these relations is then a task which concerns the criticism of the sociology and the philosophy of knowledge, or, if you prefer, of the special epistemology of these disciplines. Whatever their name is, we envisage a proceeding whose object is to determine whether or not the philosophy and the sociology of knowledge have the same aims, what is the type of reality they claim to attain and whether or not, when they say, for example, that knowledge is a practical and non-contemplative activity, this assertion has the same sense for both of them.

STRUCTURE OF A SYSTEM OF THE SOCIOLOGY OF KNOWLEDGE

The success of the physico-chemical sciences has been a constant temptation for the social scientists. Sometimes, they still dream of a sociology constructed on the model of the natural sciences. On the other hand, we would be wrong to neglect any inspiration coming from the natural sciences.[1] First because natural and social sciences have in common that they are sciences, even if the kind of facts they seek to know is different. It would not then be astonishing that their methods, that is to say their "ways" of getting at the facts are very closely related. Besides, from this point of view of methods and techniques, these disciplines — and especially

231

the physico-chemical sciences — have attained a remarkable elaboration.

Like most, if not all, of the positive sciences (in contrast with the normative) which are not only classifying (such as botany, zoology, chemistry in their taxonomic aspect), the sociology of knowledge comprises three essential stages: the research into facts, the synthesis of the results of research, and the explanatory theories.[2]

THE RESEARCH INTO FACTS

This research is the implementation of the Baconian triple method of observation, description and classification. For Sorokin and Mannheim, experimentation is excluded. One does not see how one might create an ideational culture in a group for experimental purposes. One might with difficulty set up two persons as similar as possible in all respects, except in their social affiliations, and see if one has a morphological view of reality and the other a synthetic one. But it is not incompatible for other systems of sociology of knowledge to permit a certain degree of experimentation. An example of what might be done in this respect is provided by certain very interesting experiments carried out by Sorokin and Boldyreff bearing upon the influence of suggestion on the power of distinguishing and judging values.[3]

This stage is logically first. It precedes theory. However, only *significant* facts are studied. The significant characteristic of a fact is not determined solely by the subject matter of the sociology of knowledge: Sorokin and Mannheim do not study any mental production and any social factor whatsoever. In terms of what do we estimate that one fact must be taken into consideration and not another? In terms of the relationships which, we believe, are going to be found — that is to say, in terms of a certain idea of the links which, it is thought, exist between such and such a kind of facts. The origin of this idea has little importance. It may be obtained by an imaginative work on what John Dewey calls the problematical situation, or by an analysis of the problem, as Professor Northrop thinks. This may be a sort of intuition which seems to arrange in an instant an ensemble of facts that seemed very confused. Such seems to have been the case with Sorokin. Or again, it may be the modification of a former theory, like the adaptation of Marxism by Mannheim. Or again an idea may have been suggested to someone because it is in line with his philosophy. We have noted such a harmony in regard to our authors. Whatever this harmony may be, the research into facts is already directed by an idea. This is visible in the case of Sorokin. He would never have investigated the currents of thought as he did if he had not had the three cultural types in mind.

But what difference is there between this "idea" and the guiding hypothesis which is deduced from the theory? The difference is that this "idea" is more vague and has a basis less certain than the hypothesis. Often, the fact that the new idea does not easily account for all the facts, does not stop the innovator.[4] Thus the apparent independence of the quantitative sciences in relation to the variables of Mannheim must have appeared as a very serious objection to his idea of the activistic value of knowledge. Afterwards, he made an exception of this case. Likewise, the current conception that the most ancient phases of civilizations are ideational, has not prevented Sorokin from looking for ideational cultures subsequent to sensate phases in the same current of civilization. Later he will explain that the primitive phases are not always ideational. Thus there is a sensate period from the twelfth to the ninth century B.C. in the origins of the Greek world.

If the "idea" was good, it will be, as it were, a first approximation of the hypothesis or of the theory itself.[5]

RESULTS OF RESEARCH

These results will be synthesized in a general form. The important point is that this general formulation does not extend the scope of the results obtained. For instance, if positive researches have shown that in all the cases examined political ideas corresponded to the social affiliations of the thinkers, one cannot synthesize these results by the following formula "knowledge is existentially conditioned." But there is another kind of extension which is legitimately employed in the physico-chemical sciences. It is this which remains within the limits of scientific induction. When you have established a relationship in a certain number of cases, you conclude that it will prove correct in all the other cases which present the same characteristics, all the other conditions remaining constant. Might one say that the correspondence between social affiliations and political doctrines will always prove correct? If such be the case, the synthesis of the results of research truly contributes a new knowledge — is more than a simple sum of the results acquired.

The value of scientific induction was formerly justified somewhat in the following manner. An observation of the type "water boils at a hundred degrees" expresses, they used to say, a necessary property of the profound nature of water. Consequently, once one has reached a manifestation of the essence of a thing in one of its specimens, it will necessarily be found again in all the other specimens.

Since physicists have renounced expressing themselves in terms of nature and essence in the physico-chemical sciences, induction rests especially upon a question of probability. Each time one has observed the appearance of A, that of B has followed. Whence it is probable that the next time A appears, B will follow again. This seems to imply at least the recognition of a certain constancy in the nature of things. But a solely mathematical foundation is preferred. The probability will be all the greater if it has been stated that the connection exists in *a very large number of cases* and *without exceptions*. If it has been stated that A and B were linked in ten thousand cases, the probability that this bond will exist in the ten thousand and first is stronger than if this linkage has been stated one hundred times. Furthermore, A must be linked only to B. For if A were linked to B in ten thousand cases and to C in ten thousand other cases, there would be as much probability that in the future A would be followed by C as that it would be followed by B.

It follows from this that from the point of view of induction, the sciences of observation are in a much less favorable situation than the experimental sciences. Not being able to repeat artificially certain conditions to see if the linkage is verified there, they must turn toward the past. Now history rarely furnishes the account of the very large number of cases in which a relationship can be verified. We say "rarely" because there is a considerable difference of degree between a relationship like this: "A sensate period is followed by an ideational and non-idealistic period" and another like: "An ideational thinker is an eternalist." In the first case, the sequence, sensate period-ideational period, has been verified twice (in the Graeco-Roman and the Occidental tradition); the second relationship (being an ideational and an eternalist simultaneously) can be verified thousands of times. One cannot then deprive the sciences of observation *a priori* of the benefit of scientific induction. However, scientific induction may be applied to them much more rarely. Thus the relationship established by Mannheim's research has not been checked a large enough number of times, it seems to us, for generalization by induction to be applied to it. The formula of the relationships between mental productions and premises of culture has been observed in an incomparably larger number of cases by Sorokin. However, we would not dare to say that the synthetic formula of the results, because of its complexity, really expresses a regularity guaranteed for the future.

Thus the syntheses of the results of research guarantee the results in the future only insofar as the number of concordant observations is high, at least if the variables of the sociology of knowledge are considered altogether similar to those of physics. Now we know that these variables have a meaning and that they are susceptible of relationships of logical consistency, something which is not the case with the physico-chemical variables. Hence there is another possible case for previsibility. This is not without resemblance to the natures and essences of the former physics. Let us take an example. When I have established by history that ideational thinkers are generally eternalists, I expect future ideational thinkers (or those not yet studied) to be eternalists, not only because I have established this regularity in a large number of cases without any exception, but also because I consider that logically, ideationalism and eternalism are linked.

Can it be said that this logical basis (ideationalism implies eternalism) permits one to make a real induction: the affirmation that ideationalism and eternalism are linked? We think not. In fact, we know that the establishment of logical relationships between two phenomena is not sufficient to guarantee an actual linkage, for it is possible that what appears to be a logical sequence for our minds does not appear as such to minds with another intellectual heritage than ours.[6] Or very frequently the necessary logical relationship will not be discovered. Several relationships are possible. Only recourse to observation will permit us to know if there is an actual sequence.

It seems to us then that almost all the relationships between mental productions and social factors, as they are expressed in the results of research, cannot give rise to inductions which permit the affirmation that "all the other circumstances being identical," the relationship will always prove correct. For, neither of the two possible foundations for induction is solid enough. On the one hand, the number of cases examined — and the difficulties in isolating the variables — does not permit the attainment of a very high probability. In another connection, logical linkage being rarely necessary, it is not a sufficient guarantee either that things may take place in that way only. Furthermore, the indispensable condition for the application of a scientific law, the identity of circumstances, will almost never be realized.

Let us add immediately that actual linkage and logical linkage strengthen each other considerably, so that a high degree of practical certitude in what concerns the future can be acquired. Such generalizations are still valuable guides to the prediction of events.[7] But an anticipation of this kind, as sound as it may be, is not a scientific law.

The synthetic formulation of the results of observations in the sociology of knowledge is then a sum of already known elements, expressed in a convenient way, rather than a new knowledge.

EXPLANATORY THEORY

A theory in sociology, as in most of the other scientific disciplines, is a construct of the mind explaining the synthesis of the results observed by postulating a principle from which these results can be deduced as consequences. In another connection, it serves as a directing principle for a further research.[8] These two roles of a theory constitute essentially the same intellectual procedure: laying down a principle and drawing consequences from it, then showing that these consequences have been realized in what is already known (explanatory role), and showing by new research that the things which one observes are truly realized in this way (guiding role).

Construct of the mind has no depreciatory sense here. This term means only that the theory is not a mere generalization of empirical results. Such a totalization, as we have just seen, would add nothing to what we know already and would not be at all explanatory. In theory, the mind goes beyond a pure generalization. Since it suggests other researches, the explanatory principle is not limited to the results obtained.

Theory is indispensable to the dynamism of science

It is possible for a sociologist not to concentrate on explaining the results he has obtained through his research. He can be content to show that such a relationship exists between such and such phenomena without asking why. But if theory is not indispensable in this respect, it is from the point of view of the progress of science.

We have seen in fact that it is not possible to venture into research for facts without "anticipating nature," as T. H. Huxley used to say. It is enough to think about the almost infinite multiplicity of mental productions on the one hand, and of social factors on the other, to be convinced that we cannot deal with these realms with a mind free from presuppositions and the intention of letting ourself be guided solely by the facts. There are altogether too many guides. . .

That there is a certain danger in prejudging the type of relationships we want to find is evident.[9] We shall risk believing too quickly that we perceive the relationships we are seeking, and that may easily blind us to the other relationships. To be sure, few investigators do not succumb somewhat to these temptations. But there are certain remedies for these dangers: the concern for facts, the criticism by other scientists, and the multiplicity of hypotheses. Besides, there is no possible choice — to obtain a response from the facts, a question must be asked of them.

Now, this anticipation of nature can be accomplished in two ways. One way is in having a more or less precise, more or less intuitive idea of the relationships which you think exist between the facts you intend to study. This is the method we have described in connection with the first stage of research. It is very imperfect but it is the only one which is possible at that moment. The other way is by the means the theory furnishes of guiding you among the facts.

To really understand this means, it is important to distinguish clearly "theory" and "hypothesis." Professor Conant indicates that in the physico-chemical sciences, these two terms do not have a very precise meaning and that often the word theory is utilized for a concept and its explanation.[10] Thus, one will call theory both the expression which Boyle gave to the compressibility of air which he had discovered, "there is a spring in the air," and the different conceptual schemes by which one sought to explain it (particles with elastic qualities, etc.).[11]

Because of the ambiguity of these terms, Professor Conant prefers not to utilize them.[12] However, since two important aspects of the intellectual proceeding must be distinguished and it is not easy to find new vocables, we believe we may keep these two terms by clarifying them in the following manner, which we think is the most common. The theory is the principle which produces hypotheses.[13] Thus Mannheim's theory is the principle of activistic knowledge. From this principle, numerous consequences or hypotheses can be drawn. One of them is that political ideas correspond to social affiliation. This hypothesis has been confirmed by positive research, but it is not the only one.[14] In like manner, the theory of Sorokin is composed of his three principles of immanent change, logical consistency and incomplete truth. The relationship of logical consistency which he establishes between the premises of culture and mental productions is one of the hypotheses one can draw from these principles.[15]

This shows the difference there is between the "anticipation of nature" by a vague intuition and by a hypothesis. The intellectual proceeding is then the following one. Desiring to clarify the relationships between society and knowledge, one studies certain facts considered significant in terms of a certain more or less intuitive and not very precise idea. The results are synthesized in a general form which will very often express the original idea somewhat modified and clarified. Then, one will look for an explanation of the results obtained by laying down a theoretical principle from which a certain number of consequences or hypotheses can be deduced. One of them will be the synthesis of the positive results which, thus, are explained. The others will be the hypotheses which will guide further research. We see the superiority of the latter over intuitions. Starting with a well-defined principle, they can generally be more precise and their foundation will be more certain, since some of the logical consequences of this principle have been confirmed by the facts.

If, in their turn, these new hypotheses are confirmed, the sociology of knowledge will gradually be established around a few important theories which will play as central a role as Newtonian mechanics, the atomic theory and the theory of relativity have played, and are playing, in modern physics.

Selectivity of theory in the social sciences

A theory is indispensable. But all theories are not equally valuable. The choice of them is very important. The results attained will be very different according to the theory chosen. Indeed, it will immediately direct the investigator's attention not only to a certain variety of relationships, but also to a certain category of facts. Thus Sorokin's theory leads him to consider, among mental productions, more especially philosophic currents and the fundamental aspect of physical theories. Mannheim, on the contrary, concentrates his attention on political doctrines.

This selectivity of facts contrasts theory in *Wissenssoziologie* very strongly with theory in the physico-chemical sciences, and gives, it seems, even more importance to theory in our field. In the physico-chemical sciences, there are certain very precise facts which have to be explained. To take an example provided by Conant, the physicists before Lavoisier explained combustion by the phlogiston theory. Lavoisier explained this by the role of oxygen. But both of them examined exactly the same facts: Some "earths" when heated with charcoal produce metals.[16] The two theories we have examined in *Wissenssoziologie* have on the contrary a selective power over facts. Let us suppose that you desire to determine how knowledge was socially influenced in the France of the eighteenth century. If we adopt Mannheim's theory, we will very likely examine[17] two categories of facts: social structure and political ideas. If we accept that of Sorokin, we will consider above all the French philosophic currents in their relationships to cultural premises. If the facts on which Mannheim centers his attention are not completely neglected, their importance will be judged secondary. You see how it can be said that the choice of a theory can be more important in sociology than in the physico-chemical sciences.

This great selectivity of theory in the sociology of knowledge probably has two reasons. First, experimental facts are generally more determined than observed facts. Furthermore, the field of the young sociology of knowledge has not yet been completely explored. Thus clearly defined problems have not yet crystallized.

Such are the three stages of a system of sociology of knowledge. A different method and different criteria of validity correspond to each one of them. This shows, it seems, that this distinction is not arbitrary. On the level of positive research, techniques permitting us to seize the facts without distorting them are necessary. These techniques are qualitative and quantitative analyses. At the following level of the formulation of results, one must express them in a synthesis which does not extend their scope unduly. Finally, one must be able to deduce logically from the explanation a series of consequences of which one will be the synthetic formulation of the results.[18]

Here is how the two systems we have studied stand in this respect, schematically.

	Positive research:	Synthesis of the results (or confirmed hypothesis):	Theory:
MANNHEIM:	Monographs on the political currents in Germany in the 19th century.	Correspondence between political ideas and class affiliations.	Knowledge is activistic; struggle of classes.
SOROKIN:	Qualitative and quantitative study of currents of thought through 25 centuries.	Logical consistency between currents of thought and premises of culture.	Principle of partial truth, logical consistency and immanent change.

THE PHILOSOPHY OF KNOWLEDGE

As has been noted above, epistemology and gnosiology do not have clearly defined borders.[19] The principle of distinction concerns the point of view and method of these disciplines. Epistemology turns its attention to the value of knowledge and attempts to solve the problem by a critical method. Gnosiology tries to determine the nature of knowledge by locating it in the ontological structure of the real. On the one hand, it is asked to what degree knowledge (or such a type of knowledge) realizes its ideal objective; on the other, we question the ideal type itself in terms of a complete system of philosophy.[20]

This distinction may appear clear enough. But, in reality, one passes easily from one field to the other. Our two authors raise an epistemological problem, but they both solve it partly in terms of their gnosiology. By philosophy of knowledge, we shall allude then especially to gnosiology, but also to epistemology insofar as it merges into gnosiology in borrowing the latter's methods.

To consider a thing, an activity, from the philosophic point of view, means to relate it to what is considered authentic reality. Any philosophy tends to give an explanation of the structure of the real. As a consequence it will have to account for the various aspects of human experience in terms of its conception of reality. Thus, what is called in our current speech "matter" may be interpreted as a "solidification of the vital impulse falling down again" in Bergson's philosophy, as an "inferior degree of being" by St. Thomas Aquinas, as identifying itself with "being" for J. P. Sartre, as the principle of evil for the Manicheans. In an elaborate philosophy like that of the Scholastic tradition, one will construct rather complicated theories like that of the hylemorphic composition (prime matter and substantial form) to account for the changes in material realities in terms of Aristotelian conceptions of movement.

It is the same with knowledge. Ordinary language generally distinguishes, at least in a civilized group, a certain order of human activities different from other activities, which is called "knowledge." The philosopher must ask himself what the meaning of this phenomenon is in terms of his conception of the real, that is to say he will seek to determine what knowledge is, not on the psychological and phenomenal plane, but on the ontological and noumenal one. If he considers that there is no noumenal plane, he will, however, give a status to what is called "knowledge" in respect to what he considers real.

Of course, from this status, which expresses the nature of knowledge, certain consequences will be deduced concerning the aim of this activity (such as: being a participant in the existence of others; being a contemplator of pure ideas; being a means of adapting oneself practically to situations, etc.) and concerning the ideal to which it can lay claim, and hence concerning what truth may be.

The method employed will often be a mixture of empirical descriptions and logical deductions from the fundamental principles of the philosophy in question. But this second approach will often prevail over experience, which will serve rather as confirmation. One will frequently say: "The profound nature of man and of reality being such, it follows that man must possess a certain activity corresponding to what is vulgarly called "knowledge," which has such and such a purpose. This is confirmed by such and such a fact which is completely explained according to our conception of knowledge, or which implies our conception." Of course, there will be a fairly large number of differences between the various philosophic systems. Certain ones will be more empirical, others more *a priori*. But it seems that the ultimate criterion for all will be the logical consistency with what they consider the fundamental principles of their philosophy, while the accord with experience will be secondary. Moreover, these philosophic conceptions of the nature and value of knowledge not being empirically verifiable in a direct way, it is normal for the proof of such matters to be, above all, in harmony with philosophic principles rather than with experience.

Thus a philosophy of knowledge is characterized first by the plane on which it moves: It aims to discover what the real nature of knowledge is — the meaning of this activity in terms of the ontological structure of the real. Then, it is characterized by the method of proof which is mainly deduction from the general principles of the philosophy in question.

Its elaboration comprises schematically the following stages. Point of departure: the principles of the philosophic system concerning the nature of reality and of man. Whether or not the origin of these principles is a profound experience of the real in a privileged intuition of being (thus the Christian existentialists) or of contingency (thus Sartre and the atheistic existentialists); whether or not it is reason in its postulates and laws — are questions we are not going to deal with here. We are considering these philosophic principles as data. The second stage will consist in showing that such and such a conception of the nature of this phenomenon which we call in our experience "knowledge" can be deduced from, or at least is very harmonious with, the adopted ontological principles. Finally, a third stage, more or less secondary, will consist in showing that, moreover, the facts, or certain facts observed, suggest or imply this interpretation.

Let us note once more that our two authors scarcely make their metaphysical concepts explicit and make no claim whatever to forming rigorous deductions. However, as has been more clearly shown before, there is a harmony, not to say more, between point of departure, philosophy of knowledge and confirmation by the facts.

We might indicate this schematically as follows:

	Ontological point of departure:	*Philosophic conception of knowledge:*	*Confirmation by the facts:*
MANNHEIM:	Reality is dialectical, non-transcendental becoming.	Knowledge is a non-theoretical but practical activity.	Political doctrines do not express an objective reality but the social affiliations of the thinker.
SOROKIN:	Reality is infinite manifoldness.	Knowledge is a theoretical activity inadequately attaining authentic reality. However the three systems of knowledge partly attain scientific reality.	The three systems of truth (linked to the three premises of culture) have subsisted for a long time and repeat themselves.

RELATIONSHIP BETWEEN THE PHILOSOPHY OF KNOWLEDGE AND THE SOCIOLOGY OF KNOWLEDGE

The examination to which we have just devoted our attention has clearly shown the differences between these two disciplines. The objective is, on the one hand, to determine as precisely as possible the degree of influence of social factors upon ideas; on the other, to determine the nature and value of our cognitive activity. The level is, on the one hand, that of positive science aiming at the establishment of relations between phenomena; on the other, it is that of philosophy seeking to locate knowledge in the structure of true reality.

However, the two tables ending the preceding sections show an astonishing resemblance. The content of the "Theory" column in the table of *Wissenssoziologie* (p. 240) is partly found again in the "Philosophic conception of knowledge" column of the table on the philosophy of knowledge (p. 243). The same holds true for the column "confirmation by the facts" (p. 243) and "syntheses of the results" (p. 240). This suggests that, for Sorokin and Mannheim at least, the two disciplines partly overlap each other and are, so to speak, in continuity. How is this possible then when the objectives and levels of reality of the two disciplines are so different?

In examining the explanatory theories, it was said that they had to be principles from which the synthesis of research can be deduced as a consequence. Now this explanatory principle has a sense in itself. It can be either a mathematical, chemical, mechanical, psychological or ontological principle. In reality, the possibilities are limited by the kind of facts one is considering and the formulation of the results of observations on these facts. When these facts are not expressed in mathematical form, one cannot evidently deduce them from a mathematical principle. Likewise, a chemical principle can never explain anything but chemical combinations.

In the *Wissenssoziologie* existing up to the present time, the formulation given of the relations between social factors and mental productions seems hardly to admit other kinds of explanatory principles than logical, psychological, "culturological" or philosophical ones. In fact, we have encountered these various kinds. Sorokin's principle of limits and the dialectical principle of immanent change are logical (the latter at least partly); the tendency of the human mind toward consistency and, in Mannheim, the struggle for political and economic power are rather of a psychological order. Our interpretation of Mannheim by a cultural personality type gives an idea of what a "culturological" theory might be.[21] Finally, "knowledge is activistic" and "the principle of the three truths" express the profound nature of human knowledge and its value.

Such is the reason why, in the systems we have examined, one can pass so easily from sociology to philosophy. The meeting point is located in the scientific explanation when it is susceptible of bearing a philosophic sense.

Must such a bridge necessarily exist in *Wissenssoziologie?* It seems not. If certain relationships between social factors and mental productions were translated mathematically, the principle of explanation could be mathematical. In this case, there would no longer be any passage to the philosophy of knowledge. Likewise, if the explanatory principles were purely psychological. Here, however, it would perhaps be possible to pass to philosophy because of the close relationship between psychology and the philosophic study of man.

Let us recall that certain sciences, like the physico-chemical ones, which used to include principles of explanation susceptible of a philosophical sense,[22] having become mathematized, have lost this "bridge" to the philosophy of nature. This, moreover, is a point where these sciences are clearly distinguished from the social sciences.

When the "bridge" exists, is there perfect continuity? Can one conceive that the two disciplines are united as perfectly as the following outline indicates?

(a) Philosophic principles concerning the nature of reality and of man.
(b) Philosophic conception of knowledge which can be deduced from (a) and from which (c) can be deduced.
(c) Synthesis of research which is a consequence of (b) confirmed by (d).
(d) Research into facts.

We have seen that the systems of our two authors tend to conform to such a scheme. Indeed, both conceive that positive results imply a philosophy of knowledge.

Here is the sequence for Mannheim:

(a) Dialectical and non-transcendental ontology of becoming.
(b) Knowledge is activistic relationism.
(c) Political ideas correspond to class affiliations.
(d) Monographic researches.

For Sorokin:

(a) Authentic reality is an infinite manifoldness.
(b) Integralism (the three truths).
(c) Currents of thought logically consistent with premises of culture present recurrences.
(d) Quantitative and qualitative observations of currents of thought during twenty-five centuries.

For such a continuity to be admissible, each one of the stages must have exactly the same significance, whether it is attained from philosophic principles or from facts observed.

Now we have seen that such is not the case. The meeting point stage, if we may say so, is (b). Even if its *content* is identical when it is attained as an explanation of research (c), or as a consequence of philosophic principles (a), its objective and, consequently, *its criteria of validity,* are not the same. As theory, (b) belongs to the order of "as if" and as philosophy (b) is on the level of a non-hypothetic reality.[23] For (b) to be a satisfactory theory, it is merely necessary for one to be able to deduce from it the results of observation (c) and other hypotheses. For (b) to be a satisfactory philosophy, it must be a valid expression of reality, which normally will be measured by the degree of concordance with the ontological principles of the system (a).

We could not overestimate the importance of the distinction possible between two values of the same assertion. However, this does not prevent them from sustaining any relation.

First, it does not seem impossible for the facts to imply only a single explanation. If this explanation is of an ontological nature, we are in the presence of a form of reasoning very commonly employed by the Occidental philosophers: inference, which consists in concluding from a fact its necessary conditions. Those who do not question the correspondence of the fundamental principles of traditional logic with the structure of the real must admit that such an explanation is not only good but philosophically true.

But the necessary inferences are infrequent. They are especially rare in the disciplines which, like the sociology of knowledge, deal with particularized facts.

So let us leave aside this case, which, if it ever occurs in our field, is certainly not very frequent. In the other instances, can it be said that when a good theory is also a true philosophy, it is so by pure chance?

It seems not. In fact, it is admissible with difficulty that the "true" nature of things, of knowledge, for example, has no discernible influence upon their empirical manifestations. This is tantamount to saying: "Things are fundamentally such. Whence it follows logically that one can expect them to appear empirically either so or so. But, in reality, there are just as many chances that they will present themselves in still another way."

Thus the regularity and the previsibility in human action is a pertinent objection to address to a philosopher who holds that men are free. In like manner, if in human activity we discover only a practical knowledge adapted to immediate ends, we have a right to ask the philosopher who affirms the theoretical character of our knowledge to account for this apparent contradiction.

This is what we have called the principle of probable conformity. If one holds as a philosopher that man is determined in his activity and that, empirically, one can observe that the actions of men are determined, there is nothing to explain. If, on the contrary, a philosopher holds that man is free, and if, on the other hand, one can better deduce the way in which men actually act from a determinist philosophy, this antinomy must be explained by the philosopher.

It is such a situation we have found in our two authors. Their philosophies and their scientific explanations form a coherent whole. We have not criticized their philosophic principles ("knowledge is activistic," "the three systems of truth give an at least partly valid knowledge of reality"), but we have attempted to see if one could admit these principles as explanations without admitting them as philosophies. It was necessary then to explain, how such an apparent contradiction was possible.

In Mannheim's case, it was shown that the activity of the human agents originates in certain psychological types (created by the culture of their time) more than in their ontological nature, and that the facts studied by Mannheim are situated right in an epoch and in a country where the culture led men to make use of knowledge for practical, rather than theoretical, ends.

For Sorokin, the distinction between two planes of adaptation, to the material environment and to the nature of reality, has permitted us to show how it is possible to admit integralism as an explanation without admitting it as a philosophy.

Summary of the Relationship between the Sociology and Philosophy of Knowledge

1. These two disciplines have different objectives, different methods and move on different planes of reality.
2. However, the kind of explanatory principle utilized in the sociology of knowledge, although it is not the only conceivable type, furnishes a passage: scientific explanation has a sense as philosophy.

3. Two principles play a part in regulating these relationships:
   a. The function and the criteria of validity for a scientific theory and a philosophic principle are different.
   b. The phenomenal is manifested in harmony with the noumenal.

4. Whence the following applications:
   a. If the bond between the synthesis of results and its explanation is necessary, the explanation, because it is good, is a true philosophy.
   b. In the other cases, it is possible for a valid scientific explanation not to be a philosophically valid principle. But such a situation is paradoxical and must be explained.

5. Two corollaries follow from this principle of probable conformity:
   a. The sociologist of knowledge who seeks an explanation of the real type (not psychological or mathematical) will do well to take his inspiration from a philosophy which seems valid to him, since normally a "true philosophy" will be also a "fruitful theory." However, the ultimate criterion remains always the explanatory value of the theory. This means that the sociologist will not choose as a hypothesis a philosophically true proposition because it is true, but because its truth is an indication of its probable fruitfulness.
   b. The philosopher of knowledge will be attentive to the function of a scientific hypothesis which his conception of the nature of knowledge can perform. If this concept is at the same time a fruitful scientific hypothesis, this will not be the proof of its truth, but a clue of good omen. If, on the contrary, it proves to be a poor scientific explanation, one will not be allowed to say that "the facts deny any value to his philosophy," but merely that they invite a critical re-examination.

Epistemology and Sociology of Knowledge

Whatever may be the philosophic conception of knowledge, there will always be room for the study of the significance, either of knowledge in general or of the various types of knowledge (general epistemology and special epistemology).

The epistemologist will attempt to determine to what extent the ideal which knowledge aspires to realize is actually reached and is accessible to the processes which the knowing subject has, in present circumstances, at his disposal. In this respect, the degree of influence of the social factors upon knowledge will be of the utmost importance. Thus if knowledge claims to be objective, it will be essential for the epistemologist to know that political doctrines are strongly determined by social affiliations or that the fundamental categories of logic are dependent upon cultural premises. On this basis he will have to resolve some problems. For instance: Does this conditioning not prevent the attainment of objectivity in this field? Or rather, what is the kind of objectivity which can be reached under such conditions?

It is in this sense that it can be said that the results of the sociology of knowledge will be among the most useful data for epistemology.

CHAPTER FIFTEEN

Results and Prospects for the Sociology of Knowledge

CLARIFICATION OF THE NOTION OF THE SOCIOLOGY OF KNOWLEDGE

THE SOCIOLOGY of knowledge has as its objective the determination of the conditioning of mental productions by social and cultural factors. Such is the definition we have taken as the point of departure for our research. It seems that we can now make it somewhat more precise.

KNOWLEDGE, VALUES AND NORMS

The term "mental productions" was chosen to cover the diversity of dependent variables whose social conditioning the sociologists have actually analyzed: ideas, religious and ethical beliefs, philosophy, literature, artistic productions, technology, etc.

It seems that there would be an advantage in considering in *Wissenssoziologie* those of the mental productions which are really "cognitive." But, before indicating the reasons why such a restriction would be opportune, a preliminary question arises: Is it possible to define what is "really cognitive" apart from a philosophy? Perhaps not very accurately, nor in a definite manner, but certainly in such a way that cognitive mental productions can be distinguished from those which are not.

A mental production will be cognitive when it has as its primary aim the description of reality. Here, reality signifies any datum (phenomenal as well as noumenal, if this distinction is accepted).

To describe means that the foremost aim of a certain mental production is not to communicate what is desirable, nor what we must do, nor to create an affective state in ourselves, but simply to tell what things are. Knowledge is expressed in the indicative, never in the optative or the imperative.[1]

Such a definition is very trite, but it claims only to permit us to distinguish, by using the current language, knowledge on the one hand, and values, norms, art, poetry, etc., on the other.[2] The criterion of common sense employed here does not claim to be critical. It is simply a practical principle of distinction at this stage of the research. In fact, this vulgar notion of knowledge and what it implies (for instance, that the aim is objectivity) are at the point of departure of theories which even afterwards arrive at another notion of knowledge. Thus Mannheim.

The utility of this precision from the point of view of the sociology of knowledge results from the fact that the social factors will act differently upon mental productions which claim to be imperative or to communicate emotions. In the discussion of Mannheim, we saw that this is very important. The essential defects of his system stem from the fact that he considered political doctrines (such as Marxism or Fascism) as if they were only cognitive. Whence he could very easily prove the existential conditioning of those mental productions. Furthermore, he attempted to apply to them criteria of objectivity which are suitable only for knowledge.[3]

However, this distinction between knowledge and the other mental productions must not be exaggerated. Art and religion bring also, secondarily, a certain knowledge. Besides, generally, the norms are justified by judgments which tell us what things are. Values are values only because they are real.[4] Furthermore, arts, religions, moral values, etc., are mental productions whose social and cultural determination will be studied by disciplines closely related to *Wissenssoziologie,* such as the sociology of art, of religion, etc. Despite these close relationships between cognitive productions and other mental productions, it seems preferable to us to maintain this distinction and, in the expression "sociology of knowledge," to take the term knowledge in its proper sense.[5]

Social Factors and Cultural Factors

In our definition — point of departure, we contemplated the conditioning of knowledge by social factors and cultural factors.

This distinction has hardly been emphasized in the course of our study. Let us see if it is advisable to maintain it in our definition.

Society and culture are concepts which have been defined in a multitude of ways. However, all these definitions usually include the same essential elements. It is only in secondary clarifications that authors disagree. These few essential elements are, it seems, the following. A society is an organized group of individuals who work together.[6] A culture is a social heritage.[7] It is the ensemble of ideas and behavior which an individual acquires, not by his own activity,[8] nor by biological transmission,[9] but by his education, formal or not, in such a group. They are the capacities and habits acquired by man as a member of society.[10]

The distinction is clear: The society is the group; the culture is the group's ways of living and thinking.[11] The separation appears sharp especially if society is considered in its aspect of social structure.

Thus the same social structure can be found linked to two different cultures. For instance, the Catholic church in Spain and the United States has the same social structure: the same hierarchy, the same relationships with the central authorities at Rome, the same rights and duties of the different groups of Christians within the church, etc. However, it can be said that the culture of the American Catholic church is different from that of the Spanish Catholic church: another kind of behavior is expected of the priests, the education given in the Catholic schools is sensibly different, the attitude toward higher education, the movies, etc., is far from being identical.

Reciprocally, the same culture can be found in two different social structures. A few peasant families belonging to the same Polish village come to settle in an agricultural community in the Middle West. These immigrants have lost their status in the social structure of the Polish state and even of their local Polish community. They have gained another status in the American social structure. However, at least for a certain time, they will have the same culture (language, religion, family status) as those who remained in Europe.

But these two notions are correlative too. There is no group without a culture and no culture without a group. The understanding of the rights and obligations ascribed to the individual by his culture is impossible without taking the social system into account. On the other hand, the structure of any society is a part of the culture of that society.[12]

Sorokin is one of the sociologists who unite these two aspects the most completely. The subject matter of the social sciences is the sociocultural phenomenon. This latter term indicates very well both the union of the two aspects and their duality (in the sense that one is not reducible to the other). The basis of this union is that one cannot, in the phenomena studied by the social sciences, consider meaning and the interacting human agents separately. A social science wishing to study culture without society would be equivalent to a "zoology that would concern itself only with the skin of organisms, leaving all the internal organs and tissues to another field of science."[13] However, Sorokin admits that, at a certain level of abstraction, the two aspects can be considered separately (actually the first and second books of the Dynamics are cultural and the third is social). In this case, society means the totality of interacting persons and their relations whereas culture envisages meanings, values and norms and also their material vehicles (which constitute the material culture).[14]

This conception of the "sociocultural" closely depends upon the fundamental concepts of Sorokin's general sociology. In order to discuss it, we would have to see to what degree there are meanings only in the cultural field. If by definition all meanings are placed in culture, it becomes impossible evidently to speak about social structure without speaking about culture. Such a discussion exceeds the scope of the present monograph.

Moreover, whatever this unity of society and culture may be, the two aspects can be considered separately. In this case, it can be said that Sorokin's independent variables are, on the whole, cultural, while those of Mannheim are, on the whole, social. This really shows that this distinction is founded. It appears preferable, consequently, to maintain the two concepts in the definition.

We propose the following form for this: The sociology of knowledge is the study of mental productions insofar as they are related to social or cultural factors.

UNITY OF THE SOCIOLOGY OF KNOWLEDGE

This discipline is not yet a science constituted by a well-synthesized ensemble of positive results. The two systems which we have analyzed evidently do not constitute all the sociology of knowledge, but they seem very representative of the kind of constructs which are found there. Each author has concentrated his attention upon a social or cultural factor and has attempted to show how profound and extensive its influence was upon certain spheres of knowledge. Sorokin and Mannheim, although they admit that other factors also play a part, have not paid any more attention to them.

These tactics seem to be well adapted to a discipline which is still at the stage of exploration of new territory. It is preferable, at this stage, to take a hypothesis which is known to be incomplete (without knowing to what degree it is incomplete) and get to its roots by considering it, for the moment, as if it were the only explanatory factor. It is not before a certain number of results of this type have been attained that one may undertake research having several social and cultural factors in view at the same time.

But if there is little reason for taking a plural hypothesis (comprising a constellation of factors) as a guide for research, one is not forbidden to attempt to synthesize provisionally the results which have been obtained by the separate study of a few factors. Thus one would probably see that there is more apparent than real contradiction between the various systems. We cannot, in any way, after the analysis of the two systems of sociology of knowledge, claim to sketch the main lines of such a synthesis. We can only indicate that these two systems which do not seem very harmonious are more complementary than contradictory.

The first reason why these systems are but little opposed to each other is because they are turned toward different objects. This stems partly from the fact that Mannheim's research bears upon a point so delimited in time and space: philosophic ideas in nineteenth century Germany, whereas those of Sorokin are directed rather toward vast philosophic currents.

However, the lack of contradiction between the two systems rests upon reasons less negative than the fact they turn their attention toward different things. In the first place, as was noted above,[15] the relationship Mannheim establishes between political doctrines and social affiliations has value only in a certain culture. For men to use their cognitive faculties principally with an aim to gaining economic and political power, what is often called "ethos" must be of a certain type.[16] One of Mannheim's errors was not to realize that the relationships he discovered in his research were not to be attributed to human nature but to men formed by a culture whose ethos is sensate. One sees how Sorokin can complete Mannheim. Probably Sorokin's sensate culture is a frame a bit too large for Mannheim's system to be located in it. One would have to make the sensate ethos more precise, something which is perfectly possible. Thus Sorokin himself gives a description of what he calls an "ethos of competition" which expresses exactly the cultural framework in which the relationships between knowledge and social factors as conceived by Mannheim are possible.[17]

On the other hand, Mannheim's approach can also complete Sorokin's system in a felicitous way. First, we know that various minority currents maintain themselves within large cultures of the Sorokin type. It seems that we would learn a great deal about the reasons for which these minority currents persist and why certain of them become majority currents in the following epoch if we knew what the social groups are which adopt the different currents of thought.[18] Then, while recognizing the influence of Sorokin's cultural premises, we can, by means of a somewhat enlarged Mannheim system, attempt to see whether or not these premises themselves are not influenced somewhat by social factors.

This shows that a synthesis of the systems of Mannheim and Sorokin might be made, either by integrating Mannheim's system in that of Sorokin, or vice versa. However, at least in the actual state of these systems,[19] the synthesis would be made more easily by giving preeminence to Sorokin's system, which is the most complete and the most general, and by making it more specific with that of Mannheim.

These brief indications of the possible complementary quality of the systems of Mannheim and Sorokin suggest that it would probably be possible to establish a provisory synthesis of the results obtained by these systems, each of which insists upon one social or cultural factor without paying any attention to the others.

However, what up to the present forms the unity of the sociology of knowledge, is less this possible synthesis than the problem this discipline raises. All the systems, as far removed as they appear to be in their directing hypotheses and the facts they investigate, are closely united in that they all attempt to answer the problem or, more accurately, the three questions of the sociology of knowledge. What are the social or cultural factors which influence knowledge? What are the cognitive mental productions influenced? What is the degree and kind of conditioning between the two? These three questions clearly define the point of view of *Wissenssoziologie*. It is the point of view which constitutes the unity of a science.

IDEALISTIC AND MARXIST APPROACHES

In spite of the possibilities of reconciling and synthesizing the systems of Mannheim and Sorokin, there remains at least one important divergence of accent between them. If they are in agreement on the fact that the cultural premises and the social affiliations influence ideas, they are opposed to each other on the respective importance of these factors. Thus let us suppose that one desires to study the liberalism of the nineteenth century. For Mannheim, the most important element which will explain the origin of this movement is its correspondence to the aspirations and necessities of the *bourgeoisie*. For Sorokin, it will be above all a manifestation of the dominant sensate premise. This is what we expressed in saying in a rather simplified way that Sorokin's system was "idealistic" and Mannheim's "Marxian." These two terms meaning here no more than the attribution of the primary role either to ideas, or to existential economic and political factors.[20]

Is it not advisable to ask ourselves which of these two points of view is the better? It is unwise to answer this question without clarifying it. It seems indeed that it may have three very distinct meanings.

First, it can mean simply: What is the most fruitful approach as regards the techniques of research which we have at our disposition, and the fields which have not yet been explored, etc.? It seems that, from this point of view, it is rather difficult to give any clear preference to one of the two approaches. Seeking the economic and political antecedent has been done rather widely in history these past seventy-five years, but much less in the field of knowledge. As for the idealistic approach, it is very old if we mean by that that the antecedents of ideas are ideas, but very new, we believe, if it is specified that the antecedent ideas are premises of culture or ethos. It seems then that the territory which remains to be explored by the two approaches is considerable. From the point of view of the techniques of research — the "logico-meaningful" method — the qualitative and quantitative study can be used in both of them.

The second meaning of this question concerning the relative value of the "idealistic" and the "Marxist" approach has reference to the philosophic implications of these two currents. It is meant: Is the philosophy implied by Sorokin's approach truer than that implied by Mannheim's approach? This question has been discussed at great enough length for it to be sufficient to recall here that one can have an idealistic system of *Wissenssoziologie* and profess a positivistic philosophy or a Marxist system and profess a spiritualist philosophy, although the reverse situation is more harmonious. As for the discussion of materialism and spiritualism as philosophic positions, it evidently exceeds the purpose of this work.

A third meaning of the question is concerned with the respective importance of the factors. Are Sorokin's premises of culture a more determining influence upon cognitive mental productions than Mannheim's social affiliations? For example, does the liberal doctrine of the nineteenth century find its origin more in the fact that it corresponded to the interests and ambitions of the *bourgeoisie* than in the fact that it was logically consistent with the sensate cultural premise?

If one limits the question raised in these terms to the systems of Sorokin and Mannheim, it seems that we can only answer: We do not know. In order to be able to judge, the *same* current of thought would have had to be studied by the two approaches. Then one might judge that *in that case, at least,* such a factor has been more determinant than the other. But, as has been indicated already, Mannheim studied positively only an extremely restricted field, so, indeed, we see no case in which one can really compare the conditioning of the same idea by the two factors.

But this question of the respective importance of the factors must be enlarged beyond the systems of Sorokin and Mannheim. The sociology of knowledge was born of a movement greatly emphasizing the role of irrationality in human activity.[21] In what concerns knowledge, it has been considered that ideas had not only ideal and logical antecedents (immanent interpretation) but also extra-theoretical ones. The latter can be found in the psychology of the individual. These determining psychological factors were the best known, as we have seen above. Another kind of non-immanent influence upon knowledge is located in society. Mannheim's system is a good example of this. Finally, knowledge can also be conditioned by culture. This factor is often of an ideal nature. However, even in Sorokin, where the cultural premises are very ideal, it is clearly distinguished from the immanent conditioning of ideas.[22]

Thus we have four groups of factors which each have a certain influence upon the origin of ideas: immanent, psychological, social and cultural. The sociology of knowledge turns its attention only to the last two groups. It seems that the contrast between the "Marxist" and the "idealistic" approach is but an aspect of the contrast between social and cultural factors. This is why we think it is preferable to translate our question into these terms: What is the comparative importance of the social and cultural antecedents in the conditioning of ideas?

However, this formulation is not yet completely satisfactory. Actually, when four factors act upon one thing, it is rather ineffectual to ask oneself what the respective importance of two of these factors is, when one ignores the possible importance of the other two. Hence it is necessary to formulate the problem in the following way: Four groups of antecedents are found at the origin of certain cognitive mental productions (or maybe all). What is the respective importance of these four groups?

The solution of this problem assumes that the realm of the sociology of knowledge has been investigated, if not completely, at least to a greater degree than it has been up to the present. The immanent determinants are fairly well known. They have been brought to light by numerous studies of the history of ideas. The study of the psychological determinants of ideas appears mainly in the form of the relationships between personality and opinion.[23]

One sees, therefore, that even a simple sketch of the answer to this question is premature. The research has not been pushed far enough in these four directions for us to have the least certainty about the respective importance of these four determinants of knowledge.

However, it is possible and opportune to add a few remarks.

1. It is very probable that one will never succeed in discovering an order of importance for these four factors valid for knowledge in general because it is not very probable that such an order exists.

For example, let us take, on the one hand, a politico-social theory like Marxism or Fascism. It includes a cognitive part: an interpretation of history. On the other hand, let us consider a system of geometry. It is probable that the position in the social structure of the partisans of a certain philosophy of history more greatly influences this philosophy of history than the social affiliations of the experts in geometry influence geometry. Likewise, it may be suspected that the psychological complexes of a metaphysician will appear more in his philosophy than those of a mathematician in his speculations.

It seems indeed that there is no valid order of importance for the whole of knowledge, but that certain types of knowledge are more sensitive to such factors and other types to other factors. These four factors may be considered as elements which can form different constellations for each type of knowledge. But, of course, it is only the positive study which can clarify these constellations.

2. Besides, it is very probable that the four factors will never completely take account of a cognitive mental production. There will always remain a certain margin of indeterminability due to the human agent which is the necessary intermediary. Now this human agent will not be just an aristocrat of German culture having a narcissistic type of personality and confronted with a certain philosophy containing in itself only certain possibilities of development. He will be to a certain degree an aristocrat different from the other nobles, a German different from all the other Germans, a narcissist different from all the others. It is, so to speak, necessary to add a fifth factor: the particular individuality.

This fifth factor is different from the others in the sense that it is an unknown which it does not seem possible to treat otherwise than as a residuary factor. Its importance, moreover, will diminish insofar as the social, cultural and psychological typologies are enriched.[24]

3. It is probable that the influence upon knowledge of this constellation of four factors cannot be conceived as a direct conditioning of each one of them on such knowledge, but that they act in a chain, so to speak. This, naturally, will make the appreciation of their respective importance difficult. The interpretation of the culture of Alor by Kardiner furnishes an example of a sequence of this type. The cultivation of the land falls on women (economico-social factor). There follows from this a certain type of education in which maternal care has but a small part (cultural factor). This tends to develop insecure personalities (psychological factor). This will have a certain influence upon their mental productions.[25]

4. Finally, it is interesting to note that the solution of the problem of the relative importance of the four factors exceeds each one

of the disciplines which is competent for the study of one or two of these factors: sociology of knowledge, psychology, and history of ideas.

How is one to designate the level on which this problem must be solved? It cannot be philosophy. We are, indeed, dealing with the comparison and synthesis of scientific results. We do not claim to attain the ultimate reality of things, nor to deduce the solution from metaphysical principles. What then?

It seems that our problem is one of those which do not respect the frontiers accepted between scientific disciplines. It can be solved neither by sociology nor psychology, nor intellectual history, but by a synthesis of the results of these different disciplines.

It matters little whether or not one gives a name to this field regrouping territories already distributed, but it is significant that more than one problem of social science necessitates a cross-disciplinary treatment.[26]

Notes

The references are abridged. The title of a book or an article is indicated solely by the author's name (without mentioning the first name unless it is indispensable) and by a figure indicating the page of his work. When an author has written several books or articles which are cited in this study, the capital letter (A, B, C, . . .) following his name indicates the book or article in question. Complete references are to be found in the bibliography, which is drawn up in alphabetical order (p. 298). Recourse to that bibliography will show that the reference "Mannheim: R, 45" means: "Karl Mannheim: *Diagnosis of Our Time,* Oxford University Press, New York, 1944, p. 45."

Chapter 1

INTRODUCTION

1. Cf. Lalande: art. *Connaître, Connaissance, Savoir, Science.* Professor Parsons sometimes translates *Wissenssoziologie* by "Sociology of Ideas" (Parsons: B, 680). Dr. Gerard DeGré has suggested the term "Gnosio-sociology" which would have the advantage of being shorter than "sociology of knowledge" and of providing an adjective form (DeGré: A. 110 n). He himself has readopted "sociology of knowledge" in his book following this article (DeGré: B). In French, *Sociologie du savoir* has been used. Thus Aron: 75. In Dutch, *Sociologie der kennis* is used by Hofstra, 39, while *Sociologie van het denken* is employed by Schmid. In Italian, *Sociologia del sapere* is made use of by K. Wolff (*La sociologia del sapere,* ricerca di una definizione, tesi, manoscritto, Biblioteca della Facultà di Lettere, Università degli Studi di Firenze, 1935. Cited by Mannheim: P, 303).
2. See Merton: I, 366. Grünwald in his definition of the sociology of knowledge adds *erkennen* to *wissen* (Grünwald: 2, 80).
3. "Lehre von der Verbundenheit des Wissens und Erkennens mit dem sozialen Sein," Grünwald: 12, 16, 52. "Seinsverbundenheit des Wissens," Mannheim: H, 239. The context indicates that in this formula, "existential" means nothing but social. See also Dahlke: 65. For Merton (I, 366), our discipline has to deal with the relations between knowledge and the other existential factors in society or culture. Barnes and Becker (vol. 2, 922) narrow the objective of the sociology of

knowledge to the determination of the precise ways in which the societies within which thinkers live, condition their social theories in their
form and content. For Lovejoy (p. 17), the sociology of knowledge
claims that the "modes of thought" of all individuals are related to and
conditioned by the nature of the social groups to which the individuals
belong. Social group means not merely economic classes, but also
professional, religious, educational groups, etc. Lovejoy's definition is
repeated by J. S. Roucek (art. *Wissenssoziologie* in Fairchild's *Dictionary of Sociology*).

4. See Kluckhohn and Kelly: 79.
5. Certain sociologists would like to embody in the sociology of knowledge
the study of the relation opposed to what we have just described: the
influence of ideas upon society. Thus for J. B. Gittler, the sociology
of science (he alludes to the natural sciences) ought to study the degree
to which science *influences* and is influenced by the dominant values,
attitudes, mores, habits, institutions and customs of society (Gittler:
351). In like manner Hofstra: 39. If I understand him correctly,
Znaniecki leans in the same direction. The sociology of knowledge
would study not only how the participation of men in certain social
systems determines their participation in certain systems of knowledge,
but also how their participation in systems of knowledge influences
their participation in social systems (Cf. Znaniecki: B, 8-10). However,
we believe it is preferable to keep a more limited aim for the sociology
of knowledge because almost all the sociologists of knowledge have
done so and because this discipline gains a great deal in unity of method
and purpose.
6. Cf. the paradigm for the sociology of knowledge in Merton: I, 372,
from which our scheme takes its inspiration.
7. The most complete appear to be: Grünwald, 1933, and Dahlke, 1940.
One may find valuable additions to it in Merton: C (1937), H (1941);
Speier: C (1938), and DeGré: B (1943).
8. Znaniecki: B, 1-2.
9. Mannheim: G, 56.
10. *Novum Organum,* §§ 38, 43, 46, 49, 52, 59. See a commentary on the
theory of the Idola from the point of view of the sociology of knowledge
in Grünwald: 4-5; Mannheim: G, 55; Barth: 37-54.
11. Cf. Speier: C, 204.
12. On the *Priestertrugtheorie* of the *Aufklärung* as a function of the
sociology of knowledge, Cf. Grünwald: 5 f. On Voltaire, from the same
point of view, Merton: C, 494. Another forerunner is Destutt de Tracy,
who invented the word "idéologie." Cf. Barth: 15-35.
13. Gorer: A, 37; Lovejoy: 16-17. There are certain kinds of irrational
factors such as inspiration, grace, and *caritas* whose influence has always
been stressed by different mystic philosophies and religions. From the
point of view of those philosophies and religions, that kind of irrationality has a very high cognitive value.
14. On the significance of Pareto from the point of view of the sociology
of knowledge, see DeGré: B, 23-53; Grünwald: 9-13. On Sorel: De-

Gré: B, 45-50; Grünwald: 14 f. On Nietzsche: DeGré: B, 2-9; Grünwald: 7-9; Barth: 207-282. On Marx: Merton: I, passim; Dahlke: 77-81; Grünwald: 33-42; Barth: 73-190.

15. Cf. Wirth: B, xxiv ff.; Mannheim: P, 30-48; Merton: I, 367-371; Dahlke: 64 f; Speier: B, 55. See various descriptions of this state of *anomie* in Mannheim: R, 15-18; Sorokin: AN, 247-252; Wirth: A.

16. Such is the case with Marx. He is considered as a Wissenssoziologist by Merton and Dahlke, and as a precursor by Grünwald and Mannheim. See references, note 14. Durkheim is a precursor for Grünwald, and a sociologist of knowledge for Merton, Dahlke and DeGré. See references, note 19.

17. Grünwald: 107.

18. The best documented exposition of German Wissenssoziologie is in Grünwald: 107-234. See also Aron: 75-96, and the bibliography of Mannheim, which is general but gives a large place to German authors (P, 281-304 and especially 299-303). On the sociology of knowledge of Wilhelm Jerusalem, Georg Lukàcs, and Max Scheler, see Dahlke, 72-77. On Lukàcs, see also Child: A, 213-216; C, 160-167. On Scheler, see also Merton: I, passim; Becker: B; Small; Child: B, 407-410, C, 154-159; Gurvitch: A, 129-137. The studies on Mannheim will be cited in the chapters to follow. On the Wissenschaftslehre of Weber, a field close to Wissenssoziologie, Cf. Schelting: A. A general discussion and an elaborate one of Weber (and of Durkheim and Pareto) is to be found in Parsons: C, G, I. On the philosophical problems raised by the concept of "ideology," see Barth's *Wahrheit und Ideologie*, 1945.

19. The French sociology of knowledge as such has been less studied. The best bibliography is probably that of Merton: H, 125n-126n. On Durkheim, insofar as he is a sociologist of knowledge, see Dupréel: A, B; Schaub; Grünwald: 16-23; DeGré: B, 54-84; Dahlke: 66-71; Merton: I, passim. The two important studies by Gurvitch (B and C) should be mentioned here. Unfortunately, they came to the notice of the author too late to be taken into account in this book. See also Gurvitch's forthcoming *Introduction à la sociologie de la connaissance*.

20. Thus, during the year 1947-1948, courses in the sociology of knowledge were given at the University of Chicago (Prof. Louis Wirth), at the University of Wisconsin at Madison (Prof. H. Becker), at the University of Colorado at Boulder (Prof. Reinhart Bendix), and at the New School for Social Research in New York (Prof. Alfred Schütz).

21. Thorstein Veblen, *The Higher Learning in America: A Memorandum on the Conduct of Universities by Businessmen*, 1918. Academic organization has also been studied from the sociological point of view in positive studies like those of Logan Wilson, *The Academic Man*, 1942, and of Hubert Park, *Men Who Control Our Universities*, 1947 (this is a study of the professions of 734 trustees of 30 institutions of higher learning in the United States).

22. Wirth: B, xix f.; Mills: A, B; DeGré: B, 81-84; Child: B, 416 ff., C, 182-183. These last three authors have shown, but in a very concise

way, all that the sociology of knowledge might utilize of certain constructions of the social psychology of G. H. Mead (*Mind, Self, and
Society*, 1934), like the "generalized other."

23. The studies on Sorokin will be cited in the course of the chapters concerning him. On Znaniecki, cf. Merton: G, and DeGré: B, 89-94.
Apart from the brilliant theoretical analyses published in various re-
views by Merton, Child, Mills, DeGré and others (which are worthy of
leading to more ample works), American sociology in this field seems
to remain faithful to one of its constants: the positive and very exact
study of distinctly restricted facts. (On the relative importance of
this tendency among others in American sociology during recent years,
see Shils: B; Parsons: H.) In our field, we might really be satisfied if
a theoretical concern always directed this research (it is, for instance,
the case with Merton: E): that is to say, if the positive researches were
conducted with a view to controlling in a restricted field such-and-such
an hypothesis concerning the relationship between science and society.
But even when such a concern is lacking, the positive researches can
provide valuable material for the sociology of knowledge. Thus, Harshorne, *The German Universities and National-Socialism*, 1938; Woodward, *Making Government Opinion Research Bear Upon Operation*,
1944; Lazarsfeld, *The People's Choice:* how the voter makes up his mind
in a presidential election, 1944; Merton, *Mass Persuasion*, 1946, and in
general the numerous monographs having to do with propaganda.

24. "In the first place, it is a purely empirical investigation through description and structural analysis of the ways in which social relationships,
in fact, influence thought," Mannheim: H, 239. On the positive character of sociological research, cf. Leclercq: A, 38 ff.; Joussain: 56 ff.;
Haesaert: 9 f.; Lalande: art. *Science, Philosophie.*

25. Thus Durkheim, in *Les formes élémentaires de la vie religieuse*, elaborates a sociological theory of knowledge (see especially the philosophical level where he raises the question, p. 18 ff.). Jerusalem, also, whose
ideas bear a strong resemblance to those of Durkheim (Jerusalem: C,
406-431). Scheler (Cf. A, Preface), Mannheim and Sorokin, although
very differently, also draw philosophical implications from the results
of their positive research. Mills also defends the philosophical relevance of the sociology of knowledge (B).

26. On the double aspect, positive and philosophical, of Wissenssoziologie,
see Mannheim, especially H, 237 ff., 256 ff.; Dahlke (relative and sub-
stantive approach, 65 f.); DeGré: A; Speier: B.

27. The following can be linked more or less clearly to this tendency:
Schelting: B, 634; Parsons: B, 677 f.; Lovejoy: 17 f.; Sabine: 172 f.;
Dahlke: 85 ff.; Speier: B, 159.

28. It would be necessary to have proved previously that there is a very
special relationship between society and knowledge. If the social nature
of knowledge is admitted, it may then be legitimate to give a privileged
place in the constitution of a philosophy of knowledge to the social
determinants of knowledge (cf., on a subject linked with this, note 30).
But this is not what the holders of this opinion generally do.

29. For example, Pierre Duhem: *La théorie physique*, 1906; H. Poincaré:

Science et Hypothèse, 1912; A. Eddington: *The Nature of the Physical World,* 1928; L. de Broglie: *Recueil d'exposés sur les ondes et les corpuscules,* 1930; F. Renoirte: *Eléments de critique des sciences et de cosmologie,* 1945, etc.

30. Besides the two points of contact with philosophy which have been indicated (the results of the sociology of knowledge raise problems for philosophy; they imply a philosophy), the philosophy of knowledge would have a third. Here is how:

This discipline, it is said, rests upon the postulate that social factors can influence knowledge. If we do not accept this postulate, we may reject all of the sociology of knowledge. Now we are never compelled to accept a postulate. We may prefer to interpret ideas as functions of other non-theoretical factors (race, geography, climate, psychology, etc.) or, of course, we may prefer a pure immanent interpretation also. Such is the radical position of Grünwald (65 ff.).

Thus it would not be sufficient to show by way of the methods usually employed in the social sciences that such a factor influences such an aspect of mental productions, but it would still be necessary to show beforehand the theoretical possibility of such an influence. This is what Child attempts to do by means of the theory of G. H. Mead. If mind emerges in the process of communication, if the exercise of thought consists fundamentally in the manipulation of generalized attitudes, if, in a word, mind is, by its origin and nature, ineluctably social, it follows from this that the fundamental supposition of the sociology of knowledge is not a postulate, a simple schema of possible interpretation which we are free to accept or refuse according to our preferences (Child: B, 416-418).

It seems to us that Child has conceded too much to the "postulational skepticism" of Grünwald. The latter's requirements would render all science impossible. Imagine somebody refusing to accept the results of physics because the regularity of the phenomena of nature is but a postulate! We judge a science not by its postulates but by its results. When a sociologist shows that a certain social factor has a certain influence on a certain aspect of mental productions, we may reject this result if it has been obtained by a process which is open to criticism, but we cannot reject it on any other basis. Grünwald's position implies that we accept the results, not because of their proofs but simply because we *believe* in a general way that we must interpret ideas as a function of society. Such skepticism of the value of scientific proofs condemns all positive science. In the same sense, see Speier: A, 682.

A reply of this type seems enough. To attempt to prove, as Child does, that knowledge is social by nature, and that the fundamental supposition of the sociology of knowledge is not a pure postulate, is a very neat attitude with regard to the opponent, but it implies the acceptance of a certain philosophy of knowledge. This is either another postulate which we can reject as readily as the first, or this requires the exposition and proof of a whole system. After having taken all this trouble, nothing guarantees that the "postulational skeptic" will not say that a sociological theory of knowledge makes only *probable,* but not *certain,* the special relationships which a positive study may discover between certain social factors and certain mental productions.

31. Bacon, Aphorism xxvi. This, as well as the opinion of T. H. Huxley, is cited in Northrop: B, 5, 10 f. We will return to this role of the "anticipations" in the progress of science.

PART ONE: KARL MANNHEIM

Chapter 2

MANNHEIM'S SOCIOLOGY OF KNOWLEDGE

1. For example, Aron (75-95) and Hofstra (40 ff.) limit their account of the German *Wissenssoziologie* to Mannheim.
2. About all these influences: Ernst Mannheim: 471 f.; Merton: H, 126-128; Salomon: 352 ff. About the Marxist influence: Ascoli: 101; Barnes and Becker: vol. II, 924; Merton: H, 126, B, 377; Schelting: B, 664; Speier: B, 156; Aron: 80; Wirth: C, 357; Mandelbaum: 67. On the attitude of the Marxist orthodoxy toward him: Guthrie: 230 n; Feuer: 419.
3. Mannheim: P, 47.
4. Mannheim: P, 47, Q, 32.
5. Mannheim: H, 237 ff., 256 ff.
6. Mannheim: G, 49, 66, 67, H, 238.
7. Mannheim: D, G, 50.
8. Mannheim: G, 50 f. He defines noology as the study of the contents and forms of thought in their purely cognitive interrelations (P, 314).
9. Mannheim: G, 51.
10. Mannheim: G, 52.
11. Mannheim: H, 239.
12. Mannheim: G, 62.
13. Let us recall that the theoretical justification of that view lies in Marx's philosophy of history. The proletariat, because of its historical mission, considers reality in its true perspective. Hence its thought cannot be ideological.
14. As the translators indicate it, the German expression *Seinsverbundenheit des Wissens* leaves the exact nature of the determinism open. Mannheim: H, 239 n.
15. The arrangement in this chapter does not pretend to follow the historical sequence of Mannheim's studies. We attempt to follow an "order of methodical invention"—i.e., a sequence as logical as possible of problems and solutions. Cf. Van Steenberghen, 14.
16. Mannheim: G, 173-174, N.
17. Mannheim: G, 108-110, 197-206.
18. Mannheim: G, 190-197.
19. Mannheim: E, G, 106-108, 206-215.
20. *Marx-Engels Archiv.,* ed. by D. Ryazanov, Frankfurt a.M., Vol. I, 252. Quoted by Mannheim: G, 112.

21. Lenin: *What Is To Be Done?*, New York and London, 1931. Quoted by Mannheim: G, 116.
22. Mannheim: G, 110-119, 215-222. See a psychoanalytic interpretation of the vagueness of the classless society in Lasswell: 134.
23. Mannheim deals here only with Italian fascism (G, 119-126). The three quotations from Mussolini are taken from B. Mussolini: *Reden,* ed. by H. Meyer, Leipzig, 1928, 74, 105, 13. Quoted by Mannheim: G, 121, 119.
24. Mannheim: G, 126, 225.
25. Mannheim: H, 245 f. In a subsequent book, Mannheim elaborates three conceptions of freedom, each of them corresponding to a different stage of social and intellectual technique: casual discovery, invention, and planification (Q, 369-381).
26. Mannheim: H, 246 f.
27. Mannheim: L, 20 f.
28. Mannheim: H, 248 f.
29. Mannheim: P, 2 f.
30. Mannheim: G, 116. Italics added.
31. Mannheim: H, 248. In a monograph (F), Mannheim considers the history of ideas as affected by competition and succession of generations.
32. Mannheim: H, 248.
33. Cf. interpretation of Merton: I, 377.
34. Mannheim: H, 244.
35. Mannheim: G, 71.
36. Mannheim: G, 150.
37. Mannheim: H, 250.
38. Mannheim: H, 261.
39. Mannheim: P, 1.
40. Mannheim: H, 243 f. Cf. Merton: I, 383.
41. Mannheim: H, 245-250.
42. Mannheim: H, 239 n.
43. Here are some of them (the italics are ours): "The chiliastic experience is *characteristic* of the lowest strata of society. *Underlying* it is a mental structure peculiar to oppressed peasants . . ." (G, 204). "This extreme need for theory is the *expression* of a class society. . . . The essential irrationality which *goes with* revolution . . ." (G, 117). "This *is* the ideology *of* a 'putschist' group . . ." (G, 125). "[The conservatives] tend to use morphological categories . . . the analytical approach [is] *characteristic* of the parties of the left" (H, 246). The mobile types, in society, *are generally* more abstract and more reflexive (L, 21). "It is *never an accident* when a certain theory fails to develop . . ." (H, 248). "The ethics of the earliest Christian communities . . . was *primarily intelligible* in terms of resentment of oppressed strata" (P, 40). "The liberal conception of freedom *was that of* a group which sought to overthrow . . . the social order. The conservative idea of freedom *was that of* a stratum which did not wish to see any changes . . ." (H, 245).
44. Mannheim: H, 249.

45. Mannheim: H, 239 n.
46. The last three quotations are from Mannheim: G, 72, 76, 223. Italics added.
47. Mannheim: Q, 15. Italics added.
48. Aron: 83.
49. It seems that, for the Marxists, the idea, if not abstract from the total historical life and if not "autonomous," could have another reality than that of being a mere superstructure of economic relationships. "It is not true that the economic situation is the only cause and alone active, and that all other phenomena are only a passive effect" (Engels to Starkenburg, 1894. Quoted by Merleau-Ponty, 175. This paper is an interpretation of Marx in that direction). Cf. Koestler: 165.
50. Van Steenberghen: 14.
51. Mannheim: H, 246. Cf. L, 21.
52. Merton: H, 137; Aron: 75.
53. Mannheim: H, 275-278.
54. Mannheim: H, 276.
55. Mannheim: H, 277 f.

Chapter 3

EVALUATION OF MANNHEIM'S SOCIOLOGY OF KNOWLEDGE

1. See different versions of this scheme in recent books dealing with the methodology of sciences. Renoirte: *Eléments de critique des sciences et de cosmologie,* 1945; Conant: *On Understanding Science,* 1947; Northrop: *The Logic of the Sciences and the Humanities,* 1947.
2. See above: 35 ff.
3. Child: A, 206-207.
4. Merton: H, 140.
5. For instance, see Myrdal: 8-9.
6. Mannheim: H, 276.
7. Weber: E, 294.
8. Weber: F, 110.
9. Weber: E, 324. Concerning the Ideal types, see Parsons: G, 12-15; Gerth and Mills, in Weber: E, 59-60; Abel: 155-156.
10. Mannheim: P, 40-42. The influence of phenomenology and particularly of Max Scheler is clear in these pages. Cf. Max Scheler: A.
11. Mannheim: J, 19-20.
12. Mannheim: H, 277. For another interpretation of Mannheim's method of imputation, cf. Child: A, 204-207.
13. Mannheim's thought-totalities are different from Weber's ideal types inasmuch as the logic of ideal types is purely rational. Cf. Weber: F, 92. We shall comment later on that important distinction between the different types of logic. On the internal comprehension of literature, see Maquet: A.
14. Mannheim: H, 275-276.

15. Mannheim: H, 239 n.
16. Grünwald: 92-93.
17. Cf. the different notions of "social class" and their discussion in Sorokin: AR, 261-271, BU; for Sorokin's very elaborate notion, see AR, 271-275.
18. Speier: B, 163-164.
19. Linton: A, 110 ff.
20. Mannheim: H, 244. Cf. Lasswell: 7, 112.
21. Cf. Warner and Lunt: A, 81-91; B, 2-5, 27-66; Warner and Srole: 67-102. Class is considered here rather as a cultural unit (cf. Gordon). For an example of the permeation of the middle-class mentality in the "upper-crust" of Plainville, see West: 119. Cf. Gorer: B, 212.
22. Sorokin: AD, 578-588; on the difference between political parties and occupational-economic groups, Sorokin: AR, 219-225.
23. Mannheim: H, 248.
24. Cf. above: 92 ff., and in the conclusions, 242-248.
25. Mannheim: H, 280.
26. Mannheim: G, 228-229, I, 276-281, J, 29-33. These texts were written in 1929, 1932, 1934, respectively.
27. Mannheim: Q, 207-208.
28. F. Neumann: *Koalitionsfreiheit und Reichsverfassung,* Berlin, 1932, p. 53; J. W. Heidemann, *Die Flucht in die General Klanzeln,* Tubingen, 1933; K. Geiler, *Beiträge zum Wirtshaftsrecht,* Mannheim, 1932. Cited by Mannheim: Q, 181.
29. Mannheim: Q, 181-182.
30. Max Scheler: A, 123 n., gives a good example of anarchist and humanitarian ideas having their source in the personal history of their exponent — in this case, Prince Kropotkin. After the death of his mother, whom he adored, his father married again. The resulting conflict led Kropotkin to adopt the cause of his father's servants and finally to switch to anarchist ideas.
31. Mannheim: P, 22, 24, 25. Cf. also P, 26, 27 and G, 97.
32. Mannheim: D. Cf. Falk: 272.
33. Mannheim: H, 240.
34. Schelting: B, 664.
35. Mannheim: J, 13, 14, 17.
36. Lalande: art. *Condition,* sens B.
37. Cf. Mannheim: G, 119, 125.
38. We shall deal with that question again, in the general conclusions, pp. 257-260.

Chapter 4

MANNHEIM'S PHILOSOPHY OF KNOWLEDGE

1. A difficulty of terminology arises here. The word *epistemology* has two different usages in English. (a) In a broad sense, it means at the same time *Erkenntnistheorie* (in French: *théorie de la connaissance*)

and *Wissenschaftslehre* (in French: *épistémologie*). (b) In a narrow sense, it means *Wissenschaftslehre*, and the translation for *Erkenntnistheorie* will be *theory of knowledge* (Lalande: art. *épistemologie*, note by Bertrand Russell). However, there is no unanimity on that question. Thus, cf. Baldwin: art. *Epistemology* and *Gnosiology*.

Mannheim uses the word *Erkenntnistheorie* in reference to the conceptions dealt with in this chapter. The American translators Wirth and Shils have translated it by *epistemology* (sense a). As in the criticism of Mannheim's conceptions in that field (next chapter) it has been found advisable to distinguish between *Erkenntnistheorie* and *Wissenschaftslehre*, it would be misleading to understand *epistemology* in a broad sense in this chapter and a narrow sense in the following. So *Erkenntnistheorie* should be translated *theory of knowledge*. Unfortunately in the present monograph, the word *theory* has a well-defined meaning: the third stage of a scientific system. To avoid any confusion, in reference to *Erkenntnistheorie*, we shall use the terms: philosophical theory of knowledge, gnosiology (the German *gnoseologie* being a synonym of *Erkenntnistheorie*).

2. For instance, Schelting: A, 94-100; 117-167, B; Stern; Hofstra: 39-51; Tillich; Marcuse; Aron: 80-94; Ascoli; Speier: B, C; Parsons: B, 678.
3. Mannheim: Q, 27.
4. Mannheim: H, 237.
5. Another interpretation: Merton: H, 140-141.
6. Mannheim: H, 239.
7. Mannheim: H, 256-257.
8. Mannheim: H, 259.
9. Mannheim: H, 240.
10. Mannheim: G, 87.
11. For instance, Mannheim: H, 259, 270. Cf. Mandelbaum: 79.
12. For instance, Mannheim: H, 267, 268.
13. Mannheim: G, 166.
14. Mannheim: G, 166-167, H, 272, 273.
15. For instance, Mannheim: H, 266, 270.
16. Mannheim: H, 252-253.
17. Mannheim: H, 253.
18. Mannheim: H, 256.
19. Ibid.
20. Mannheim: G, 70.
21. Mannheim: H, 261, 263, 265.
22. Mannheim: H, 265-266. He adds, in parentheses: "It is interesting to note that the connotations of the designation 'impure knowledge' seem to point to a magical origin of the term."
23. Mannheim: H, 267.
24. Mannheim: H, 258-260.
25. Mannheim: H, 266.
26. Mannheim: G, 71.
27. Mannheim: H, 268.
28. Mannheim: H, 269.
29. Mannheim: H, 262-264, 270-271.

30. Mannheim applies his relationism to ethics also. Relativism in that realm would mean that there are no objective values and that, consequently, the moral obligation cannot exist. For the relationism, there is a moral obligation, but it is derived from the concrete situation to which the obligation referred. Values and ideas are not considered separately any more but are constantly related to social situations and structures. Mannheim: J, 16.
31. Mannheim: H, 270.
32. Ibid.
33. See above: 60.
34. Mannheim: G, 131-132.
35. Ibid.
36. Mannheim: G, 135.
37. Mannheim: G, 136.
38. Mannheim, G, 134. Here are the references for the examples: for bureaucratic conservatism: G, 104-106, 132; for conservative historicism: G, 106-108, 132-133; for bourgeois liberalism: G, 108-110, 133; for Marxism: G, 110-119, 133-134; for fascism: G, 119-130, 134.
39. The measure in which he succeeds is indicated by the following scheme:

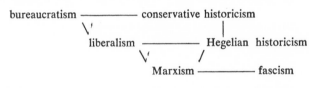

The antithesis of the first triad which reappears in the antithesis of the second one does not look like a success from the point of view of logical esthetics.
40. Mannheim: G, 137.
41. Mannheim: G, 138.
42. Mannheim: G, 137-142. An historical example of the synthesis-role of the intellectuals is given by the Renaissance humanists. Cf. Mannheim: N. On Mannheim's personal attitude, cf. Wirth: C and Mannheim: Q, 4.
43. Mannheim: H, 271.
44. Mannheim: G, 174-176.
45. Mannheim: G, 175.
46. Mannheim: G, 184.
47. Mannheim: G, 85. See a similar interpretation of these facts in Tawney: 39 ff.
48. Mannheim: G, 85.
49. Merton: H, 145. He has very skillfully compared some texts by Mannheim about the intelligentsia with Marxist texts concerning the proletariat. Merton: H, 140.
50. Mannheim: H, 237.
51. Mannheim: G, 169. Cf. Salomon: 357.
52. Mannheim: G, 142. Cf. Wirth: B, xxvii.

Chapter 5

EVALUATION OF MANNHEIM'S PHILOSOPHY OF KNOWLEDGE

1. See above, chapter 4, note 1, pp. 269-270.
2. Van Steenberghen: 9; Van Riet: v, 645 ff.
3. Van Riet: 637, 658.
4. Lalande: art. *Epistémologie.*
5. Lewis: 10-11.
6. Parsons: C, 20-27 and especially 23-24.
7. Mandelbaum: 1-2.
8. Van Riet: 659; Lalande: ibid.; Parsons (C, 24 n) and Lewis insist on the general aspect of epistemology.
9. Cf. analytical and critical stage of epistemology as they are described by Van Steenberghen: 23-24 and Van Riet: 655-656.
10. Baldwin: art. *Gnosiology.*
11. Noël: A, 24, 233, 234, 241, B, 159-178 (especially 163, 164).
12. Cf. Northrop: A, 274-275.
13. Certain philosophers have reduced epistemology to that. See, for example, in Van Riet: 656-657 (the metaphysical method).
14. Cf. Lewis: 9, 27.
15. See above: 58.
16. Mannheim: H, 265. See above: 61-62.
17. Mannheim: H, 259-260.
18. Mannheim: G, 87.
19. See above: 59.
20. See above: 60.
21. Merton: H, 143-144.
22. Mannheim: P, 42-43.
23. Mannheim: G, 141. We are not concerned here with the Chinese or the Medieval intellectuals who seem to have constituted real social groups, but rather with the modern Western intelligentsia. Cf. Koestler: 166-167; Wolpert; Blàha. For an extensive bibliography on that question, see Michels: 124-126; Lasswell: 113 n.
24. Schelting: B, 664; Parsons: B, 680; Speier: B, 163; Mandelbaum: 67, 82, 89.
25. Cf. Lalande: art. *Relativité de la connaissance,* especially Hamilton's third sense.
26. Parsons: B, 680.
27. See above: 72 ff.
28. Mannheim: P, 22. See above: 64.
29. Mannheim: H, 263.
30. Cf. Leclercq: B, 602.
31. See above: 19.
32. Engels: 453.
33. Mannheim: G, 84.

34. Mannheim: G, 86.
35. Mannheim: G, 179. See also: 87, 88, 178. Mandelbaum: 89, stresses also the fact that Mannheim sees beyond every concrete event the ultimate reality of change.
36. Engels: 453.
37. Mannheim: G, 217.
38. Cf. Mannheim: G, 229.
39. Mannheim: H, 267.
40. Mannheim: B, 54 and in general 52-60. Aron: 83 and Schelting: B, 669, suggest a criticism in that direction. See also Brinkmann: 53-54.
41. Hegel: 10.
42. Cf. Hegel. 22.
43. Mannheim: G, 179-180.
44. Hegel: 54.
45. Hegel: 63. See Grégoire, especially 40-70.
46. Raphaël: 12-33.
47. Marx: 2d thesis on Feuerbach, 471.
48. Mandelbaum: 72-73.
49. See above: 70 ff.
50. Mannheim: G, 179.
51. See above: 29, 32.

Chapter 6

CONCLUSIONS DRAWN FROM THE STUDY OF MANNHEIM

1. It could be objected that Mannheim, starting from the observed facts, has not explicitly reached ontological dynamism. This is true, but, as we have shown above, it is not impossible to go further than the affirmation of the activistic nature of thought. Moreover, it is certain that Mannheim passes from the empirical level to the philosophic one. That is essential.
2. See above: 33-35.
3. See above: 87-88, 90-91.
4. See above: 48.
5. Mannheim passes from the results of his positive researches to that principle, rather through the problem of the value of perspective knowledge than directly. But this does not change the bearing of his proceeding.
6. See above, chapter 1, note 29, pp. 264-265.
7. Duhem: A, 26. Cf. Renoirte: 153 ff.
8. Here we do not follow Duhem's terminology. For him, a mathematical proposition is not an explanation: to explain is but to unveil the nature of reality either hypothetically or with certainty. Cf. Duhem: A, 24. However, his acceptance of natural classification reintroduces somewhat a relationship with reality. Cf. A, 38.
9. Renoirte: 153.

10. We shall meet other types of phenomenal explanation in the sociology of knowledge: logical and even what Leslie A. White terms "culturological." Cf. his paper cited in the bibliography.

11. Cf. above: 51 ff.

12. A similar problem is raised when a spiritualistic philosopher is confronted with the fact that the actions of a being endowed with free-will can be expressed in laws according to which it is possible to predict his behavior. For a solution of that question, see Leclercq: A, 71-87.

13. Leclercq: B, 603.

14. The determination of cultural personality types raises many difficult problems that we can just mention here. Cultures, ways of life of a group, are indeed on different levels. We can say that each family has a culture, but we can also talk about the culture of the United States, or even of the Occident. To which one of cultural unities does a particular psychological structure correspond? May we speak of "the personality type of the X family," of the "Spanish character" or of the "Occidental personality?" The answer to this problem is closely related to another: How do we conceive of the way in which this cultural personality type is formed? Thus, if the *basic personality type* is constituted mainly during the individual's early experience, as it is for Dr. Kardiner and Professor Linton, we shall tend to take as the cultural unity to which a basic personality type corresponds, the unity in which child training is performed along the same patterns.

   The notion of the *basic personality type* is expounded by Linton (in Kardiner: A, vi ff., C, vii ff.) and Kardiner: B. For the analysis of concrete cultures along this line, see Kardiner: A and C; Cora DuBois.

15. Whatever the solutions of the problems raised in note 14 may be, it seems safe, however, to assume the existence of a capitalistic culture as a basis for a personality type. The best proof being the descriptions of that personality. Here are a few of them. Sombart: 13 ff. (production for exchange instead of production for use), 168-189 (character of the modern businessman). Sorokin: AC, 508-529 (psychological consequences of social mobility), AK, 104-118 (contractual instead of familistic relationships), AR, 121-122 (the moral norms of competition and rivalry), 515-516 (ethos of competition). Mannheim: R, 168-169 (competition and inferiority complex), 170-173 (gregarious mentality). Weber: D, 21-22 (rational organization of the enterprise and rationalized life). Margaret Mead: B, 138 ff. (economic depression and aggressiveness), 159 (metropolitan life and passivity). Horney: A, 286-287 (competitiveness, potential hostilities and feeling of isolation), B, 173 (idem), C, 24 (neurotic conflicts and types of culture). Knight: 41-75 (ethics of competition). Lasswell: 261 ff. (psychological strains of the contemporary middle-class). Etc.

16. Weber: A, vol. I, 94. Cited by Mannheim: Q, 202.

17. Mannheim: Q, 19.

18. This solution of the paradox is not very far from what has been called above (see n. 10, above) a culturological principle of explanation. Instead of a philosophical principle (as "the nature of knowledge is activistic") we could use a culturological one (as "the capitalistic per-

sonality type uses knowledge as an instrument for practical aims"), to explain the results of observation. Our solution evokes also Mannheim's *principium medium* which he uses in his last books. It is a principle which is not to be applied to human conduct as such, but which is tied up to a particular stage of society (Mannheim: Q, 181). However, there is no question here of substituting another one for Mannheim's theory, but only of showing how his theory, which is good, has, at the same time, a philosophical meaning which we suppose false. A substitution of theories would change the data of the problem. This is not a good way to solve it.

19. Weber: A, vol. I, 94 ff. Cited by Mannheim: Q, 201n-202n. Cf. Weber: C, 355.
20. See Mannheim: K, L, O, Q, R.
21. See above: 74.
22. See above: 81.
23. Ascoli: 106.

PART TWO: PITIRIM A. SOROKIN

Chapter 7

GENERAL FRAMEWORK OF SOROKIN'S SOCIOLOGY OF KNOWLEDGE

1. *Crime and Punishment,* 1914 (in Russian); *Leo Tolstoï as Philosopher,* 1915 (in Russian).
2. Sorokin: AQ, 7-8.
3. Block: 782.
4. *Systema soziologii,* 2 vol., 1920-21 (in Russian). Some of the theses of this work are mentioned in the Introduction of the German edition of AB (*Die Soziologie der Revolution,* München, 1928) by Hans Kasspohl. *The Influence of Inanition on Human Behavior, Social Organization and Social Life* was an empirical study of the consequences of the 1921 starvation in Russia. The edition, in course of publication in Petrograd, was destroyed by the Soviet Government (1922). A short summary of this work is given in *Contemporary Social Theories* (AD, 629 ff.).
5. Sorokin: BA, 64-65, AD, 617-635.
6. Sorokin: AA, 119, 123, 145, 202.
7. Sorokin: AI, ix.
8. See specially Sorokin: AB, 17-31.
9. Barnes and Becker: vol. II, 1056.
10. Sorokin: AC, ix.
11. Sorokin: AC, 215-316.
12. Cf. especially Sorokin: AL, 89-125. Some traces of behaviorism can be found in later books. Thus in AK, 174, his analysis of human liberty suggests the "freedom reflex" of dogs studied by Pavlov.

13. Sorokin: AD, 600.
14. Sorokin: AD, 433.
15. Laserson: 687.
16. See also Sorokin: AR, 18.
17. Sorokin: AM, 40-44, AP, 4-12, AR, 47-51. Cf. Laserson: 687-688.
18. Sorokin: AR, 7.
19. Sorokin: AI, xi.
20. As, for instance, BB, BD, BF, BJ.
21. In addition to the books cited here, Sorokin wrote *Principles of Rural-Urban Sociology* (with Carle C. Zimmerman, 1929) and *Systematic Source Book in Rural Sociology* (with Carle C. Zimmerman and Charles J. Galpin, 3 vol., 1930-1932).
22. Sorokin: AM, 775-779.
23. Sorokin: AR, 119, 131. That concern for social action was probably pre-existent to its explicit manifestation. Although Professor Sorokin has condemned the intrusion of value judgments in sociology (AC, ix, AE, vi, BC, 316), he has vigorously expressed his preferences and dislikes for certain scientific doctrines and even certain forms of culture. For instance, see what he thinks concerning "fact-finders" in AM, 434, 435n, 766-767, BH, 95-96; concerning psychoanalysis in AJ, 115, AK, 152, AS, 191, etc. Hence the controversies about his works have been too often very emotional and out of focus. Some critics have attacked him violently only because they did not like his evaluations (for instance, Guthrie, Mumford). Others have praised him for the same reason (for instance, Hanley, LaFarge). Even certain specialists seem to have overlooked the essentials because they were so anxious to reject his evaluations (see for instance: Brinton, Goldenweiser, and the answers to these: BO, BP). Granted that such value judgments are undesirable, in the case of Sorokin they are incidental and do not interfere with the scientific significance of his work.
24. Sorokin: AR, 3.
25. Sorokin: AR, 5.
26. Sorokin: AR, 39-40.
27. See C. I. Lewis: *The Modes of Meaning*, in *Philosophy and Phenomenological Research*, vol. IV, p. 236. Quoted by Sorokin: AR, 40.
28. Sorokin: AR, 42n.
29. Sorokin: AP, 4-12; AR, 41-63. For the first form of these notions, cf. AM, 3-44.
30. Sorokin: AR, 42.
31. Sorokin: AP, 5, AR, 47.
32. Sorokin: AM, 13, AP, 6, AR, 51, 61.
33. Sorokin: AR, 58, 556-562. See above: 189.
34. Sorokin: AM, 55. Cf. 53-56.
35. Sorokin: AE, 3-8, AR, 7-8.
36. Sorokin: AR, 14, 65.
37. Sorokin: AR, 64.
38. Sorokin: AR, 16-17.

39. See its place in Dynamics: "From Art, we pass now to the next fundamental 'compartment' of culture . . ." Sorokin: AJ, 3.

40. In AR, Sorokin expresses these ideas by distinguishing three levels in the culture of a person or group. The *ideological culture* is the totality of meanings, values and norms possessed by an individual or a group. The term "ideology" indicates only the most spiritual aspect of culture. It does not convey the special sense given to it by Marx and Mannheim (see above: 21 ff.). In this part, it will be used only in Sorokin's sense. The *behavioral culture* is the totality of the actions and reactions of the person or the group through which the ideological culture (meanings, norms and values) are objectified and socialized. The *material culture* is the totality of all the vehicles, other than the behavior of the human agents, through which the ideological culture is manifested (AR, 313). One can see also that Sorokin's notion of "culture" is more inclusive than the usual conception of that term (cf. above: 252-253).

41. Sorokin: AR, 314-316.

42. Sorokin: AR, 321-324. Those definitions and distinctions are extremely important as conceptual tools for the solution of the problem of the integration of culture which is sometimes overlooked even by the students of culture (AM, 102-105, AR, 337-341, BS, 380-383). Merton (H, 139n, J, 396) stresses also the relevance of Sorokin's *Dynamics* (whose contemplated title was *The Integrated Culture,* BI, 520n) in that respect.

43. Sorokin: AM, 106-124, AR, 317-319.

44. Northrop: A, 21-28.

45. Sorokin: AM, 137, 164-195, AR, 580-582, 668-673.

46. In the first exposition of this system, Sorokin speaks of seven types of culture (AI, 55-101). There are the three we have just mentioned, and four combined forms: the mixed cultural systems. We shall overlook the latter which are only qualifications of the three essential ones. Sorokin himself generally uses the classification with three types in his *Dynamics* (cf. AM, 137) and subsequent books (AN, 19-21, AR, 319-321, etc.).

47. Sorokin: AI, 55-101, 112-134, 140.

48. Sorokin: AI, 143-150.

49. Sorokin: AR, 320.

50. This interpretation is in conformity with Sorokin's ideas on knowledge, as we shall see later. He assigns to intuition a great role in intellectual creation (AM, 759, AP, 228) and even in the scientific method (AR, 18, 546-547).

51. Sorokin: AR, 537-592.

52. Sorokin: AM, 737.

53. See the graphs in *Dynamics,* especially AI, 404, AJ, 189, 190, 629, 630.

54. See the second part of Sorokin: AI (195-688) and the summary (671-681).

55. Sorokin: AI, 22-47, AP, 18, 39.

Chapter 8

SOROKIN'S SOCIOLOGY OF KNOWLEDGE

1. Sorokin: AJ, vii, 3. Sorokin being much more systematic than Mannheim, our description of his sociology of knowledge will follow his own exposition closely. However, we have changed his arrangement or his divisions when these modifications appeared advisable.
2. The term *truth* does not mean here more than *validity*. It leaves open the question of the kind of validity knowledge can reach. As the three conceptions of truth are deduced from philosophical positions concerning the ultimate nature of reality, we are dealing with gnosiology rather than epistemology according to our previous definitions. See above: 75.
3. Sorokin: AJ, 4-7.
4. Sorokin: AC, x, AE, vii, AI, 369-370.
5. Sorokin: AF, 15-16, 20 n.
6. N. O. Lossky and I. I. Lapshin.
7. Cf. especially: AJ, 27-28 n, 267-270 n, 439 n, 635 n.
8. Sorokin: AJ, 19. Let us take two curves representing the same current of thought. One is based on an equal evaluation of the thinkers (the value of each equals 1); the other is based on a differential evaluation of each thinker (each evaluated from 1 to 12). The difference between the two curves is that the amplitude of the fluctuations of the second one is wider than that of the first one (Sorokin: AJ, 18 n). In AJ, Sorokin does not present curves based on an equal evaluation of the thinkers but he gives some such curves in BJ. Concerning a similar question (the inventions in the Arabian world), Sorokin presents three curves. The first is based on an equal evaluation of the particular cases, the second on a differential evaluation of the particular cases, weighted according to a scale 1-3 and in the third, the cases are weighted according to a scale 1-15. The resulting graph is in BF, 520-521 and AJ, 127.
9. Here are the eight criteria:
   1. The number of special monographs devoted to a philosopher. The monographic studies are arranged according to a progression beginning with 5 and doubling the number each time (10, 20, 40, 80, etc.). To each of these numbers, one of the values 1-12 corresponds.
   2. The approximate frequency with which the philosopher's name has been mentioned, in the works of the contemporary and subsequent thinkers in this field.
   3. Whether he has founded a school of philosophic thought.
   4. Whether his name is mentioned in the most elementary texts of history, epistemology and theory of knowledge.
   5. The number of his avowed followers.

6. Whether his works have been translated into foreign languages.
7. Whether his works have been republished again and again after his death.
8. Whether he was a creator of an original and complete system of philosophy and epistemology (AJ, 17-18).

10. Thus Loyola is cited in connection with ethics and not with the problem of universalia. Cf. Sorokin: AJ, 711.

11. Thus Peter Abelard appears in connection with the following currents: rationalism (AJ, 637), pluralistic idealism (AJ, 658), equilibrium of temporalism and eternalism (AJ, 673), nominalism (AJ, 676), universalism-singularism (AJ, 690), indeterminism (AJ, 702) and ethics of Love (AJ, 707). In these different currents (which will be defined later), Abelard always has the value 4.

12. Sorokin: AJ, 23.
13. Sorokin: AJ, 24.
14. Sorokin: AJ, 25.
15. Sorokin: AJ, 23-27.

16. As an example, here are a few names from the list of the philosophers falling into these categories.
Period 380-360 B.C.: *Rationalism:* Euclid 3, Phaidon 2, Eubulides 1, Aeschines 3, Plato 12, Eurytos 1, Archytas 1, Hiketas 1 (total 24); *Fideism:* Antisthenes 5 (total 5); *Skepticism:* Gorgias 5, Alkidamos 4, Metrodoros 1, Aristippos 6 (total 16); *Empiricism:* Democritus 8, Nessas 1, Xenophon 7 (total 16). Cf. AJ, 635, 642, 643, 645. During that 20-year period, there were no philosophers falling into the currents of mysticism and criticism.
Period 1280-1300 A.D.: *Rationalism:* Albertus Magnus 8, Ragmundus Lullus 5, Witelo 2, Guilelmus de la Mere 1, Henricus Gandav. 4, Gottfried (Font.) 3, Bernardus de Trilia 2, Aegidius (Lessines) 2, Remigio di Ch. d. G. 2, Ionnes (Genua) 1, Ramberto dei Prim. 1, Aegidius Romanus 3, Georgios Pachymeres 2, Sophonias 2, Hugo Ripelin 3, Matthaeus ab G 2, Nicolaus (Ockham) 1, Roger (Marston) 2, Guilelmus (Ware) 2, Guilelmus (Hothun) 1, Richard (Clapwell) 1, Siger of Brabant 4, Boethius de Dacia 2 (total 56). *Mysticism:* Ioannes Peckham 1, Walter of Bruges 2, Fr. Eustachius 2, Dietrich of Friberg 2 (total 7). *Empiricism:* Roger Bacon 6, Richard of Mediav. 3 (total 9). Cf. AJ, 638, 641, 646. No representatives of other currents.
Period 1880-1900 A.D.: *Rationalism:* Cicerin 4, Bradley 7, Bosanquet 4, Rehmke 7, Penjon 3, Schasler 2, Strachov 3, Fiorentino 2, Erkole 2, Debolsky 1, Jevons 5, Lasson 3, Michelet 2, Cantor 4, Dedekind 2, Zeller 5, K. Fischer 4, Cohen 7, Schroder 4, Edgeworth 4, Bakunin 2, Hamelin 4, McTaggart 5, Bugaiev 3, Vatke 1 (total 90). Cf. AJ, 639. For this period the five other currents are represented by a great number of philosophers. See AJ, 642, 643, 644, 647.

17. Sorokin: AJ, 29-32. As an example, here is the table of the indicators of fluctuation of influence in six main systems of truth by hundred-year periods. We reproduce only the percentages, and not the absolute figures (AJ, 31).

Period	Empir.	Ration.	Mystic.	Critic.	Skeptic.	Fideism
600-500 B.C.	19.4	80.6	0	0	0	0
500-400	19.2	50.8	0	0	30.0	0
400-300	14.6	42.0	8.0	0	25.4	10.0
300-200	21.7	21.7	0.6	0	17.8	38.2
200-100	19.6	28.6	1.8	0	21.4	28.6
100-0	24.3	24.3	6.5	0	6.5	38.4
0-100 A.D.	2.3	14.6	30.3	0	0	52.8
100-200	6.7	23.0	46.0	0	8.0	16.3
200-300	24.8	12.8	57.1	0	4.5	0.8
300-400	15.2	34.4	50.4	0	0	0
400-500	11.7	44.7	43.6	0	0	0
500-600	1.6	72.6	25.8	0	0	0
600-700	0	65.0	35.0	0	0	0
700-800	0	100	0	0	0	0
800-900	0	67.7	32.3	0	0	0
900-1000	0	75.0	25.0	0	0	0
1000-1100	7.7	43.6	28.2	0	0	20.5
1100-1200	14.3	41.8	40.7	0	0	3.2
1200-1300	12.8	71.4	15.8	0	0	0
1300-1400	17.2	51.3	24.7	0	4.3	2.5
1400-1500	7.2	35.7	47.6	0	0	9.5
1500-1600	15.8	29.0	33.6	0	13.8	7.8
1600-1700	29.6	40.1	23.3	0	4.7	2.3
1700-1800	37.5	30.6	18.9	6.0	4.0	3.0
1800-1900	42.6	21.1	17.2	10.3	2.8	6.0

18. Sorokin: AJ, 55.
19. Sorokin: AJ, 30, 46-53.
20. Sorokin: AJ, 60. Cf. also AI, 404 and the summary written by Sorokin in Barnes and Becker, vol. I, 786.
21. Sorokin: AJ, 61-123.
22. Sorokin: AP, 40.
23. Sorokin: AJ, 13.
24. Cf. Merton: I, 378.
25. Sorokin: AP, 233 n.
26. Sorokin: AJ, 386 n.
27. Sorokin: AK, 373.
28. See Sorokin, on art: AI, 195-594; literature: AI, 595-688; human interaction: AK, 1-256; war: AK, 259-380; revolution: AK, 383-506.
29. Sorokin: AK, 375-380; AQ, 215-217; AR, 511-513.
30. Sorokin: AJ, vii.
31. Thus, for example, AP, 233, AJ, 385.
32. Sorokin: AJ, 386-387.
33. Léon Brunsvicg: L'expérience humaine et la causalité physique, Paris, 1922, p. 96. Quoted by Sorokin: AJ, 389.
34. L. Lévy-Bruhl: Les fonctions mentales dans les sociétés inférieures, Paris, 1910, p. 325. Cited ibid.
35. Durkheim: 258. Cited ibid.

36. Granet: 329-331, 334, 338, 338 n. Cited by Sorokin: AJ, 390-391.
37. Sorokin: AJ, 394-395.
38. Cf. for instance, St. Augustine's *Confessions,* Liv. I, iv.
39. Sorokin: AJ, 397-399.
40. See, for instance, Pearson: 152-178.
41. Sorokin: AJ, 402-413, AP, 38-42.
42. Duhem: B, vol. I, 244. Cited by Sorokin: AJ, 414.
43. Sorokin: AJ, 414-422.
44. See H. Poincaré: *Dernières Pensées,* 41-42; *Science et Méthode,* 95 ff. E. Mach, *The Science of Mechanics,* Chicago, 1902, p. 224. Cited by Sorokin: AJ, 426 n.
45. Sorokin: AJ, 426-427. Concerning the sociocultural time, see AP, 158-225. In BN, Sorokin criticizes some studies on *time,* because they do not consider that notion as dependent upon the type of society and culture in which such a concept is diffused (BN, 1018).
46. Sorokin: AJ, 428, AP, 97-157 and especially 123, 128.
47. Granet: 86. Cited by Sorokin: AJ, 430.
48. Durkheim: 14, 128.
49. Granet: 149.
50. Granet: 299. Quoted by Sorokin: AJ, 434.
51. Hesiod: *Works and Days,* passim. Cited by Sorokin: AJ, 436.
52. The concept of *liberty* has also an ideational meaning and a sensate one. An individual is free when the sum of his wishes does not exceed the sum of available means of gratification. When that result is obtained by diminishing the wishes until they no longer exceed the possibilities of satisfaction, the liberty will be ideational. On the contrary, the sensate freedom is obtained by the increase of the means of satisfaction (Sorokin: AK, 161 ff.). Cf. the formula of self-esteem and its interpretation by W. James: vol. I, 310-311.
53. Sorokin: AJ, 181.
54. To illustrate these categories, there are a few names chosen among thousands: *mechanistic materialism:* Leukippos 2, Voltaire 7, Condorcet 4, Marx 8, Kropotkin 4. *Hylozoistic materialism:* Thales 4, Heraclite 7, Diogenes 3, William Ockham 8, Campanella 6, Diderot 7, Espinas 4. *Monistic idealism:* Parmenides 7, Aristotle 12, David Dinantenensis 3, Siger of Brabant 4, Emerson 6, Brunschvicg 4. *Pluralistic idealism:* Pythagoras 8, Cicero 8, Erigenes 8, Thomas Aquinas 12, Berkeley 8, Kant 12, Renouvier 7. Skeptics, agnostics, etc., fall into a mixed category (AJ, 184, 648-662).
55. Sorokin: AJ, 183-209.
56. Sorokin: AJ, 211-241, 663-675. On the apparent deviation of the curve of eternalism in the graph, p. 154, see Sorokin: AJ, 628 n.
57. Sorokin: AJ, 243-260. The names of the philosophers gathered under the categories of nominalism, conceptualism and realism are in AJ, 676-684. That classification cannot avoid any subjectivism. Even about thinkers as prominent in the question of universalism as Abelard and William Ockham, the specialists disagree. Abelard is usually considered as a conceptualist. J. Reiners, however (in *Der Nominalismus in der Frühscholastik,* Munster, 1910; 41-59) indicates, and not with-

out reason, that he should be regarded as a nominalist. Ockham, almost unanimously regarded as the initiator of nominalism, is rather a conceptualist for Ueberweg (B. Geyer, *Die Patristische und Scholastische Philosophie* in Ueberweg's *Geschichte des Philosophie*, Berlin, 1928, pt. II, 575) and Gilson (*La philosophie du Moyen Age*, Paris, 1922, vol. II, 97 ff.). (Sorokin: AJ, 250-251.)

58. Cf. above: 136 ff.
59. Sorokin: AJ, 339-349, 697-703.
60. Sorokin: AJ, 261-269. The nuances of these different currents being not very easily discernible, here are a few names to characterize them. *Radical singularism:* Aristippos 6, Epicuros 8, Diderot 7 (*L'Ecole de la Volupté*), Proudhon 6, Bakunin 4, Nietzsche 9. *Moderate singularism:* (liberal trend) Socrates 9, Horatius 6, Machiavelli 6 (*Discorsi*), Locke 8, Bentham 6, J. S. Mill 8; (collectivistic trend): Thomas More 6, Fénelon 6, Robert Owen 4, Marx 8. *Radical universalism:* Pythagoras 8, Aristotle 12, Ulpianus 3, Calvin 6, Aug. Comte 8. *Moderate universalism:* Plato 12, Th. Aquinas 12, Luther 8, Machiavelli 6 (*Il Principe*), Bossuet 6, Wolf 7. *Integralism:* Cicero 8, Plotinus 12, Erigenes 8, Francis d'Assisi 6, M. Eckhart 8, N. of Cusa 8, Rousseau 8, Kant 12. (AJ, 685-696.)
61. Sorokin: AJ, 269-304.
62. Sorokin: AJ, 305-337.
63. Sorokin: AI, 181-189, AJ, 351-384, AR, 676 ff., and his comparative study of the nineteenth and twentieth centuries from that standpoint: BT.
64. Sorokin: AJ, 439-446.
65. Sorokin: AJ, 446-455.
66. Sorokin: AJ, 125. That list is based on works like Ludwig Darmstaedter: *Handbuch zur Geschichte des Naturwissenschaften und der Technik,* Berlin, 1908. It is a collective work by twenty-six German scientists. See other titles AJ, 132.
67. See above: 278, note 8; and Sorokin: AJ, 128.
68. Sorokin: AJ, 129-131.
69. Sorokin: AJ, 134-146.
70. Sorokin: AJ, 479-485.
71. Sorokin: AJ, 486-514. In the ethical field, Sorokin establishes another correlation between his independent variables and the currents that he calls *absolutism-relativism, optimism-pessimism* (AJ, 512-522). We only mention them because these currents merge partly into the ones we have considered and because Sorokin indicates that in regard to the numerical results "my feeling of uncertainty as to how accurately they reflect the reality is especially strong." (AJ, 516.)
72. Sorokin: AJ, 523-627.
73. See tables, Sorokin: AJ, 573.
74. For instance: usury, blasphemy, economic exploitation of a prostitute, etc., are considered as criminal actions. Sorokin: AJ, 560.
75. For instance, the interpretation of the following crimes is widened: usury, sacrilege, hindering religious services, etc. Sorokin: AJ, 556.
76. Sorokin: AJ, 571-572.

77. We have introduced into this survey of the dependent variables certain types of mental productions which are not primarily cognitive: technological inventions, ethical philosophies and criminal law. Sorokin treats of these two last subjects outside of the chapters he formally devotes to *Wissenssoziologie*. They have been, however, included in the present outline because those fields are closely correlated to knowledge and because they are covered by the denotation of *mental productions* by which we have, at least provisionally, defined the object of sociology of knowledge.
78. Sorokin: AJ, 386.
79. Granet: 329.
80. Durkheim: 18-21, 519-525.
81. All the terms of the Legend have been explained in the preceding pages. Mystic unity is a synonym for integralism. The relations between the various curves may be translated into correlation coefficients. As an example, here are the correlation coefficients between idealism and all the non-empirical theories of truth: 580 B.C.-520 A.D.: .51; 520-1500: 1.; 1500-1900: .86. See other coefficients in Sorokin: AJ, 631-632. The graphs are taken from Sorokin: AJ, 629-630.
82. Sorokin: AR, 314. Concerning Sorokin's classification of four types of relationships between the sociocultural phenomena, see AI, 10-21. In AR, 145-146, 333-335, there is a more elaborate classification of six types.
83. Sorokin: AI, 25-26. (Emphasis ours.)
84. The expressions often used by Sorokin: ideational *mentality,* sensate *mentality,* etc., seem significant in this respect. To say that "the ideational mentality sees the historical processus as cyclical" suggests a less rigorous logic than the formula "from the ideational premise, it results that . . ."
85. Sorokin: AJ, 250.
86. Sorokin: AJ, 352.
87. Sorokin: AM, 669-670.
88. Sorokin: AM, 587.
89. Sorokin: AM, 587-779.
90. Sorokin: AM, 738-739.
91. See Sorokin's tables: AJ, 53, 200, 240, 259, 296, 345, 513, 518, 521.
92. This argument is especially relevant if one considers not only the proposition concerning the nature of the reality, but the whole cultural system it permeates.
93. Sorokin: AJ, 122, AM, 741-744.
94. Sorokin: AR, 325. According to Speier (D, 885), Sorokin emphasized more the limited power of human reason in his earlier studies.
95. Cf. M. Sherif: *The Psychology of Social Norms,* N. Y., 1936, chap. 6. Cited by Sorokin: AR, 327 n.
96. Sorokin: AM, 595-596. See the criticism of externalistic theories: 595-600.
97. Sorokin: AM, 591. Cf. 587-620. On the history of the principle: AM, 621-668; AR, 696-699, 702-705.
98. Sorokin: AM, 599, AR, 702.

99. Toynbee: 120. Sorokin: AM, 742 ff., AN, 270-271, AR, 704-705. *The Crisis of Our Age* is the analysis of the different compartments of our declining sensate culture. In that book, Sorokin attempts to show how the sensate premise, when carried to its last consequences, is self-destroying. In the realm of knowledge, Sorokin's description of the evolution of the concept of causality from the seventeenth up to the twentieth century is a good example of the way he sees such a process of auto-destruction. If one looks only for tangible facts, if one abstracts from the category of causality the idea of necessity, then causality is reduced to a probable association between two variables and finally the border between a causal link and an incidental link disappears. See above: 138-139; Sorokin: AJ, 410-413, AP, 43-44.
100. Sorokin: AM, 701-714, 737-740.

Chapter 9

EVALUATION OF SOROKIN'S SOCIOLOGY OF KNOWLEDGE

1. In our exposition of Sorokin's system of sociology of knowledge, in the preceding chapter, we have refrained from introducing terms which are absent from his terminology, in order to avoid any confusion. In the present criticism, these terms will be used. They can be applied to Sorokin's system as well as to Mannheim's system.
2. Sorokin enumerates six types of relationship (AR: 145-146, 333-335): (1) spatial contiguity; (2) spatial contiguity and mechanical cohesion between the different parts; for example: a piece of rock perceptionally circumscribed from the rest of the world; (3) an indirect causal-functional relationship between two phenomena through the association of each of them with the same third phenomena; for example: the relationship between my pocket-book and my watch is indirect, due to the direct relationship of each of them to me; (4) direct causal-functional relationship; (5) logico-meaningful relationship; (6) meaningful-functional relationship. These six classes are only a clarification of the classification with 4 types (AI: 10-21).
3. *Causal* has here exactly the same sense as *functional*. Bierstedt's criticism — that Sorokin has a conception of causality that he himself condemns and confuses *post hoc* and *propter hoc* (Bierstedt: 822) — misses the point. Sorokin does not confuse efficient causality and antecedent-consequent relationship. He simply uses the word *causal* in the usual sense of the physico-chemical sciences.
4. See above: 111 ff.
5. It means, in Sorokin's terminology, when those phenomena exactly constitute a *congeries* (which is the contrary of a system). Sorokin: AP, 79.
6. See Sorokin: AP, 83.
7. Sorokin: AP, 95, AI, xi.

8. Sorokin: AP, 34.
9. It has been objected that logic cannot be applied to culture, but only to what is said of it, because the material objects cannot be contradictory or consistent in themselves (Bierstedt: 815-816). That criticism overlooks the fact that any sociocultural phenomenon has a meaning and meanings can be contradictory or consistent. (See Sorokin: BL, 824.)
10. This is an example and not the affirmation of a correlation.
11. Cf. Dollard: 44.
12. Cf. Kluckhohn and Kelly: 97-100.
13. It is true that if we take into account other elements (character, history, religion, etc.), we shall be able to foresee more accurately the logical sequence which will really happen in such or such circumstances. Thus in a culture in which religion forbids any suicide and in which the individuals are deeply religious, it can be foreseen that suicide as a response to an economic depression will not be so common as in a culture in which suicide is not condemned in general. Many other elements than religion will interfere. Then it will be necessary to evaluate the relative importance of the different factors to know if aggressiveness will be exteriorised in such or such a way or will be interiorised. It is very likely that such a precision will be finally due — at the present stage of our knowledge — more to intuition than to critical reasoning. And an intuition must also be checked by facts.
14. Sorokin: AJ, 503 n.
15. See above: 153 ff.
16. For instance, see Leclercq: A, 120 ff., 127 ff.; Bouthoul: 114-118, 131-137.
17. Merton: B, 396 n; Bierstedt: 818; Speier: D, 891.
18. Sorokin: AJ, 631.
19. Sorokin: AP, 229.
20. Sorokin: AP, 94, BO, 360.
21. Sorokin: AP, 95 n.
22. Sorokin: AC, x.
23. Thus in *The Configurations of Culture Growth,* A. L. Kroeber looks for the regularities that can be discovered in the highest forms of culture. He covers an impressive number of centuries and civilizations. Although he bases his conclusions on the study of many artists, musicians, philosophers, etc., he does not use a quantitative method (translating his facts into figures). This results in a lesser degree of precision in many aspects of the work. Besides, he does not seem to have overlooked the quantitative method for reasons of principle. He notes, with perhaps a bit of melancholy, that Sorokin's method requires the cooperation of a team of assistants (Kroeber: 849).
24. Many critics of the quantitative methods of the *Dynamics* limit their objections to general considerations on the impossibility of treating mathematically social phenomena because they are qualitative. See Goldenweiser: 358; Park: 827. To that general objection, Dr. Rashevsky answers that branches of mathematics such as the Boolean algebra may be used to deal with qualitative relations and besides that there is

a very large array of quantitative sociological facts (Rashevsky: iv-v).

25. See above, chapter 8, note 9, pp. 278-279.

26. Sorokin mentions that idea incidentally in connection with another question (AK, 227 n).

27. Renoirte: 107 ff.

28. See an attempt to define empirically the concept *public opinion* based on a set of positive American studies in this field in Jean Stoetzel, *Theorie des opinions.* Cf. Maquet: B, 753 ff. This distinction between empirical concepts and concepts of common experience is similar (but not identical) to Professor Northrop's distinction between concepts by postulation (the meaning of which is designated by the postulates of a theory) and concepts by intuition (which express an immediate apprehension of facts) (Northrop: B, 36, 62, 77 ff., 191 ff.).

29. Sorokin: AJ, 251.

30. Sorokin: AJ, 341.

31. Sorokin: AJ, 648, 662.

32. Sorokin: AJ, 191, BJ, 339.

33. Sorokin: AJ, 632.

34. See Barnes and Becker: 783; Usher: 8; Goldenweiser: 358; Speier: D, 842-843.

35. Brinton: 258.

36. Sorokin in Barnes and Becker: 785; AP, 233 n.

37. Sorokin: AJ, 267.

38. Sorokin: AJ, 629.

39. See Sorokin: AJ, 486-489, 704-712.

40. Professor Hart's article (whose provocative title is "Sorokin's Data Versus His Conclusions") places some of Sorokin's figures in another arrangement (for instance, grouping them in 500-year periods) in order to discover a linear increase of empiricism (Hart: 638). This dynamic aspect is of less interest for us. Besides, Sorokin's answer seems satisfactory (Sorokin: BQ). As a matter of fact, the critics of Sorokin's statistics do not indicate — as far as I know — examples of specific errors. In his *Mathematical Theory of Human Relations,* Dr. Rashevsky uses abundantly data taken from the *Dynamics* which he considers particularly permeated with the quantitative spirit of natural sciences. According to his opinion, the objection that Sorokin's data are not reliable "misses the point entirely." Because, if these data are sometimes crude (as were the facts used in the early development of physics), that does not prevent them from being the basis of very valuable generalizations.

41. Cf. Sorokin: AJ, 29-32, 53-55, 55 n.

42. See note 40.

43. Sorokin: AI, xii.

44. See, for instance, Sorokin: AI, 70.

45. Sorokin: AJ, 211.

46. Sorokin: AI, 72.

47. A distinction should be made also between what is sensory and what is

material. Democritus' atom was material but not sensory. For Sorokin, very often "sensate" means "material" (for instance: AN, 312).

48. Sorokin: AI, 73, 98.
49. Besides, a certain imprecision is perhaps necessary in the sense that to adopt, as a starting point of cultural integration, a formula perfectly elaborate and precise would not lead very far. The logic of a culture is not a rigorous one.
50. Sorokin: AM, 742 ff.
51. Sorokin: AM, 619.
52. Sorokin: BI, 510.
53. Sorokin: AM, 589, AR, 696.
54. Sorokin: AM, 595.
55. Sorokin: AM, 602-604.
56. Sorokin: AM, 600-602.
57. Sorokin: AH, 628-653 and especially 635.
58. Sorokin: AR, 460.
59. Here is how Sorokin describes the cause of the present crisis of our Occidental culture, in a book meant for a very broad audience. "The major premise of the sensory nature of the true reality and value is the root from which developed the tree of our sensate culture with its splendid as well as its poisonous fruit. Its first positive fruit is an unprecedented development of the natural sciences and technological inventions. The first poisonous fruit is a fatal narrowing of the realm of true reality and true value. . . . Anything that was supersensory, from conception of God to the mind of man . . . had to be declared unreal. . . . The rude and imperfect human organs of sense were made the supreme arbiter of what was real and what was not. . . . Man was reduced mainly to anatomy and physiology. Even as the possessor of unmaterial mind and thought . . . he was often denied. . . . Once the culture entered this path, it had to move along it, toward a greater and greater sensorization of the world of reality and of value. . . . No wonder that . . . they treat him exactly as we treat other organisms. . . . If he is useful for a given moment, we can care for him. . . . If he is unserviceable, we can eliminate him as we eliminate parasites and old animals" (AN, 308-315). Thus the sensate culture carried to its last consequences leads to the extermination camps. And through such excesses, that culture raises up reactions which will destroy it.
60. Sorokin: AM, 743, AR, 705.
61. Sorokin: AM, 587-620.
62. Sorokin: AM, 737-746.
63. Sorokin: AM, 591, 737, AR, 448-449. See an organicist interpretation of Sorokin's explanation in Barnes and Becker: vol. I, 786.
64. Sorokin: AD, 207-213, AR, 150. Cf. Dechesne: B, 428 f.
65. Sorokin: AR, 381 n. Cf. AR, 327 n, 704, etc.
66. Northrop: A, 66-164.
67. Northrop: A, 193-219. See the clarification of his method of logical and historical analysis in B, 293-305.

Chapter 10

SIGNIFICANCE OF SOROKIN'S SOCIOLOGY OF KNOWLEDGE

1. Sorokin notes that the kind of *Wissenssoziologie* which has been prevalent recently is mainly of a Marxian type (AJ, 413).
2. Sorokin: AP, 233 n.
3. Sorokin: AM, 599.
4. Sorokin: AM, 619, AR, 697.
5. Sorokin: AR, 212, 247, 343, 344, 714. See in the same sense Professor Northrop's interpretation of Sorokin (Northrop: A, 13).
6. E. Durkheim: *Le suicide*, 426-427. Cited by Sorokin: AR, 58.
7. Spencer: 831 (cited by Sorokin: AR, 557), 832. On the role of the limited possibilities in culture, see: Murdock: 137-139.
8. Sorokin: AR, 58-63; 556-562.
9. Hook: 22.
10. Sorokin: AR, 345 n, 347.
11. James: vol. I, 294 ff. Cited by Sorokin: AR, 346.
12. Sorokin: AR, 348-349. That notion of the *social ego* is very similar to the concept of *role* which is abundantly used by certain American sociologists and anthropologists. The *role* is the behavior expected from a person who enjoys a certain *status* in the society. This means that the position he occupies grants him a collection of rights and duties. Cf. Linton: A, 113-131; Parsons: E, 6-9.
13. Sorokin: AR, 349.
14. Ibid.
15. Sorokin: AR, 352, 352 n. f.
16. Sorokin: AR, 356.
17. Znaniecki: A, 16-17. His concept of the "closed system" comes principally from the French methodologists who were grouped around *La Revue de Métaphysique et de Morale* in the twenties (Znaniecki: A, 12 n.).
18. Kluckhohn and Kelly: 95.
19. Sorokin: AM, 611-615.
20. Sorokin: AI, 15.
21. Sorokin: AR, 317.
22. Sorokin: AJ, 474.
23. Sorokin: AJ, 476.
24. Sorokin: AJ, 464-467.
25. Sorokin: AG, 198, 229, etc.
26. Sorokin: AJ, 628. It is useless to emphasize that Sorokin admits the inverse relationship — the influence of the mental productions upon society — since the premises of culture influence phenomena such as the type of association (contractual, compulsory, etc.) and even the frequency of wars and revolutions. He notes also more precise and particular influences in this field such as the increase of the vertical

social mobility during periods of emergence of philosophical systems, scientific theories, new religions and forms of art (Sorokin: AR, 428).

27. See above: 49 ff.
28. See above: 152.
29. Sorokin: AJ, 466.
30. Merton: I, 378.
31. Sorokin: AJ, 5.
32. Sorokin: AI, 73.
33. Sorokin: AJ, 630. See above: 153.
34. Sorokin: AJ, 181-209.
35. See above: 155 ff., 165 ff.
36. That accounts for the somewhat disturbing fact that Sorokin never gives a statistical study of the cultural premises themselves. We have the curves of the consequences of these premises in the fields of art, science, ethics, law, etc. But we do not have the curves of the premises. Consequently, the comparison of the fluctuations of a dependent variable is made with the whole of the cultural system (the other dependent variable) rather than directly with the premise.
37. Sorokin: AJ, 465-466.
38. Sorokin: AJ, 455-459.
39. Sorokin: AN, 76, 78. Cf. BR and AQ (*Russia and the United States*). His dealing with that topic in 1944, in a popular form, suggested indeed a very high standpoint tending to minimize the differences.
40. Sorokin: AJ, 30-31.
41. Usher: 7.
42. Sorokin: BM, 22.
43. Sorokin: AJ, 186-187.
44. Sorokin: AJ, 224.
45. Sorokin: AJ, 277.
46. Sorokin: AI, xii.
47. Sorokin: AP, 233 n.
48. Sorokin: AM, 610-618.
49. Sorokin: AJ, 476.
50. For instance, see Sorokin: AJ, 628-632.

Chapter 11

SOROKIN'S PHILOSOPHY OF KNOWLEDGE

1. Sorokin: AJ, 13.
2. Sorokin: AM, 765-766. The scientists alluded to here by Sorokin are especially Poincaré, K. Pearson, E. Mach, W. James.
3. Sorokin: AR, 327 n., 381 n.
4. Sorokin: AR, 521.
5. Sorokin: AM, 630-635.
6. The term *epistemology* as used by Sorokin covers epistemology and gnosiology as they have been defined above: 75 ff. We shall see later

how to qualify the philosophical conceptions of Sorokin according to these notions.

7. Sorokin: AJ, 8-9.
8. Sorokin: AM, 765, AN, 118.
9. Sorokin: AJ, 200. See analogous comments on temporalism-eternalism (AJ, 240), realism-conceptualism (AJ, 260), universalism-singularism (AJ, 297), determinism-indeterminism (AJ, 346), ethics of happiness and of principles (AJ, 513), absolutism and relativism in ethics (AJ, 518).
10. Sorokin: AJ, 55, 299.
11. Sorokin: AP, 226-237.
12. Sorokin: AM, 746-761, AN, 105-112.
13. Cf. K. W. Wild: *Intuition*, Cambridge, University Press, 1938, cited by Sorokin: AM, 748.
14. Sorokin: AM, 747 ff.
15. Guthrie: 234.
16. Speier: D, 895.
17. Sorokin: AI, 11-12 n., AJ, 299.
18. Sorokin: AJ, 4, 474 n., AN, 103, etc.
19. Sorokin: AI, 86 n.
20. Sorokin: AJ, 208 n. He adds, however: "Since the validity of the fundamental laws of logic rests assured in both systems — in this sense, these laws are absolute and continue to be absolute. There is fluctuation, not in the validity of logical laws, but in the existential premises to which they are applied." Perhaps. But if the existential premises were excluded from the sphere of certainty and if the latter were reduced to laws of logic, the margin for relativism would be broad enough. We shall see that this is not Sorokin's conception.
21. Sorokin: AJ, 475, AM, 744.
22. Nicolas of Cusa. Quoted by Sorokin: AM, 745 n.
23. Sorokin: AM, 744 n.
24. From that point of view (the affirmation of reason's incapacity to attain any Absolute), there is a certain connection between mystical metarationalism and skepticism. That could be the reason why Sorokin has been sometimes considered a skeptic. However, the difference between the two currents is important. Modern agnosticism generally denies the reality of what reason cannot reach. The mystic metarationalism affirms the reality of the transcendental and the possibility to attain it through intuitive means.
25. Shortly before his death, he said: "I do not know what I may appear to the world; but for myself I seem to have been like a boy playing on the seashore and diverting myself now and then by finding a smoother pebble or a prettier shell than ordinary, whilst the great ocean of Truth lay all undiscovered before me." L. T. More: *Isaac Newton* (New York, 1934), 664. Quoted by Sorokin: AM, 744 n.
26. Sorokin: AJ, 475.
27. Sorokin: AM, 763. See also his interpretation of Planck's idea on the ultimate aim of science (AJ, 207 n.-208 n.).
28. Sorokin: AR, 327 n., 381 n.

29. Sorokin: AJ, 3.
30. Sorokin: AM, 763, AP, 230-231 n.
31. Sorokin: AM, 763-764.
32. Sorokin: AP, 230 n.
33. Merton: I, 389.
34. Sorokin: AI, 36, AJ, 12 n.
35. If certain critics have overlooked the threefold sphere of competence of the truth criteria, there are some extenuating circumstances. The general trend of the *Dynamics* often gives the impression that reason and intuition are not only the sources but the criteria in sciences. Moreover, if each system of truth is competent in its sphere, it seems that we could hope to reach a balanced culture where science should be scientific, philosophy rational and religion intuitive (or revealed). For, at first sight, such a culture seems to conform most with reality. Unfortunately, the idealistic culture, which is the most similar to this, disappears as rapidly as (in fact, more rapidly than) the others.
36. We have only mentioned the possible philosophic bearing of the principle of immanent change. This principle is the token of a certain Hegelianism of Sorokin. Thus on the logical level, the three central concepts of the cultural premises sustain the relationships of thesis (sensate premise), antithesis (ideational) and synthesis (idealistic). Many philosophic and scientific currents are presented in the same way: sociological singularism — universalism — integralism; eternalism — temporalism — mixed theories (some of them at least are real syntheses).

     On the ontological level, the principle of immanent change, considered as the law of reality, seems to be linked to integralism and metarationalism. Thus the reason why a system disappears is that its inadequateness to reality tends to increase. Consequently, the conjunction of the three systems of truth will always be necessary to approach the integral reality (AM, 743, AR, 705; see also above: 183). On the other hand, as we have indicated (above: 211-212), the principle of immanent change may be connected to the metalogical character of the authentic reality which is beyond any contradiction. The ultimate reality may be considered as the final synthesis in which all the contradictions are harmonized.

     It is because of the close relationship between the principle of immanent change and both integralism and metarationalism that it did not need a separate discussion.
37. For instance, see Sorokin: AM, 763, AP, 230 n., 231 n.

Chapter 12

EVALUATION OF SOROKIN'S PHILOSOPHY OF KNOWLEDGE

1. See above: 205.
2. Sorokin: AM, 742.

3. Sorokin: AM, 745.
4. Sorokin: AJ, 475.
5. Sorokin: AM, 742.
6. Sorokin: AN, 104.
7. Concerning the adaptation of the primitive peoples, cf. Sorokin: AJ, 389 n., AM, 742.
8. We are concerned here with the behavior which assures survival. Of course, the whole of the activity of a sensate personality will be different from the whole of the activity of an ideational personality. A sensate culture will urge a more complete mastery of nature than an ideational culture. But mastery of nature and adaptation are not synonymous. Does the mastery of atomic energy provide a society with more chances for survival?
9. Metarationalism is not a necessary complement of integralism. One might claim, indeed, that sense, reason and intuition are three sources of valid knowledge without granting that the ontological realm is completely beyond the reach of reason and above the principles of logic.
10. It is the reason why we have termed Sorokin's philosophy of knowledge now epistemology, now gnosiology, now, in a more neutral manner, conception of knowledge.

Chapter 13

CONCLUSIONS DRAWN FROM THE STUDY OF SOROKIN

1. See above: 168 ff.
2. See above: 176 ff.
3. It has sometimes been said that the *Dynamics* was a philosophic work. If this means that the *Dynamics* may be considered as a philosophy of history, that opinion is justifiable inasmuch as the philosophy of history is defined as the study of certain permanences and recurrences through the historical unfolding. Moreover, Sorokin agrees with such a qualification of his work (AI, x).

   Besides, we have seen that there are also in Sorokin's *Dynamics* ontological propositions concerning the infinitely manifold nature of the ultimate reality and a certain mystic metarationalism. This philosophic part, secondary in respect to the aim of the work, is not very extensive. (The importance we have assigned to this part in the present monograph is comparatively much greater than the importance it has in Sorokin's books. Because we were looking for what is significant from the point of view of the relationships between sociology of knowledge and philosophy of knowledge, we have put the emphasis on these passages.)

   But when the Sorokin work is qualified as philosophic, this term is understood rather in the derogatory sense it may convey when applied to scientific works ("what is said may be true, but is impossible to check"). Now, the abundant use of the quantitative proof and the constant concern for facts characterize Sorokin's works. How then is one to term it "speculative"? This qualification refers probably to Sorokin's value judgments. They may be characterized rather improperly as "philosophic" in the sense that they express personal opinions. These opinions may be true, but anyway they are incidental and without relevance to the scientific meaning of the work. Unfortunately, as those appreciations are generally sharply critical of contemporary culture (see above, chapter 7, note 23, p. 276), many critics resent them deeply and, instead of overlooking them, focus their attention on them.

4. For instance, to say that the new concepts of physics evolve from experiments and observations is an immanent explanation of the genesis of the concepts. Cf. Conant: 101.

5. This conception is, however, closer to the immanent history of ideas than to the "traditional" *Wissenssoziologie*, since the conditioning relationships are situated on the philosophical level. See above: 195 ff.

6. See above: 189 ff.

7. See above: 165 ff., 197 ff.

8. See Duhem: A, 20; Meyerson: 387; Davis: 36; Renoirte: 171 ff.

PART THREE: GENERAL CONCLUSIONS

Chapter 14

THE SOCIOLOGY OF KNOWLEDGE AND THE PHILOSOPHY OF KNOWLEDGE

1. For instance, see Rashevsky's mathematical biology of social phenomena and Henderson's approach to Pareto's sociology from the point of view of a physiologist.

2. It is possible to sub-distinguish or to combine these three stages in another way than it has been done here. Thus, in *The Logic of the Sciences and the Humanities*, Northrop emphasizes in what he calls the logic of the sciences (natural and social), the three following stages: (a) The analysis of the problem (Northrop: B, 19-34). This means to trace the problem back to its roots. Here is the example by which he illustrates this step. Let us consider the motion of a shell shot from a cannon. At the beginning of the seventeenth century that phenomenon was unexplainable. The projectile continues to move after the cessation of the explosion, something it should not do according to Aristotelian physics. Galileo analyzed the problem. He saw that the root of the difficulty was not in the problem of the projectiles but in the Aristotelian conception of force: what manifests itself as the motion or velocity of the object upon which it acts (ibid. 22-23). (b) The research into the facts relevant to the root of the problem (ibid. 35-58). (c) The formulation of the theory suggested by the facts (ibid. 59-76). We do not think there is a contradiction between Northrop's three stages and the sequence which has been followed in the present work.

The difference is that the former elaborates what has been called here the research into facts, and does not put any emphasis on the generalization (our second stage).

3. It is announced to a group of subjects that they will hear two variations on the same musical theme and that according to the opinion of connoisseurs of music, the first variation is better than the second. They are asked to be very attentive and to judge if they agree with the critics and why. Then exactly the same record is played twice. This experiment made on 1,484 persons showed that 96% (Sorokin: BE, 727) found that the records were different and only 15.9% disagreed with the experts' opinion. This is rather a psychological experiment. But by the comparison of the results obtained with groups of individuals of different social status, some conclusions could be drawn relevant to the standpoint of the sociology of knowledge (Sorokin: BE).

4. Cf. Conant: 95-96.

5. If I am allowed to take the present work as an example of this, a similar process has been followed. We started with a rather vague idea that the sociology of knowledge and the philosophy of knowledge could have relationships similar to that existing between physico-chemical sciences and philosophical cosmology. The examination of facts (which means here the examination of a few systems of *Wissenssoziologie*) enabled us to clarify and modify that vague idea.

6. If we say that the affirmation of the supra-sensory character of the true reality implies that it is eternal, it is because we take it for granted that (a) supra-sensory means non-material; (b) immaterial beings not having in themselves any principle of corruption, will never cease. May we say that thinkers belonging to a culture in which the dualistic view body-mind is not so deeply rooted as in ours, would so easily draw eternalism from ideationalism?

7. Linton: B, 18. Cf. Bouthoul: 159-167, Joussain: 107-125.

8. Cf. Lalande: art. "théorie"; Northrop: B, 59-76.

9. Cf. Merton: H, 136; Leclercq: A, 103; Bouthoul: 114-115.

10. Conant: 59, 102.

11. Conant: 29-64, 102-103.

12. Conant: 47.

13. For Northrop, the hypothesis is the principle of which consequences are theorems (Northrop: B, 60). So his *hypothesis* corresponds to what is called here *theory* and his *theorems* correspond to our *hypotheses*. In Meyerson's terminology, too, a theory is an hypothesis (Meyerson: 51).

14. See above: 48 f.

15. See above: 185.

Several reasons account for the confusion between theory and hypothesis. First, the synthesis of the observed results (which is thus a confirmed hypothesis) has a certain explanatory value in respect to the particular results of observation. Thus the very high correlation between the curves of materialism and nominalism seems to be "explained" by the very fact that they are two sensate variables. As a matter of fact, that affirmation locates only the simultaneous variations of nominalism and materialism among other variables of which the fluctuations have also been measured. It does not really explain but suggests the explanation. A second reason for confusion is that it is often said that theory is hypothetical, which means that it does not claim to express reality. Finally, it appears curious to term hypothesis a consequence which expresses synthetically the results of positive research.

16. For an account of that example, see Conant: 74-97.
17. These words "very likely" expresses the difference between theory and hypothesis. If one adopts Mannheim's hypothesis, it is certain that social structure and political ideas only will be taken into account. If one adopts Mannheim's theory, it is not certain that other facts will not be considered. A similar distinction may be drawn concerning Sorokin.
18. This puts the emphasis on a common mistake that Professor Northrop has denounced vigorously: the belief that the scientific method is *one*. Hence, he writes, it is a pseudo-problem to wonder whether or not Bacon, Cohen or Dewey has expounded the real scientific method. Each of these methods is useful when employed at the right stage of the inquiry (Northrop: B, ix).
19. See above: 75 ff.
20. In the present work, an attempt has been made to keep an epistemological (non-gnosiological) point of view. We have tried to make clear the significance of the sociology of knowledge independently from a system of philosophy.
21. See chapter 6, note 18, pp. 274-275. On the "culturological interpretation," see White.
22. See examples above: 94.
23. Here is an example given by Meyerson. When we say that benzene is made of six atoms of carbon, forming a hexagon, we do not mean that there is in reality a hexagon in benzene, but that benzene acts *as if* there were a hexagon of carbon atoms in it. Cf. Meyerson: 52.

Chapter 15

RESULTS AND PROSPECTS OF THE SOCIOLOGY OF KNOWLEDGE

1. Cf. Poincaré quoted by Sorokin: BC, 312.
2. The distinction between knowledge and values is, as Professor Northrop stresses it, essential. However, it tends often to be overlooked (Northrop: B, 19-22).
3. See above: 43-44, 79-80.
4. Some philosophers hope to resolve value problems by reducing them to truth problems. So, they say, we will be able to resolve value problems scientifically, because to claim that an assertion is true is to answer a question of fact (Northrop: B, 32). Hence the pragmatist attempt to identify the good with empirically tangible pleasure. But even if, as

Northrop requires, that reduction is achieved very carefully through an elaborate method, it seems that the problem of truth, especially in respect to objects not directly observable, is difficult enough to prompt us to think that the success of the scientific determination of values is still doubtful (see a more optimistic comment in Northrop: B, 328-347). On the opposite opinion (that any truth-judgment is finally based on a value judgment), see Perelman's paper.

5. It is what Sorokin does since the cultural conditioning of ethical and juridical doctrines is studied in AJ outside his chapters devoted to *Wissenssoziologie*. Of course, the classification could be established in another way. For instance, a "sociology of mental productions" could be taken as a general discipline divided into sociology of art, of knowledge, of law, etc.

6. Linton: C, 56; Kluckhohn and Kelly: 79.

7. Linton: A, 78; Malinowski: A, 621; Ogburn and Nimkoff: 63.

8. Lowie: 3.

9. Benedict: 13.

10. Tylor cited by Lowie: 199. For more elaborate definitions of culture, see: Sorokin (AI, 3): "In the broadest sense [human culture] may mean the sum total of everything which is created or modified by the conscious or unconscious activity of two or more individuals interacting with one another or conditioning one another's behavior"; Linton: C, 32-54; Boas: A, 79; Merton: B. Malinowski's functionalist conception is expounded, for instance, in Malinowski A and B, 41-51. A broad discussion of the various aspects of culture is to be found in Kluckhohn and Kelly. See some other conceptions and their discussion in Sorokin: AI, 4-7.

11. The distinction is so clear-cut for some social scientists in the English-speaking countries that they like to make of society and culture the subject-matter of two disciplines: sociology and cultural (or social) anthropology. On the notion of anthropology in relation to the concept of culture, see: Linton: B; Kroeber: A, 5-6; Boas: A, B, 4-6; Lowie: 3.

12. Cf. Linton: C, xvii.

13. Sorokin: AR, 65.

14. Sorokin: AR, 63-65. See above: 115.

15. See above: 102 ff.

16. Some American sociologists and anthropologists mean by "ethos" the part of the culture which is formed by fundamental values which, permeating the activities of the members of a society, integrate them in a certain configuration of style. (Parsons: E, 16-25 and especially 17-18.) See also: Wirth: A, 473; Merton: D, 326; Feibleman: 48-66. That term is more general than Sorokin's major cultural premise (in the sense that it has not such a logical connotation) but each of his premises may be qualified an "ethos."

17. Sorokin: AR, 515-516.

18. Sorokin himself has leaned somewhat in that direction. Thus he indicates that the groups bearing the ideational culture are the clergy and the landed aristocracy whereas the *bourgeoisie* and the secular intelligentsia are especially sensate (AH, 250). From the point of view of

cultural diffusion, Sorokin indicates that the "upper-urban-civilized-male groups" have a preponderant action (AR, 568-570). See also AM, 221-227.

19. The present stage of these systems is to be distinguished from the approaches they represent and from other *wissenssoziologisch* systems which could be drawn from certain principles of our authors. This is especially true of Sorokin. It has been shown (above: 189-193) how a traditional sociology of knowledge could find two sound starting points in Sorokin's general sociology.

20. The term "Marxian" is preferred to that of "materialistic" which is too ambiguous. Besides, "Marxian" evokes the filiation of Mannheim's system and the origin of the "traditional" trend of *Wissenssoziologie*.

21. See above: 6 ff.

22. See above: 187 ff.

23. That research has emerged somewhat as a by-product of the public opinion polls. But a shift of focus has occurred and some social psychologists have devised special techniques in order to use the public opinion polls for the study of the relationships between opinion and personality. Researches in this field are pursued by Dr. Jerome S. Bruner and his collaborators at the Psychological Clinic of the Laboratory of Social Relations, Harvard University. For a synthesis of the question, see Murphy's *Public Opinion and the Individual;* Stoetzel: 265-342 and Bruner's coming book.

24. That personal equation is not to be confused with the psychological factor — except if the differential psychology devoted to the study of the individual differences is meant. But what we have termed here the psychological factors concerns the individual only as realizing in himself certain general types. He realizes them in a certain way. It is that unique way which is considered here as a residuary element. Its importance is also variable according to the case.

25. See Cora DuBois; Kardiner: C, 146-170, 238. Similar examples may be found in some anthropological works of the trend of "Culture and Personality." See, for instance, M. Mead: A; Kluckhohn and Leighton: A, B. For some very tentative analyses of the American culture along the same line, see M. Mead: B; Gorer: B.

26. One of the most brilliant examples of these "inter-field" works is Northrop's *The Meeting of East and West.* On this trend in the American social sciences during the decade 1930-1940, cf. Cottrell and Gallagher. On the very particular problem of the possibility of collaboration between psychoanalysis and sociology, see Hollitscher: 89-99 and his bibliography: 106-116.

Bibliography

ABEL, Theodore: *Systematic Sociology in Germany,* Columbia University Press, New York, 1929.

ADAMS, James Luther: "Freud, Mannheim and the Liberal Doctrine of Man" in *The Journal of Liberal Religion* (Chicago, Ill.), Winter 1941, 107-111.

ARON, Raymond: *La sociologie allemande contemporaine,* Alcan, Paris, 1935.

ASCOLI, Max: "On Mannheim's 'Ideology and Utopia'" in *Social Research* (New School for Social Research, New York), February 1938, 101-106.

BALDWIN, James Mark, ed.: *Dictionary of Philosophy and Psychology,* 3 vol., New York, Macmillan, 1905-1911; Peter Smith, 1940.

BARNES, Harry Elmer: *An Introduction to the History of Sociology,* The University of Chicago Press, Chicago, 1948.

BARNES, Harry Elmer, and BECKER, Howard: *Social Thought from Lore to Science,* 2 vol., D. C. Heath & Company, Boston, 1938.

BARTH, Hans: *Wahrheit und Ideologie,* Manesse Verlag, Zürich, 1945.

BARZIN, Marcel: *Cours de Logique,* 2 vol. (mimeographed, Desoer, Liège), University of Brussels, 1938.

BATESON, Gregory: *Naven,* Cambridge University Press, 1936.

BECK, Hubert Park: *Men Who Control Our Universities,* King's Crown Press, New York, 1947.

BECKER, Howard:
   A. Review of *Social and Cultural Dynamics,* vol. III, in *Rural Sociology* (Baton Rouge, La.), September 1938, 356.
   B. and DAHLKE, H. Otto: "Max Scheler's Sociology of Knowledge" in *Philosophy and Phenomenological Research,* (Buffalo University, Buffalo, N. Y.), March 1942, 310-322.

BENEDICT, Ruth: *Patterns of Culture* (1st ed., 1934), Penguin Books, New York, 1946.

BIERSTEDT, Robert: "The Logico-meaningful Method of P. A. Sorokin" in *American Sociological Review* (Menasha, Wis.), December 1937, 813-823.

BLÀHA, In. Arn.: "Social Psychology of the Intelligentsia" in *Social Sciences* (Menasha, Wis.), Summer 1936, 196-201.

BLOCK, Maxime, ed.: *Current Biography 1942,* H. W. Wilson Company, New York.

BOAS, Franz:
  A. article "Anthropology" in *Encyclopaedia of the Social Sciences,* Macmillan, New York, 1930-1935, 15 vol.
  B. and others: *General Anthropology,* D. C. Heath & Company, Boston, 1938.
BRINKMANN, Carl: "The Present Situation of German Sociology" in *Publications of the American Sociological Society* (Chicago, Ill.), 1927, 47-56.
BRINTON, Crane: "Socio-Astrology" in *The Southern Review* (Baton Rouge, La.), Autumn 1937, 243-266.
BROGLIE, L. de: *Recueil d'exposés sur les Ondes et les Corpuscles,* Hermann, Paris, 1930.

CHILD, Arthur:
  A. "The Problem of Imputation in the Sociology of Knowledge" in *Ethics* (Chicago), January 1941, 200-219.
  B. "The Theoretical Possibility of the Sociology of Knowledge" in *Ethics,* July 1941, 392-418.
  C. "The Existential Determination of Thought" in *Ethics,* January 1942, 153-185.
CONANT, James B.: *On Understanding Science,* Yale University Press, New Haven, 1947.
COTTRELL, Leonard S., Jr., and GALLAGHER, Ruth: *Developments in Social Psychology (1930-1940),* Sociometry Monograph, Beacon House, Beacon, N. Y., 1941.

DAHLKE, H. Otto: "The Sociology of Knowledge" in *Contemporary Social Theory* by H. E. Barnes, H. Becker and F. B. Becker, D. Appleton-Century Co., New York and London, 1940, 64-89.
DAVIS, Harold T.: *Philosophy and Modern Science,* The Principia Press, Bloomington, Ind., 1931.
DECHESNE, Laurent:
  A. "La crise de notre civilisation selon Sorokin" in *Bulletin de la Classe des Lettres et Sciences morales et politiques* (Académie Royale de Belgique), Brussels, 5-9, 1946, 172-177.
  B. *La nouvelle Sociologie de Sorokin,* ibid., 11-12, 1947, 426-441.
DEGRE, Gerard:
  A. "The Sociology of Knowledge and the Problem of Truth" in *Journal of History of Ideas* (College of the City of New York), January 1941, 110-115.
  B. *Society and Ideology,* Columbia University Bookstore, New York, 1943.
DIACONIDE, Elie: "Sociologie et Métaphysique" in *Revue Internationale de Sociologie,* Paris, 1938, 71-84.
DOLLARD, John, and others: *Frustration and Aggression,* Yale University Press, New Haven, 1939.
DUBOIS, Cora Alice: *The People of Alor,* The University of Minnesota Press, Minneapolis, 1944.

DUHEM, Pierre:
A. *La théorie physique*, Marcel Rivière & Company, Paris, 1941 (2nd edition).
B. *Le système du monde*, Hermann & Fils, 5 vol., Paris, 1913-1917.
DUPREEL, E.:
A. "La logique et les sociologues" in *Revue de l'Institut de Sociologie* (University of Brussels), January 1924, 215-219.
B. "La sociologie et les problèmes de la connaissance," ibid., March-May 1925, 161-183.
DURKHEIM, Émile: *Les formes élémentaires de la vie religieuse*, Alcan, Paris, 1912.
DYCKMANS, G.: "Les types d'intégration socioculturelle selon Pitirim Sorokin" in *Revue des Sciences Économiques*, Liège, April 1939, 82-87.

EDDINGTON, Arthur Stanley: *The Nature of the Physical World*, Macmillan, New York, 1928.
ELLIOTT, William Yandell: "Sorokin and the Dangerous Science" in *Harvard Guardian* (Cambridge, Mass.), November 1937, 13-16.
ENGELS, Frederich: "Ludwig Feuerbach and the Outcome of Classical German Philosophy" in *Selected Works* of Karl Marx, International Publishers, Moscow and New York, n. d. (1933), vol. I, 417-470.

FAIRCHILD, Henry Pratt: *Dictionary of Sociology*, Philosophical Library, New York, 1944.
FALK, Werner: "The Sociological Interpretation of Political Ideas" in *The Sociological Review*, London, July 1934, 268-287.
FEIBLEMAN, James: *The Theory of Human Culture*, Duell, Sloan & Pearce, New York, 1946.
FEUER, Lewis S.: Review of Mandelbaum's *Problem of Historical Knowledge* in *Science and Society*, New York, 1939.

GITTLER, J. B.: "Possibilities of a Sociology of Science" in *Social Forces*, University of North Carolina Press (Chapel Hill, N. C.), March 1940, 350-359.
GOLDENWEIZER, Alexander: "Sociologos" in *Journal of Social Philosophy*, New York, July 1938, 350-358.
GORDON, Milton M.: "*Kitty Foyle* and the Concept of Class as Culture" in *The American Journal of Sociology*, University of Chicago Press, November 1947, 210-217.
GORER, Geoffrey:
A. "The American Child" in *Pilot Papers*, London, June 1947, 37-54.
B. *The American People*, Norton & Company, New York, 1948.
GRANET, Marcel: *La pensée chinoise*, La Renaissance du Livre, Paris, 1934.
GRÉGOIRE, Franz: *Aux sources de la pensée de Marx: Hegel et Feuerbach*, Institut Supérieur de Philosophie, Louvain, 1947.
GRÜNWALD, Ernst: *Das Problem der Soziologie des Wissens*, W. Braumüller, Vienna and Leipzig, 1934.

GURVICH, Georges:
  A. *Les tendances actuelles de la philosophie allemande*, Vrin, Paris, 1930.
  B. *Initiation aux recherches sur la sociologie de la connaissance* (mimeographed), Fasc. 1, Centre de Documentation universitaire, Paris, 1948.
  C. "Sociologie de la connaissance" in *L'Année sociologique*, third series, Paris, 1949, I, 463-86.
GUTHRIE, Elton P.: "Sorokin: Counsellor to Reaction" in *Science and Society*, New York, 1939, 229-238.

HAESAERT, J.:
  A. "La Sociologie" in *La Bibliothèque de l'Honnête Homme*, ed. by Pierre Wigny, Bruxelles, 1945, 411-421.
  B. *Essai de Sociologie*, Editions Lumière, Brussels, n.d. (1946).
HALBWACHS, Maurice: *Les cadres sociaux de la mémoire*, Alcan, Paris, 1925.
HANLEY, Thomas R.: "Some Interpretations of the Present World Crisis" in *The National Benedictine Educational Association Bulletin* (Atchinson, Kansas), March 1943, 115-183.
HARSHORNE, Edward Yarnell, Jr.: *The German Universities and National Socialism*, Harvard University Press, Cambridge, 1948.
HART, Hornell: "Sorokin's Data Versus His Conclusions" in *American Sociological Review* (Menasha, Wis.), October 1939, 635-646.
HEGEL, Georg Wilhelm Friedrich: *The Philosophy of History* (trans. by J. Sibree), Willey Book Co., New York, 1944.
HEISS, Robert: Review of Mannheim's *Ideologie und Utopie* in *Kölner Vierteljahrshefte für Soziologie*, Köln, 1929, 240-241.
HENDERSON, Lawrence J.: *Pareto's General Sociology*, Harvard University Press, Cambridge, 1935.
HOFSTRA, Sjoerd: *De Sociale Aspecten van Kennis en Wetenschap*, Scheltema & Holkema's Boekhandel, Amsterdam, 1937.
HOLLITSCHER, Walter: *Sigmund Freud*, Oxford University Press, New York, 1947.
HOOK, Sidney: "Man's Destiny: A Scientific View" in *The New York Times Book Review*, August 17, 1947, pp. 4 and 22.
HORNEY, Karen:
  A. *The Neurotic Personality of Our Time*, Norton & Company, New York, 1937.
  B. *New Ways in Psychoanalysis*, ibid., 1939.
  C. *Our Inner Conflicts*, ibid., 1945.
HOUSE, Floyd N.: Review of Sorokin's *Society, Culture and Personality* in *American Journal of Sociology*, University of Chicago Press, November 1947, 225-226.

JAMES, William: *The Principles of Psychology*, 2 vol., Macmillan, London, 1890.
JERUSALEM, Wilhelm:
  A. "Sociologie des Erkennens" in *Die Zukunft*, Berlin, May 1909, 236-246.

B. *Einleitung in die Philosophie,* W. Braumüller, Vienna and Leipzig, 1923.

C. *An Introduction to Philosophy* (trans. of *B* by C. F. Sanders), Macmillan, New York, 1932.

JOUSSAIN, André: *La sociologie,* Flammarion, Paris, 1945.

KARDINER, Abram:
A. *The Individual and His Society,* Columbia University Press, New York, 1939.
B. "The Concept of Basic Personality" in *The Science of Man in the World Crisis,* ed. by R. Linton, Columbia University Press, New York, 1945, 107-122.
C. *The Psychological Frontiers of Society,* Columbia University Press, New York, 1945.

KILZER, Ernest F.: Review of *Society, Culture and Personality* in *The American Catholic Sociological Review* (Loyola University, Chicago), December 1947, 296-299.

KLUCKHOHN, Clyde, and KELLY, William H.: "The Concept of Culture" in *The Science of Man in the World Crisis,* ed. by R. Linton, Columbia University Press, New York, 1945.

KLUCKHOHN, Clyde, and LEIGHTON, Dorothea C.:
A. *The Navaho,* Harvard University Press, Cambridge, Mass., 1946.
B. *Children of the People,* ibid., 1947.

KNIGHT, Frank H.: *The Ethics of Competition,* Harper & Brothers, New York and London, 1935.

KOESTLER, Arthur: "The Intelligentsia" in *Horizon,* London, March 1944, 162-176.

KROEBER, A. L.:
A. *Anthropology,* Harcourt, Brace & Company, New York, 1923.
B. *Configuration of Culture Growth,* University of California Press, Berkeley and Los Angeles, 1944.

LAFARGE, John: "A Critique of Progress" in *America,* New York, September 1937, 597.

LALANDE, André: *Vocabulaire technique et critique de la philosophie,* Alcan, 5th ed., Paris, 1947.

LASERSON, Max M.: "Russian Sociology" in *Twentieth Century Sociology,* ed. by G. Gurvitch and W. E. Moore, The Philosophical Library, New York, 1945.

LASSWELL, Harold D.: *World Politics and Personal Insecurity,* McGraw-Hill Book Co., New York and London, 1935.

LAZARSFELD, Paul, BERELSON, Bernard, and GAUDET, Hazel: *The People's Choice,* Duell, Sloan & Pearce, New York, 1944.

LECLERCQ, Jacques:
A. "Dimensions de la Sociologie" in *Bulletin de l'Institut de Recherches Économiques et Sociales,* University of Louvain, 1946, 602-608.

B. *Introduction à la Sociologie,* Institut de Recherches Économiques et Sociales, Louvain, 1948.

Lévy-Bruhl, Lucien: *La mentalité primitive,* Alcan, Paris, 1922.

Lewis, Clarence Irving: *An Analysis of Knowledge and Valuation,* The Open Court Publishing Company, La Salle, Ill., 1946.

Linton, Ralph:
- A. *The Study of Man,* D. Appleton-Century Company, New York and London, 1936.
- B. "Scope and Aims of Anthropology" in *The Science of Man in the World Crisis,* ed. by R. Linton, Columbia University Press, New York, 1945, 3-18.
- C. *The Cultural Background of Personality,* D. Appleton-Century Company, New York and London, 1945.

Lovejoy, Arthur O.: "Reflections on the History of Ideas" in *Journal of the History of Ideas* (College of the City of New York), January, 1940, 3-23.

Lowie, Robert H.: *The History of Ethnological Theory,* Rinehart & Company, New York, 1937.

Lukacs, Georg: *Geschichte und Klassenbewusstsein,* Berlin, 1923.

Malinowski, Bronislaw:
- A. article "Culture" in *The Encyclopaedia of the Social Sciences,* Macmillan, New York, 1931, vol. IV, 621-646.
- B. *The Dynamics of Culture Change,* Yale University Press, New Haven, 1945.

Manndelbaum, Maurice: *The Problem of Historical Knowledge,* Liveright Publishing Corp., New York, 1938.

Mannheim, Ernest: "Karl Mannheim" in *The American Journal of Sociology,* University of Chicago Press, May 1947, 471-474.

Mannheim, Karl. This is not an exhaustive bibliography of Mannheim's works; one may be found in E. Mannheim, *op. cit.*
- A. *Die Strukturanalyse der Erkenntnistheorie,* Reuther & Reichard, Berlin, 1922.
- B. "Historismus" in *Archiv für Sozialwissenschaft und Sozialpolitik* (Verlag J. C. B. Mohr), Tübingen, 1924, 1-60.
- C. "Das Problem einer Soziologie des Wissens," ibid., 1925, 577-652.
- D. "Ideologische und soziologische Betrachtung der geistigen Gebilde" in *Jahrbuch für Soziologie* (Verlag G. Braun), Karlsruhre, 1926, 424-440.
- E. "Das konservative Denken" in *Archiv für Sozialwissenschaft und Sozialpolitik* (Verlag J. C. B. Mohr), Tübingen, 1927, 68-142, 470-495.
- F. "Das Problem der Generationen" in *Kölner Vierteljarshefte für Soziologie,* Köln, 1928, 157-185, 309-330.
- G. *Ideologie und Utopie,* Friedrich Cohen, Bonn, 1929. Trans. into English by Louis Wirth and Edward Shils in *Ideology and Utopia,* Harcourt, Brace & Company, New York, 1936, 49-236. (Our notes refer to the English translation.)

H. "Wissenssoziologie" in *Handwörtenbuch der Soziologie*, ed. by A. Vierkandt (Verlag F. Enke), Stuttgart, 1931, 659-680. Trans. into English by L. Wirth and E. Shils in *Ideology and Utopia*, Harcourt, Brace & Company, New York, 1936, 237-280. (Our notes refer to the English translation.)

I. Review of *Methods in Social Science*, ed. by S. T. Rice, in *The American Journal of Sociology*, University of Chicago Press, September 1932, 273-282.

J. "German Sociology (1918-1933)" in *Politica* (London School of Economics and Political Science), February 1934, 12-33.

K. "The Crisis of Culture in the Era of Mass-Democracies and Autarchies" in *The Sociological Review*, LePlay House, London, April 1934, 105-129.

L. *Rational and Irrational Elements in Contemporary Society*, Oxford University Press, London, 1934.

M. "Ernest Troeltsch" in *Encyclopedia of the Social Sciences*, Macmillan, New York, 1935, vol. XV, 106-107.

N. "Utopia," ibid., 200-203.

O. *Mensch und Gesellschaft im Zeitalter des Umbaus*, A. W. Sijthoff's, Leiden, 1935.

P. "Preliminary Approach to the Problem," trans. by L. Wirth and E. Shils in *Ideology and Utopia*, Harcourt, Brace & Company, New York, 1936, 1-48.

Q. *Man and Society in an Age of Reconstruction* (translation of *O* by E. Shils, with many modifications and additions by Mannheim). New York, Harcourt, Brace & Company, 1940.

R. *Diagnosis of Our Time*, Oxford University Press, New York, 1944.

MAQUET, Jacques J.:

A. "La critique personnaliste de Charles Du Bos" in *La Revue Nouvelle*, Brussels, 1945, September 15 (216-224), October 1 (278-287).

B. "Perspectives de l'étude des opinions" in *Bulletin de l'Institut de Recherches Economiques et Sociales* (University of Louvain), 1946, 745-757.

MARCUSE, Herbert: "Zur Warheitsproblematik der Sociologishen Methode" in *Die Gesellschaft*, Berlin, October 1929, 356-369.

MARX, Karl: "Theses on Feuerbach" in *Selected Works* of Karl Marx, International Publishers, Moscow and New York, n. d. (1933), vol. I, 471-473.

MAUROIS, André: *Journal, Etats-Unis, 1946*, Editions du Bateau Ivre, Paris, 1946, 25-34.

MEAD, George Herbert: *Mind, Self and Society*, The University of Chicago Press, Chicago, 1934.

MEAD, Margaret:

A. *From the South Seas*, W. Morrow & Company, New York, 1939.

B. *And Keep Your Powder Dry*, ibid., 1942.

MERLEAU-PONTY, Maurice: "Marxism and Philosophy." trans. by Eva and Harold Orlansky in *Politics*, 4, New York, 1947, 173-176.

MERTON, Robert K.:
A. "Puritanism, Pietism and Science" in *The Sociological Review*, LePlay House, London, January 1936, 103-113.
B. "Civilization and Culture" in *Sociology and Social Research*, University of Southern California, Los Angeles, 1936, 103-113.
C. "The Sociology of Knowledge" in *Isis* (Saint Catherine Press, Bruges, Belgium), November 1937, 493-503.
D. "Science and the Social Order" in *Philosophy of Science* (Williams & Wilkins Company, Baltimore, Md.), July 1938, 321-337.
E. "Science, Technology and Society in the XVIIth Century England" in *Osiris* (ed. by G. Sarton, Saint Catherine Press, Bruges, Belgium), 1938, 360-632.
F. "Science and the Economy in the XVIIth Century England" in *Science and Society*, New York, 1939, 3-27.
G. Review of F. Znaniecki's *The Social Role of the Man of Knowledge* in *American Sociological Review* (Menasha, Wis.), 1941, 111-115.
H. "Karl Mannheim and the Sociology of Knowledge" in *The Journal of Liberal Religion* (Chicago, Ill.), Winter 1941, 125-147.
I. "The Sociology of Knowledge" in *Twentieth Century Sociology*, ed. by G. Gurvitch and W. E. Moore, The Philosophical Library, New York, 1945, 366-405.
J. *Mass Persuasion*, Harper & Brothers, New York and London, 1946.
MEYERSON, Emile: *Identity and Reality*, trans. by Kate Loewenberg; G. Allen & Unwin, London; Macmillan, New York; 1930.
MICHELS, Roberto: article "Intellectuals" in *Encyclopaedia of the Social Sciences*, Macmillan, New York, 1932, vol. VIII, 118-126.
MILLS, C. Wright:
A. "Language, Logic and Culture" in *American Sociological Review* (Menasha, Wis.), October 1939, 670-680.
B. "Methodological Consequences of the Sociology of Knowledge" in *The American Journal of Sociology*, University of Chicago Press, November 1940, 316-330.
MUMFORD, Lewis: "Insensate Ideologue" in *The New Republic*, New York, July 1937, 282-284.
MURDOCK, George Peter: "The Common Denominator of Cultures" in *The Science of Man in the World Crisis*, ed. by R. Linton, Columbia University Press, New York, 1945, 123-142.
MURPHY, Gardner: *Public Opinion and the Individual*, Harper & Brothers, New York and London, 1938.
MYRDAL, Gunnar: *An American Dilemma*, Harper & Brothers, New York and London, 1942.

NOËL, Léon:
A. *Notes d'épistémologie thomiste*, Alcan, Paris, 1925.
B. *Le réalisme immédiat*, Institut Supérieur de Philosophie, Louvain, 1938.

NORTHROP, F. S. C.:
   A. *The Meeting of East and West,* Macmillan, New York, 1946.
   B. *The Logic of the Sciences and the Humanities,* Macmillan, New York, 1947.

OGBURN, William F., and NIMKOFF, Meyer F.: *Sociology,* Houghton Mifflin Company, Boston, 1940.

PARK, Robert E.: Review of Sorokin's *Sociocultural Dynamics* in *American Journal of Sociology,* University of Chicago Press, March 1938, 824-832.

PARSONS, Talcott:
   A. "The Place of Ultimate Values in Sociological Theory" in *The International Journal of Ethics,* University of Chicago Press, April 1935, 282-316.
   B. Review of Alexander von Schelting's *Max Weber's Wissenschaftlehre* in *American Sociological Review* (Menasha, Wis.), August 1936, 675-681.
   C. *The Structure of Social Action,* McGraw-Hill, New York and London, 1937.
   D. "The Role of Ideas in Social Action" in *American Sociological Review* (Menasha, Wis.), 3, 1938, 652-664.
   E. and DUNLOP, J. T.; GILMORE, M. P.; KLUCKHOHN, C. K.; TAYLOR, O. H.: *Toward a Common Language for the Area of Social Science* (mimeographed, Harvard University, Social Relations Library), n. d.
   F. "The Present Position and Prospects of Systematic Theory in Sociology" in *Twentieth Century Sociology,* ed. by. G. Gurvitch and W. E. Moore, The Philosophical Library, New York, 1945, 42-69.
   G. Introduction to Max Weber's *The Theory of Social and Economic Organization,* Oxford University Press, New York, 1947.
   H. and BARBER, Bernard: "Sociology, 1941-1946" in *The American Journal of Sociology,* University of Chicago Press, January 1948, 245-257.
   I. "Max Weber's Sociological Analysis of Capitalism and Modern Institutions" in *An Introduction to the History of Sociology,* ed. by H. E. Barnes, Chicago, 1948.

PEARSON, Karl: *The Grammar of Science,* vol. 1, 3d ed., 1911, A. & C. Black, London.

PERELMAN, Chaïm: "Le statut social des jugements de vérite" in *Revue de l'Institut de Sociologie* (University of Brussels), 1, 1933, 17-23.

POINCARÉ, Henri: *Science et hypothèse,* Flammarion, Paris, 1912.

PRALL, D. W.: "Sorokin and the Dangerous Science" in *Harvard Guardian* (Cambridge, Mass.), November 1937, 8-13.

RAPHAEL, Max: *La théorie marxiste de la connaissance (Zur Erkenntnistheorie des concrete Dialektik,* trans. by L. Gara) Gallimard, Paris, 1937.

RASHEVSKY, N.: *Mathematical Theory of Human Relations*, The Principia Press, Bloomington, Ind., 1947.

RENOIRTE, Fernand: *Éléments de critique des sciences et de cosmologie*, Institut Supérieur de Philosophie, Louvain, 1945.

ROHEIM, Geza, ed.: *Psychoanalysis and the Social Sciences*, Imago Publishing Company, London, 1947.

ROUCEK, Joseph S.: "Wissenssoziologie" in *Dictionary of Sociology*, ed. by H. P. Fairchild, Philosophical Library, New York, 1944.

SABINE, George H.: "Logic and Social Studies" in *The Philosophical Review* (Cornell University, Ithaca, N. Y.), March 1939, 155-176.

SALOMON, Albert: "Karl Mannheim" in *Social Research* (New School for Social Research, New York), September 1947, 350-364.

SCHAUB, Edward L.: "A Sociological Theory of Knowledge" in *The Philosophical Review* (Cornell University, Ithaca, N. Y.), July 1920, 319-339.

SCHELER, Max:
  A. *L'homme du ressentiment* (translation of *Vom Umsturz der Werte*), Gallimard, Paris, 1933.
  B. *Versuche zu einer Soziologie des Wissens*, Duncker & Humblot, Munich and Leipzig, 1924.
  C. *Die Wissensformen und die Gesellschaft*, Der Neue Geist Verlag, Leipzig, 1926.

SCHELTING, Alexander von:
  A. *Max Weber's Wissenschaftlehre*, Verlag J. C. B. Mohr, Tübingen, 1934.
  B. Review of Karl Mannheim's *Ideologie und Utopie* in *American Sociological Review* (Menasha, Wis.), August 1936, 664-674.

SCHMID, J. J. von: "Sociologie van het Denken" in *Mensch en Maatschappij* (Vereeniging voor Wijsbegeerte des Rechts, Groningen), 1936, 252 ff.

SHILS, Edward:
  A. "Irrationality and Planning" in *Journal of Liberal Religion* (Chicago, Ill.), Winter 1941, 148-153.
  B. "The Present Situation in American Sociology" in *Pilot Papers*, London, June 1947, 8-36.

SMALL, Albion: Review of Scheler's *Versuche zu einer Soziologie des Wissens* in *The American Journal of Sociology*, University of Chicago Press, 1925, 262-264.

SOMBART, Werner: *Der Bourgeois*, Duncker & Humblot, Munich and Leipzig, 1913. English translation by M. Epstein: *The Quintessence of Capitalism*, T. F. Unwin, London, 1915. (Our notes refer to the English translation.)

SOROKIN, Pitirim A. (This is not an exhaustive bibliography of Sorokin's works.)
  AA. *Leaves from a Russian Diary*, E. P. Dutton & Company, New York, 1924. (Enlarged edition, The Beacon Press, Boston, 1950.)

AB. *The Sociology of Revolution*, J. B. Lippincott & Company, Philadelphia and London, 1925.

AC. *Social Mobility*, Harper & Brothers, New York and London, 1927.

AD. *Contemporary Sociological Theories*, ibid., 1928.

AE. and ZIMMERMAN, Carle C.: *Principles of Rural-Urban Sociology*, Henry Holt & Company, New York, 1929.

AF. and ZIMMERMAN, Carle C., and GALPIN, Charles J.: *A Systematic Source Book in Rural Sociology*, University of Minnesota Press, Minneapolis, 1930, vol. I.

AG. idem, 1930, vol. II.

AH. idem, 1932, vol. III.

AI. *Social and Cultural Dynamics*, vol. I: *Fluctuation of Forms of Art*, American Book Company, New York, 1937.

AJ. *Social and Cultural Dynamics*, vol. II: *Fluctuation of Systems of Truth, Ethics and Law*, American Book Company, New York, 1937.

AK. *Social and Cultural Dynamics*, vol. III: *Fluctuation of Social Relationships, War and Revolution*, American Book Company, New York, 1937.

AL. and BERGER, Clarence Q.: *Time-Budgets of Human Behavior*, Harvard University Press, Cambridge, Mass., 1939.

AM. *Social and Cultural Dynamics*, vol. IV: *Basic Problems, Principles and Methods*, American Book Company, New York, 1941.

AN. *The Crisis of Our Age*, E. P. Dutton & Company, New York, 1941.

AO. *Man and Society in Calamity*, ibid., 1943.

AP. *Sociocultural Causality, Space, Time*, Duke University Press, Durham, N. C., 1943.

AQ. *Russia and the United States*, E. P. Dutton & Company, New York, 1944.

AR. *Society, Culture and Personality*, Harper & Brothers, New York and London, 1947.

AS. *The Reconstruction of Humanity*, The Beacon Press, Boston, 1948.

BA. "Russian Sociology in the Twentieth Century" in *Publications of the American Sociological Society*, Chicago, 1927, 57-69.

BB. "Leaders of Labor and Radical Movements in the United States and Foreign Countries" in *American Journal of Sociology*, University of Chicago Press, November 1927, 382-411.

BC. "Sociology and Ethics" in *The Social Sciences and their Interrelations*, ed. by F. Ogburn and A. Goldenweiser, Houghton Mifflin Company, Boston, 1927, 310-318.

BD. and others: "An Experimental Study of Efficiency of Work under Various Specified Conditions" in *American Journal of Sociology*, University of Chicago Press, March 1930, 765-782.

BE. and BOLDYREFF, J. W.: "An Experimental Study of the Influence of Suggestion on the Discrimination and the Valuation of People" in *American Journal of Sociology*, University of Chicago Press, March 1932, 720-732.

BF. and MERTON, R. K.: "The Course of Arabian Intellectual Development, 700-1300 A.D." in *Isis* (Saint Catherine Press, Bruges), February 1935, 516-524.

BG. "Is Accurate Social Planning Possible?" in *American Sociological Review* (Menasha, Wis.), 1936, 12-25.

BH. "Some of the Basic Factors in the Improvement of Scholarship among American Students of the Social Sciences" in *Social Science* (Menasha, Wis.), April 1936, 93-99.

BI. "Le concept d'équilibre est-il nécessaire aux sciences sociales?" in *Revue Internationale de Sociologie*, Paris, September 1936, 497-529.

BJ. in collaboration with LOSSKY, N. O., and LAPSHIN, I. I.: "The Fluctuations of Idealism and Materialism in the Graeco-Roman and European Cultures from 600 B.C. to 1920 A.D." in *Reine und angewandte Soziologie*, Hans Buske Verlag, Leipzig, 1936, 321-362.

BK. and MERTON, R. K.: "Social Time: A Methodological and Functional Analysis" in *American Journal of Sociology*, University of Chicago Press, March 1937, 615-629.

BL. Rejoinder to Bierstedt's review in *American Sociological Review* (Menasha, Wis.), December 1937, 823-825.

BM. Rejoinder to "Sorokin and the Dangerous Science" in *Harvard Guardian* (Cambridge, Mass.), December 1937, 21-25.

BN. Review of *The Concept of Time* by L. R. Heath, and of *The Problem of Time* (University of California publications) in *American Journal of Sociology*, University of Chicago Press, May 1938, 1016-1018.

BO. "Pseudo Sociologos" in *Journal of Social Philosophy*, New York, July 1938, 359-364.

BP. "Histrionics" in *The Southern Review* (University of Louisiana, Baton Rouge), Winter 1938, 554-564.

BQ. "Comments on Professor Hart's Paper" in *American Sociological Review* (Menasha, Wis.), October 1939, 646-651.

BR. "Sociocultural Trends in Euro-American Culture During the Last Hundred Years" in *A Century of Social Thought* (Duke University Press, Durham, N. C.), 1939, 98-125.

BS. "Arnold J. Toynbee's Philosophy of History" in *The Journal of Modern History*, University of Chicago Press, September 1940, 374-387.

BT. "Sociocultural Dynamics and Evolutionism" in *Twentieth Century Sociology*, ed. by G. Gurvitch and W. E. Moore, Philosophical Library, New York, 1945, 96-120.

BU. "Qu'est-ce qu'une classe sociale?" in *Cahiers Internationaux de Sociologie*, II, Éditions du Seuil, Paris, 1947, 57-87.

SPEIER, Hans:

A. Review of E. Grünwald's *Das Problem einer Soziologie des Wissens* in *American Sociological Review* (Menasha, Wis.), August 1936, 681-682.

B. Review of *Ideology and Utopia* by K. Mannheim in *American Journal of Sociology,* University of Chicago Press, July 1937, 155-156.

C. "The Social Determination of Ideas" in *Social Research* (New School for Social Research, New York), May 1938, 182-205.

D. "The Sociological Ideas of P. A. Sorokin: 'Integralist Sociology'" in *An Introduction to the History of Sociology,* ed. by H. E. Barnes, Chicago, 1948, 884-901.

SPENCER, Herbert: *The Principles of Sociology,* vol. I, D. Appleton & Company, New York, 1891.

STERN, Gunther: "Uber die sog. 'Seinverbundenheit' des Bewusstseins" in *Archiv für Sozialwissenschaft und Sozialpolitik* (Verlag J. C. B. Mohr), Tübingen, 1930, 492-509.

STOETZEL, Jean: *Théorie des Opinions,* Presses Universitaires de France, Paris, 1943.

TAWNEY, R. H.: *Religion and the Rise of Capitalism* (1st ed., 1926), Penguin Books, New York, 1947.

TILLICH, Paul: "Ideologie und Utopie" in *Die Gesellschaft* (J. H. W. Dietz, Berlin), October 1929, 348-355.

TOYNBEE, Arnold J.: *A Study of History,* vol. IV, Oxford University Press, New York, 1939.

USHER, Abbot Payson: "Sorokin and the Dangerous Science" in *Harvard Guardian,* Cambridge, Mass., November 1937.

VAN RIET, Georges: *L'epistémologie thomiste,* Institut Supérieur de Philosophie, Louvain, 1946.

VAN STEENBERGHEN, Fernand: *Épistémologie,* Institut Supérieur de Philosophie, Louvain, 1945.

VEBLEN, Thorstein: *The Higher Learning in America,* B. W. Huebsch, New York, 1918.

WARNER, W. Lloyd, and LUNT, Paul S.:
A. *The Social Life of a Modern Community,* Yale University Press, New Haven, 1941.

B. *The Status System of a Modern Community,* Yale University Press, New Haven, 1942.

WARNER, W. Lloyd, and SROLE, Leo: *The Social Systems of American Ethnic Groups,* Yale University Press, New Haven, 1945.

WEBER, Max:
A. *Gesammelte Aufsätze zur Religionssoziologie,* J. C. B. Mohr, Tübingen, 1920-1921.

B. *Wirtschaft und Gesellschaft,* J. C. B. Mohr, Tübingen, 1925.

C. *General Economic History,* trans. by F. H. Knight, Greenberg, New York, 1927.

D. *The Protestant Ethics and the Spirit of Capitalism,* trans. by T. Parsons, Charles Scribner's Sons, New York, 1930.

E. *From Max Weber: Essays in Sociology,* trans. and ed. by H. H. Gerth and C. W. Mills, Oxford University Press, New York, 1946.

F. *The Theory of Social and Economic Organization,* trans. by A. M. Henderson and T. Parsons, introd. by T. Parsons, Oxford University Press, New York, 1947.

WEST, James: *Plainville, U. S. A.,* Columbia University Press, New York, 1945.

WHITE, Leslie A.: "Culturological vs. Psychological Interpretations of Human Behavior" in *American Sociological Review* (Menasha, Wis.), December 1947, 686-698.

WILSON, Logan: *The Academic Man,* Oxford University Press, New York and London, 1942.

WIRTH, Louis:
A. "Ideological Aspects of Social Disorganization" in *American Sociological Review* (Menasha, Wis.), August 1940, 472-482.

B. Preface to "Ideology and Utopia" in Karl Mannheim's *Ideology and Utopia,* Harcourt, Brace & Company, New York, 1936.

C. "Karl Mannheim" in *American Sociological Review* (Menasha, Wis.), June 1947, 356-357.

WOLFF, Kurt H.: "The Sociology of Knowledge: Emphasis on an Empirical Attitude" in *Philosophy of Science* (Baltimore, Md.), April 1943, 104-123.

WOLPERT, J. F.: "Notes on the American Intelligentsia" in *Partisan Review,* New York, September-October 1947, 472-485.

WOODWARD, Julian L.: "Making Government Opinion Research Bear Upon Operations" in *American Sociological Review* (Menasha, Wis.), 1944, 670-677.

ZNANIECKI, Florian:
A. *The Method of Sociology,* Farrar & Rinehart, New York, 1934.

B. *The Social Role of the Man of Knowledge,* Columbia University Press, New York, 1940.

Index

Abelard, Peter, 172
Abiogenesis, 198-199
Absolute principles, 151, 176
Abstraction, 51; level of, 28, 31, 175
Activistic knowledge, 63, 78, 84, 88, 244; principle of, 93; theory of, 64; value of, 233
"Aged" theory. *See* Knowledge
Agents, human, 112-113, 115-116, 120, 140, 180, 189, 202, 206, 216, 247, 253, 259
Agnosticism, 130, 158
Anarchists, anabaptist, 24
Anaximander, 198
Aquinas, Saint Thomas, 77, 120, 126, 241
Aristotelians, 171
Aristotle, 77, 128, 130, 137-138, 140, 145, 158, 168, 182
Atomism, 144, 148
Australian aborigines, 136, 141

Bach, Johann Sebastian, 116, 157
Bacon, Francis, 6, 15, 118, 138
Baconian method, 232
Bede, Venerable, 138
Beethoven, Ludwig van, 113
Behaviorism, 108-110
Berger, Clarence Q., 109
Bergson, Henri, 7, 140, 241
Berkeley, George, 138
Bernard of Chartres, 145
Bernoulli, J., 138
Blondel, Georges, 7
Boethius, Anicius Manlius Severinus, 138
Boldyreff, J. W., 232

Bourgeoisie, 11, 24, 29, 35, 67, 70-71, 256-257
Boyle, Robert, 237
Brahmanism, 175
Brunschvicg, Léon, 136
Buddhism, 175
Burke, Edmund, 24

Caesar, Gaius Julius, 120
Cajetanus, 126
Calvinism, 102
Capitalism, 199; culture of, 101-102; principle of law of, 52; system of, 182
Cartesians, 138
Causal relationships. *See* Relationships
Causality, 138, 153; concepts of, 136-139, 153; principle of, 12
Change, principle of immanent, 160-162, 178, 181-184, 188-189, 193-194, 205, 211, 238, 244; corollary, 187
Chinese, 141, 153; civilization, 136; concept of causality, 136-137, 153; concept of number, 141; concept of space, 141; thought, 12
Christian concept of causality, 138
Christians, 130, 175, 179
Civilizations: Chinese, 136; Graeco-Roman, 121-122, 127, 137, 142, 150-151, 157, 174, 186, 199; Occidental, 121-122, 127, 137, 142, 151, 157, 174, 186, 199
Clarenbaud, 145
Communism, 25, 199
Communists, 45

Comte, Auguste, 5, 115, 121, 135, 148
Conant, James Bryant, 237-239
Conceptualism, 145, 157
Condorcet, Marquis de, 24
Conformity, principle of probable, 96-97, 247
Confucianist: attitude, 120; mentality, 136
Conservatives, 24-25, 27, 67
Contradiction, 116-117, 120
Copernicus, Nicolaus, 138
Correlation, 31, 132, 136, 140
Correspondences, 32, 34-36, 41, 43-47, 55
Coste, Adolphe, 118
Criminal law, 151-152
Criticism, 176; defined, 129
Cultural integration. See Integration
Cultural personality types, 100-103, 247
Cultural premises, 132-135, 142, 180-181, 187-188, 194, 202-204, 225, 238-239, 255-257; fluctuation of, 198; inadequacy of, 161-162; influence of, 152, 195-196
Cultural realm, 116-122
Cultural systems. See Supersystems
Culture: capitalistic, 101-102; concept of, 252; correlation between concepts and types of, 136; definition of, 4; Mexican, 118
Currents of thought, 126-128, 175; American, 9; Aristotelian, 77; idealistic, 173; influence of, measured, 170-173; materialistic, 173; relationships between, 170
Cyclical processes, 148, 157

Darwin, Charles Robert, 148
Definitions: communism, 25; culture, 4; empiricism, 129; epistemology, 75-78; error, 72; fideism, 129; freedom, 27; gnosiology, 76-77; "historic," 29; hypothesis, 237-238; ideology, 21-22; interaction, 112; meaningful, 112; mental production, 4; mysticism, 129; broad-

est perspective, 70; philosophy of knowledge, 97; rationalism, 129; qualitative study, 168; quantitative study, 168; skepticism, 129; society, 4; sociology of knowledge, 5, 23, 97; theory, 237-238
Democracy, 27, 80
Democritus, 144
Dependent variable, 46, 135-142, 152, 155, 157, 195-197, 203
Descartes, Rene, 77, 95, 138-139, 228
Determinism, 146, 156
Development, laws of immanent, 193
Dewey, John, 10, 232
Diderot, Denis, 175
Dilthey, Wilhelm, 40
Divine immutability, principle of, 95
Dominant culture, 134, 201; concept of, 200; fluctuations of, 137
Duhem, Pierre, 139
Durkheim, Emile, 8-9, 99, 136, 141, 153, 189, 225

Eckhart, Johannes, 209
Egyptians, ancient, 120
Empiricism, 130-131, 176; defined, 129; development of, 200; linked with nominalism, 145
Engels, Friedrich, 86-87
Epicurus, 148
Epistemology, 12, 204, 215, 219, 231, 240-241, 248-249; integralist, 222; meaning of, 75-78; methodology of, 76
Erigena, John Scotus, 138, 184, 210-211
Error: causes of, 10; sources of, 6, 59; defined by Mannheim, 72; Mannheim's, 254-255
Espinas, Alfred Victor, 175
Eternalism, 143-144, 201; linked to ideationalism, 235
Eternalists, 235
Euclid, 116, 157
Existentialists, 242
Explanation, Mannheim's principle of, 34-35

Fact, judgments of, 46-47, 83
Fascism, 26, 68, 83, 199, 251, 258
Faust, 117
Fideism, 130, 176; defined, 129
France, Anatole, 207
France: political freedom in, 70-71;
  sociologists in, 9
Francis of Assisi, Saint, 151
Freedom, two meanings of, 27; liberal concept of, 35
Freud, Sigmund, 6, 7, 191

Geocentrism, 194, 196, 198
Germany: sociologists in, 9; sociology in, 50-51, 54; sociology of knowledge in, 11
Girondins, 24
Goethe, Johann Wolfgang von, 117
Gounod, Charles Francois, 117
Gnosiology, 75, 78, 145, 204, 215, 217-218, 220, 222-223, 240-241; meaning of, 76-77; relations between sociology of knowledge and, 92, 96-97
Graeco-Roman world. See Civilizations
Granet, Marcel, 9, 136, 141, 153
Greeks, 122, 149, 175; concept of number of, 141
Group, 22, 28; principle of competition of, 48, 93; correspondences between political conception and, 34-36, 41-45
Grünwald, Ernst, 5, 9
Gualterus of Mauretania, 145

Halbwachs, Maurice, 9
Harmony, 12, 32
Hegel, Georg Wilhelm Friedrich, 19, 73, 86-87, 184-185, 192
Hegelian: dialectics, 68; process, 87; synthesis, 66
Hegelianism, 86, 205
Heliocentrism, 194, 196, 198
Herder, Johann Gottfried von, 24
Hesiod, 141
Hindus, 139
History: concepts of, 23-28, 87

Hobbes, Thomas, 138
Homo economicus, 114
Homo socius, 114
Hume, David, 138
Husserl, Edmund, 19
Huxley, Thomas Henry, 15, 237
Hypothesis, meaning of, 237-238

"Ideal types," 39
Idealism, 142-143, 200-201, 207
Idealistic: approach, 256-258; culture, 131-132; current of thought, 173; premise, 121, 143, 220; mentality, 120, 125, 136, 144, 151; periods, 122, 140, 148, 175; system, 119, 256; theory of knowledge, 63-64
Ideas: Aristotelian, 140; meaning of, 85; Mannheim's interpretation of, 53-54; origin of, 11-12, 55, 85-86; Platonic, 78, 142; social determination of, 11; sociological interpretation of, 54-55; validity of, 11-13, 58, 64-65, 72-73, 83-88
Ideational: art, 122; category, 75; characteristics, 119-120; concepts, 137, 141, 153; culture, 131-132, 148, 182, 219, 233; individuals, nervous system of, 209; mentality, 119-120, 124, 136, 144, 150-151, 220, 235; periods, 122, 138, 148, 194, 233; premise, 121, 156; system, 119; theory of knowledge, 220
Ideationalism, 235
Ideology, 58, 70-71, 90; distinction between utopia and, 71; theory of, 19, 31; two meanings of, 21-22
Impressionism, 199
Independent variable, 28, 30, 133-135, 155, 159, 185, 187-189, 225-226, 253; concept of ultimate reality as, 159; premises of culture as, 142; relationships between dependent and, 157, 195-197; relationship between mental productions and, 160; social factor as, 28

Indeterminism, 146, 156
Individual, the, 22; ideational, 209; sensate, 209
Integralism, 147, 176, 207, 209, 214, 217-218, 221-223, 247; arguments in favor of, 216; epistemological, 208
Integration, 116-118, 120, 155, 179, 202, 226
Intellectuals, 69, 73, 82
Interaction, 112-113, 115-116, 134, 161, 193
Interest, Marxist principle of, 34
Intuition, 125, 206-208, 211, 213-214, 232. *See also* Truth of faith
Intuitionalism, 25-27
Isadore of Seville, Saint, 138

James, William, 3, 10, 191
Jerusalem, Wilhelm, 4, 9
Jesus Christ, 151
Jews, 28
Judgments: of fact, 46-47, 83; of strategy, 79-80; of value, 46-47, 83, 79-80
Juridical personality, 147, 188

Kant, Immanuel, 116, 146
Kantianism, 11-12. *See also* Neo-Kantianism
Kardiner, Abram, 259
Kerensky, Aleksandr Feodorovich, 108
Kluckhohn, Clyde, 193
Knowledge: activistic, 63-64, 78, 84, 88, 93, 233, 244; "aged" theory of, 61-62, 80-81; "existential determination" of, 23, 32, 47-50; function of, 90, 94; idealistic theory of, 63-64; ideational theory of, 220; perspective, 58, 61, 66, 78-81, 83-84; philosophy of, 13-14, 97; principle of practical, 48, 93; qualitative, 31; sociology of, 10-11, 13-14, 23, 33, 95, 97

Lavoisier, Antoine Laurent, 239
Law, criminal, 151-152
Laws of immanent development, 193

Leibnitz, Baron Gottfried Wilhelm von, 138-139
Lenin, Nikolai, 25-26, 108, 120
Leucippus, 144
Lévy-Bruhl, Lucien, 9, 136
Liberalism, 67, 147, 256-257
Liberals, 24-25; concept of freedom of, 35
Limits, principle of, 160-162, 244
Linear processes, 148, 157
Locke, John, 77, 185
Logical consistency, 155, 157, 159-160, 178-179, 185, 226, 235, 242; principle of, 205, 238
Louis, Saint, 175
Lukács, Georg, 9, 19
Lumpenproletariat, 45

Machiavelli, Niccolo, 6
MacIver, Robert Morrison, 118
Malebranche, Nicolas de, 6, 138, 171
Mandelbaum, Maurice, 76, 88
Manicheans, 241
Manifoldness, 209, 216-217, 223
Marx, Karl, 6-7, 19, 21, 23, 25, 34, 45, 58, 73, 86-88, 118, 152, 192
Marxism, 19, 29, 31, 35, 45, 68, 83, 90, 232, 251, 258
Marxist: approach, 256-258; criticism, 208; ideological analysis, 21; origin, 22-23, 187, 192; philosophy, 88, 94; principle of interest, 34; system, 257; theory of ideology, 7, 23, 28; thinkers, social perspective of, 68; tradition, 44
Materialism, 143, 173, 175, 200-201, 207, 257
Maurus, Rhabanus, 138
Maxwell, James Clerk, 138
Meaningful relationships. *See* Relationships
Meanings, 112-113, 115-116, 119-120, 140, 189-190, 253
Mechanism, 149-150
Mental production, definition of, 4
Mentality: Buddhist, 119-120; early Christian, 119-120; Hindu, 119-120; idealistic, 120, 125, 144, 151;

ideational, 124, 136, 144, 150-151, 220, 235; sensate, 125, 135-136, 144, 149-151, 209; Taoist, 119-120
Merton, Robert K., 10, 38, 73, 196, 213
Metarationalism, 209-210, 212-214, 217, 222-223
Methodology, 76
Mexico, colonial, 118
Meyerson, Emile, 208
Mixed processes, 148, 157
Montaigne, Michel de, 138
Montesquieu, Baron de, 139
Moses, 24
Münzer, Thomas, 24
Mussolini, Benno, 26
Mysticism, 129-131, 176

Nazianzen, Gregory, 209
Neo-Kantianism, 19
Neoplatonic trend, 126
Neo-Thomism, 75
Newton, Sir Isaac, 139-140, 171, 208, 210
Nicolas of Cusa, 184, 210-211
Nietzsche, Friedrich Wilhelm, 7, 53, 148
Noël, Leon, 76
Nominalism, 145, 157
Non-integration, 116-117, 120
Norms. See Meanings
Northrop, F. S. C., 118, 185, 200, 232
Number, 142, 153; concepts of, 141

Objectivity, 10, 68, 88; criteria of, 65, 69-70, 72-73, 84, 251; new concept of, 11
Occidental civilization. See Civilization
Ockham, William, 172, 175
Ogburn, William F., 118
Osiander, Andreas, 138

Pareto, Vilfredo, 6, 7
Parsons, Talcott, 76
Particularization: method of, 60; principle of, 81
Pasteur, Louis, 198

Pavlov, Ivan, 108
Pearson, Karl, 138
Peirce, Charles Sanders, 10
Pericles, 120, 175
Personality: cultural types of, 100-103, 247; structure of, 190-193
Perspective, 23, 30, 48, 67; awareness of, 81; broadest, 70; compared with visual perception, 59; Hegelian, 32; historico-social, 30; idealistic, 209; ideational, 209; knowledge linked to, 58, 61, 66, 78-81, 83-84; objectivity of, 65, 68; of intellectuals, 82; of Marxist thinkers, 68; thought linked to, 59-60, 63, 84
Phenomenology, 19
Plato, 128, 130, 137-138
Platonists, 171
Platonic idea, 78, 142
Poincaré, Jules Henri, 208
Political doctrines, 27, 30, 66-67, 83, 90, 233, 239, 251, 254; fascist, 26; liberalism, 256-257; socialist, 35. See also Communism, Marxism, Totalitarianism
Positivism, 45, 126
Predestination, doctrine of, 167. See also Calvinism
Premises of culture. See Cultural premises
Principle of: activistic knowledge, 93; causality, 12; competition of groups, 48, 93; explanation, 34-35; harmony, 12; immanent change, 160-162, 178, 181-184, 188-189, 193-194, 205, 211, 238, 244; incomplete truth, 238; interest, Marxist, 34; limits, 160-162, 244; logical consistency, 205, 238; particularization, 81; perfect bodies and divine immutability, 95; practical knowledge, 48, 93; probable conformity, 97, 247; the three truths, 244
Proletariat, 22, 25, 28, 34, 45
Pseudo-Dionysius, 138, 209
Pythagoreans, 139-140

Qualitative study, 125-132, 136, 169-170, 173, 240, 256; defined, 168

Quantitative study, 125-132, 151, 169-170, 172, 224, 240, 256; defined, 168

Rashevsky, Nicolas, 177

Rationalism, 25, 34, 67, 130-131, 157, 176, 222; defined, 129; linked with conceptualism, 145

Realism, 144-145, 157, 175

Reality: concept of, 133, 241; conformity with, 58, 88; nature of, 153, 155, 159-161, 178-179, 242; ultimate, 87, 119-120, 133, 135, 142-143, 148, 150, 153, 155-156, 158-159, 161, 179-180, 188, 197, 209-211, 216-217, 219-220, 223

Reason, 207-208, 211, 213-214. See also Truth of reason

Reconstruction a priori, 38-40

Relationism, 61-64, 72, 83-84, 86, 89

Relationships, 4, 7, 31, 198-199, 254; between currents of thought, 170; between dependent and independent variables, 157, 195; between independent variables and mental productions, 160; causal, 164, 168; central, 20; logical, 143, 145, 168, 214, 235; logico-meaningful, 166, 197; meaningful, 112, 123-124, 133, 164, 167, 169, 172-174, 196, 226; of correspondence, 45-47; of power, 29

Relativism, 11, 61-62, 74, 78, 83-84, 89, 208-209

Renaissance, 20

Rickert, Heinrich, 19

Robespierre, Maximilien de, 192

Romans, 130, 149

Russian Revolution, 109

Saint Pierre, Bernardin de, 192

Sartre, Jean Paul, 241-242

Savigny, Friedrich Karl von, 24

Scheler, Max, 9, 19, 225

Scholastics, 6, 140, 174, 241. See also Abelard, Aquinas

Sensate: concept of causality, 137-138; concept of number, 141; concept of space, 140; culture, 131-132, 148-150, 196, 199, 219, 255; individual, 120, 209; mentality, 125, 135-136, 144, 149-151, 209; periods, 121-122, 138, 140, 148, 194, 199, 201, 233; premise, 121, 147, 256-257; system, 119

Senses, 207-208, 211, 213-214. See also Truth of the senses

Singularism, 147, 201

Skepticism, 11, 129-130, 158, 176

Social sciences, 111-114

Socialism, 67-68

Socialists, 25, 45; concept of historical evolution of, 28; concept of time of, 26

Society, definition of, 4, 252

Sociologists, 9-10

Sociology, 114; divisions of, 115-116; in Germany, 50-51, 54; in the United States, 11

Sociology of knowledge: ambition of, 10; attitude defined, 97; definitions of, 5, 23; elements necessary to, 33; gnosiology and, 92, 96-97; in Germany, 11; in the United States, 11; mathematization of, 95; philosophy of knowledge and, 13-14

Sombart, Werner, 21

Sorel, Georges, 7

Space, concepts of, 140, 141, 153

Spanish Catholicism, values of, 118

Spencer, Herbert, 148, 190

Spengler, Oswald, 161

Spinoza, Benedict de, 138

Spiritualism, 175, 257

Strategy, judgments of, 79-80

Superorganic realm, 111, 114-115

Supersystems, 119-122, 132, 160, 183, 202, 211, 216; fluctuations, 194

Systems: capitalistic, 182; defects of Mannheim's, 251; differences between Mannheim's and Sorokin's, 14; represented schematically,

240, 243; synthesis of Mannheim's
and Sorokin's, 254-255

Taine, Hippolyte Adolphe, 7
Tao, 137, 148
Taoism, 175
Taoist mentality, 136
Temporalism, 143-144, 201
Thales, 173, 175
Theory: atomistic, 144; definition
of, 237-238; Mannheim's, 48-49;
of ideology, 19, 31; of knowledge,
63-64, 220; of time, 139; Sorokin's,
179, 238
Time, 142, 153; anabaptist concept
of, 35; Aristotelian concept of,
140; Bergson's qualitative, 140;
correlation of concepts of, 140;
ideational, 139; Newton's absolute, 140; Pythagoreans' concept
of, 140; Scholastics' concept of,
140; socialist concept of, 26; sensate concept of, 139; theories of,
139
Totalitarianism, 147
Toynbee, Arnold Joseph, 161
Transition, periods of, 134
Troeltsch, Ernst, 21
Truth, concepts of, 124, 128-130,
132, 204-206; integralist, 213; sensate, 208, 219
Truth of faith, 125, 130-131, 145,
157, 176, 207, 212. See also Fideism, Intuition, Mysticism, Rationalism, Realism
Truth of reason, 125, 130-131, 176,
206-207, 212. See also Idealism,
Rationalism
Truth of the senses, 125, 130, 157,
196, 200, 206-207, 212. See also
Empiricism, Materialism
Truth, principle of incomplete, 238
Truth, sources of, 207, 211
Truth, systems of, 124-126, 132-133,
135, 176, 212-213, 216-217, 222;
periods of, 130; validity of, 207-
208
Truths, principle of three, 244

Ultimate reality. See Reality
United States: sociologists in, 9-10;
sociology in, 51; sociology of
knowledge in, 11
Universalism, 147, 176, 201
Utopias, 23-24, 27, 70-71, 90; anabaptist, 29; communist, 25-26;
definition of, 24; fascist, 26; liberal, 24; socialist, 34

Validity, 13, 58, 61, 83, 88, 205; of
ideas, 11-12, 64-66, 72-73, 84-86;
of three concepts of truth, 207-
208, 220
Values: fundamental, 8; of Spanish
Catholicism, 118. See also Mean-
ings
Variable. See Dependent variable,
Independent variable
Veblen, Thorstein, 9
Vehicles, 112-113, 115-116, 119-120,
140, 189-190, 253
Vierkandt, Alfred, 50, 65
Voltaire, Francois, 6

Walter of Montagne, 145
Weber, A., 118
Weber, L., 118
Weber, Max, 9, 19, 21, 39-40, 102,
167
Weltanschauung, 8, 26, 30, 36, 38,
40-41, 43, 46, 66, 79, 142, 156,
170
Wild, K. W., 207
Wissenssoziologie, 7, 9-11, 14, 19,
50, 65, 124, 162-163, 189-190,
193, 196, 199, 203-204, 212, 222-
223, 227, 239, 244, 250-251, 257;
definition of, 3-4; of Marxist origin, 192; relationship between
philosophy of knowledge and, 12;
Sorokin's system of, 187; systems
of, 225, 228
World War I, 8, 109

Znaniecki, Florian, 5, 10, 193